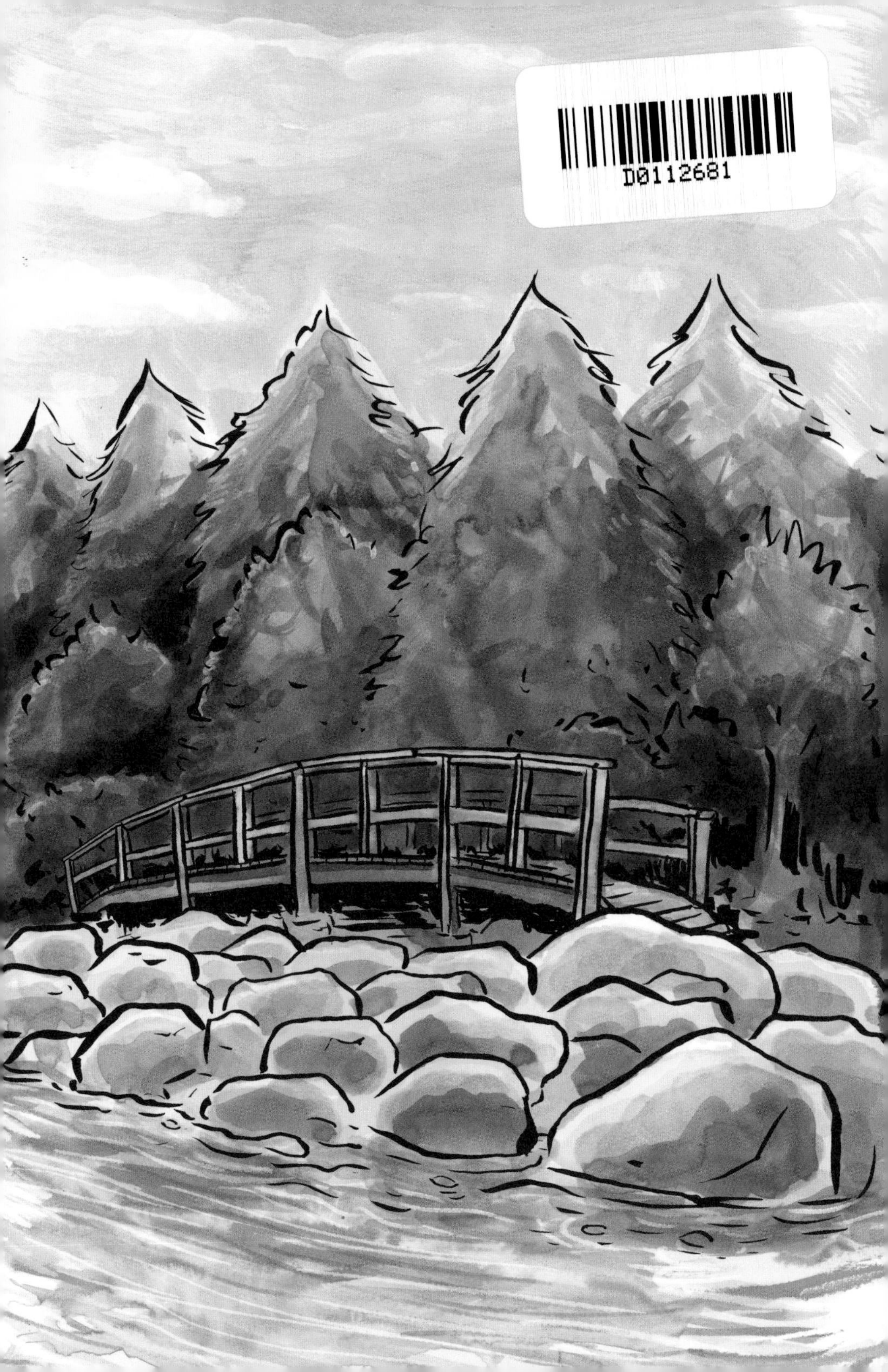

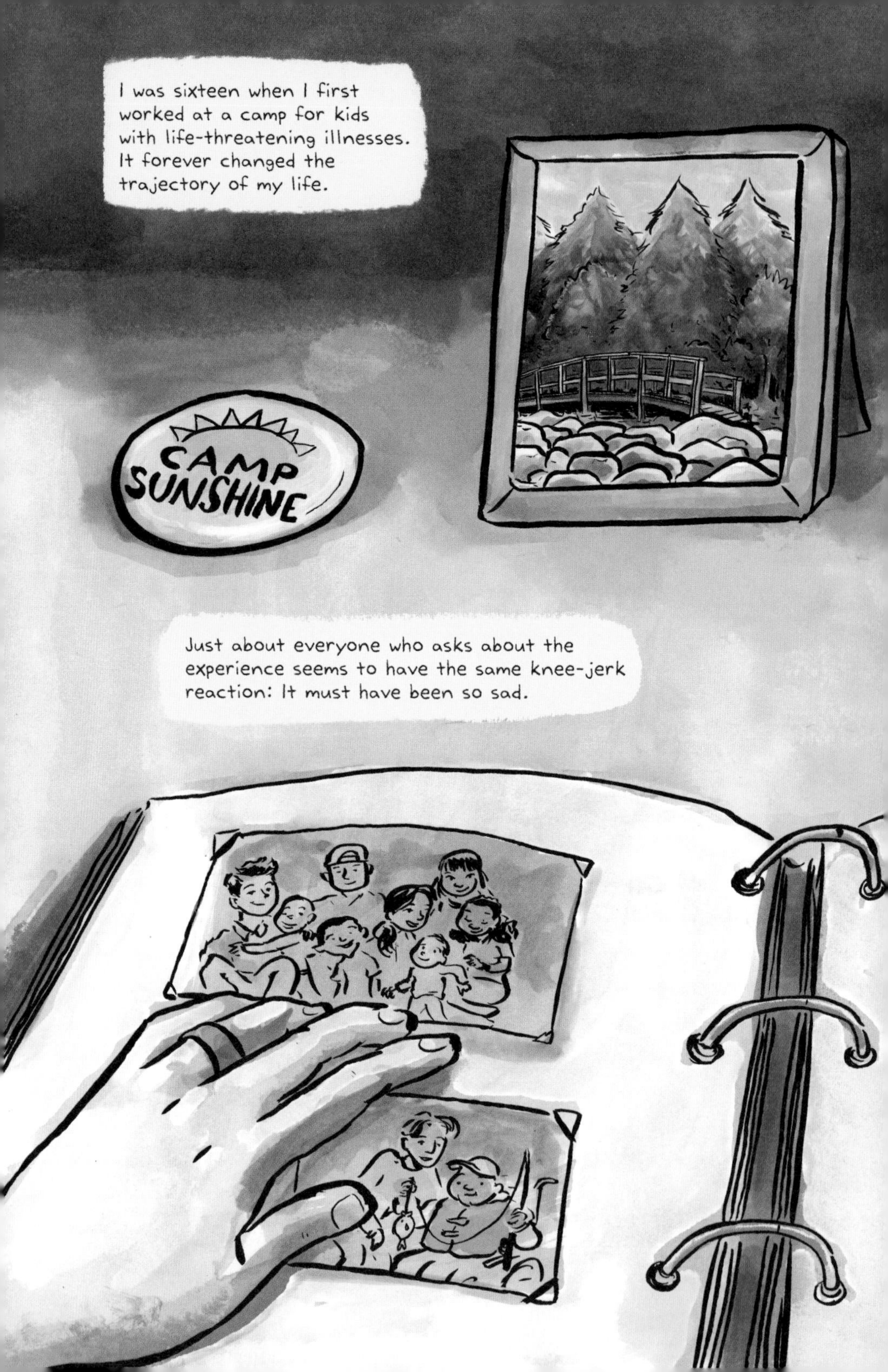
I was sixteen when I first worked at a camp for kids with life-threatening illnesses. It forever changed the trajectory of my life.
CAMP SUNSHINE
Just about everyone who asks about the experience seems to have the same knee-jerk reaction: It must have been so sad.

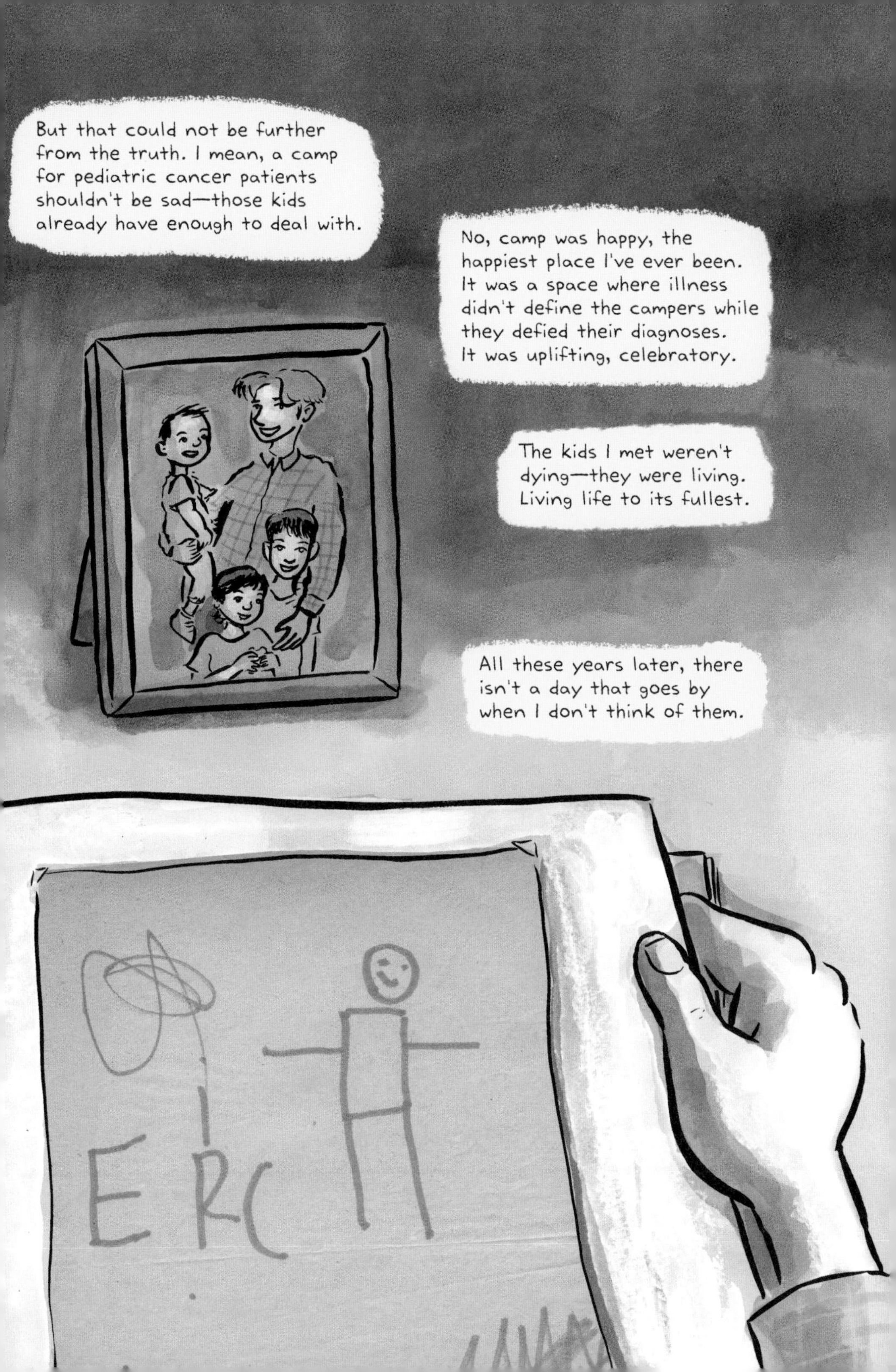
But that could not be further from the truth. I mean, a camp for pediatric cancer patients shouldn't be sad—those kids already have enough to deal with.
No, camp was happy, the happiest place I've ever been. It was a space where illness didn't define the campers while they defied their diagnoses. It was uplifting, celebratory.
The kids I met weren't dying—they were living. Living life to its fullest.
All these years later, there isn't a day that goes by when I don't think of them.
ERC

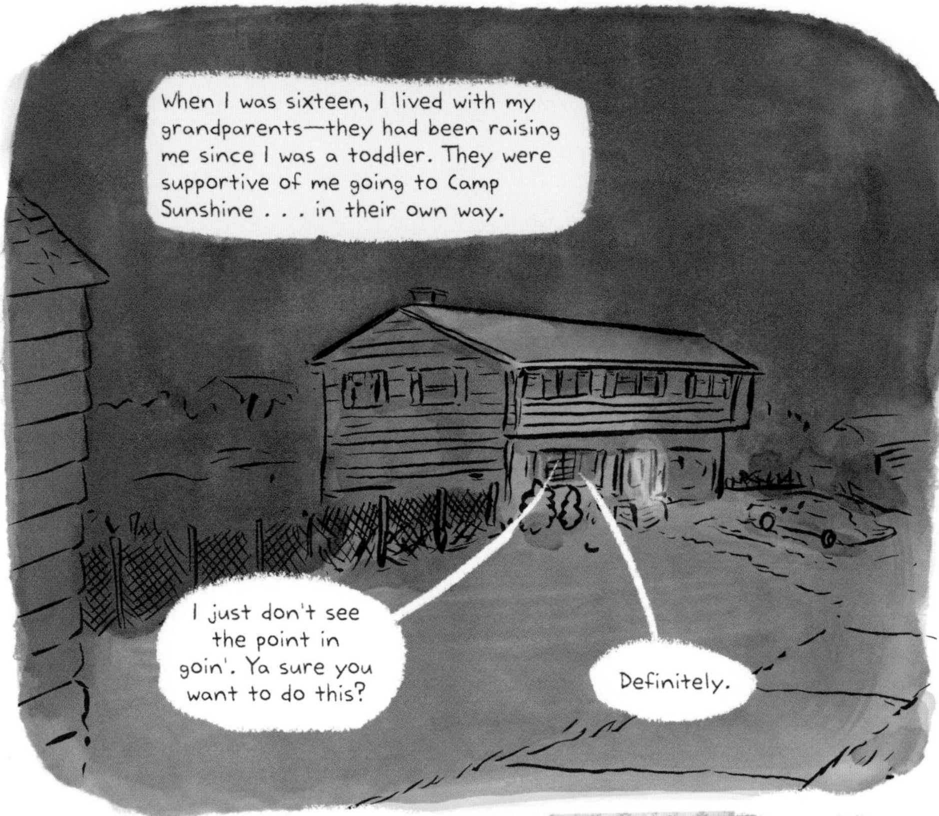
When I was sixteen, I lived with my grandparents—they had been raising me since I was a toddler. They were supportive of me going to Camp Sunshine . . . in their own way.
I just don't see the point in goin'. Ya sure you want to do this?
Definitely.

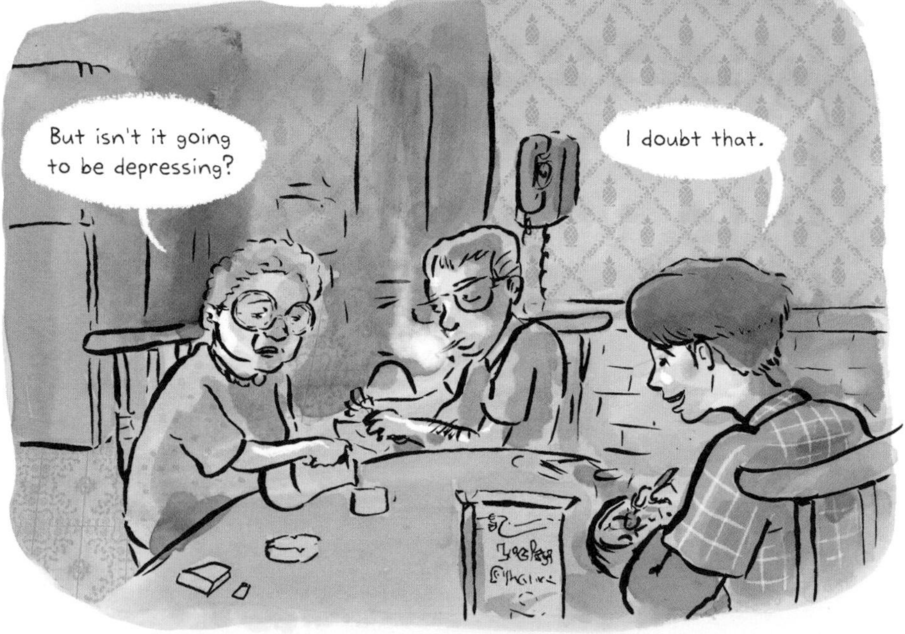
But isn't it going to be depressing?
I doubt that.

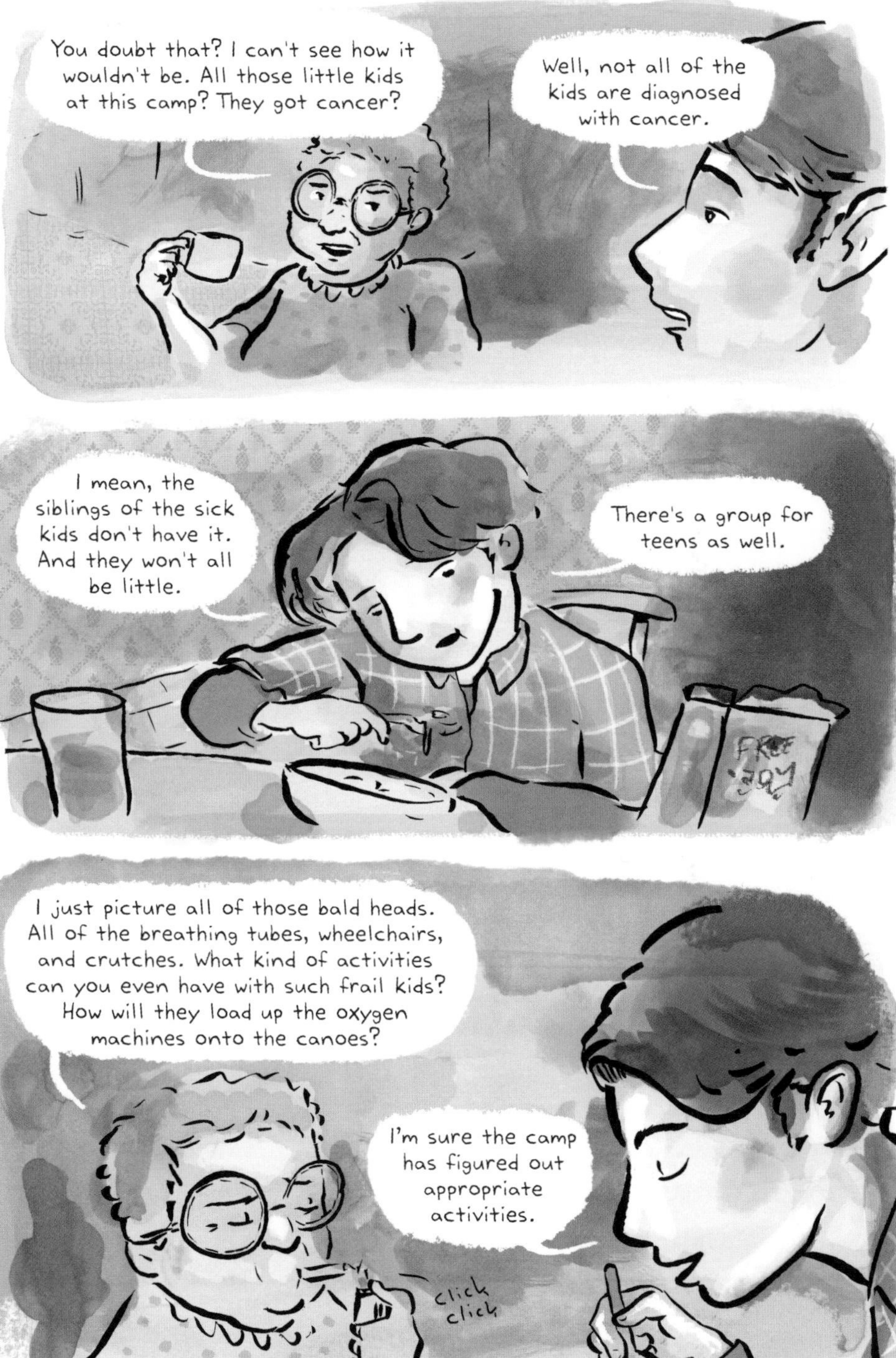
You doubt that? I can't see how it wouldn't be. All those little kids at this camp? They got cancer?
Well, not all of the kids are diagnosed with cancer.
I mean, the siblings of the sick kids don't have it. And they won't all be little.
There's a group for teens as well.
I just picture all of those bald heads. All of the breathing tubes, wheelchairs, and crutches. What kind of activities can you even have with such frail kids? How will they load up the oxygen machines onto the canoes?
I'm sure the camp has figured out appropriate activities.
click click

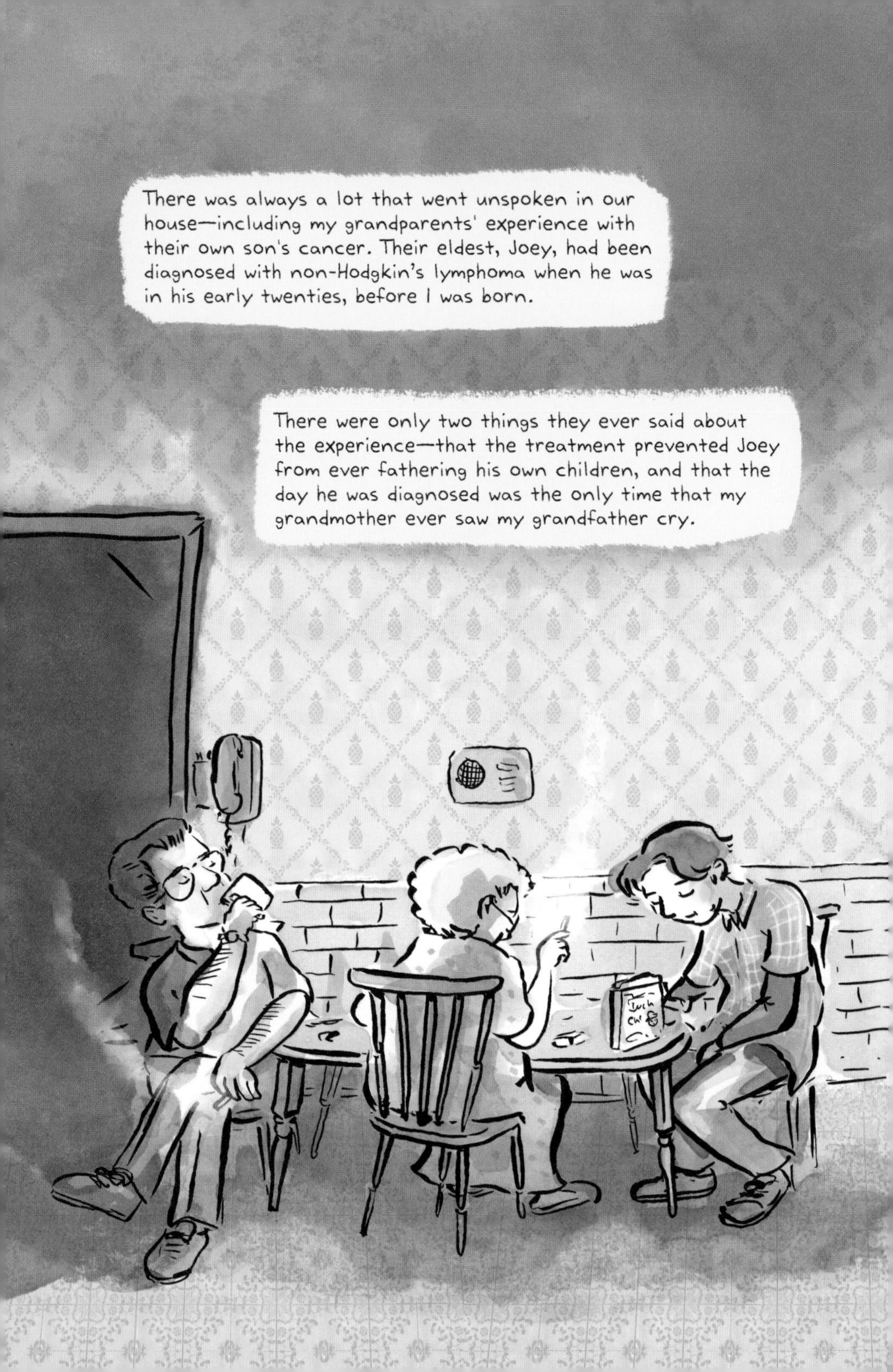
There was always a lot that went unspoken in our house—including my grandparents' experience with their own son's cancer. Their eldest, Joey, had been diagnosed with non-Hodgkin's lymphoma when he was in his early twenties, before I was born.
There were only two things they ever said about the experience—that the treatment prevented Joey from ever fathering his own children, and that the day he was diagnosed was the only time that my grandmother ever saw my grandfather cry.

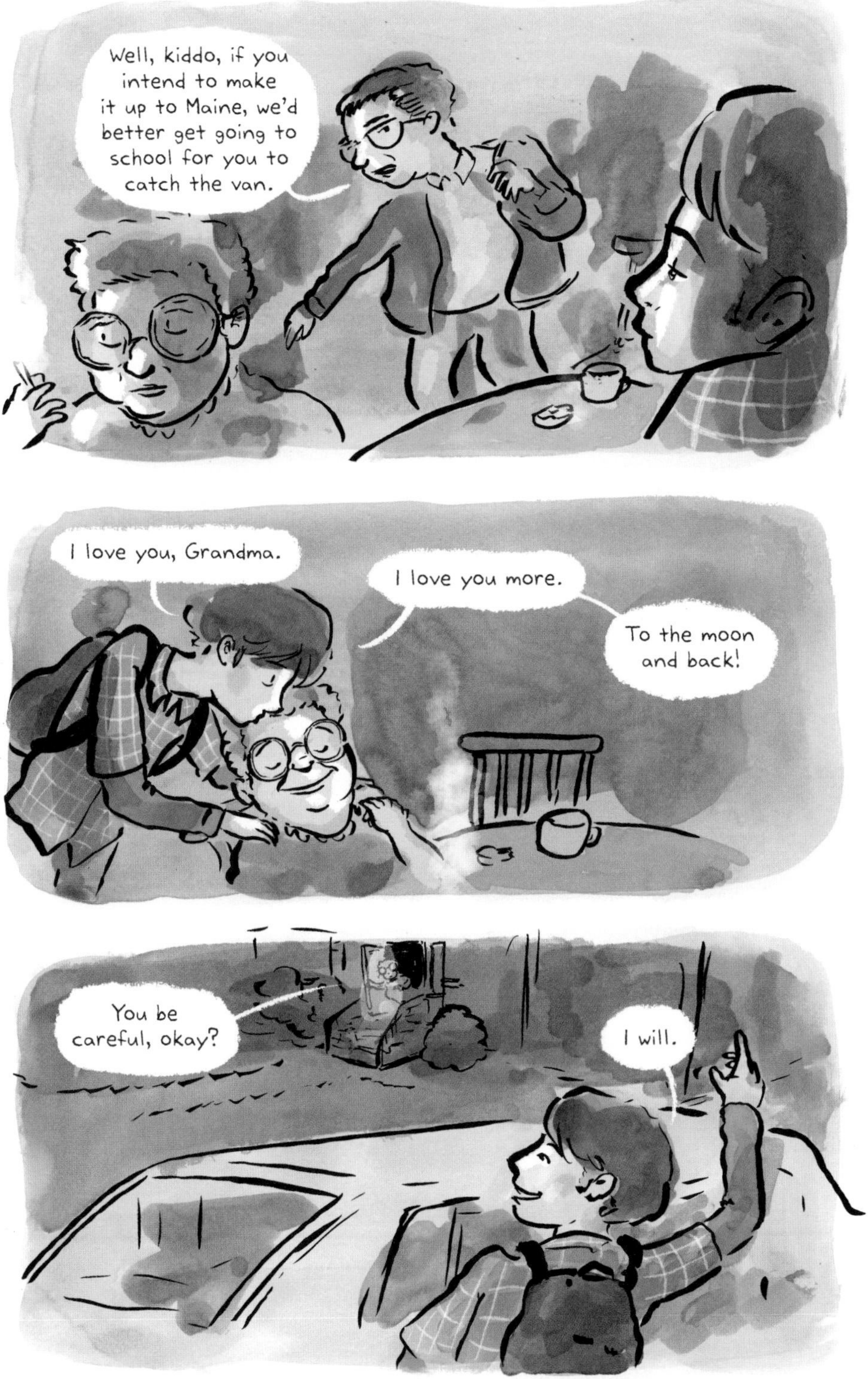
Well, kiddo, if you intend to make it up to Maine, we'd better get going to school for you to catch the van.
I love you, Grandma.
I love you more.
To the moon and back!
You be careful, okay?
I will.

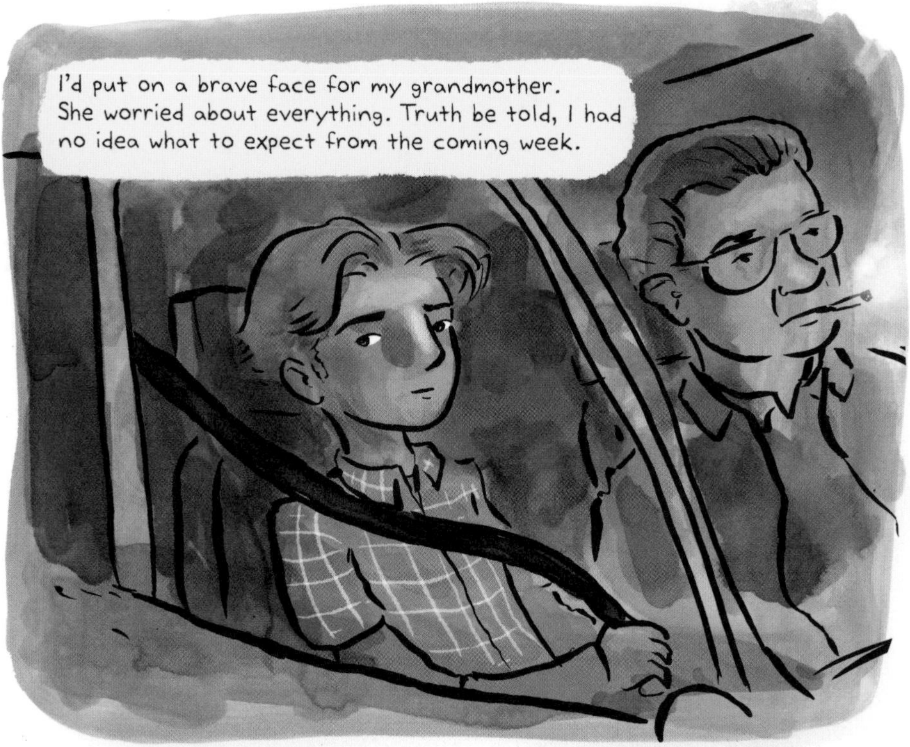
I'd put on a brave face for my grandmother. She worried about everything. Truth be told, I had no idea what to expect from the coming week.

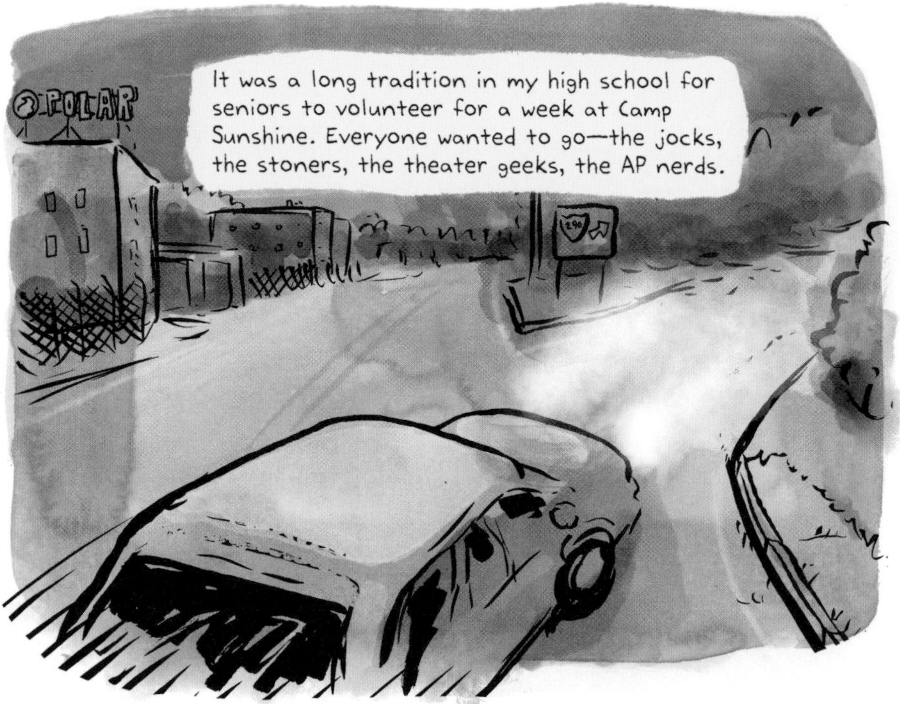
POLAR
It was a long tradition in my high school for seniors to volunteer for a week at Camp Sunshine. Everyone wanted to go—the jocks, the stoners, the theater geeks, the AP nerds.

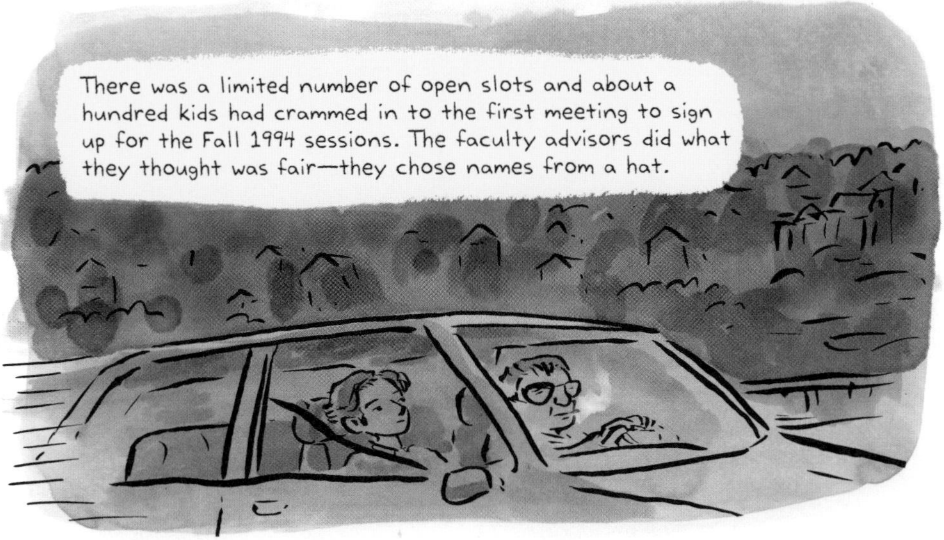
There was a limited number of open slots and about a hundred kids had crammed in to the first meeting to sign up for the Fall 1994 sessions. The faculty advisors did what they thought was fair—they chose names from a hat.

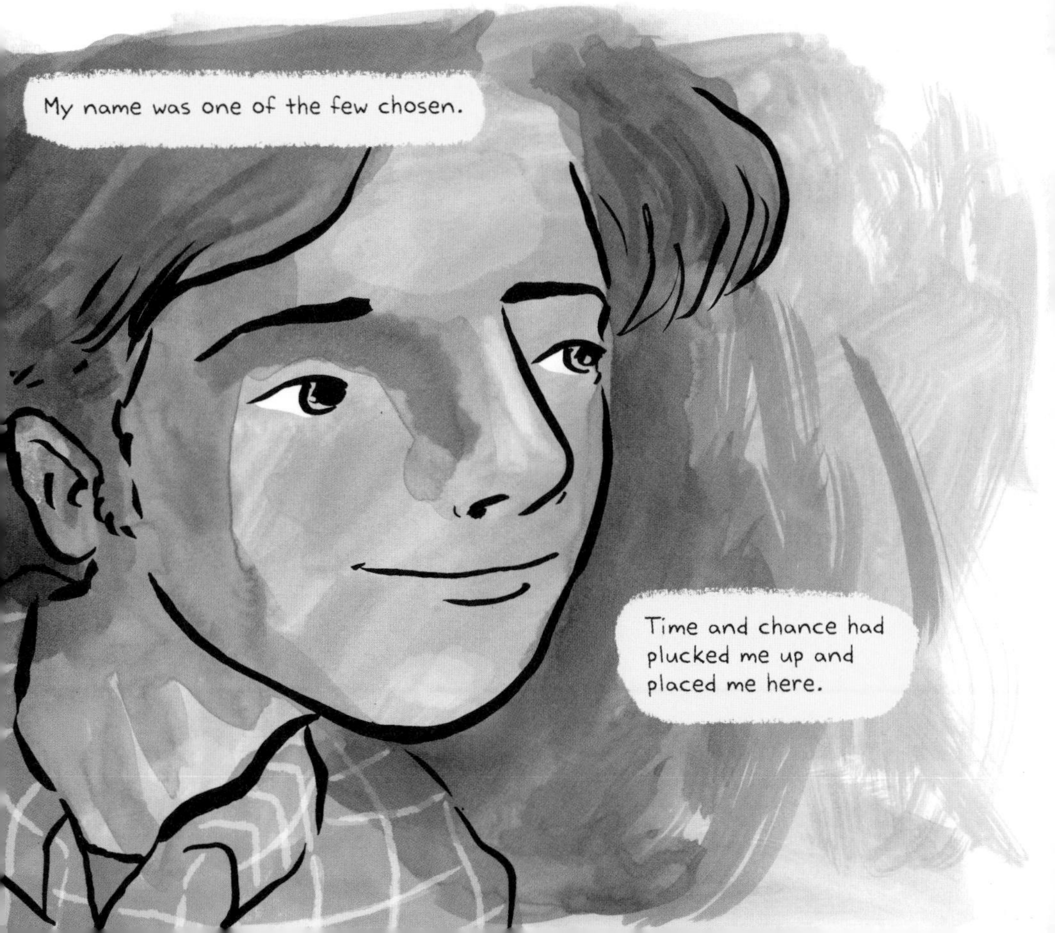
My name was one of the few chosen.
Time and chance had plucked me up and placed me here.

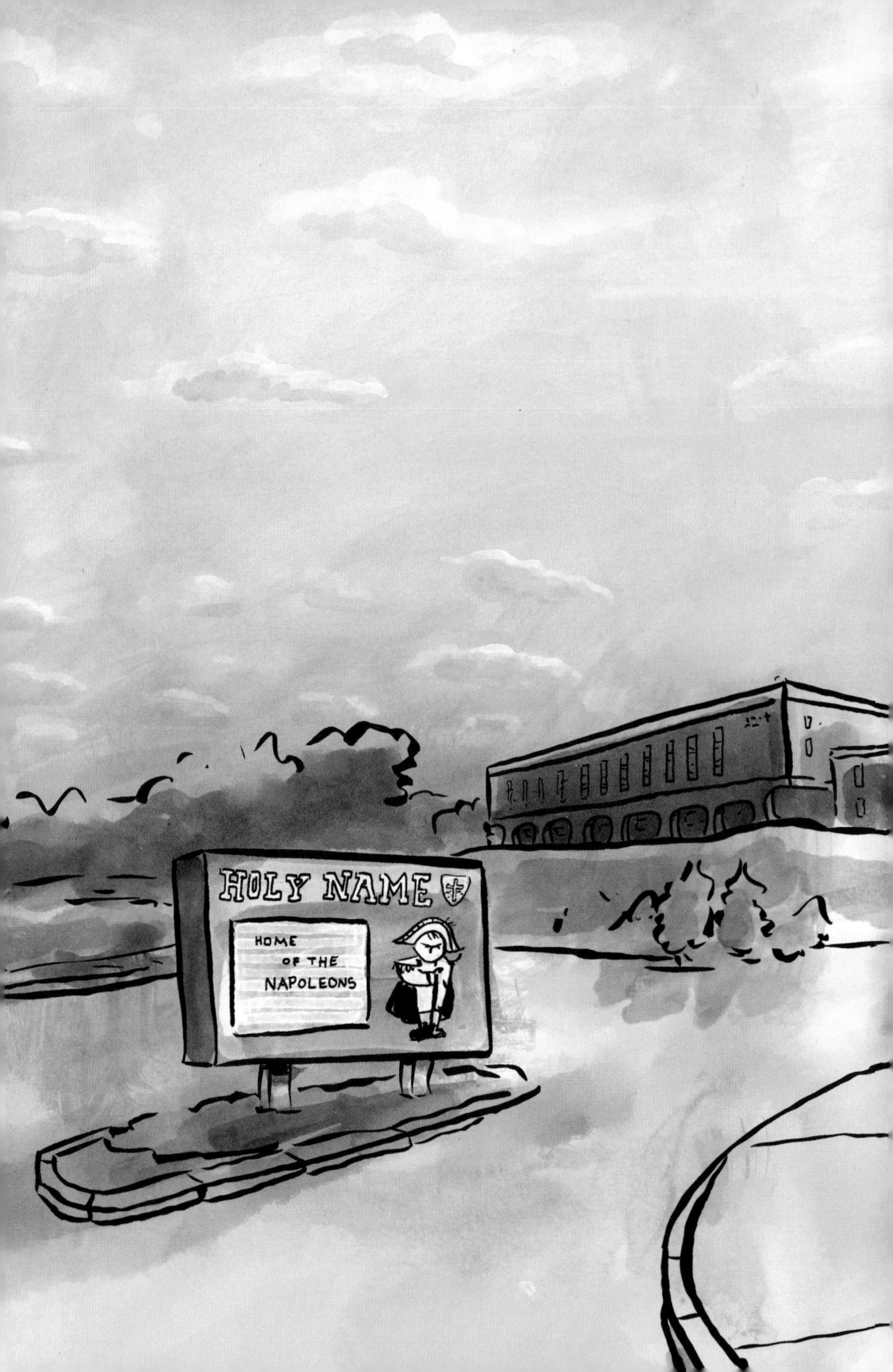
HOLY NAME
HOME
OF THE
NAPOLEONS

SUNSHINE

by Jarrett J. Krosoczka

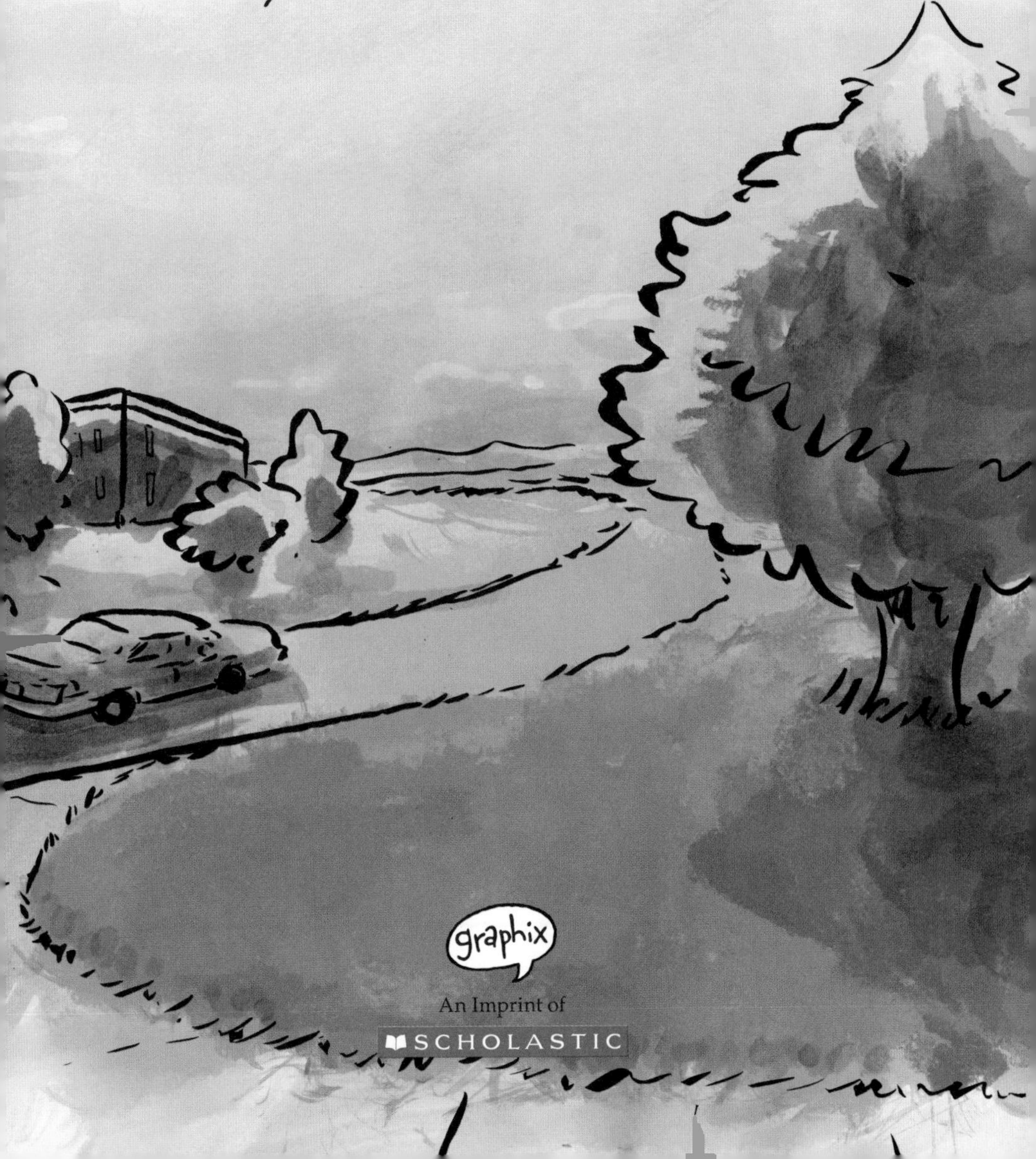

graphix
An Imprint of
SCHOLASTIC

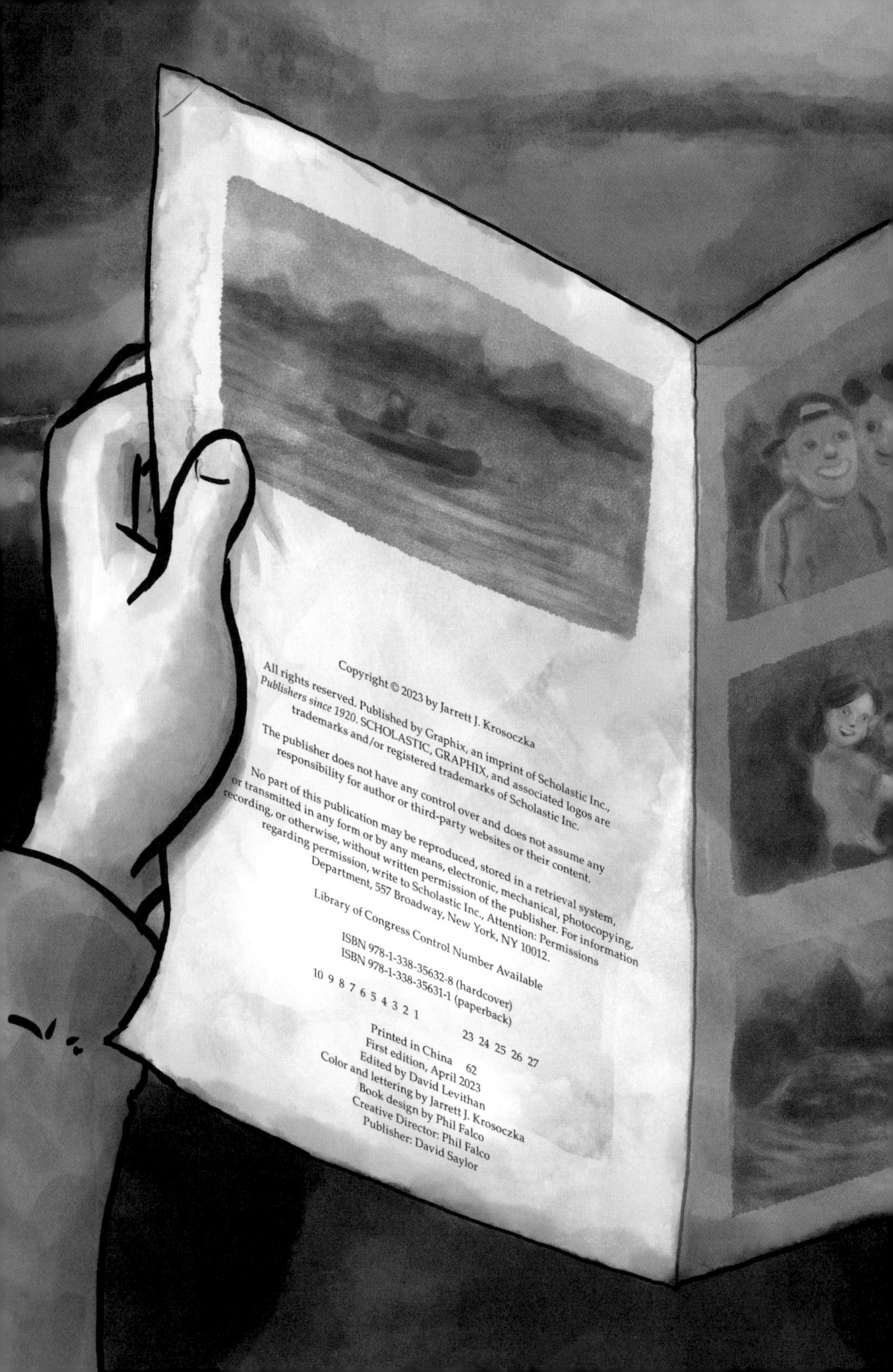

Library of Congress Control Number Available

ISBN 978-1-338-35632-8 (hardcover)
ISBN 978-1-338-35631-1 (paperback)

10 9 8 7 6 5 4 3 2 1 23 24 25 26 27

Printed in China 62
First edition, April 2023
Edited by David Levithan
Color and lettering by Jarrett J. Krosoczka
Book design by Phil Falco
Creative Director: Phil Falco
Publisher: David Saylor

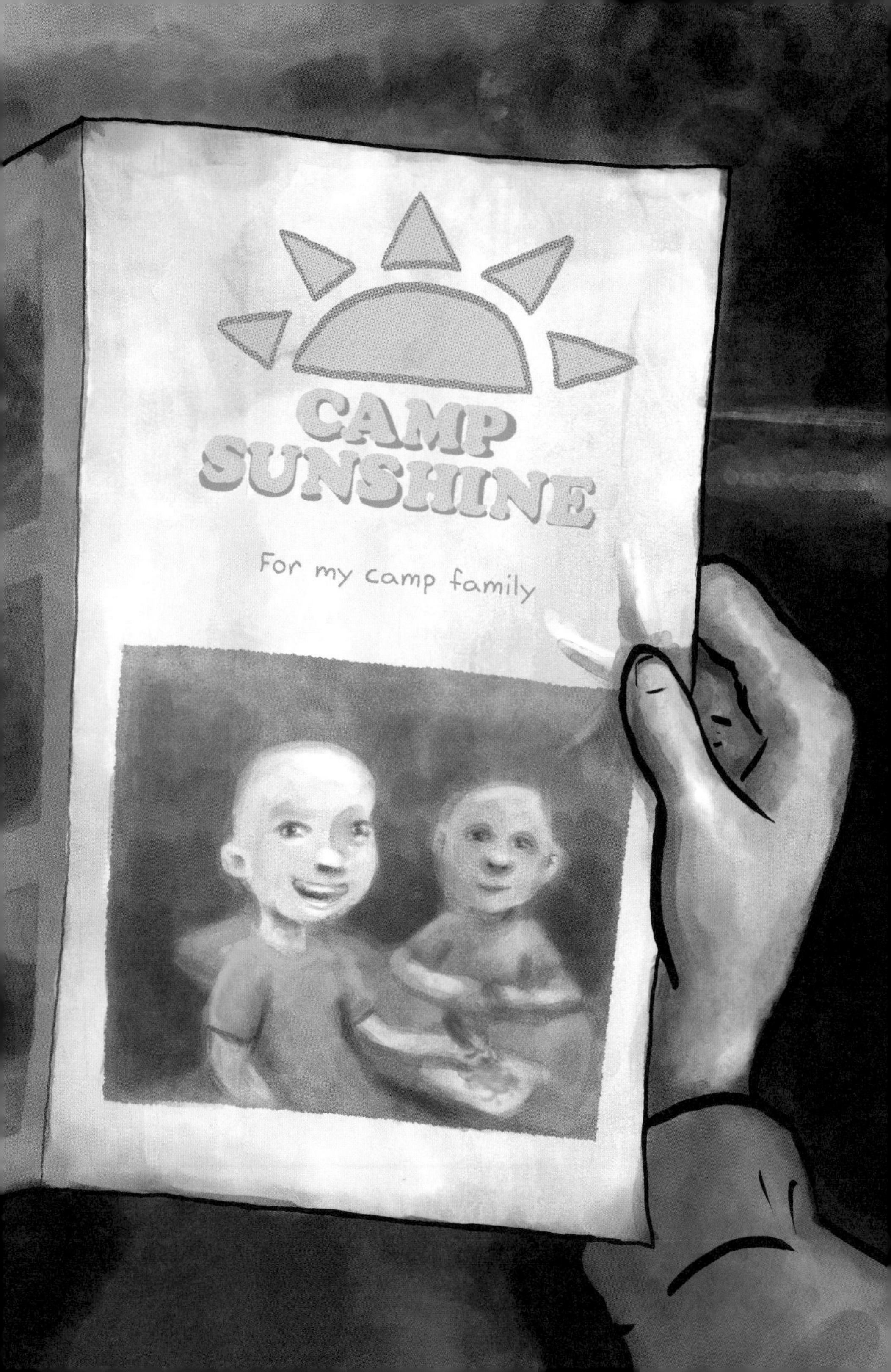
CAMP
SUNSHINE
For my camp family

CAMP SUNSHINE

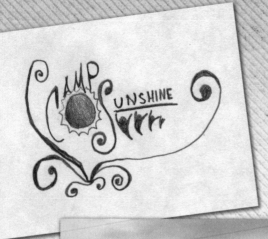

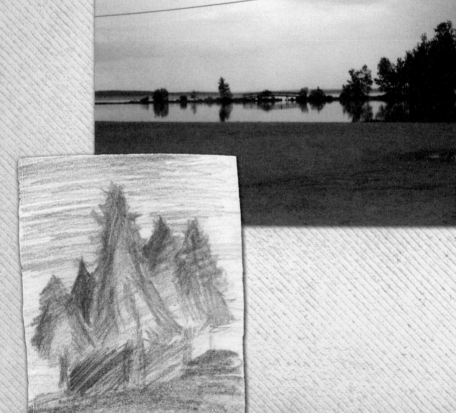

CHAPTER 1
ROAD TRIP

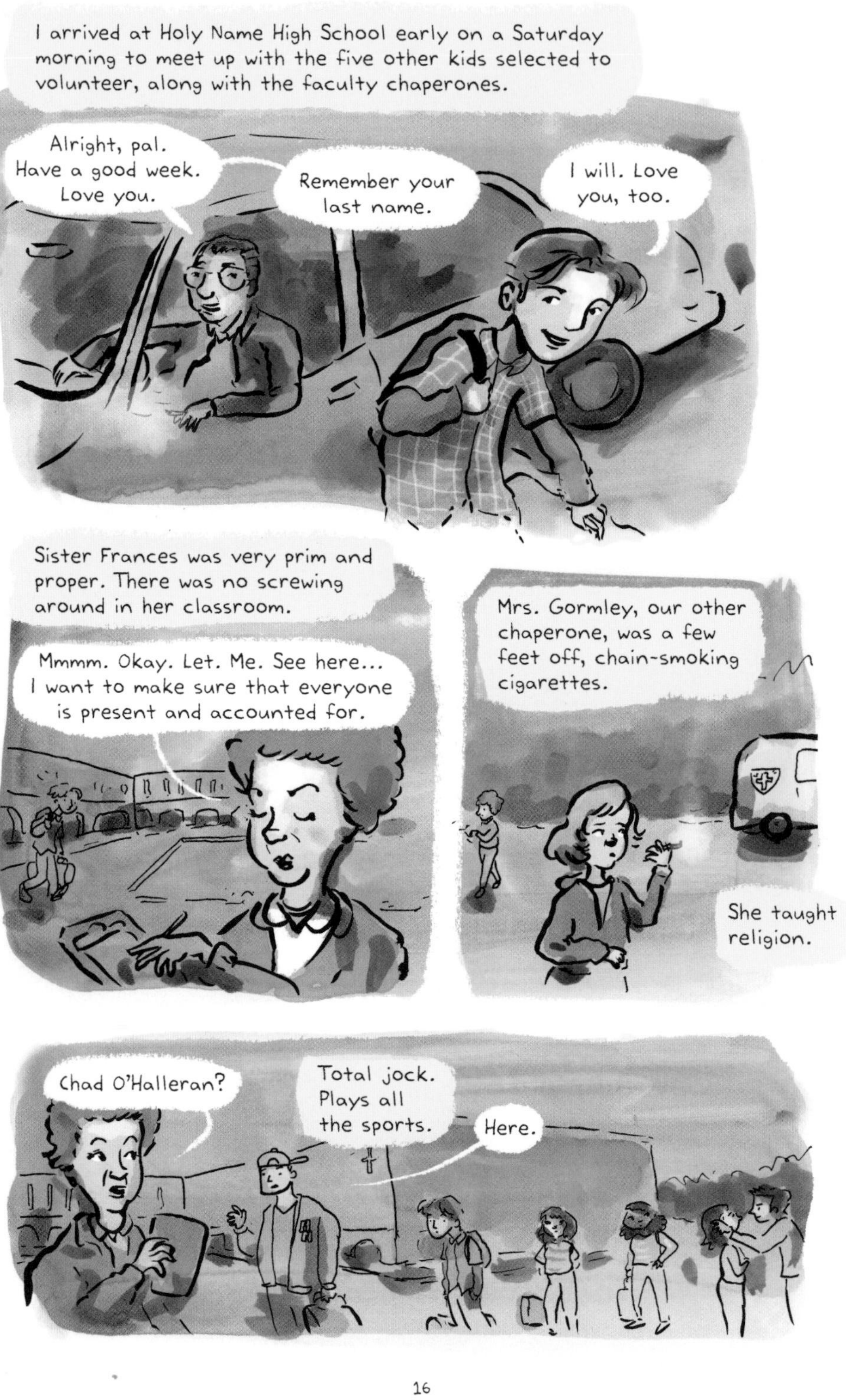
I arrived at Holy Name High School early on a Saturday morning to meet up with the five other kids selected to volunteer, along with the faculty chaperones.
Alright, pal. Have a good week. Love you.
Remember your last name.
I will. Love you, too.
Sister Frances was very prim and proper. There was no screwing around in her classroom.
Mmmm. Okay. Let. Me. See here... I want to make sure that everyone is present and accounted for.
Mrs. Gormley, our other chaperone, was a few feet off, chain-smoking cigarettes.
She taught religion.
Chad O'Halleran?
Total jock. Plays all the sports.
Here.

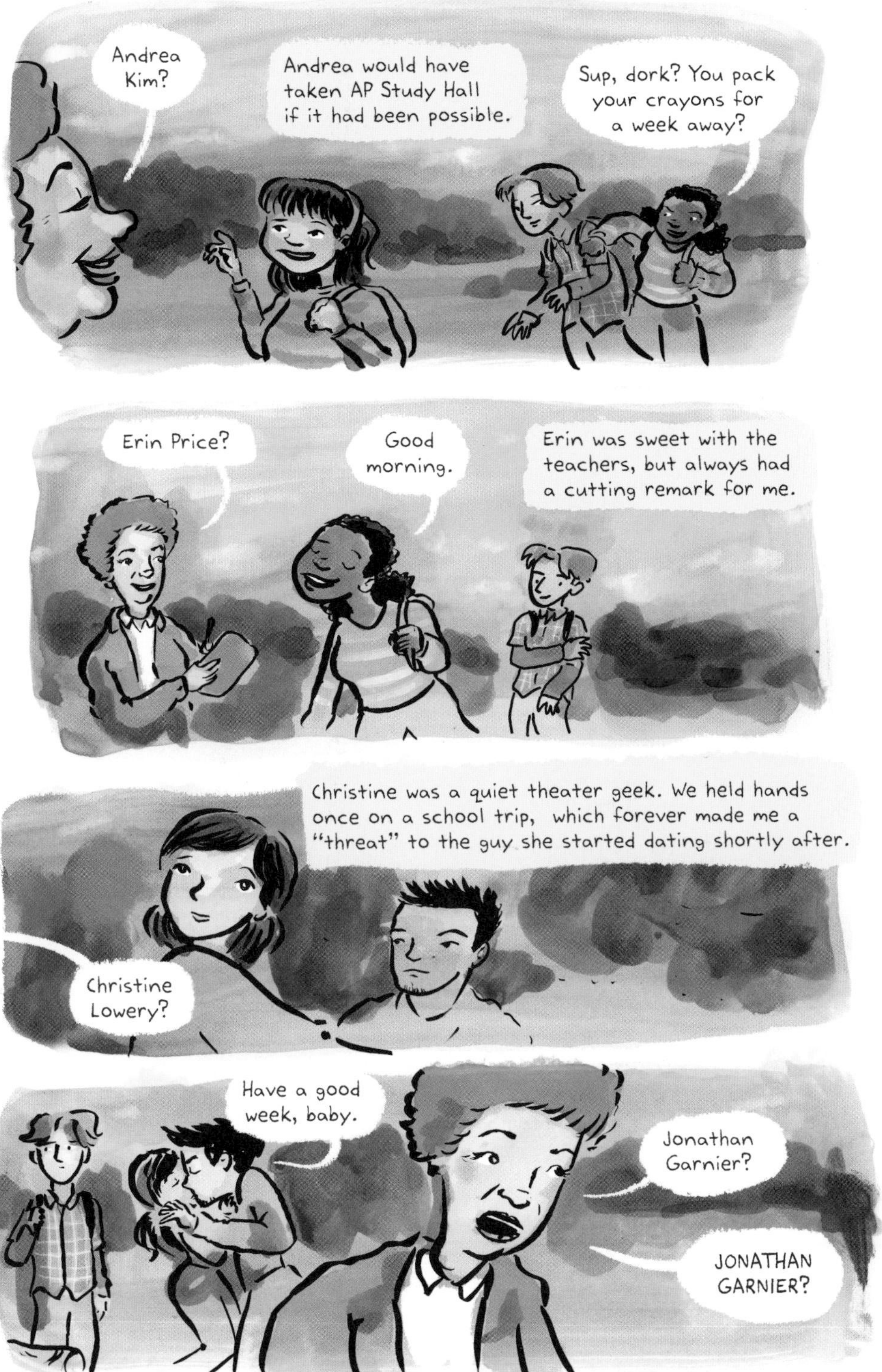
Andrea Kim?
Andrea would have taken AP Study Hall if it had been possible.
Sup, dork? You pack your crayons for a week away?
Erin Price?
Good morning.
Erin was sweet with the teachers, but always had a cutting remark for me.
Christine was a quiet theater geek. We held hands once on a school trip, which forever made me a "threat" to the guy she started dating shortly after.
Christine Lowery?
Have a good week, baby.
Jonathan Garnier?
JONATHAN GARNIER?

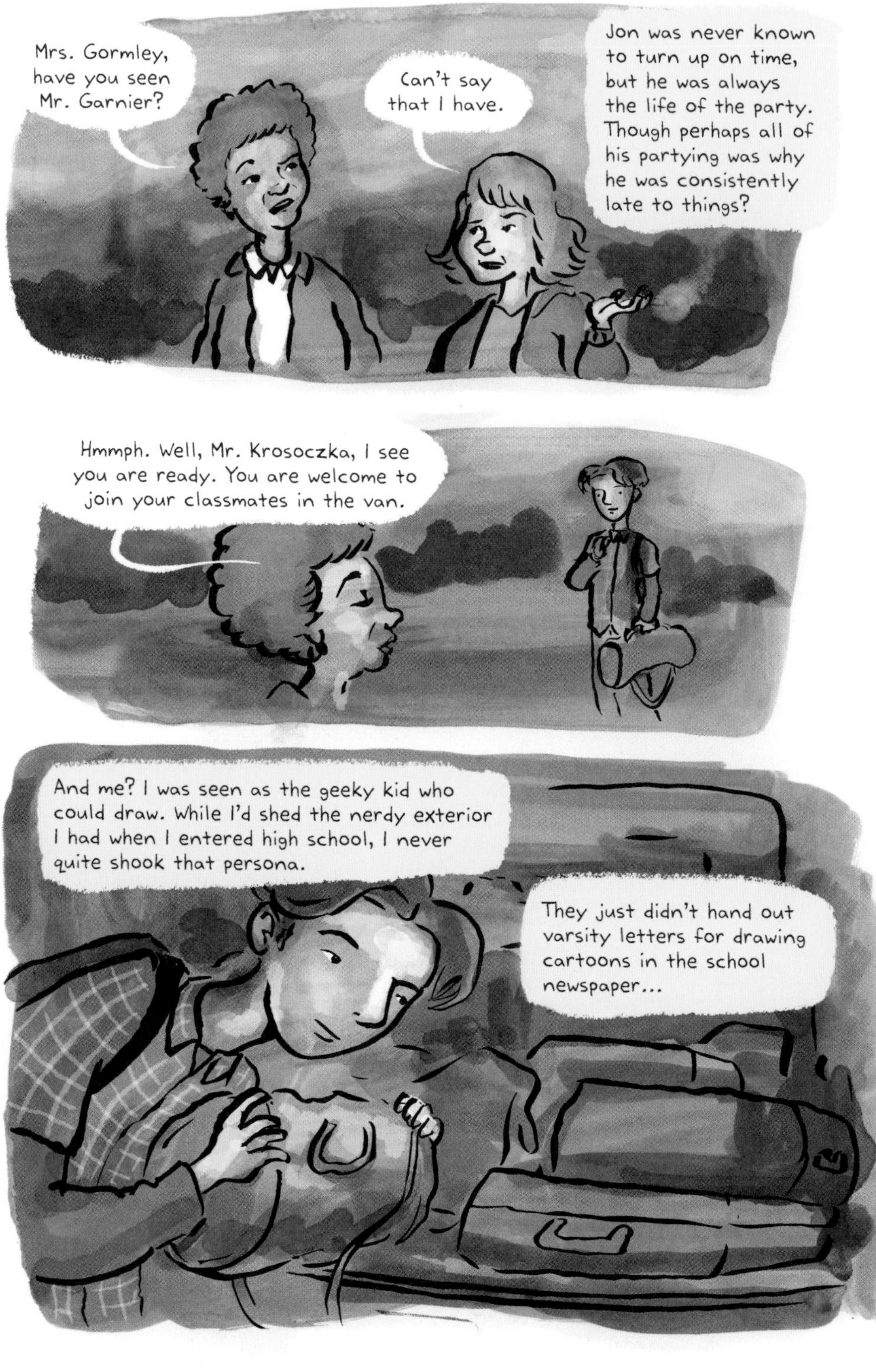
Mrs. Gormley, have you seen Mr. Garnier?
Can't say that I have.
Jon was never known to turn up on time, but he was always the life of the party. Though perhaps all of his partying was why he was consistently late to things?
Hmmph. Well, Mr. Krosoczka, I see you are ready. You are welcome to join your classmates in the van.
And me? I was seen as the geeky kid who could draw. While I'd shed the nerdy exterior I had when I entered high school, I never quite shook that persona.
They just didn't hand out varsity letters for drawing cartoons in the school newspaper...

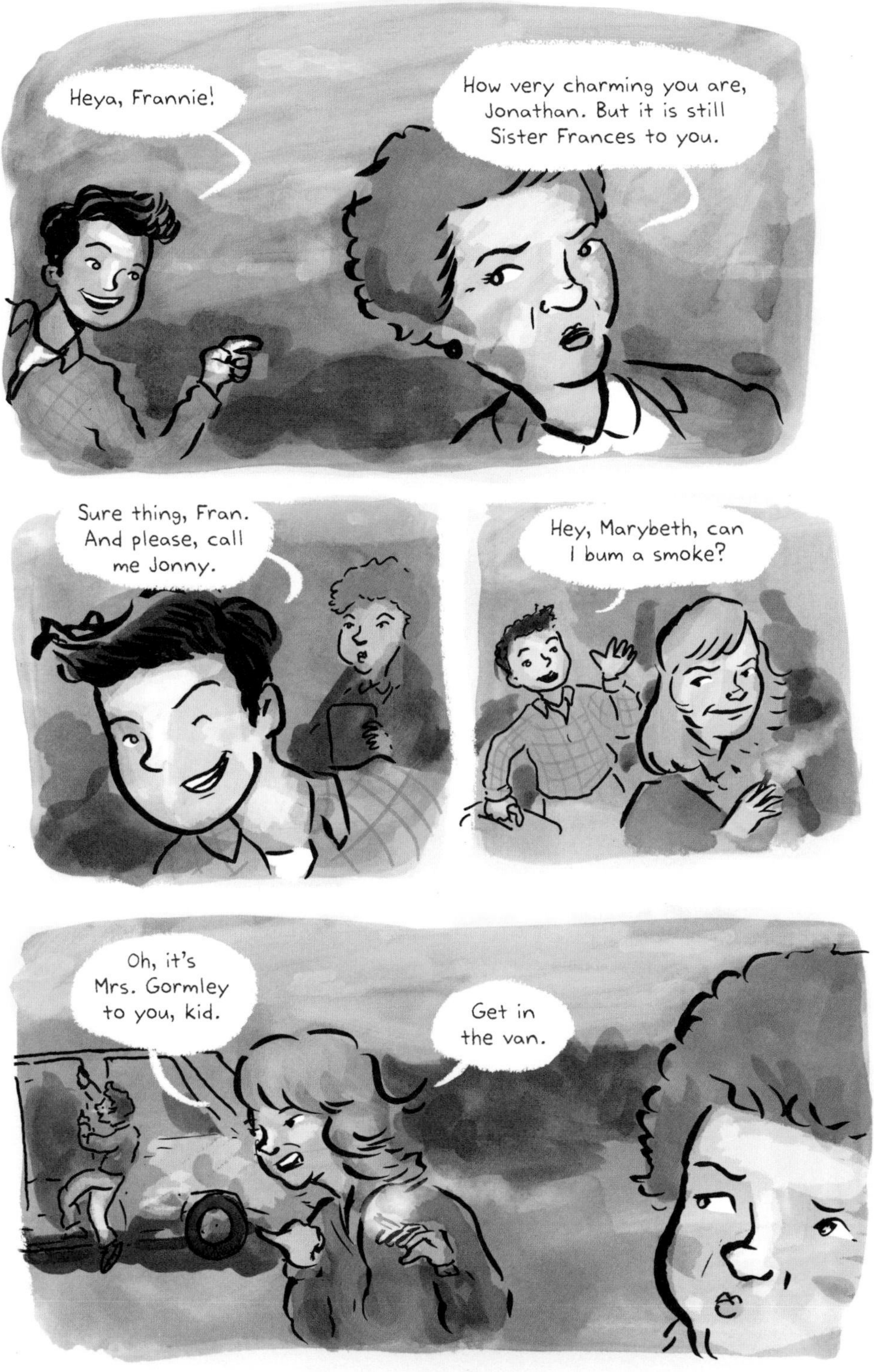
Heya, Frannie!
How very charming you are, Jonathan. But it is still Sister Frances to you.
Sure thing, Fran. And please, call me Jonny.
Hey, Marybeth, can I bum a smoke?
Oh, it's Mrs. Gormley to you, kid.
Get in the van.

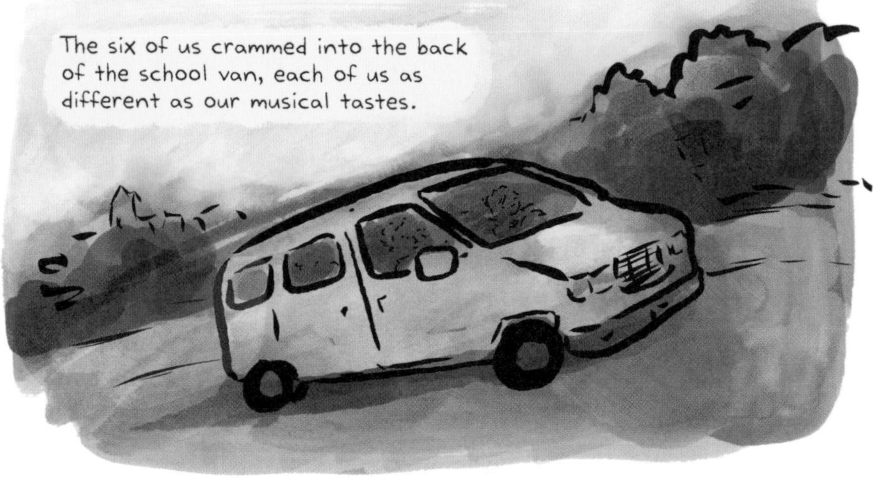
The six of us crammed into the back of the school van, each of us as different as our musical tastes.

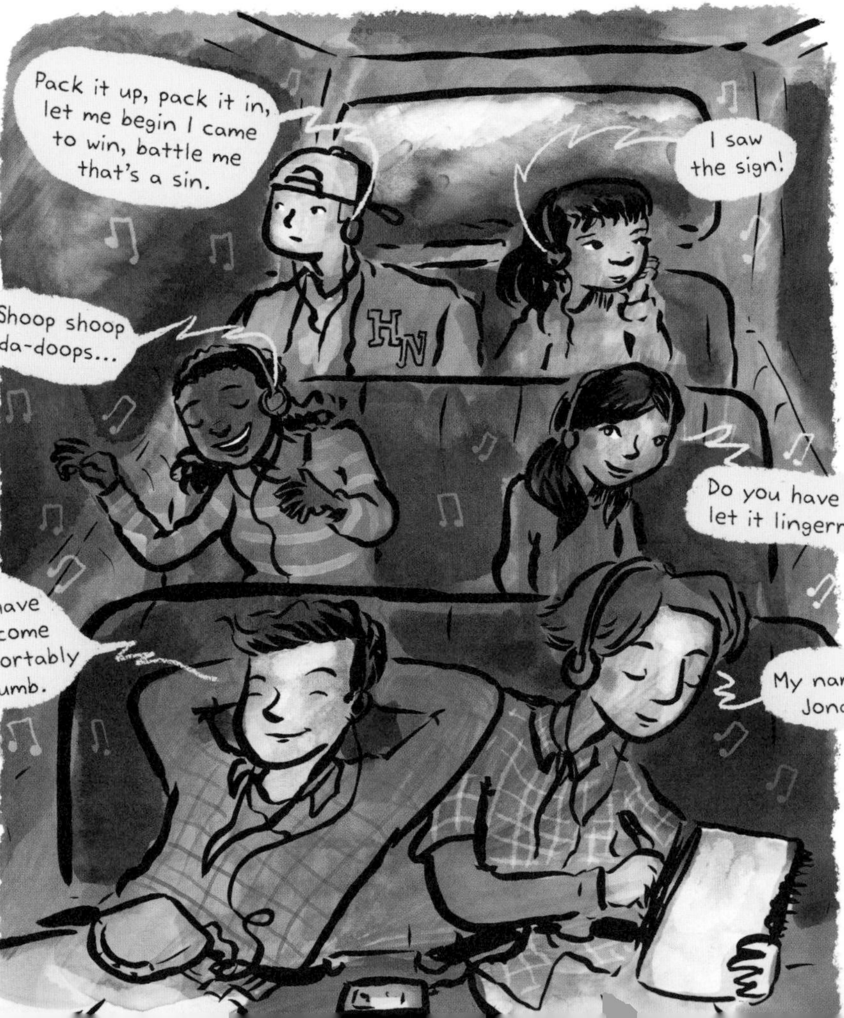
Pack it up, pack it in, let me begin I came to win, battle me that's a sin.
I saw the sign!
HN
Shoop shoop da-doops...
Do you have to let it lingerrr?
I have become comfortably numb.
My name is Jonas!

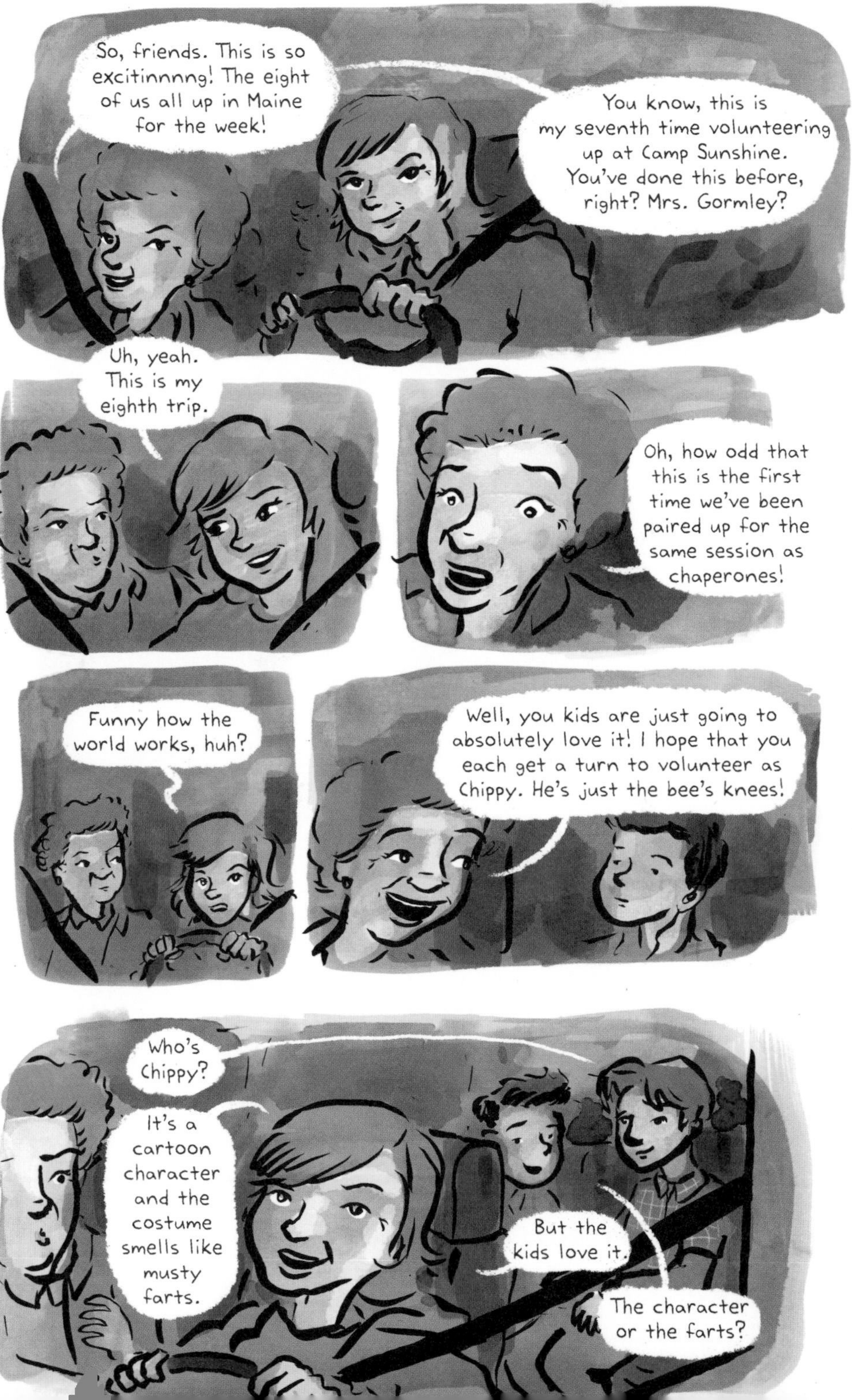
So, friends. This is so excitinnnng! The eight of us all up in Maine for the week!
You know, this is my seventh time volunteering up at Camp Sunshine. You've done this before, right? Mrs. Gormley?
Uh, yeah. This is my eighth trip.
Oh, how odd that this is the first time we've been paired up for the same session as chaperones!
Funny how the world works, huh?
Well, you kids are just going to absolutely love it! I hope that you each get a turn to volunteer as Chippy. He's just the bee's knees!
Who's Chippy?
It's a cartoon character and the costume smells like musty farts.
But the kids love it.
The character or the farts?

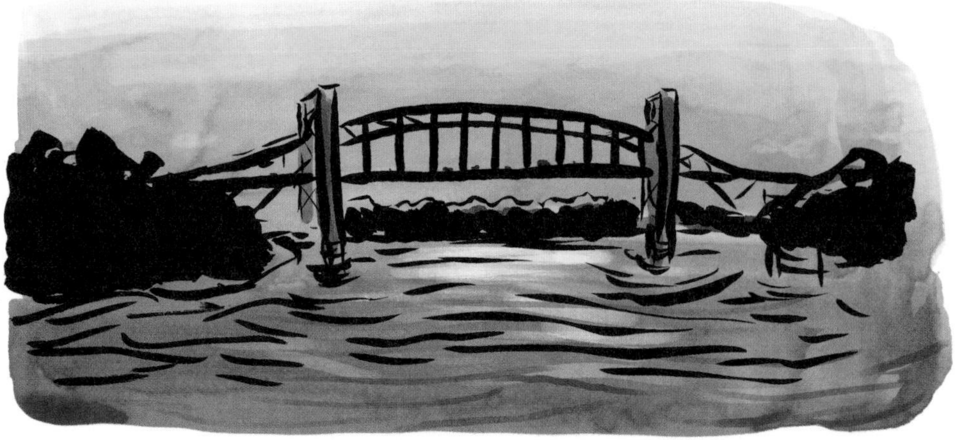

After about three hours in the car, we were at camp. The van pulled up to the administrative offices.

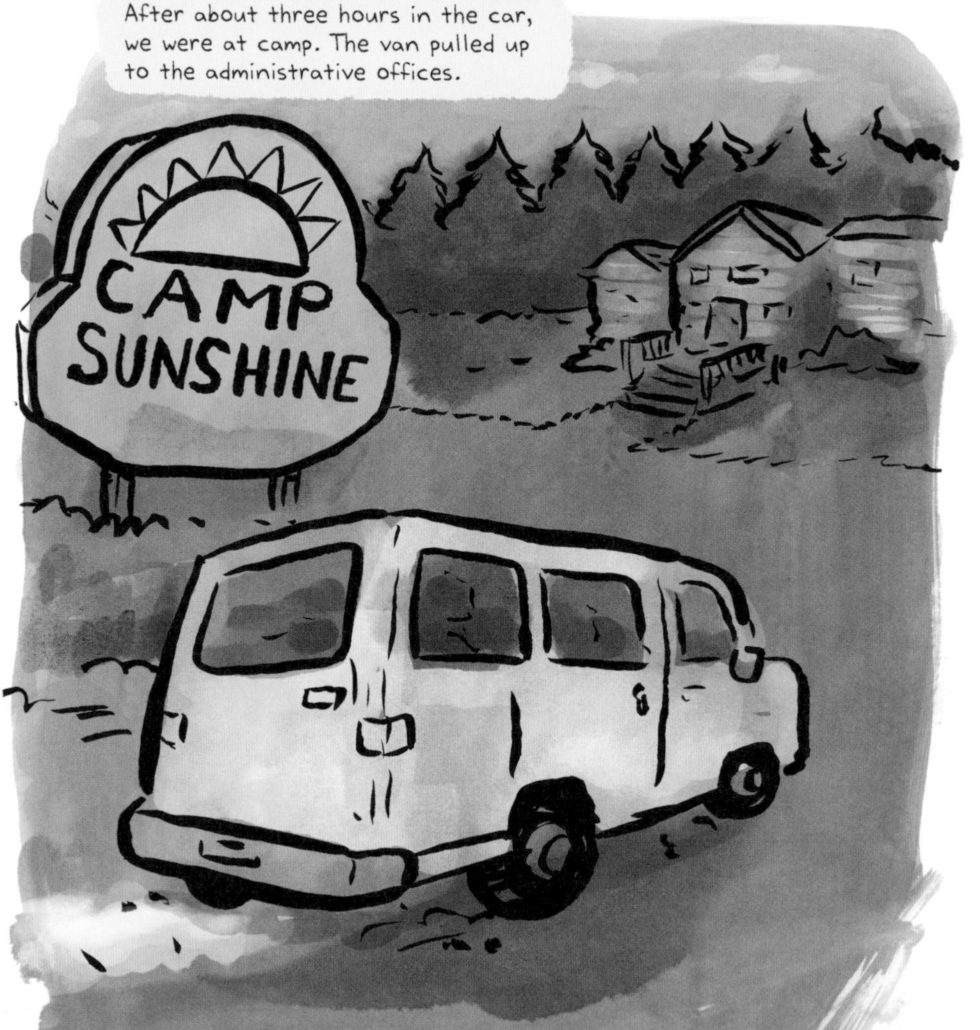
CAMP SUNSHINE

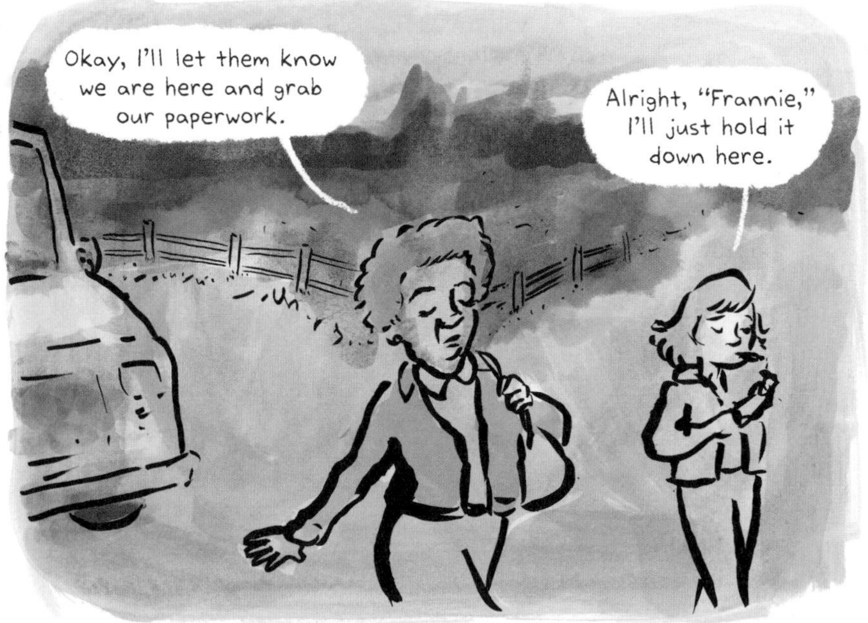
Okay, I'll let them know we are here and grab our paperwork.
Alright, "Frannie," I'll just hold it down here.

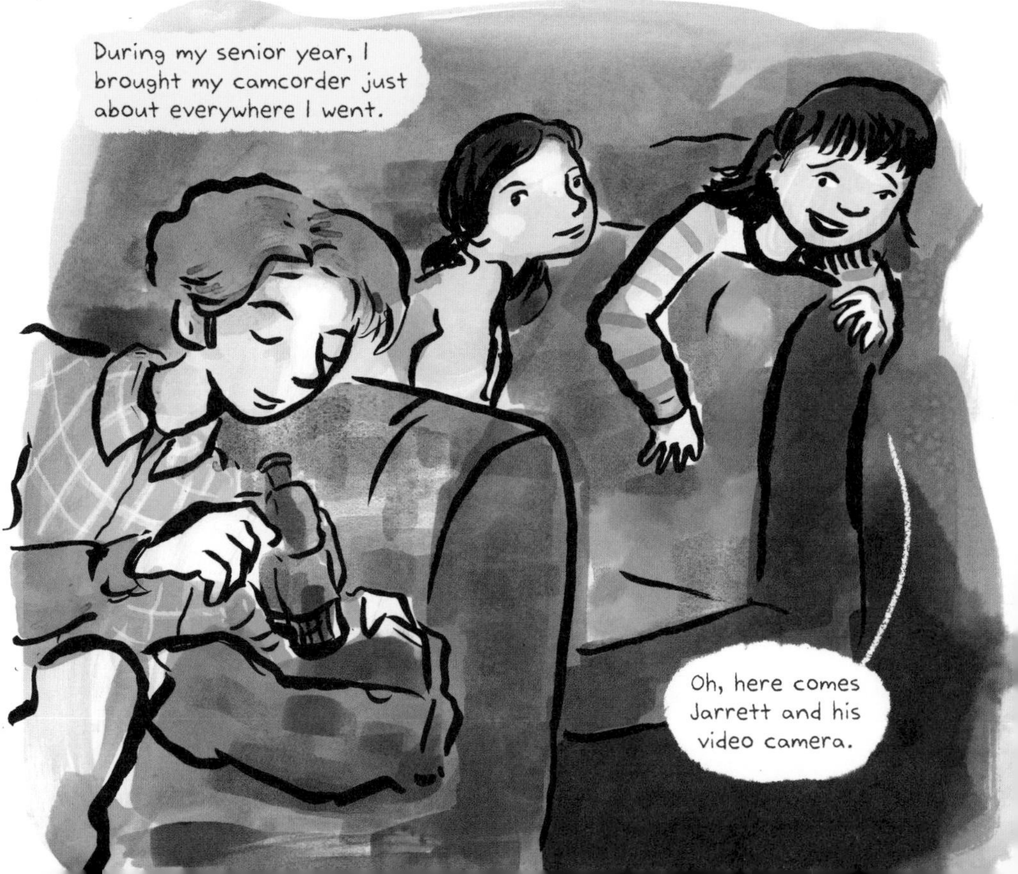
During my senior year, I brought my camcorder just about everywhere I went.
Oh, here comes Jarrett and his video camera.

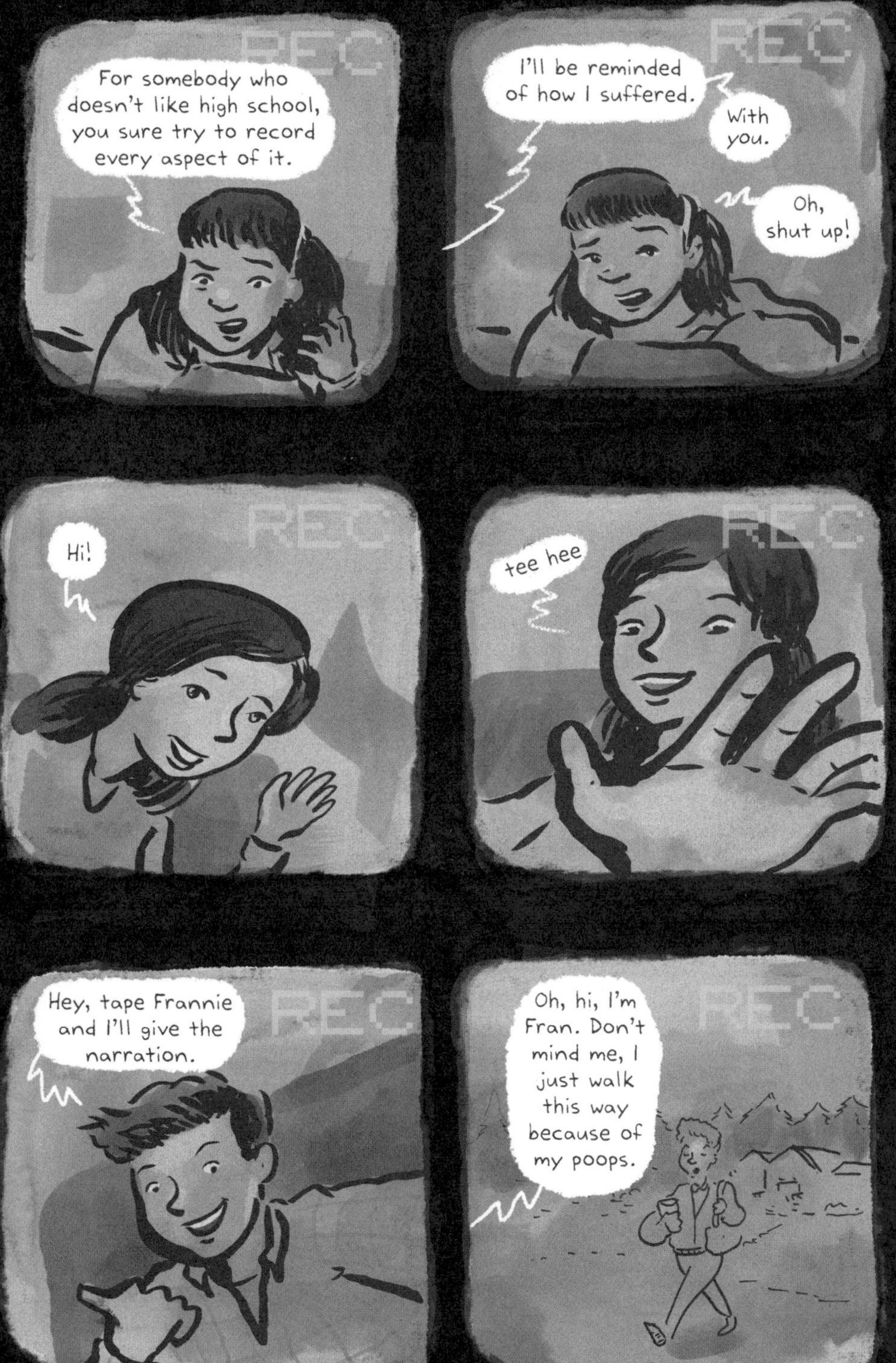
REC
For somebody who doesn't like high school, you sure try to record every aspect of it.
REC
I'll be reminded of how I suffered.
With you.
Oh, shut up!
REC
Hi!
REC
tee hee
REC
Hey, tape Frannie and I'll give the narration.
REC
Oh, hi, I'm Fran. Don't mind me, I just walk this way because of my poops.

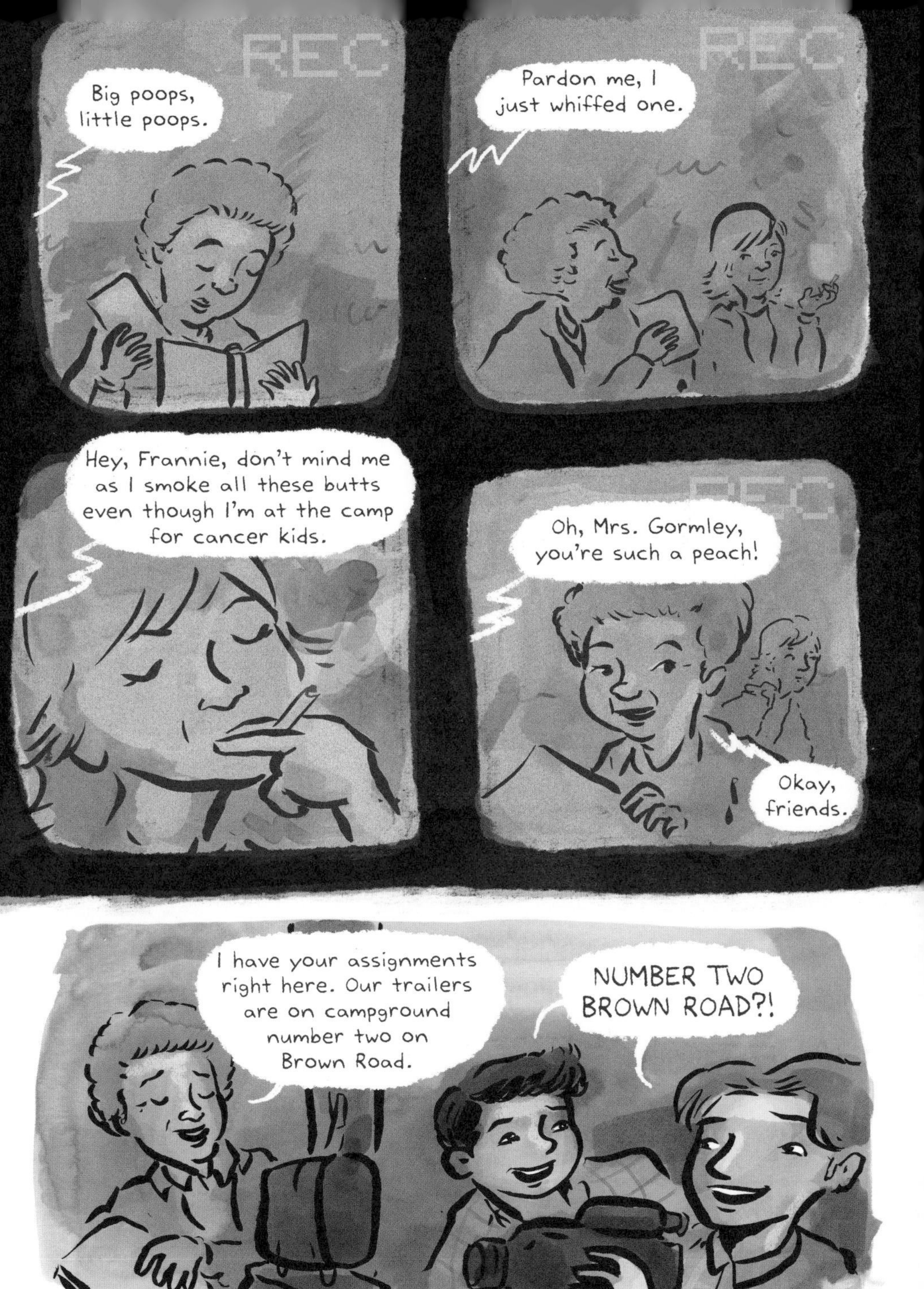
REC
Big poops, little poops.
REC
Pardon me, I just whiffed one.
Hey, Frannie, don't mind me as I smoke all these butts even though I'm at the camp for cancer kids.
REC
Oh, Mrs. Gormley, you're such a peach!
Okay, friends.
I have your assignments right here. Our trailers are on campground number two on Brown Road.
NUMBER TWO BROWN ROAD?!

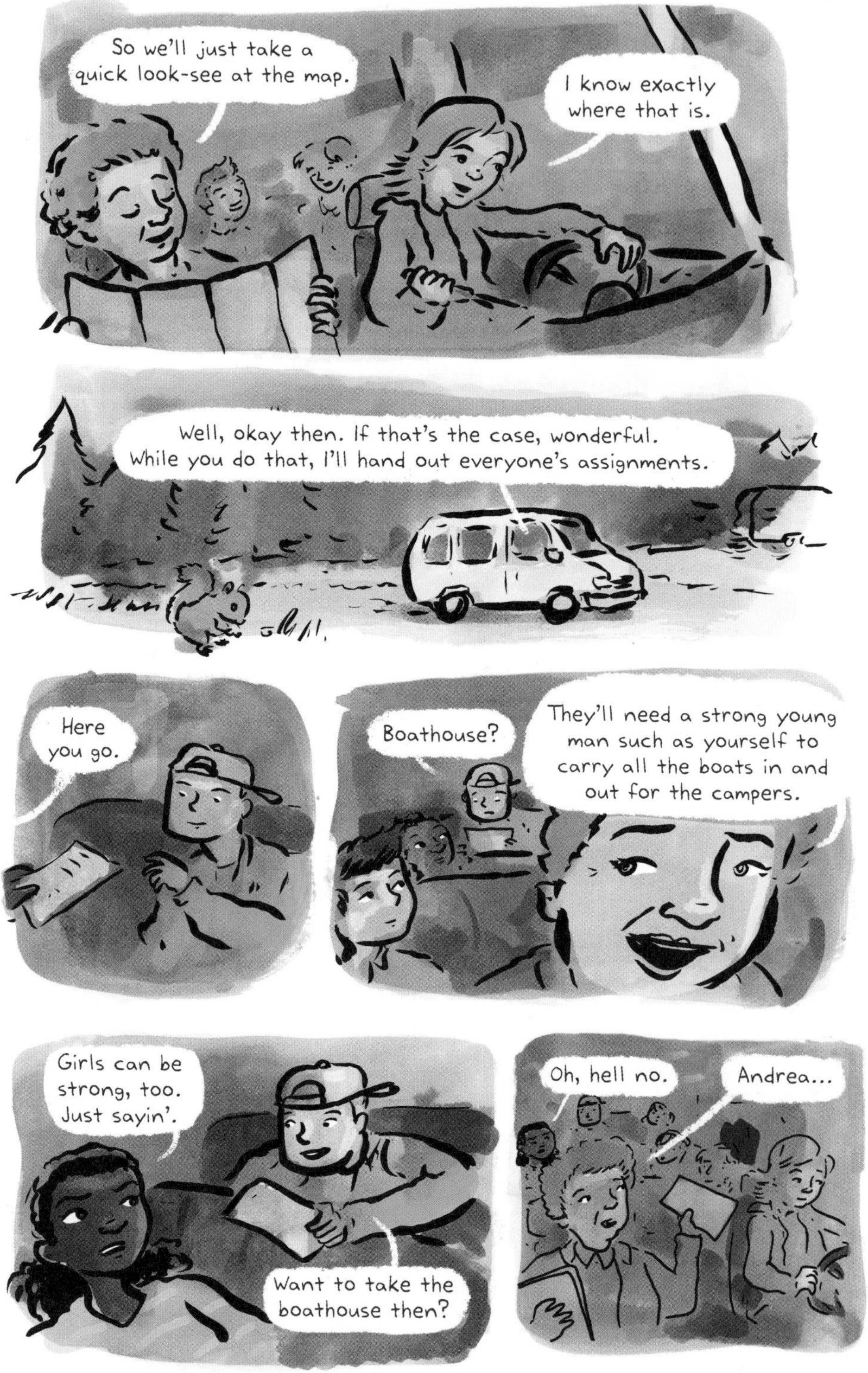

So we'll just take a quick look-see at the map.
I know exactly where that is.
Well, okay then. If that's the case, wonderful. While you do that, I'll hand out everyone's assignments.
Here you go.
Boathouse?
They'll need a strong young man such as yourself to carry all the boats in and out for the campers.
Girls can be strong, too. Just sayin'.
Want to take the boathouse then?
Oh, hell no.
Andrea...

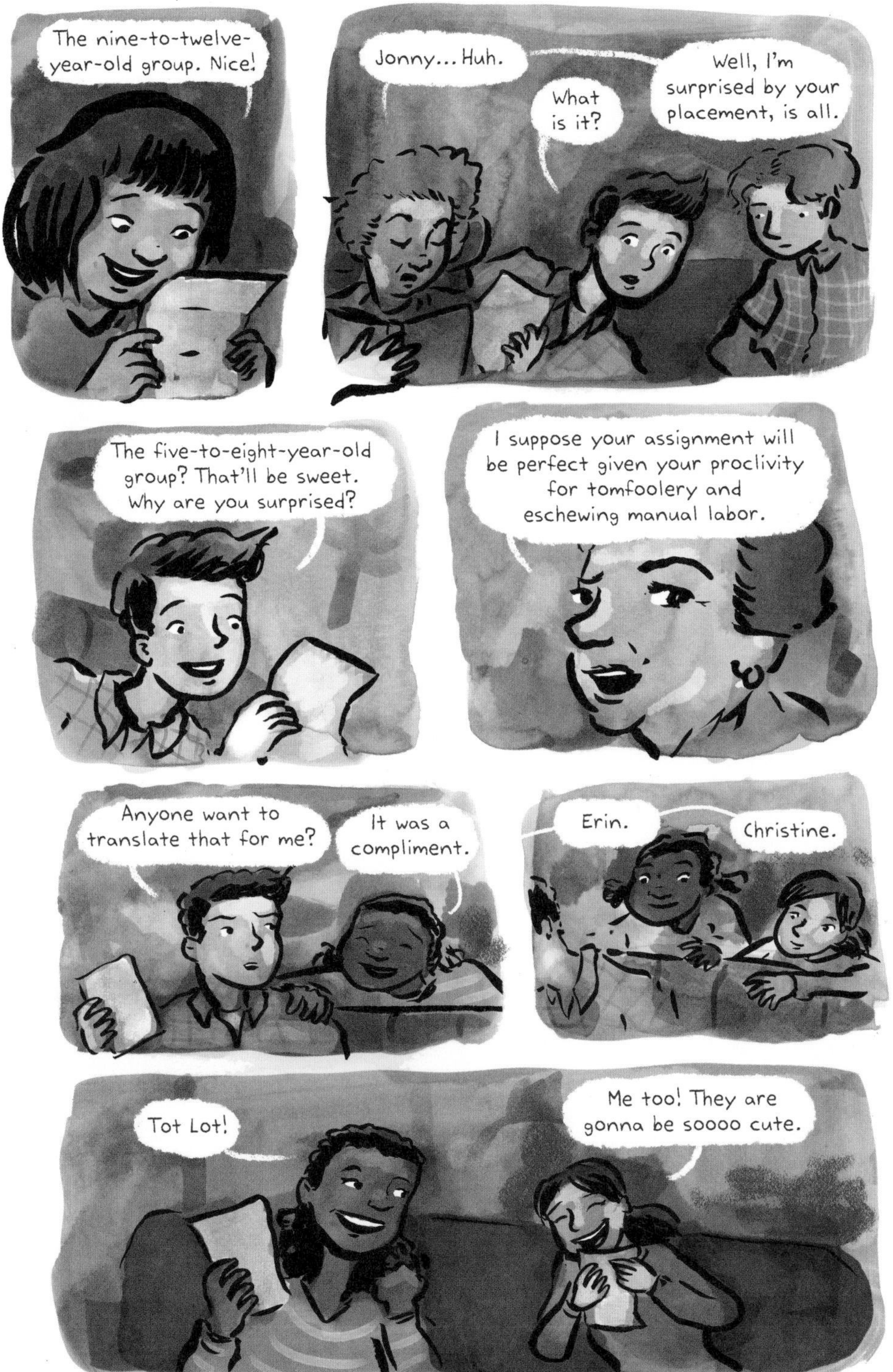
The nine-to-twelve-year-old group. Nice!
Jonny... Huh.
What is it?
Well, I'm surprised by your placement, is all.
The five-to-eight-year-old group? That'll be sweet. Why are you surprised?
I suppose your assignment will be perfect given your proclivity for tomfoolery and eschewing manual labor.
Anyone want to translate that for me?
It was a compliment.
Erin.
Christine.
Tot Lot!
Me too! They are gonna be soooo cute.

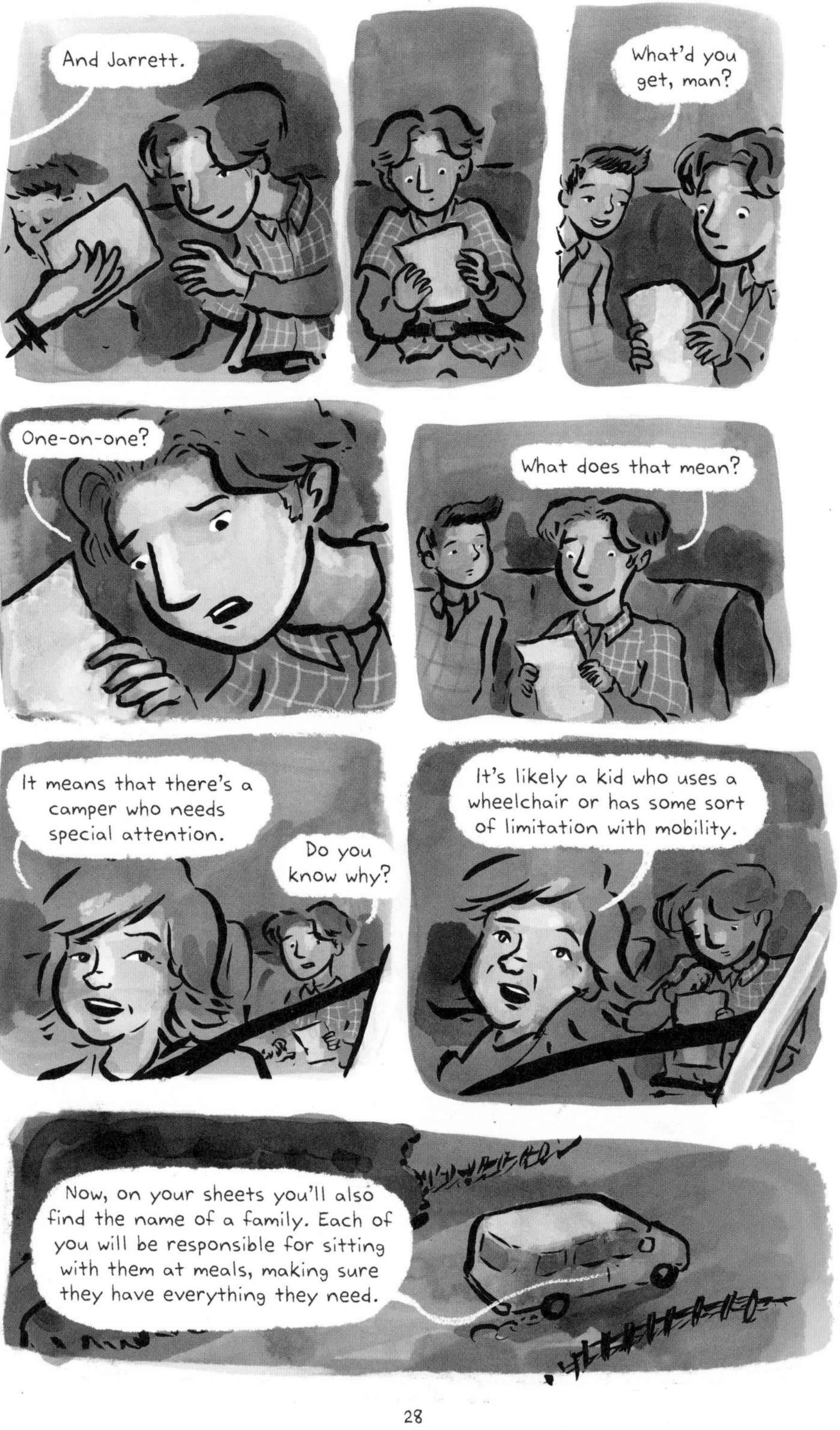

And Jarrett.
What'd you get, man?
One-on-one?
What does that mean?
It means that there's a camper who needs special attention.
Do you know why?
It's likely a kid who uses a wheelchair or has some sort of limitation with mobility.
Now, on your sheets you'll also find the name of a family. Each of you will be responsible for sitting with them at meals, making sure they have everything they need.

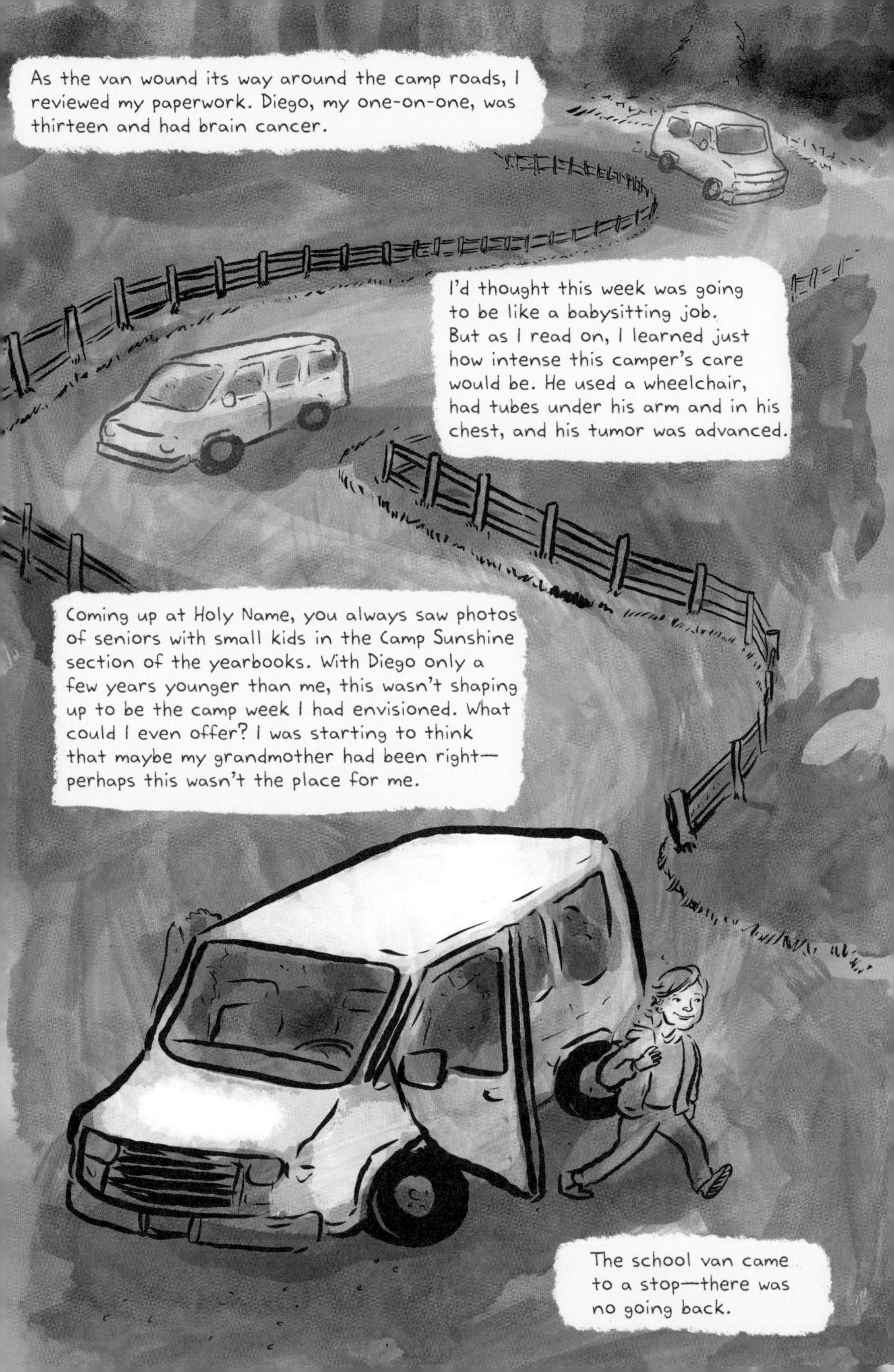
As the van wound its way around the camp roads, I reviewed my paperwork. Diego, my one-on-one, was thirteen and had brain cancer.
I'd thought this week was going to be like a babysitting job. But as I read on, I learned just how intense this camper's care would be. He used a wheelchair, had tubes under his arm and in his chest, and his tumor was advanced.
Coming up at Holy Name, you always saw photos of seniors with small kids in the Camp Sunshine section of the yearbooks. With Diego only a few years younger than me, this wasn't shaping up to be the camp week I had envisioned. What could I even offer? I was starting to think that maybe my grandmother had been right—perhaps this wasn't the place for me.
The school van came to a stop—there was no going back.

We arrived at the pod of trailers where we'd be living for the week.

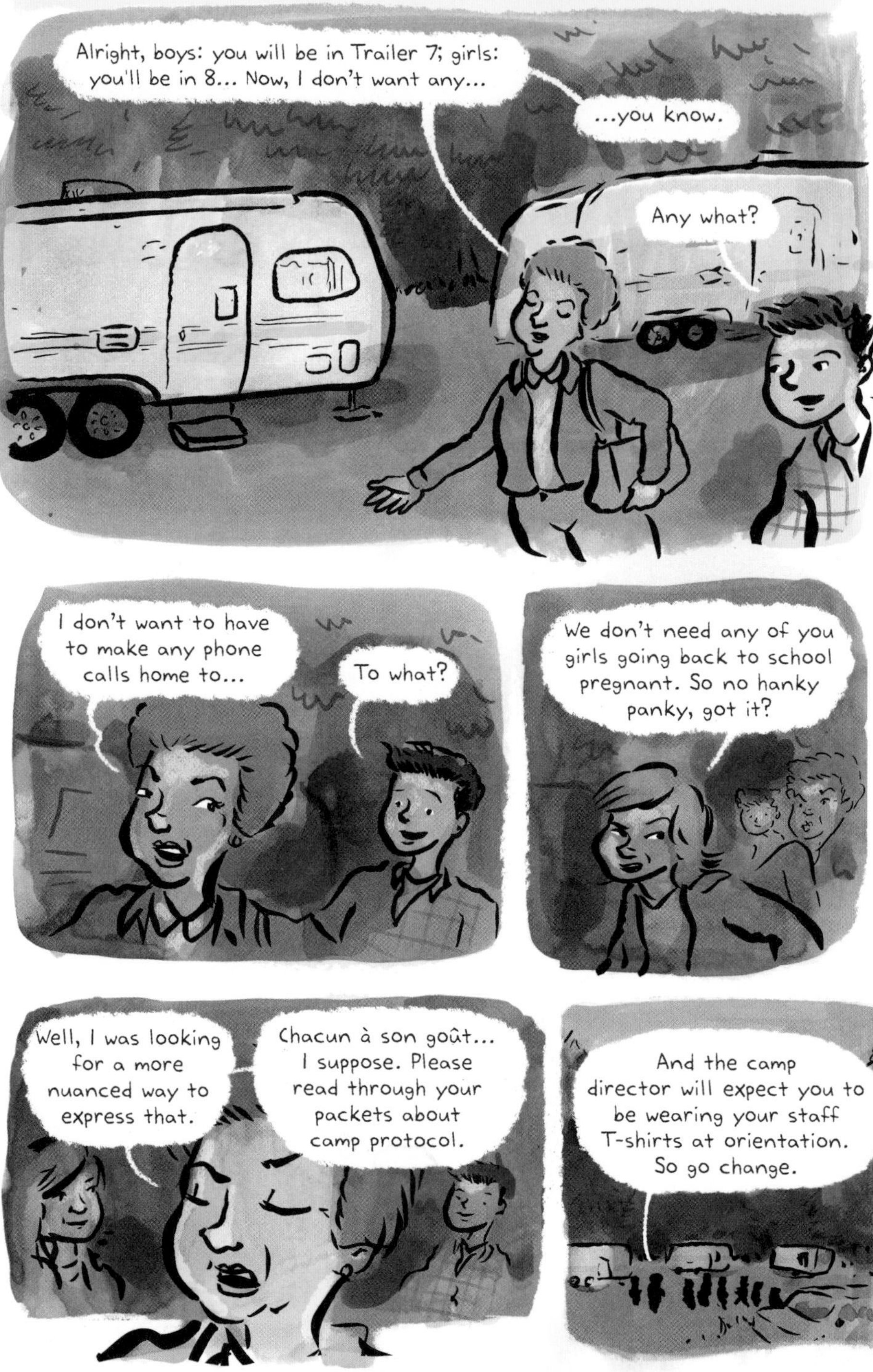
Alright, boys: you will be in Trailer 7; girls: you'll be in 8... Now, I don't want any...
...you know.
Any what?
I don't want to have to make any phone calls home to...
To what?
We don't need any of you girls going back to school pregnant. So no hanky panky, got it?
Well, I was looking for a more nuanced way to express that.
Chacun à son goût... I suppose. Please read through your packets about camp protocol.
And the camp director will expect you to be wearing your staff T-shirts at orientation. So go change.

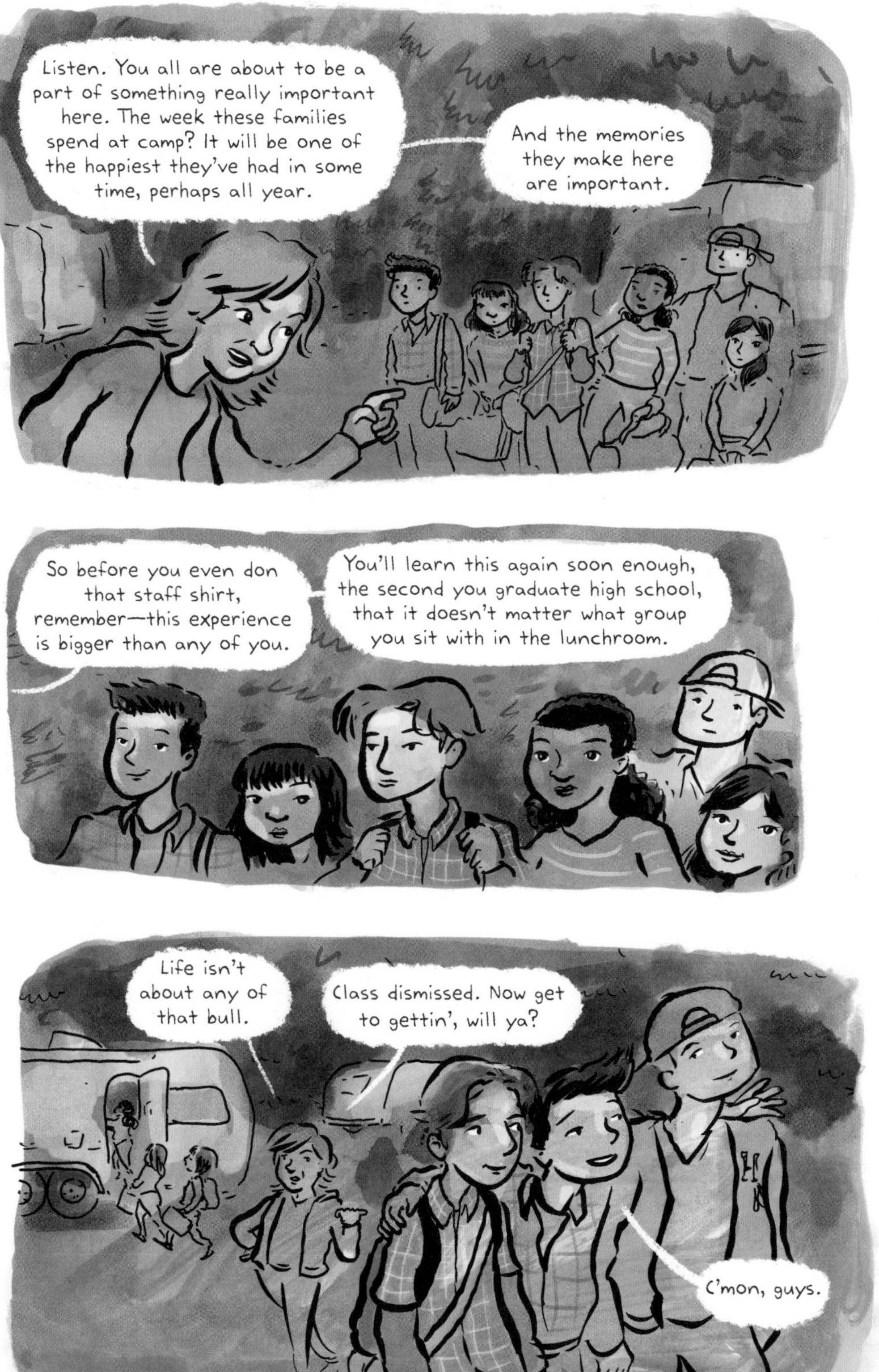
Listen. You all are about to be a part of something really important here. The week these families spend at camp? It will be one of the happiest they've had in some time, perhaps all year.
And the memories they make here are important.
So before you even don that staff shirt, remember—this experience is bigger than any of you.
You'll learn this again soon enough, the second you graduate high school, that it doesn't matter what group you sit with in the lunchroom.
Life isn't about any of that bull.
Class dismissed. Now get to gettin', will ya?
C'mon, guys.

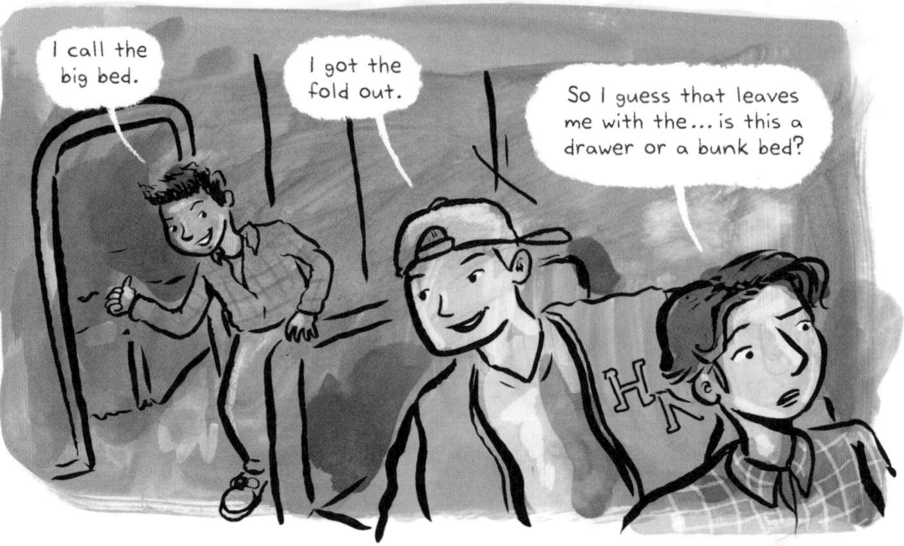
I call the big bed.
I got the fold out.
So I guess that leaves me with the... is this a drawer or a bunk bed?

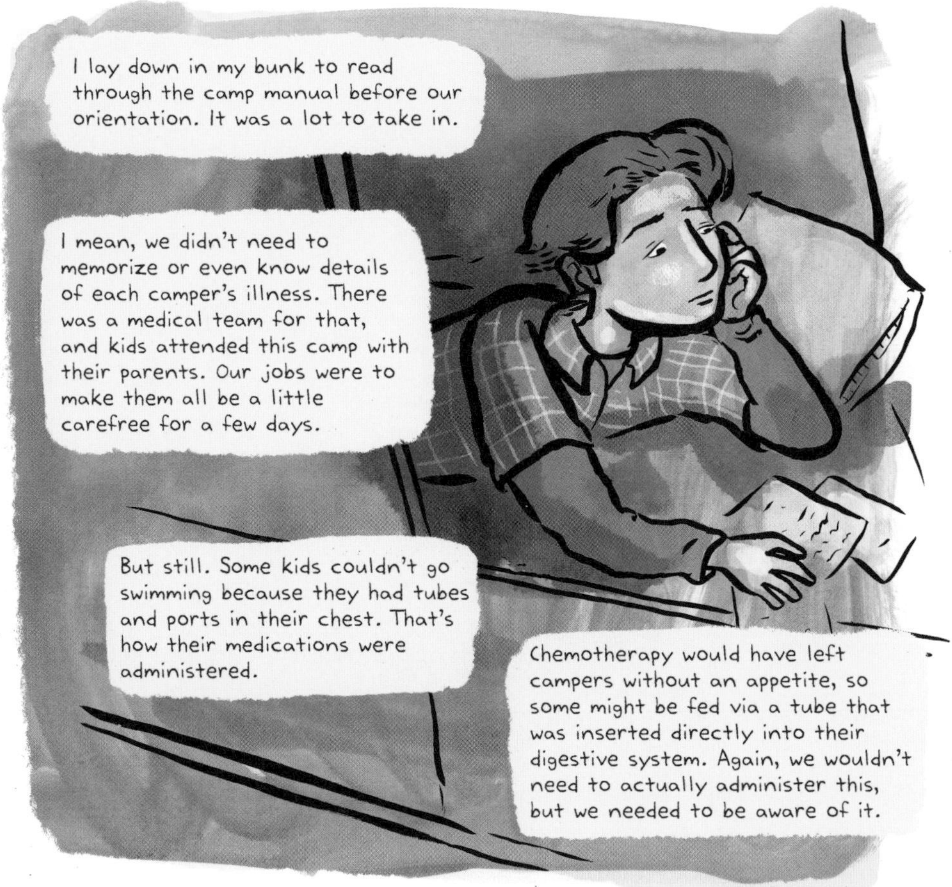
I lay down in my bunk to read through the camp manual before our orientation. It was a lot to take in.
I mean, we didn't need to memorize or even know details of each camper's illness. There was a medical team for that, and kids attended this camp with their parents. Our jobs were to make them all be a little carefree for a few days.
But still. Some kids couldn't go swimming because they had tubes and ports in their chest. That's how their medications were administered.
Chemotherapy would have left campers without an appetite, so some might be fed via a tube that was inserted directly into their digestive system. Again, we wouldn't need to actually administer this, but we needed to be aware of it.

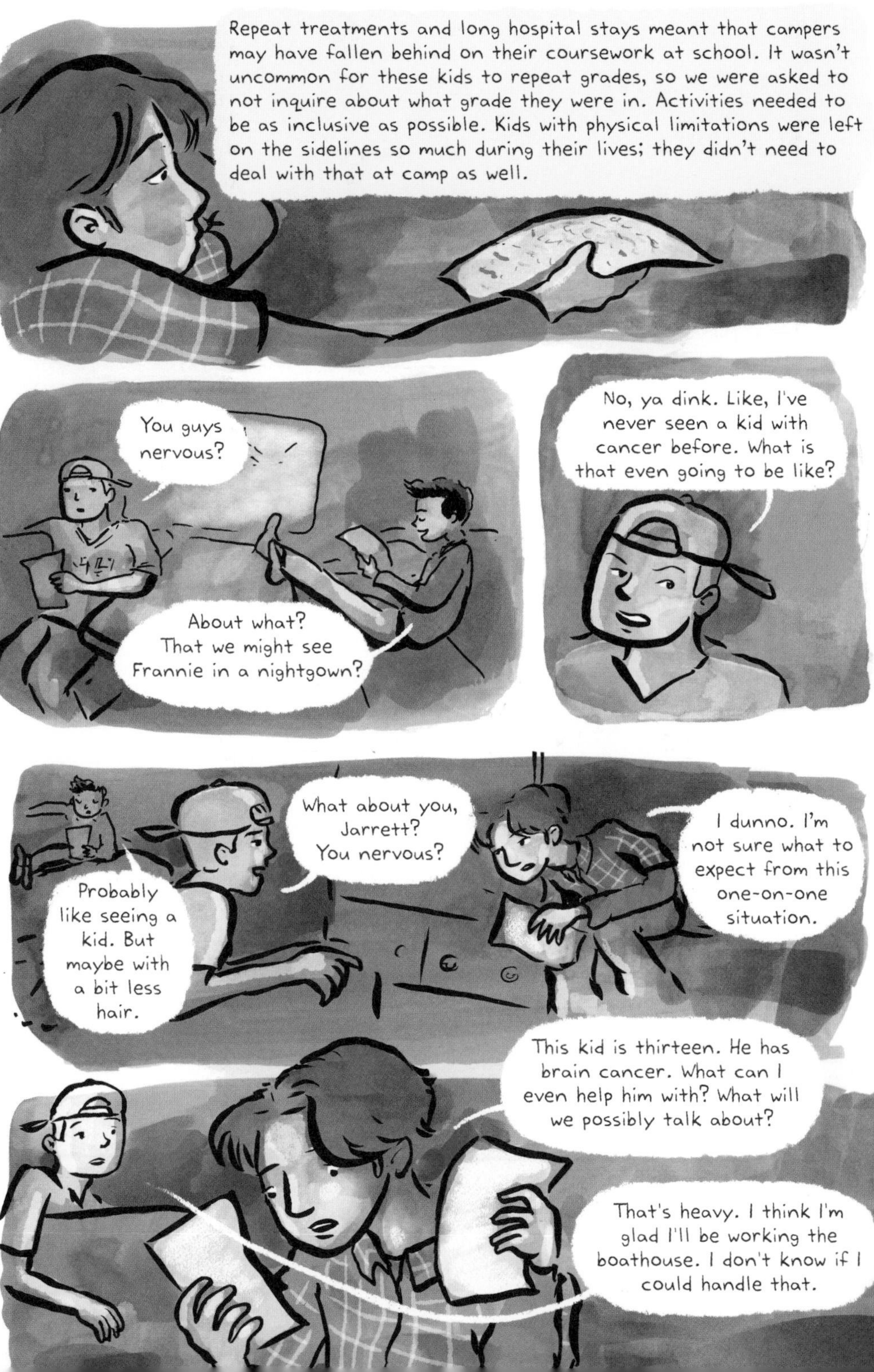
Repeat treatments and long hospital stays meant that campers may have fallen behind on their coursework at school. It wasn't uncommon for these kids to repeat grades, so we were asked to not inquire about what grade they were in. Activities needed to be as inclusive as possible. Kids with physical limitations were left on the sidelines so much during their lives; they didn't need to deal with that at camp as well.
You guys nervous?
About what? That we might see Frannie in a nightgown?
No, ya dink. Like, I've never seen a kid with cancer before. What is that even going to be like?
Probably like seeing a kid. But maybe with a bit less hair.
What about you, Jarrett? You nervous?
I dunno. I'm not sure what to expect from this one-on-one situation.
This kid is thirteen. He has brain cancer. What can I even help him with? What will we possibly talk about?
That's heavy. I think I'm glad I'll be working the boathouse. I don't know if I could handle that.

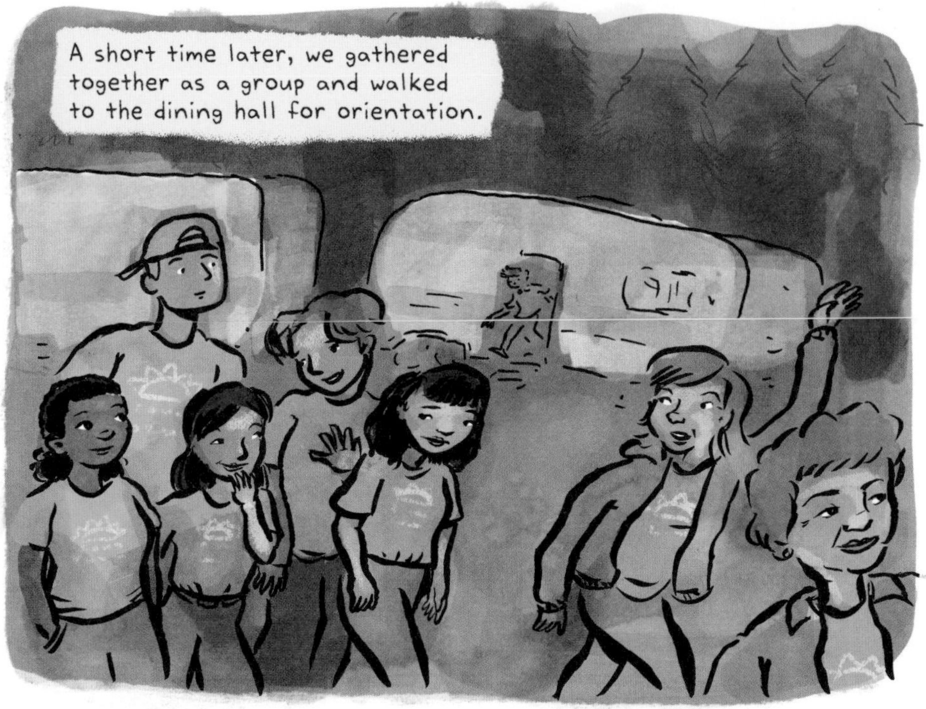
A short time later, we gathered together as a group and walked to the dining hall for orientation.

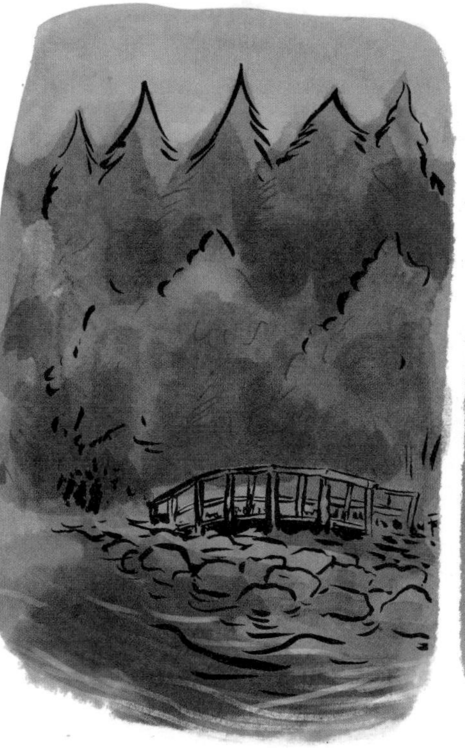

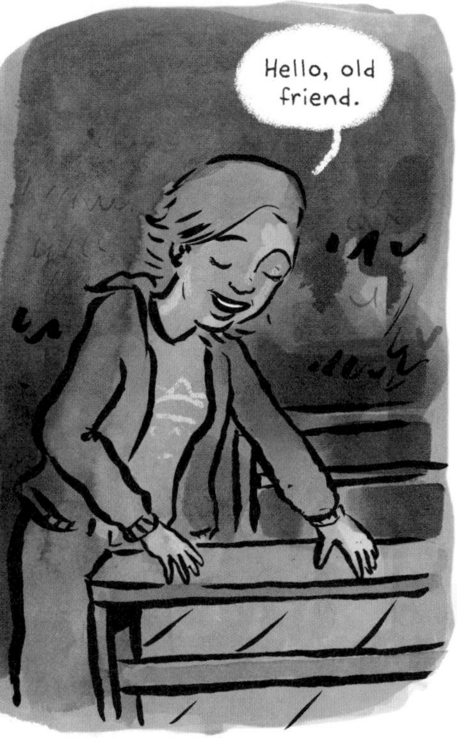
Hello, old friend.

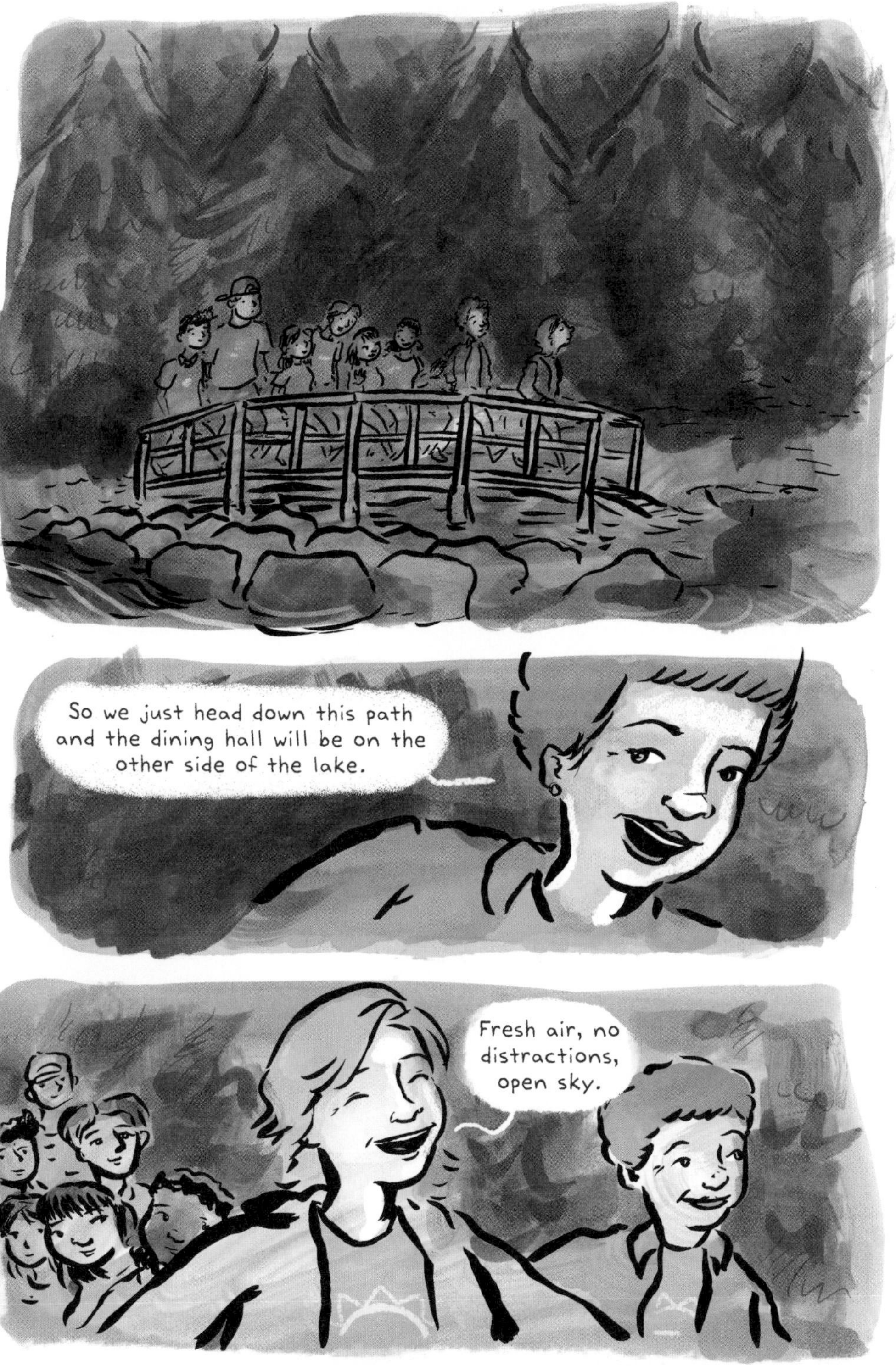
So we just head down this path and the dining hall will be on the other side of the lake.
Fresh air, no distractions, open sky.

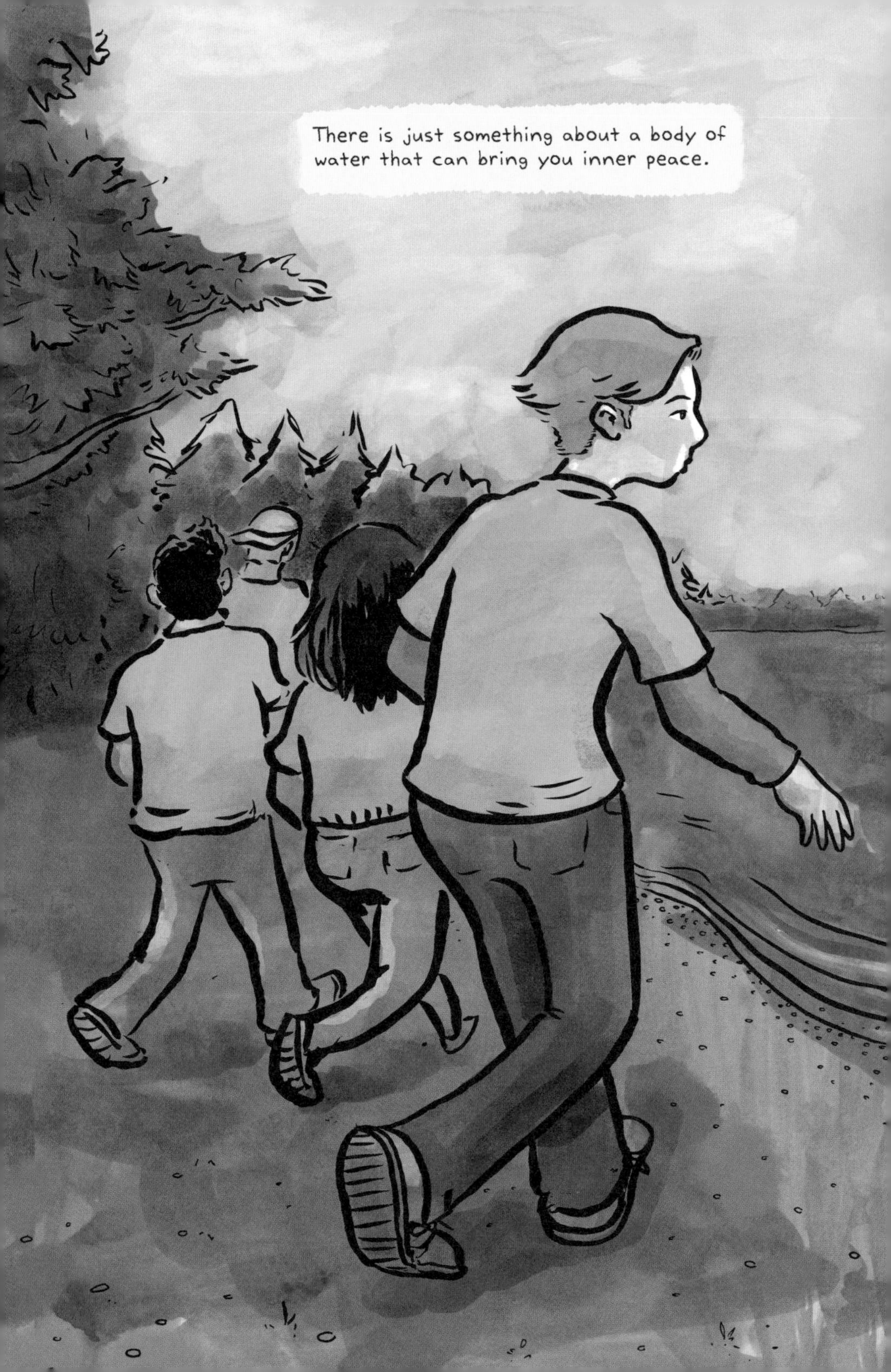
There is just something about a body of water that can bring you inner peace.

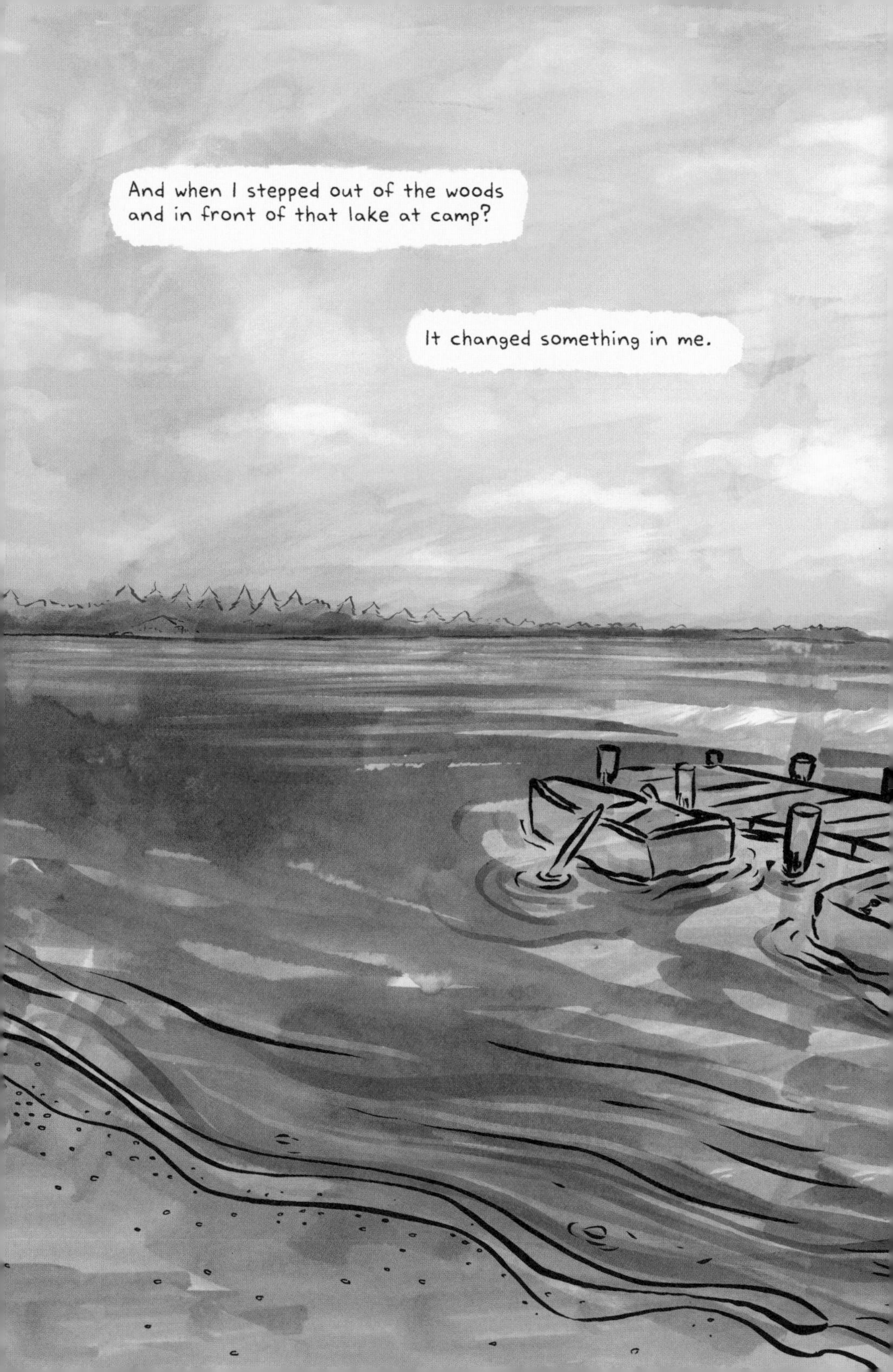
And when I stepped out of the woods and in front of that lake at camp?
It changed something in me.

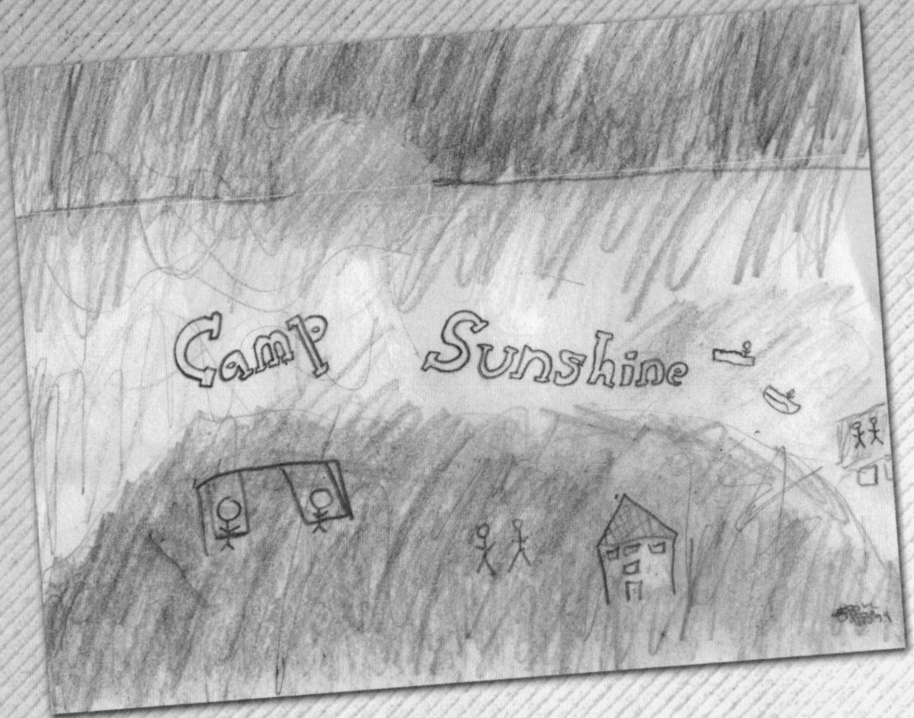
Camp Sunshine

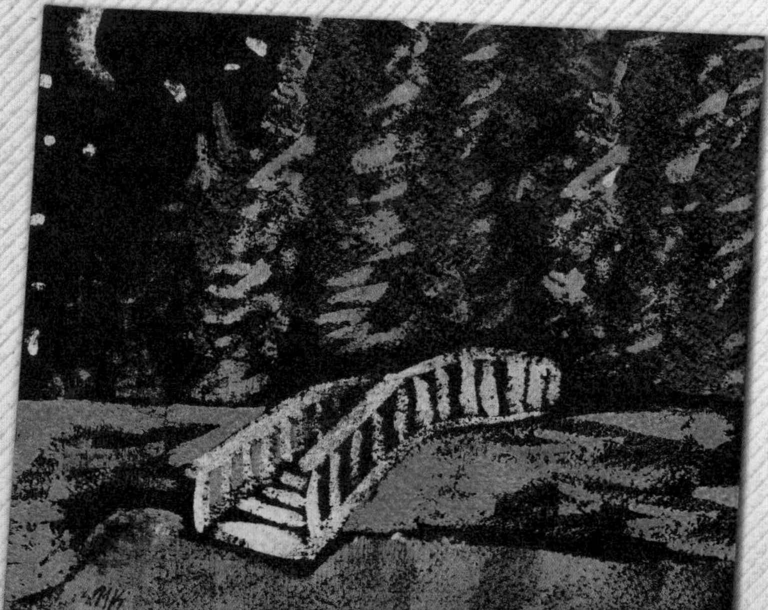
MK

CHAPTER 2
ICE BREAKERS

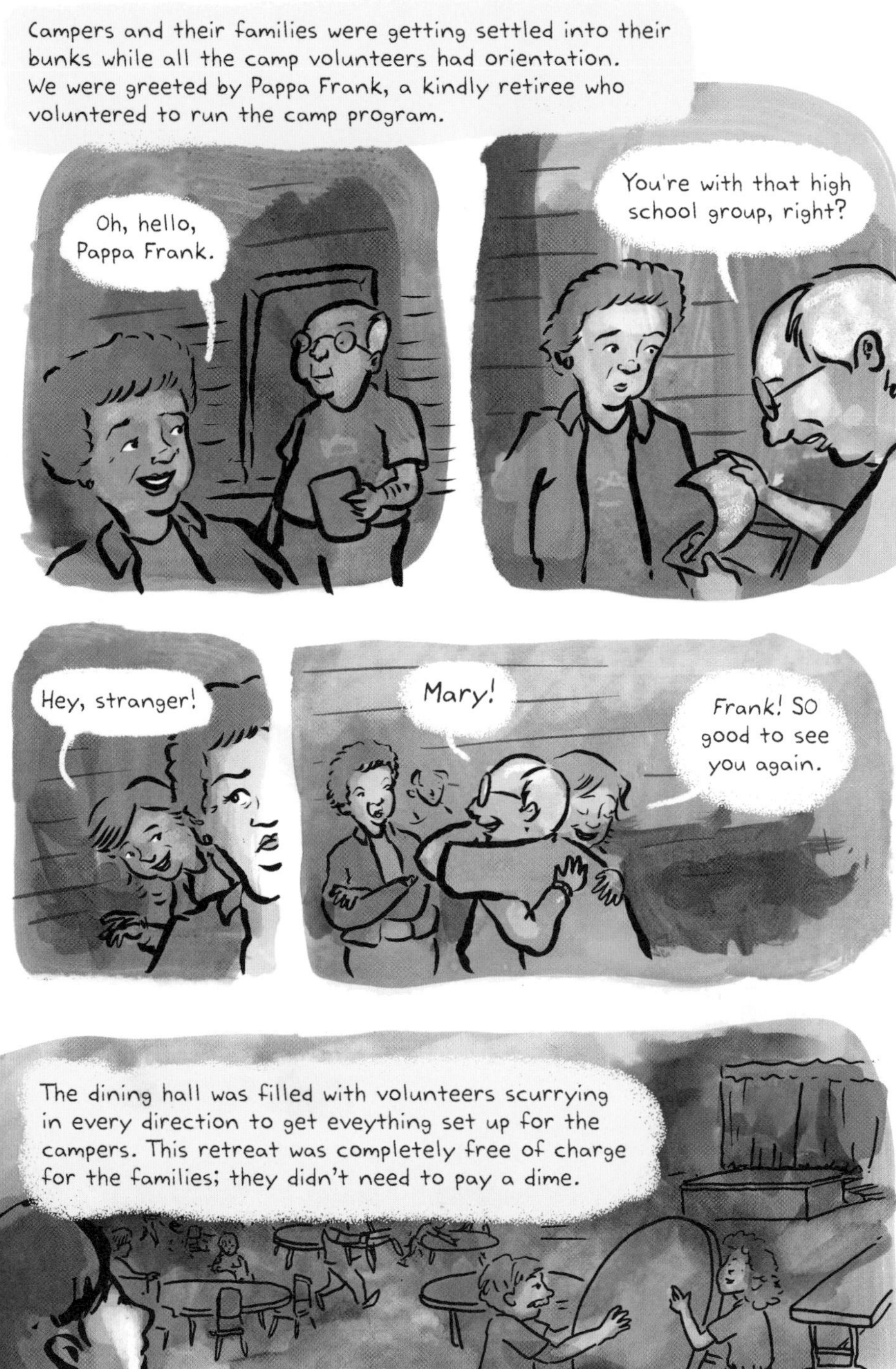
Campers and their families were getting settled into their bunks while all the camp volunteers had orientation. We were greeted by Pappa Frank, a kindly retiree who volunteered to run the camp program.
Oh, hello, Pappa Frank.
You're with that high school group, right?
Hey, stranger!
Mary!
Frank! SO good to see you again.
The dining hall was filled with volunteers scurrying in every direction to get eveything set up for the campers. This retreat was completely free of charge for the families; they didn't need to pay a dime.

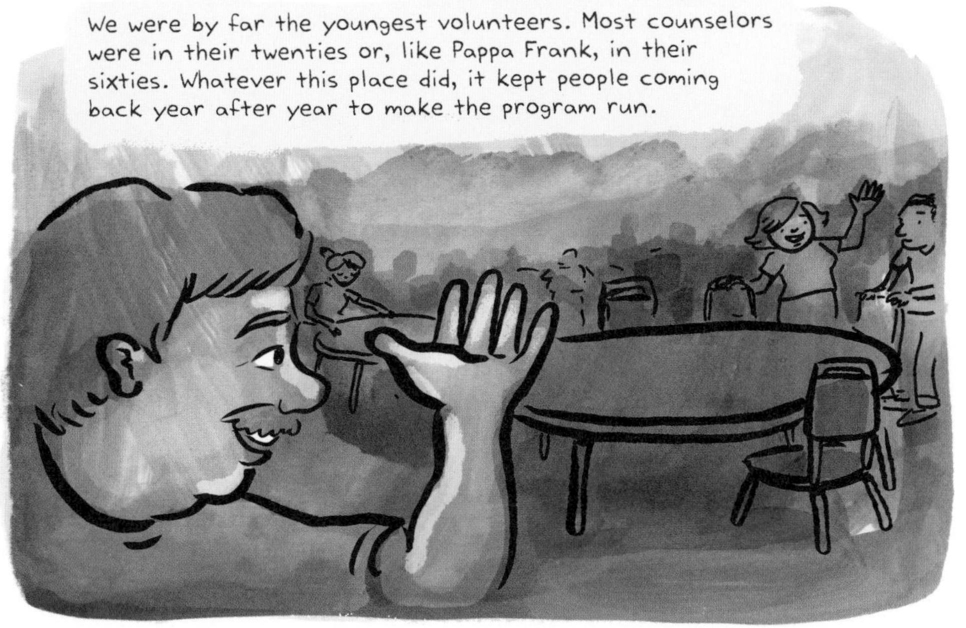
We were by far the youngest volunteers. Most counselors were in their twenties or, like Pappa Frank, in their sixties. Whatever this place did, it kept people coming back year after year to make the program run.

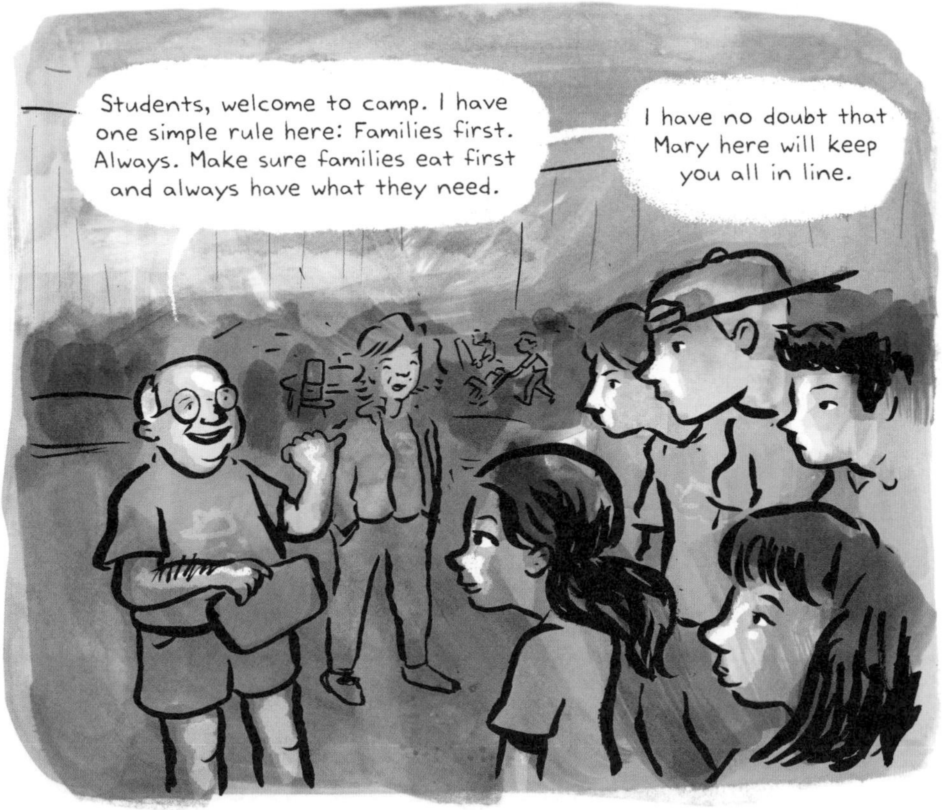
Students, welcome to camp. I have one simple rule here: Families first. Always. Make sure families eat first and always have what they need.
I have no doubt that Mary here will keep you all in line.

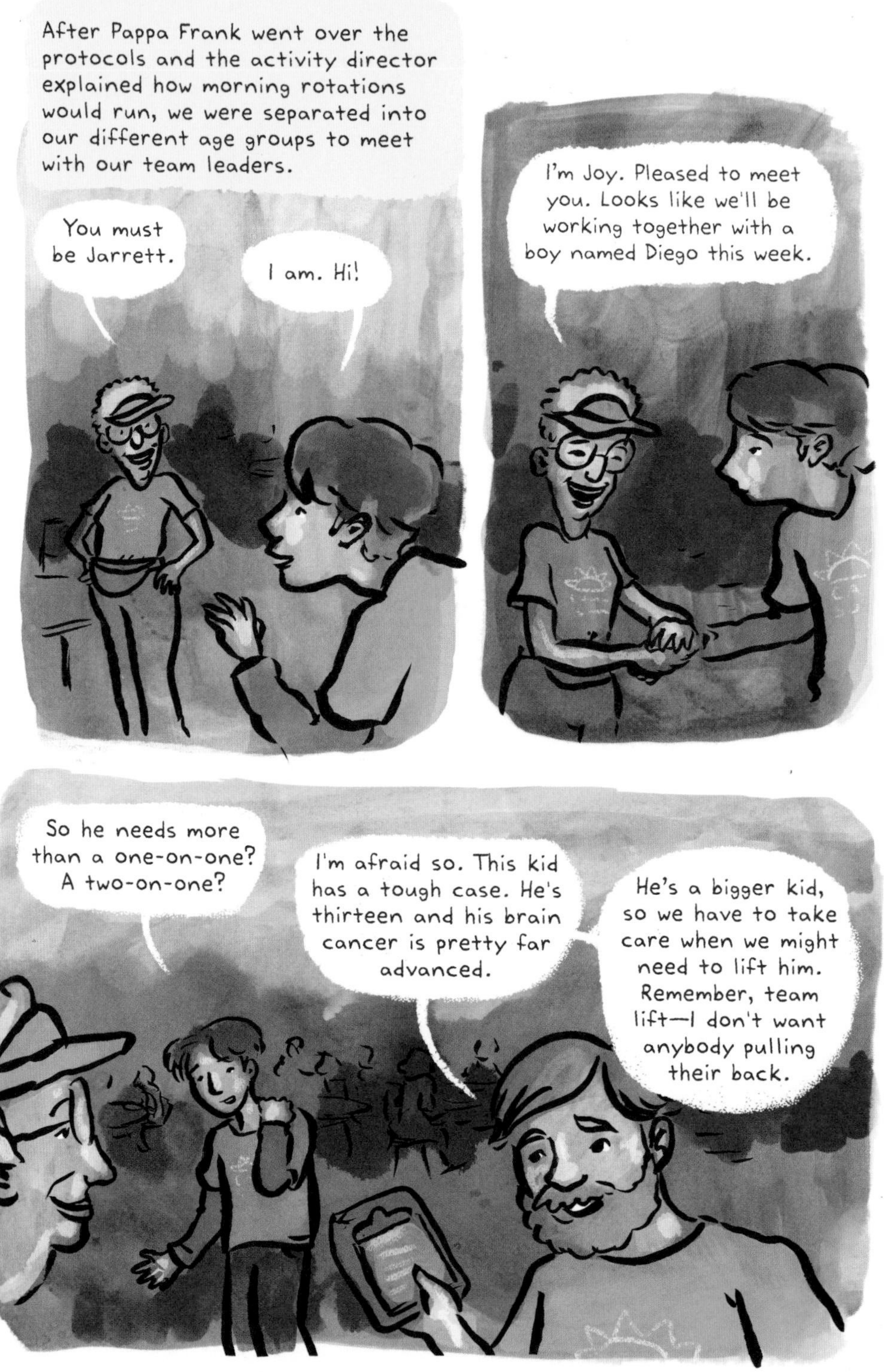
After Pappa Frank went over the protocols and the activity director explained how morning rotations would run, we were separated into our different age groups to meet with our team leaders.
You must be Jarrett.
I am. Hi!
I'm Joy. Pleased to meet you. Looks like we'll be working together with a boy named Diego this week.
So he needs more than a one-on-one? A two-on-one?
I'm afraid so. This kid has a tough case. He's thirteen and his brain cancer is pretty far advanced.
He's a bigger kid, so we have to take care when we might need to lift him. Remember, team lift—I don't want anybody pulling their back.

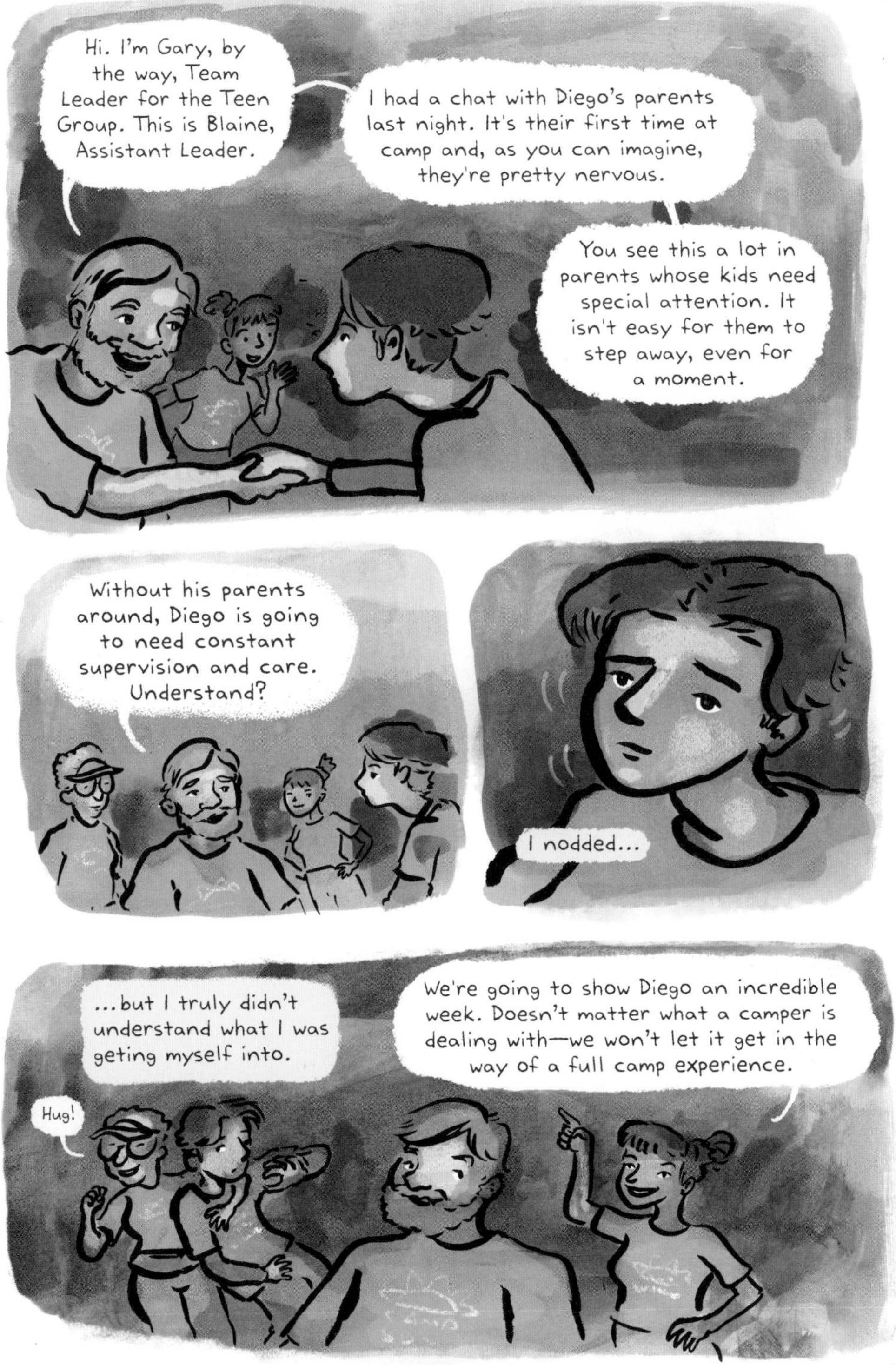

Hi. I'm Gary, by the way, Team Leader for the Teen Group. This is Blaine, Assistant Leader.
I had a chat with Diego's parents last night. It's their first time at camp and, as you can imagine, they're pretty nervous.
You see this a lot in parents whose kids need special attention. It isn't easy for them to step away, even for a moment.
Without his parents around, Diego is going to need constant supervision and care. Understand?
I nodded...
...but I truly didn't understand what I was geting myself into.
We're going to show Diego an incredible week. Doesn't matter what a camper is dealing with—we won't let it get in the way of a full camp experience.
Hug!

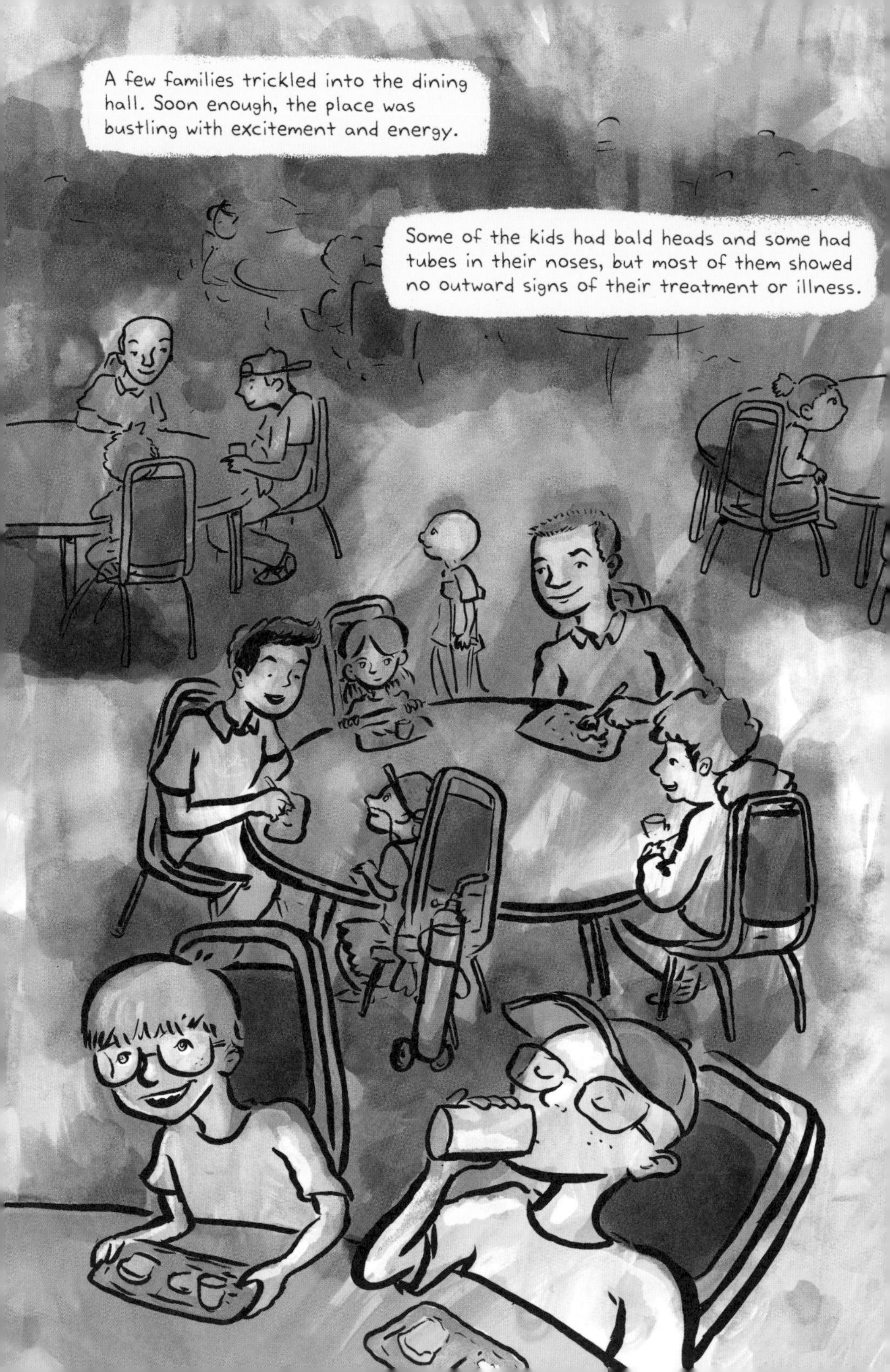
A few families trickled into the dining hall. Soon enough, the place was bustling with excitement and energy.
Some of the kids had bald heads and some had tubes in their noses, but most of them showed no outward signs of their treatment or illness.

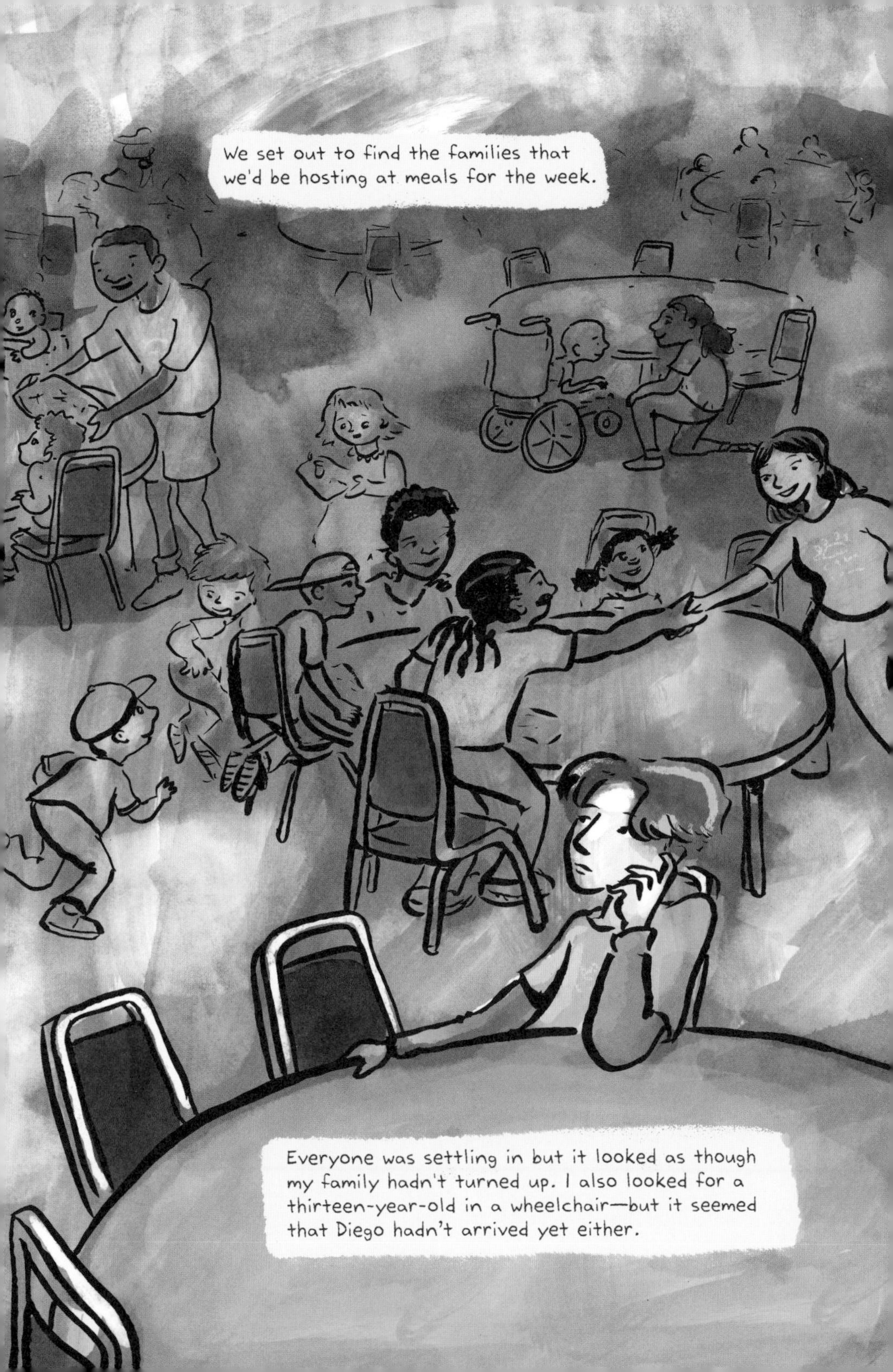
We set out to find the families that we'd be hosting at meals for the week.
Everyone was settling in but it looked as though my family hadn't turned up. I also looked for a thirteen-year-old in a wheelchair—but it seemed that Diego hadn't arrived yet either.

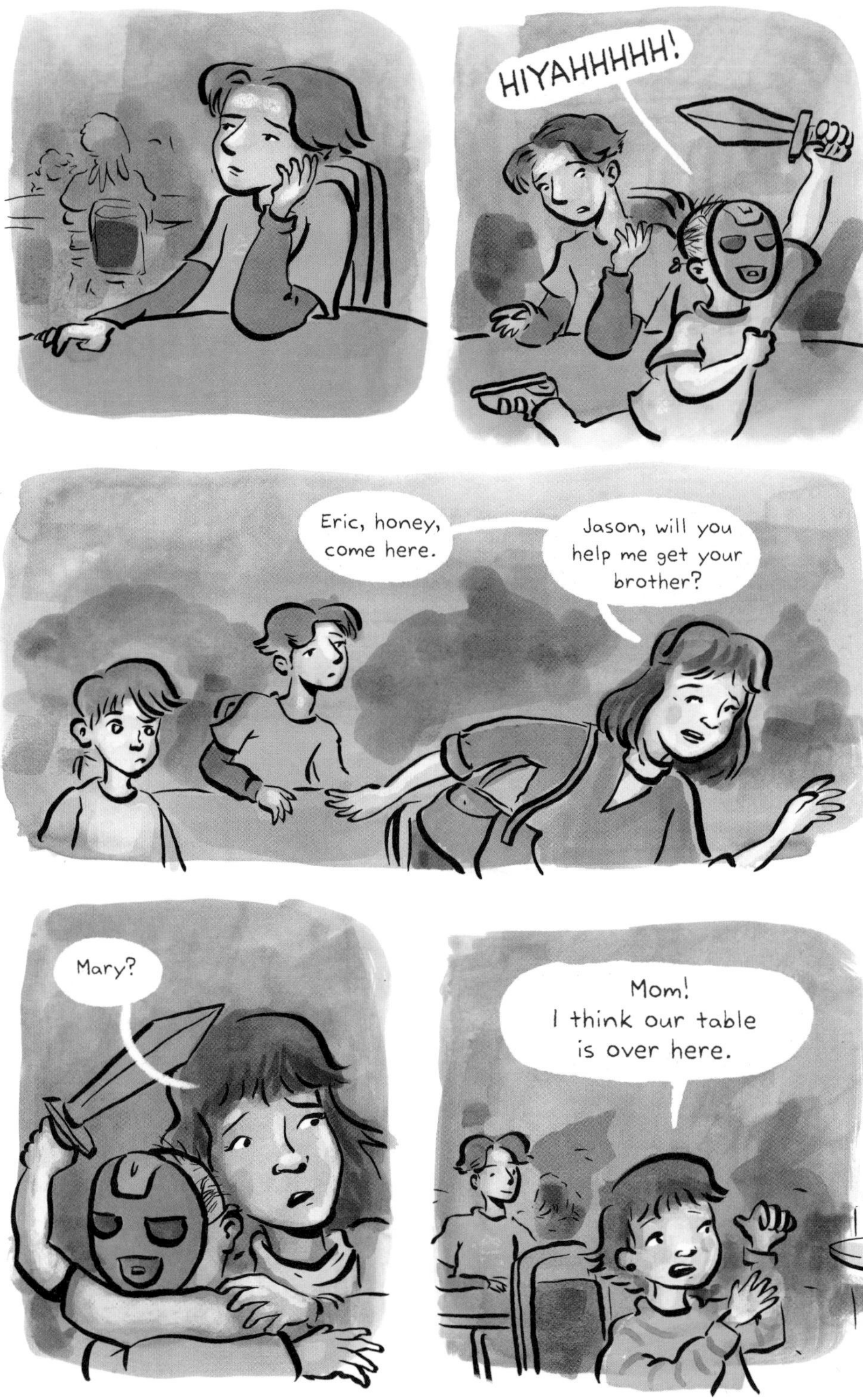
HIYAHHHHH!
Eric, honey, come here.
Jason, will you help me get your brother?
Mary?
Mom! I think our table is over here.

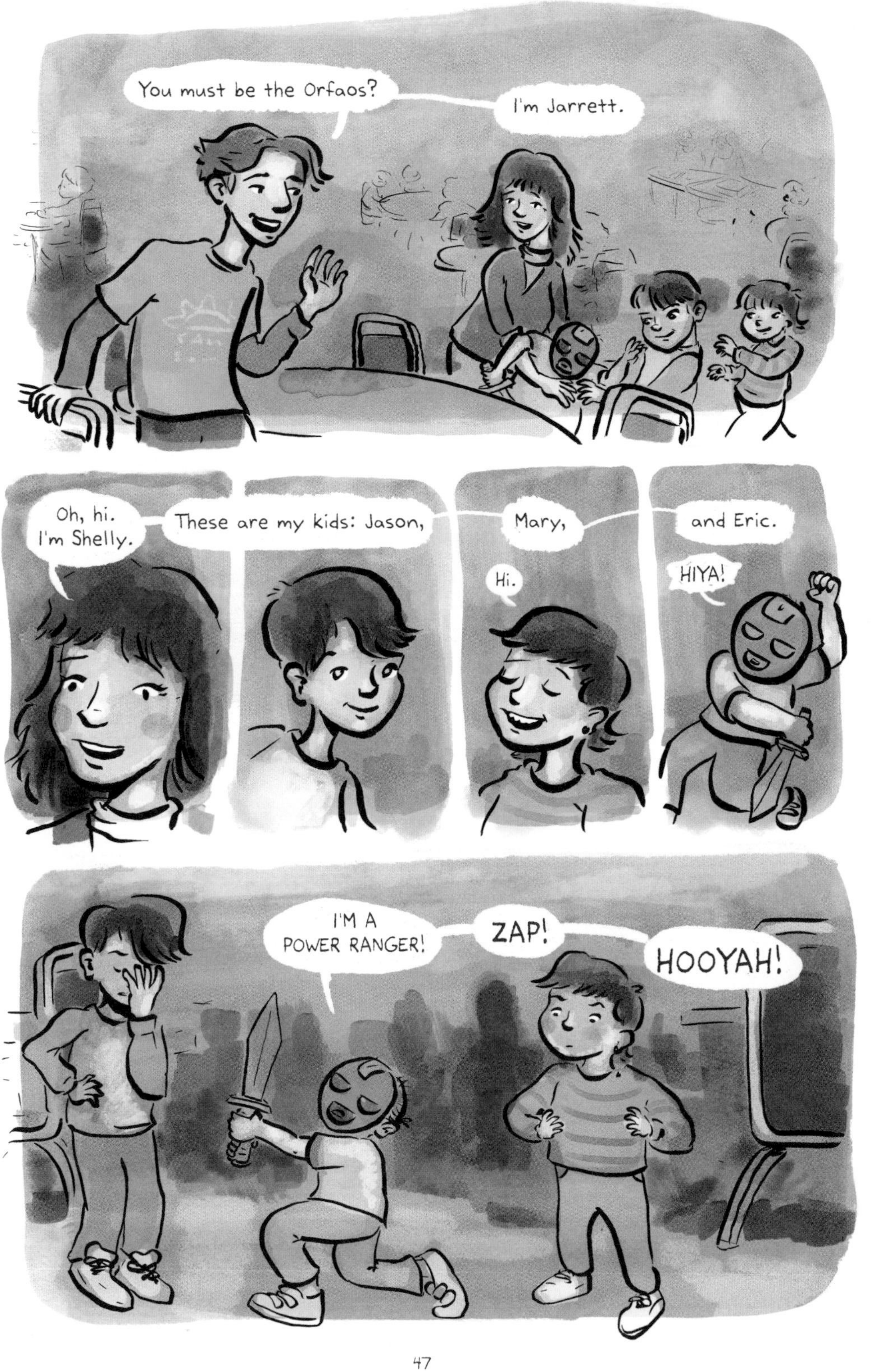
You must be the Orfaos?
I'm Jarrett.
Oh, hi.
I'm Shelly.
These are my kids: Jason,
Mary,
Hi.
and Eric.
HIYA!
I'M A
POWER RANGER!
ZAP!
HOOYAH!

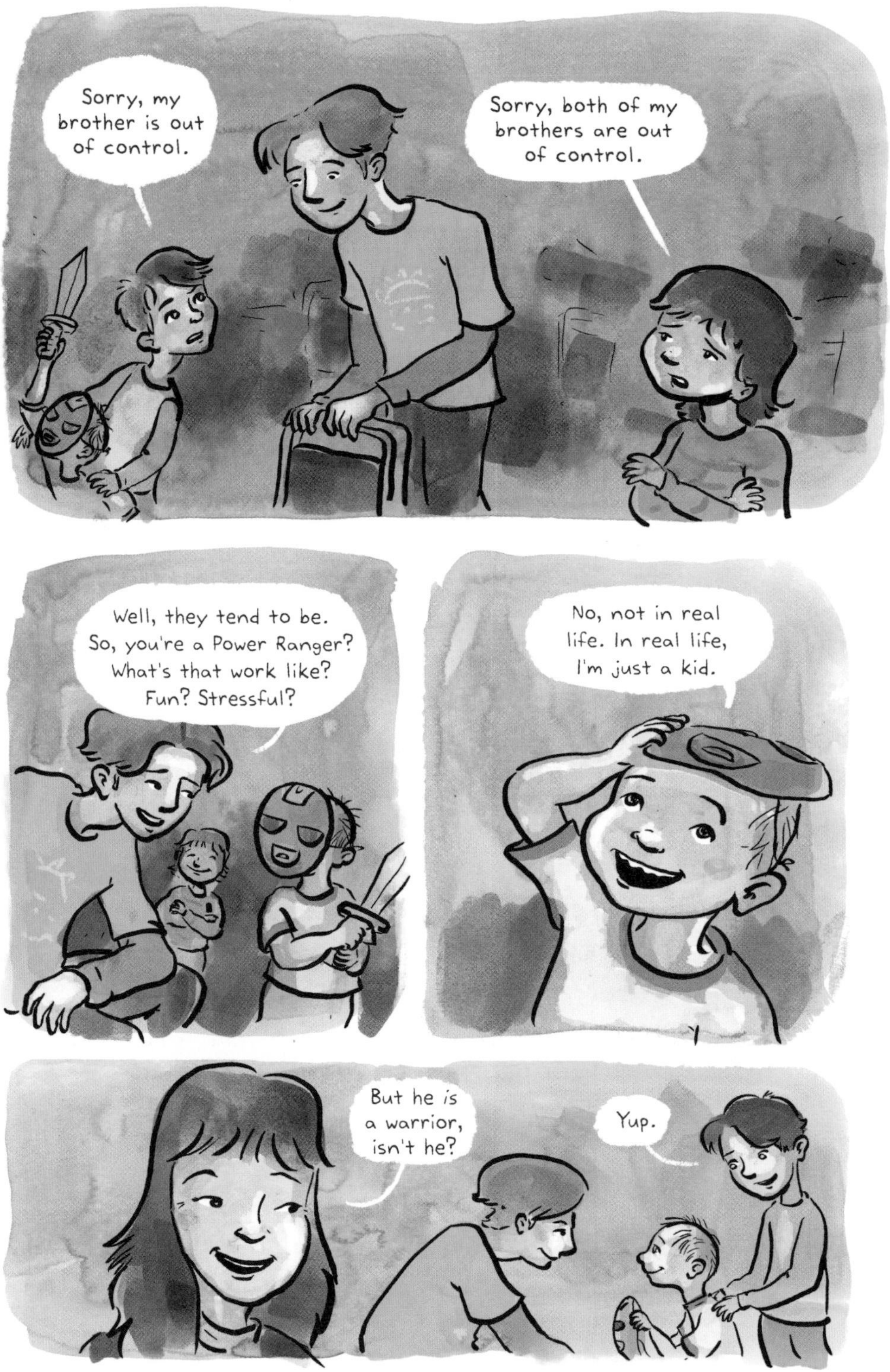
Sorry, my brother is out of control.
Sorry, both of my brothers are out of control.
Well, they tend to be. So, you're a Power Ranger? What's that work like? Fun? Stressful?
No, not in real life. In real life, I'm just a kid.
But he *is* a warrior, isn't he?
Yup.

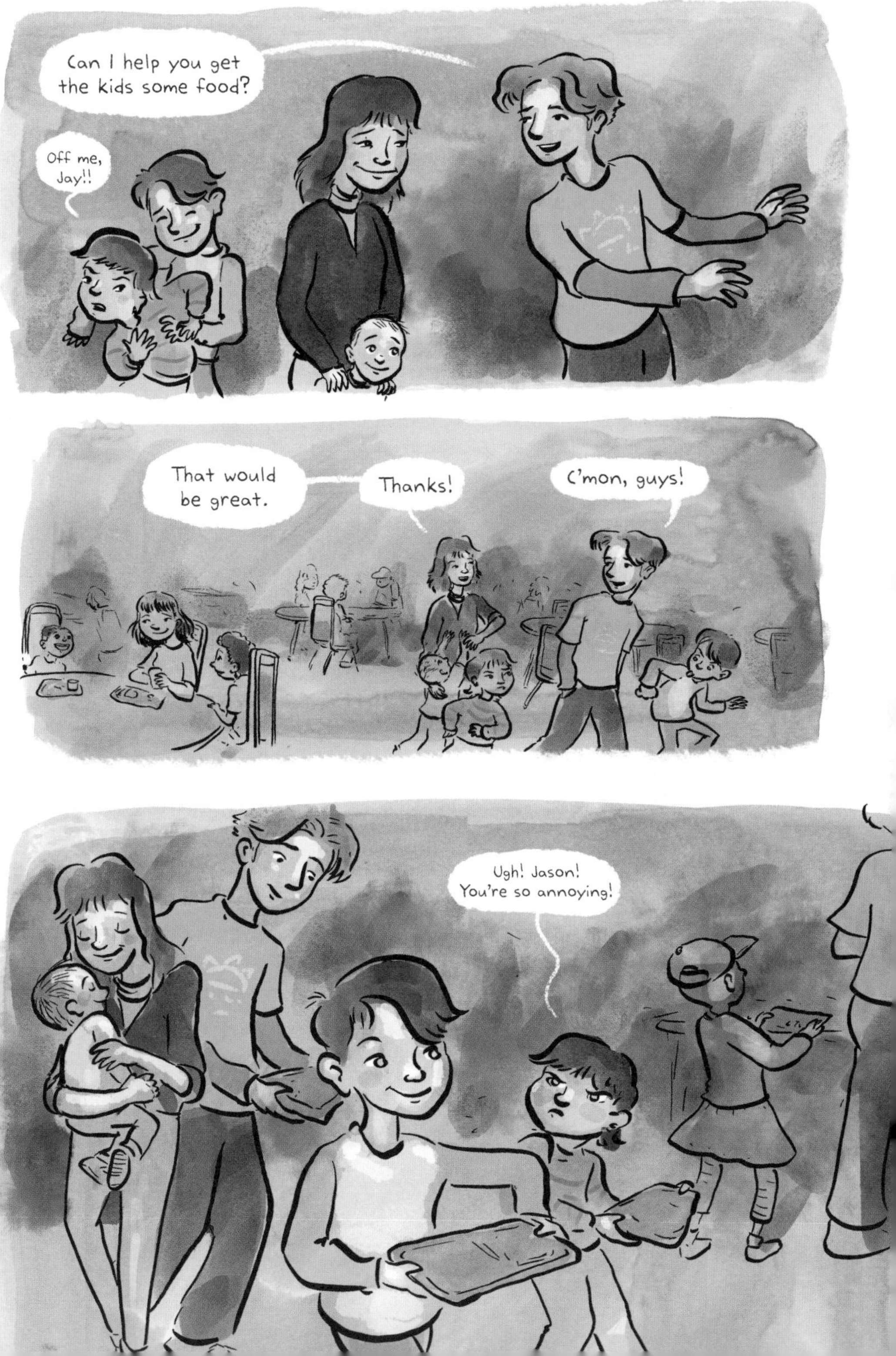
Can I help you get the kids some food?
Off me, Jay!!
That would be great.
Thanks!
C'mon, guys!
Ugh! Jason! You're so annoying!

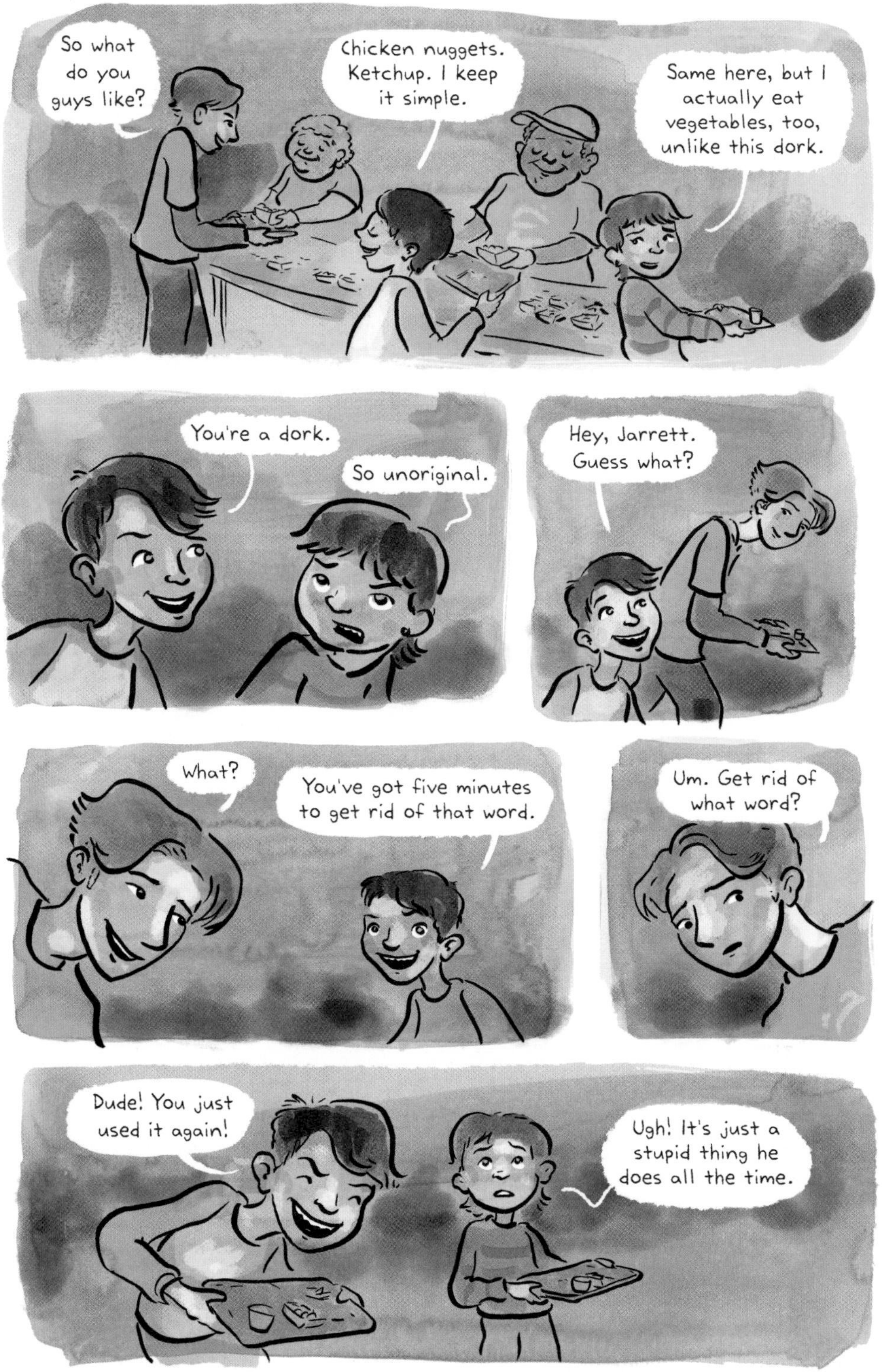
So what do you guys like?
Chicken nuggets. Ketchup. I keep it simple.
Same here, but I actually eat vegetables, too, unlike this dork.
You're a dork.
So unoriginal.
Hey, Jarrett. Guess what?
What?
You've got five minutes to get rid of that word.
Um. Get rid of what word?
Dude! You just used it again!
Ugh! It's just a stupid thing he does all the time.

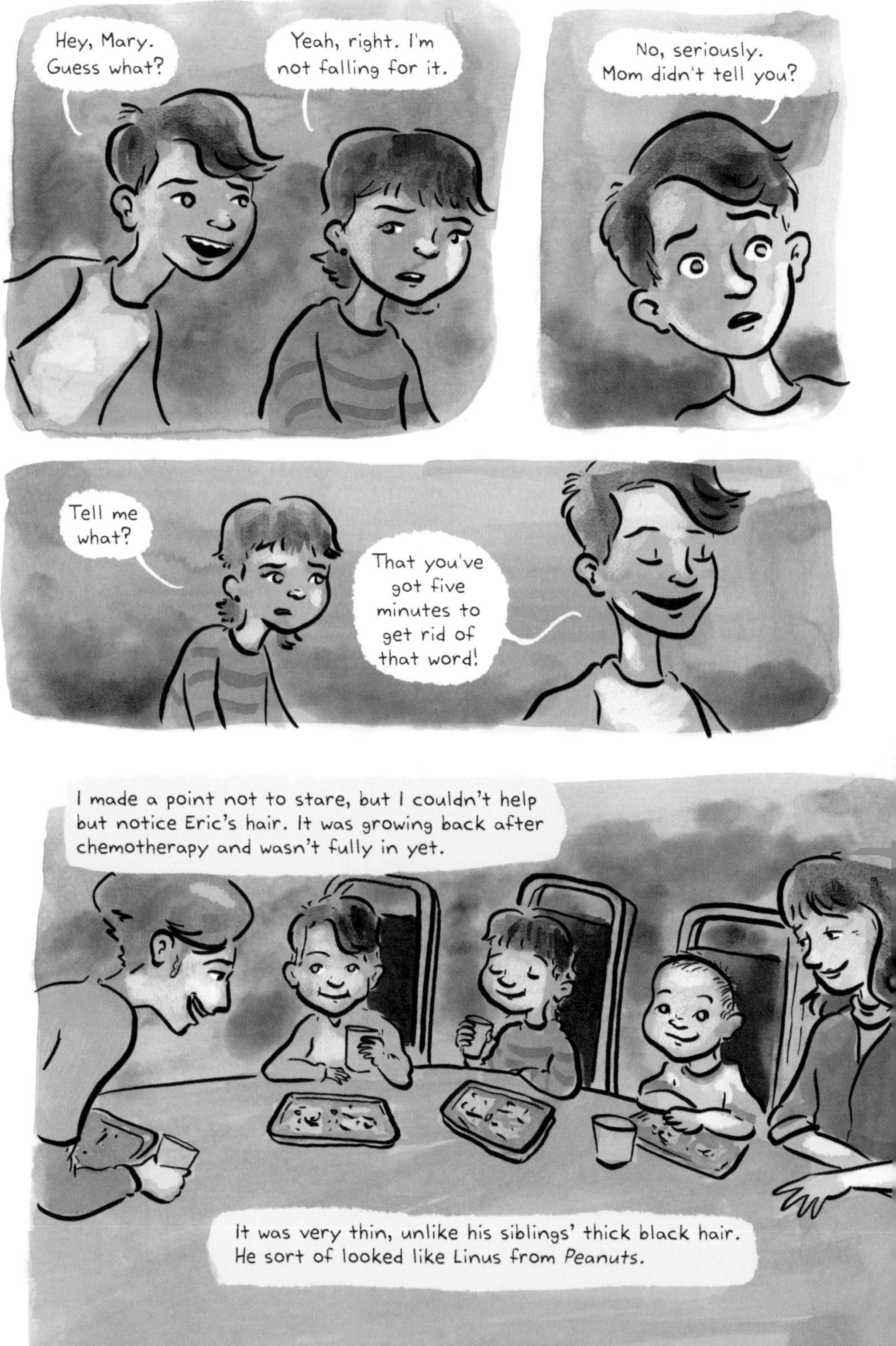
Hey, Mary. Guess what?
Yeah, right. I'm not falling for it.
No, seriously. Mom didn't tell you?
Tell me what?
That you've got five minutes to get rid of that word!
I made a point not to stare, but I couldn't help but notice Eric's hair. It was growing back after chemotherapy and wasn't fully in yet.
It was very thin, unlike his siblings' thick black hair. He sort of looked like Linus from *Peanuts*.

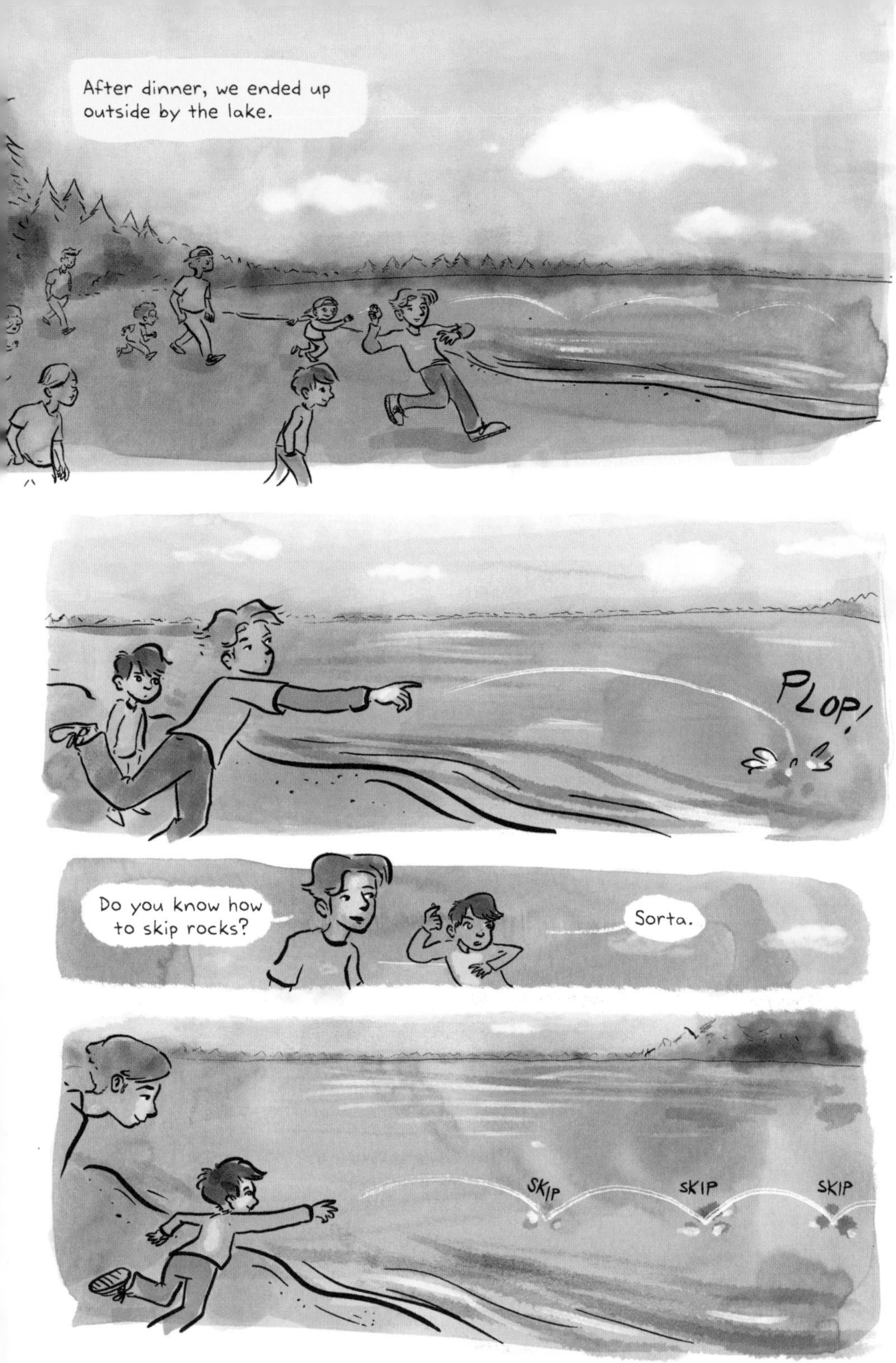
After dinner, we ended up outside by the lake.
PLOP!
Do you know how to skip rocks?
Sorta.
SKIP
SKIP
SKIP

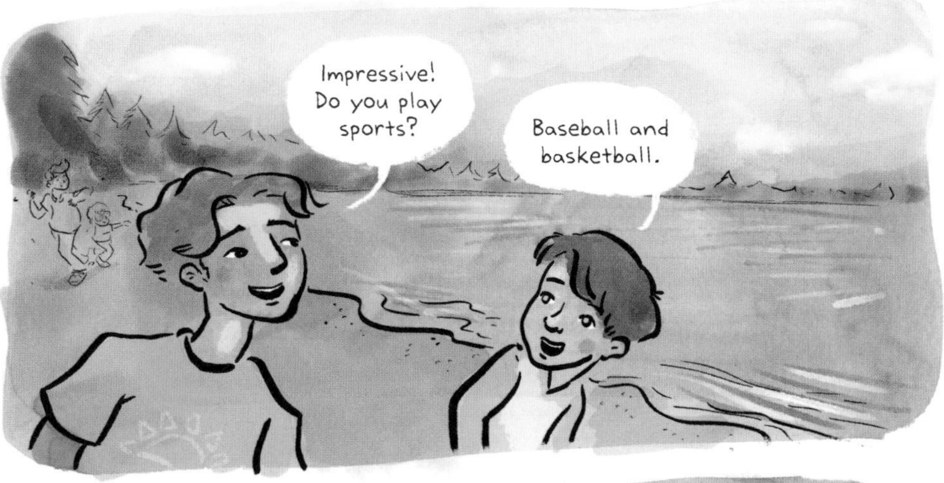
Impressive! Do you play sports?
Baseball and basketball.

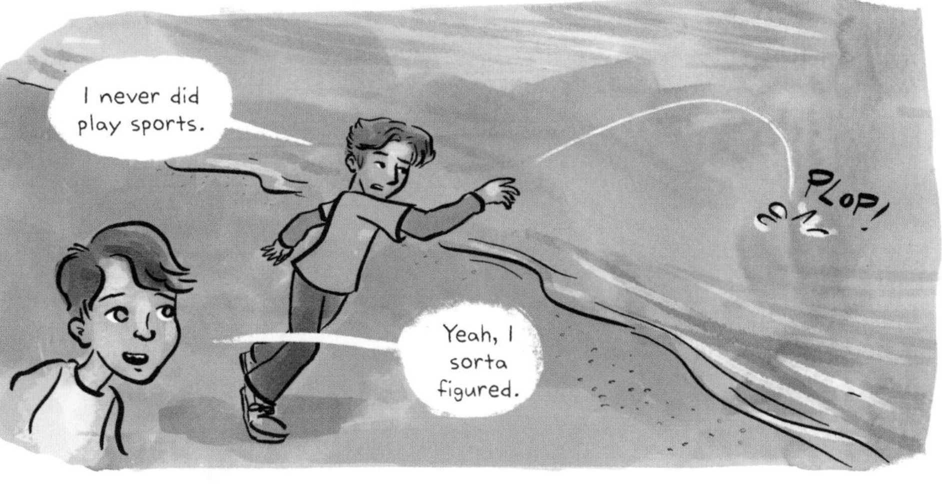
I never did play sports.
PLOP!
Yeah, I sorta figured.

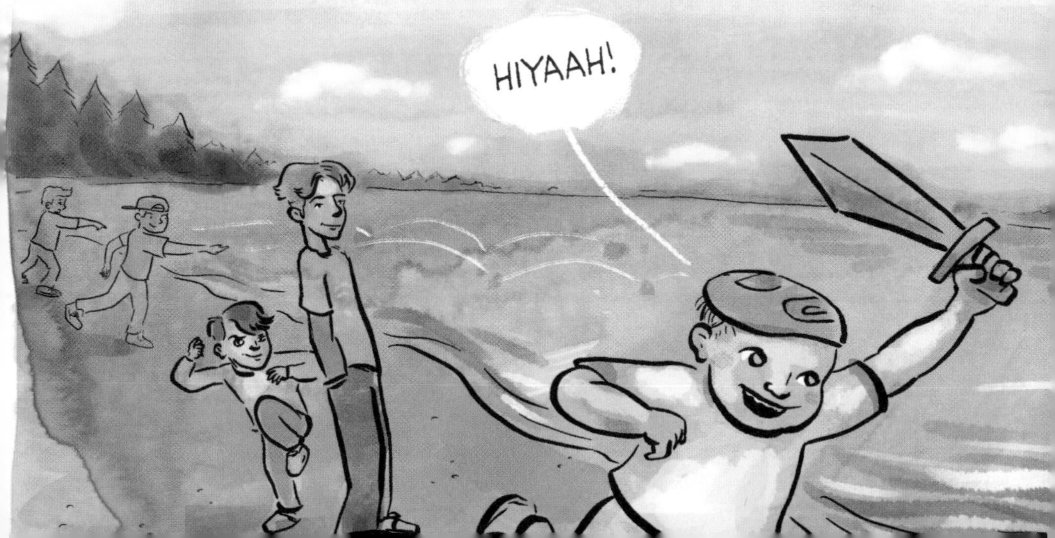
HIYAAH!

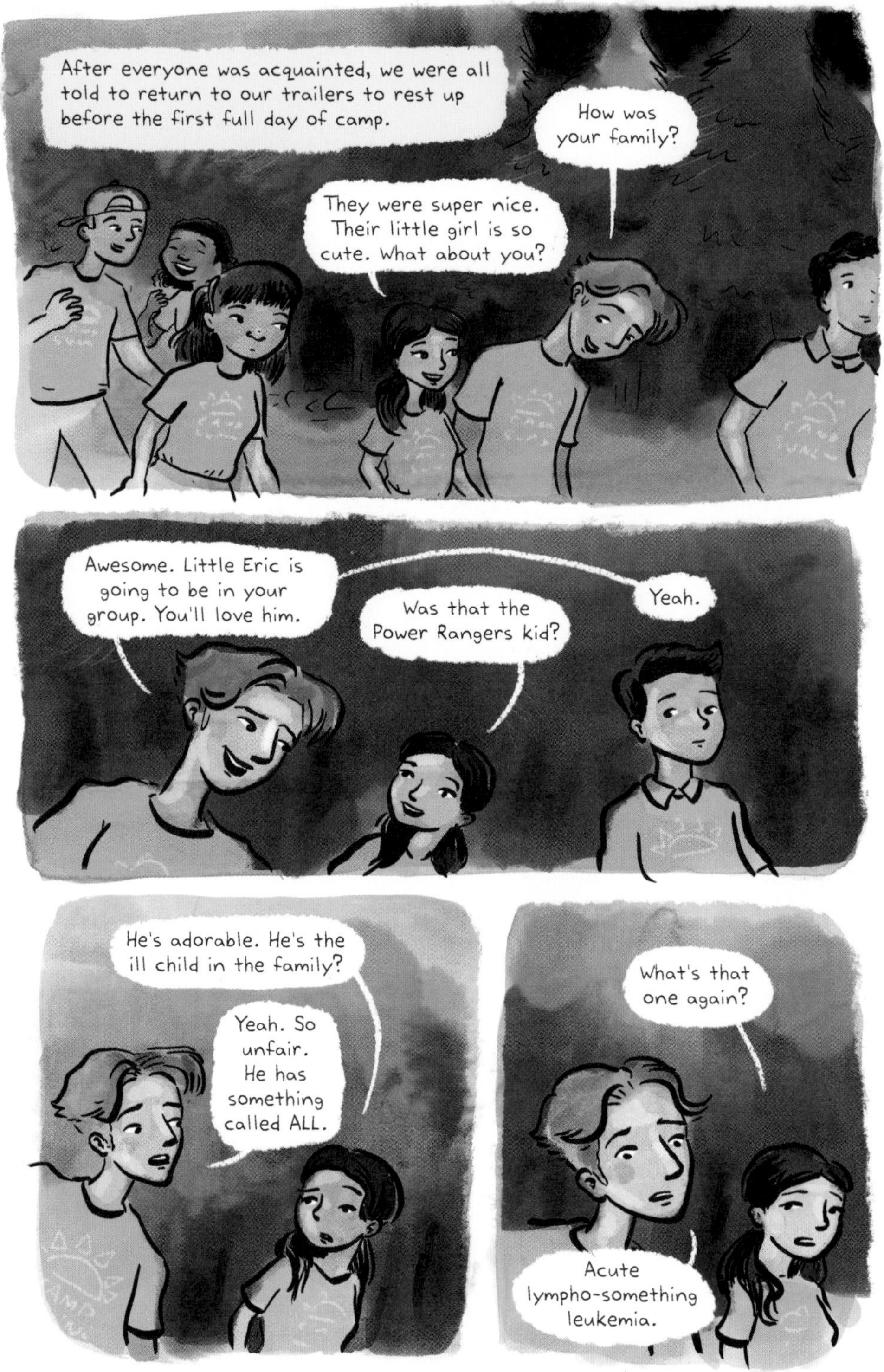
After everyone was acquainted, we were all told to return to our trailers to rest up before the first full day of camp.
How was your family?
They were super nice. Their little girl is so cute. What about you?
Awesome. Little Eric is going to be in your group. You'll love him.
Was that the Power Rangers kid?
Yeah.
He's adorable. He's the ill child in the family?
Yeah. So unfair. He has something called ALL.
What's that one again?
Acute lympho-something leukemia.

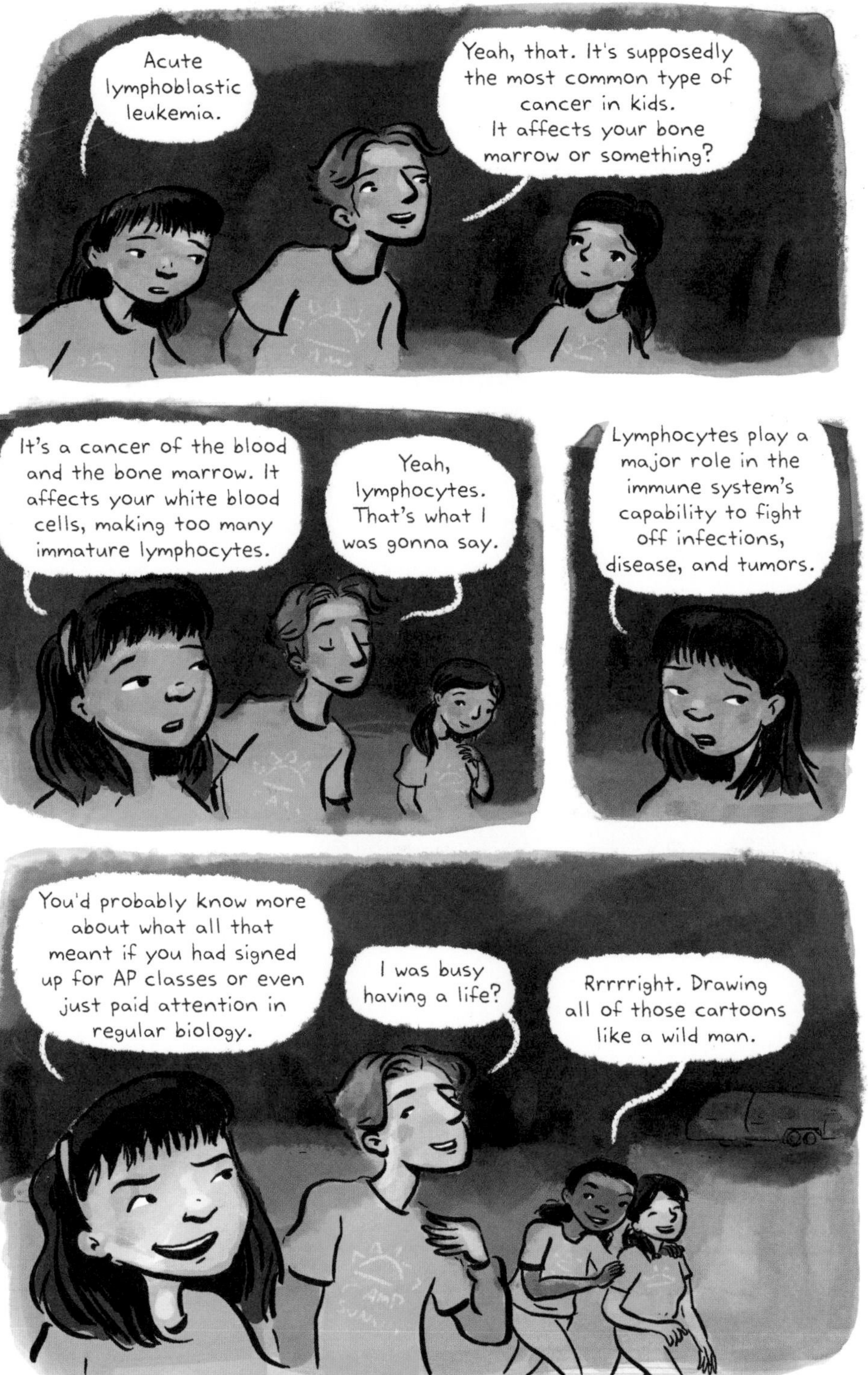

Acute lymphoblastic leukemia.
Yeah, that. It's supposedly the most common type of cancer in kids. It affects your bone marrow or something?
It's a cancer of the blood and the bone marrow. It affects your white blood cells, making too many immature lymphocytes.
Yeah, lymphocytes. That's what I was gonna say.
Lymphocytes play a major role in the immune system's capability to fight off infections, disease, and tumors.
You'd probably know more about what all that meant if you had signed up for AP classes or even just paid attention in regular biology.
I was busy having a life?
Rrrrright. Drawing all of those cartoons like a wild man.

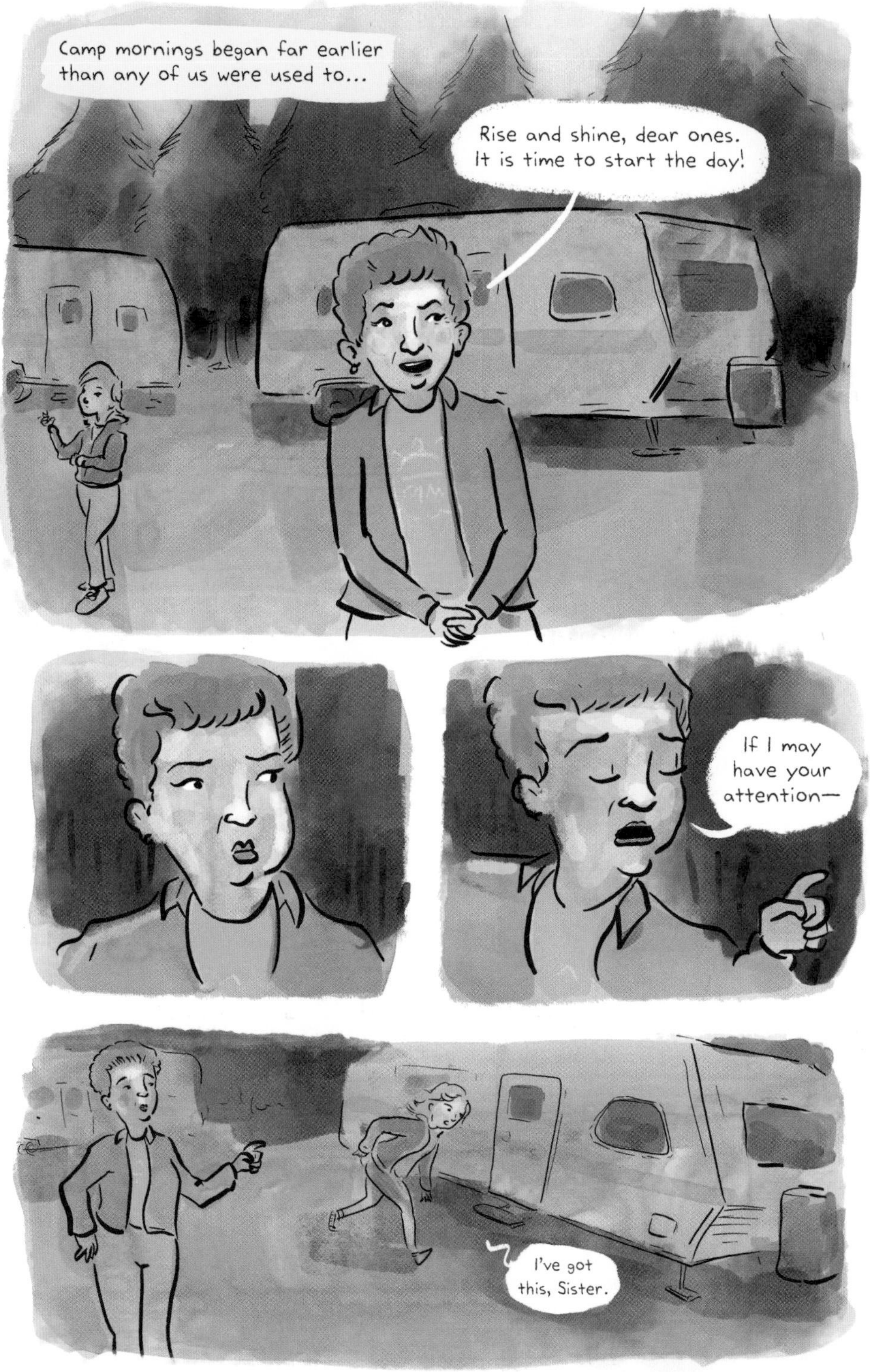
Camp mornings began far earlier than any of us were used to...
Rise and shine, dear ones. It is time to start the day!
If I may have your attention—
I've got this, Sister.

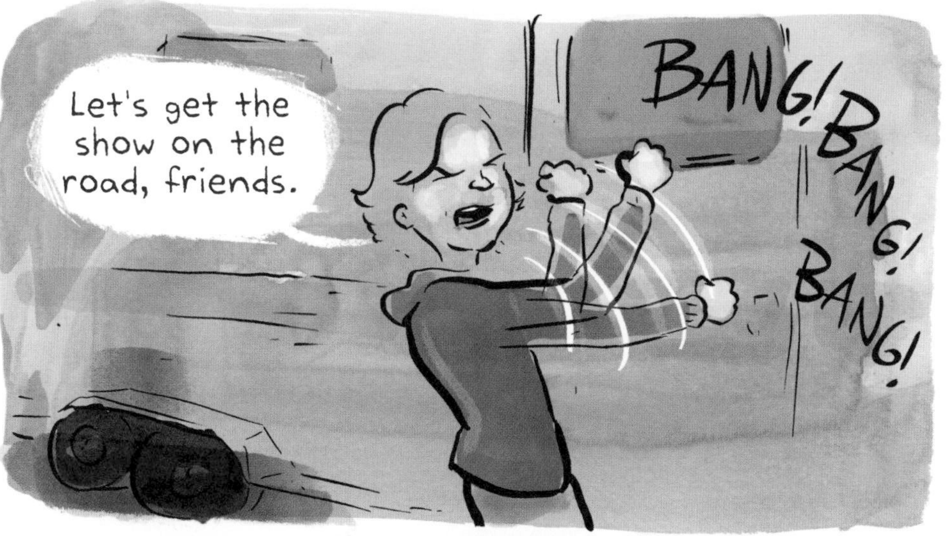
Let's get the show on the road, friends.
BANG! BANG! BANG! BANG!

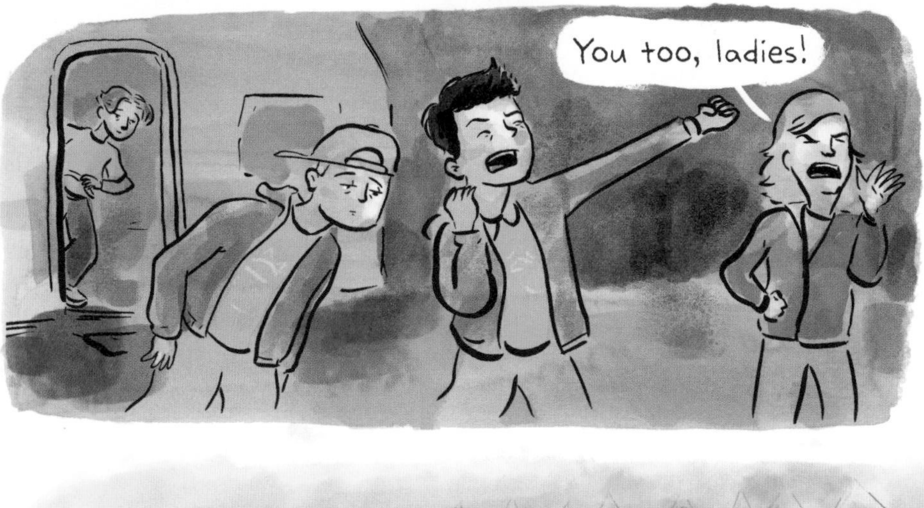
You too, ladies!

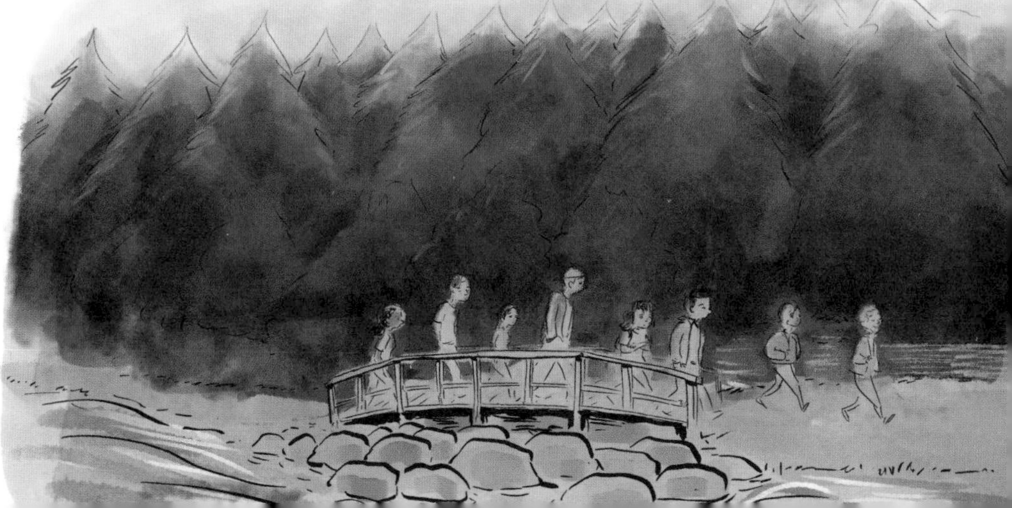

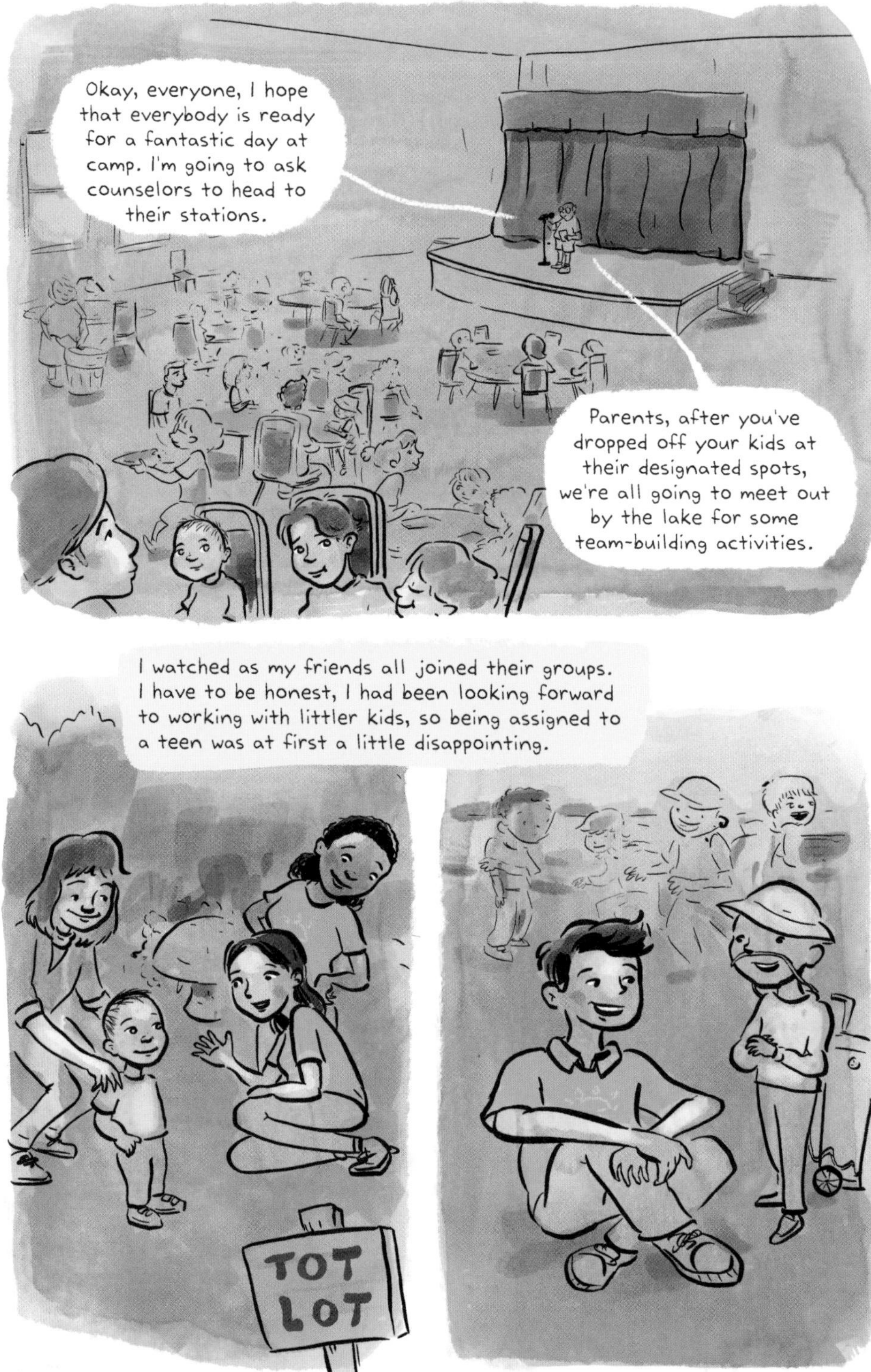

Okay, everyone, I hope that everybody is ready for a fantastic day at camp. I'm going to ask counselors to head to their stations.
Parents, after you've dropped off your kids at their designated spots, we're all going to meet out by the lake for some team-building activities.
I watched as my friends all joined their groups. I have to be honest, I had been looking forward to working with littler kids, so being assigned to a teen was at first a little disappointing.
TOT LOT

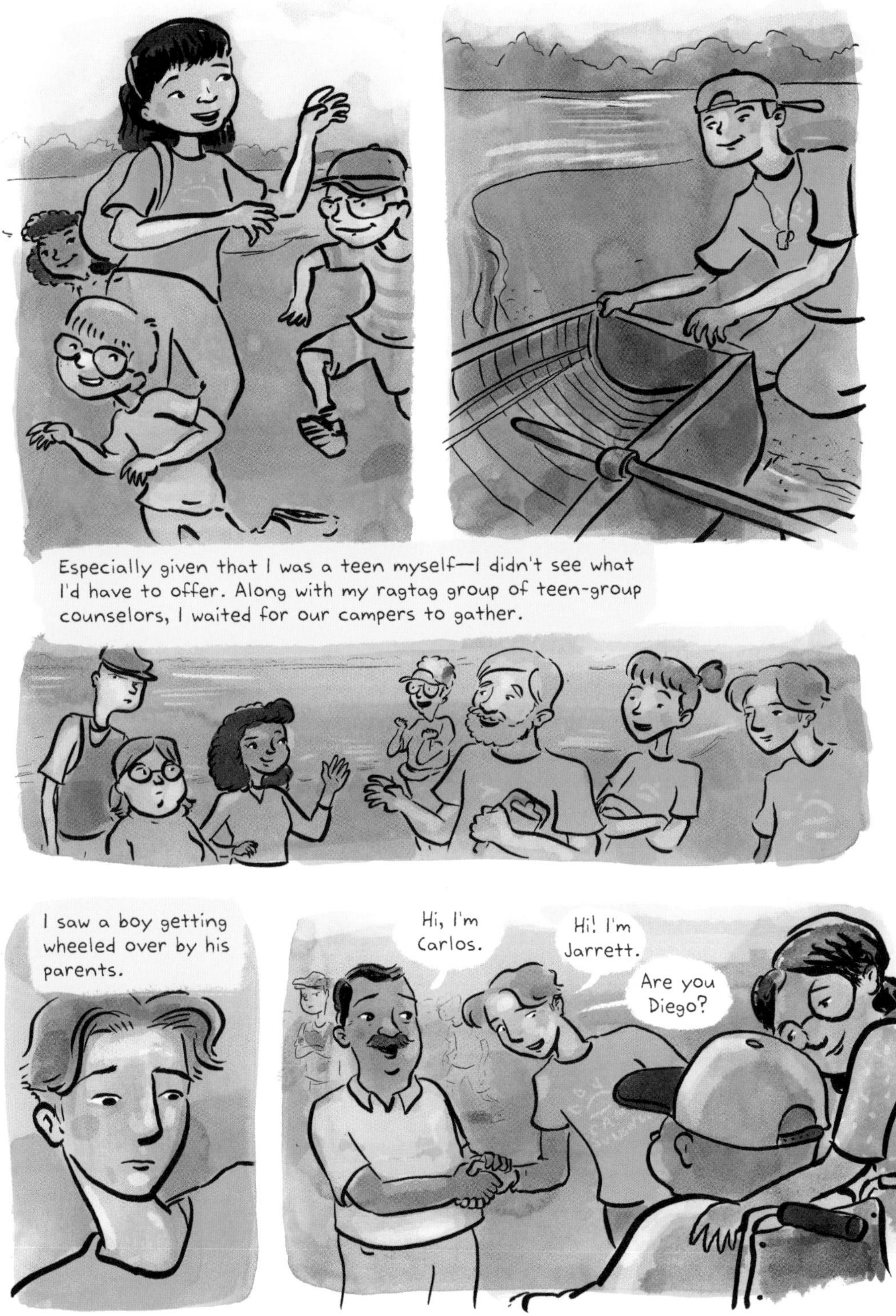
Especially given that I was a teen myself—I didn't see what I'd have to offer. Along with my ragtag group of teen-group counselors, I waited for our campers to gather.
I saw a boy getting wheeled over by his parents.
Hi, I'm Carlos.
Hi! I'm Jarrett.
Are you Diego?

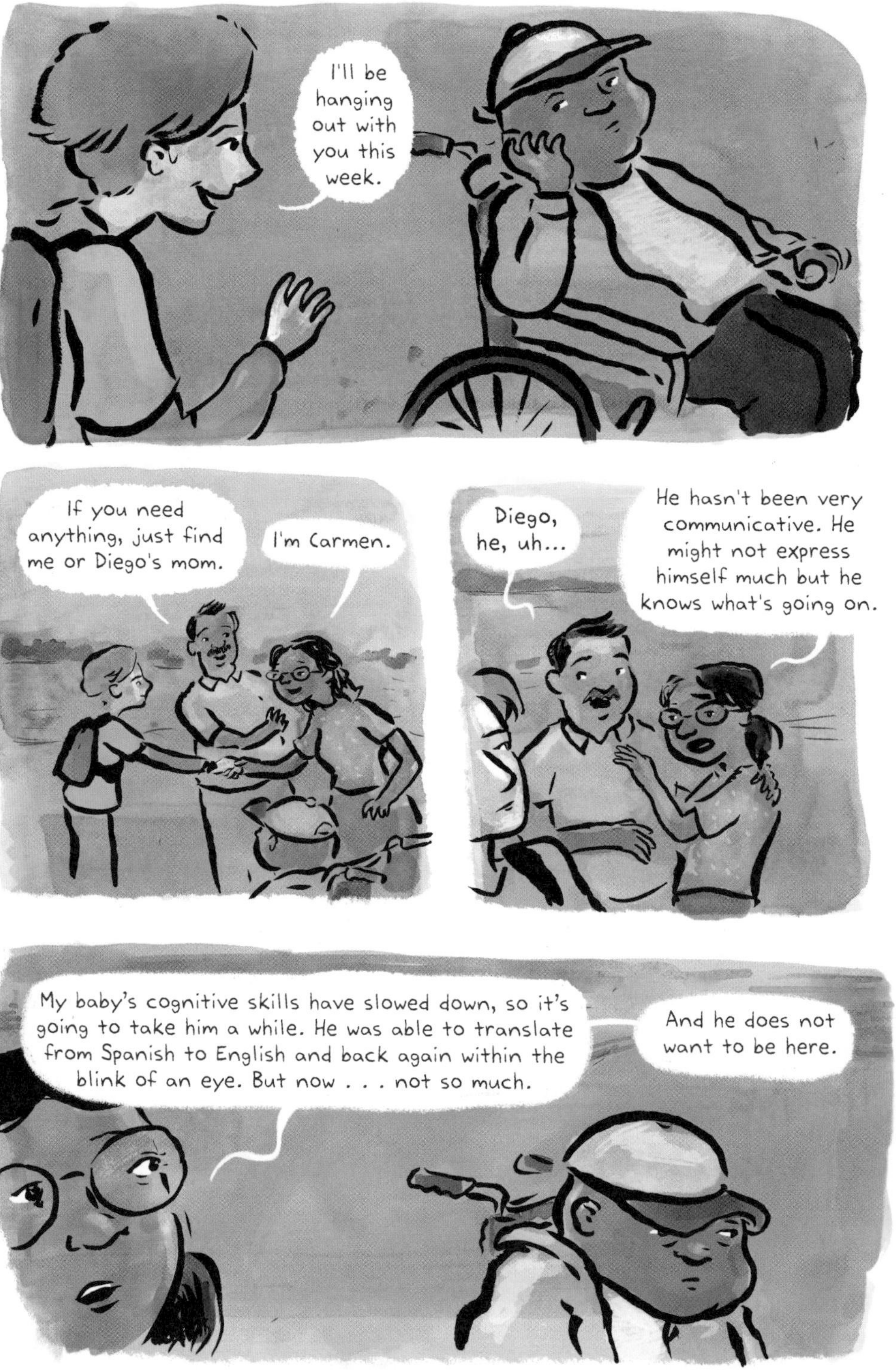
I'll be hanging out with you this week.
If you need anything, just find me or Diego's mom.
I'm Carmen.
Diego, he, uh...
He hasn't been very communicative. He might not express himself much but he knows what's going on.
My baby's cognitive skills have slowed down, so it's going to take him a while. He was able to translate from Spanish to English and back again within the blink of an eye. But now . . . not so much.
And he does not want to be here.

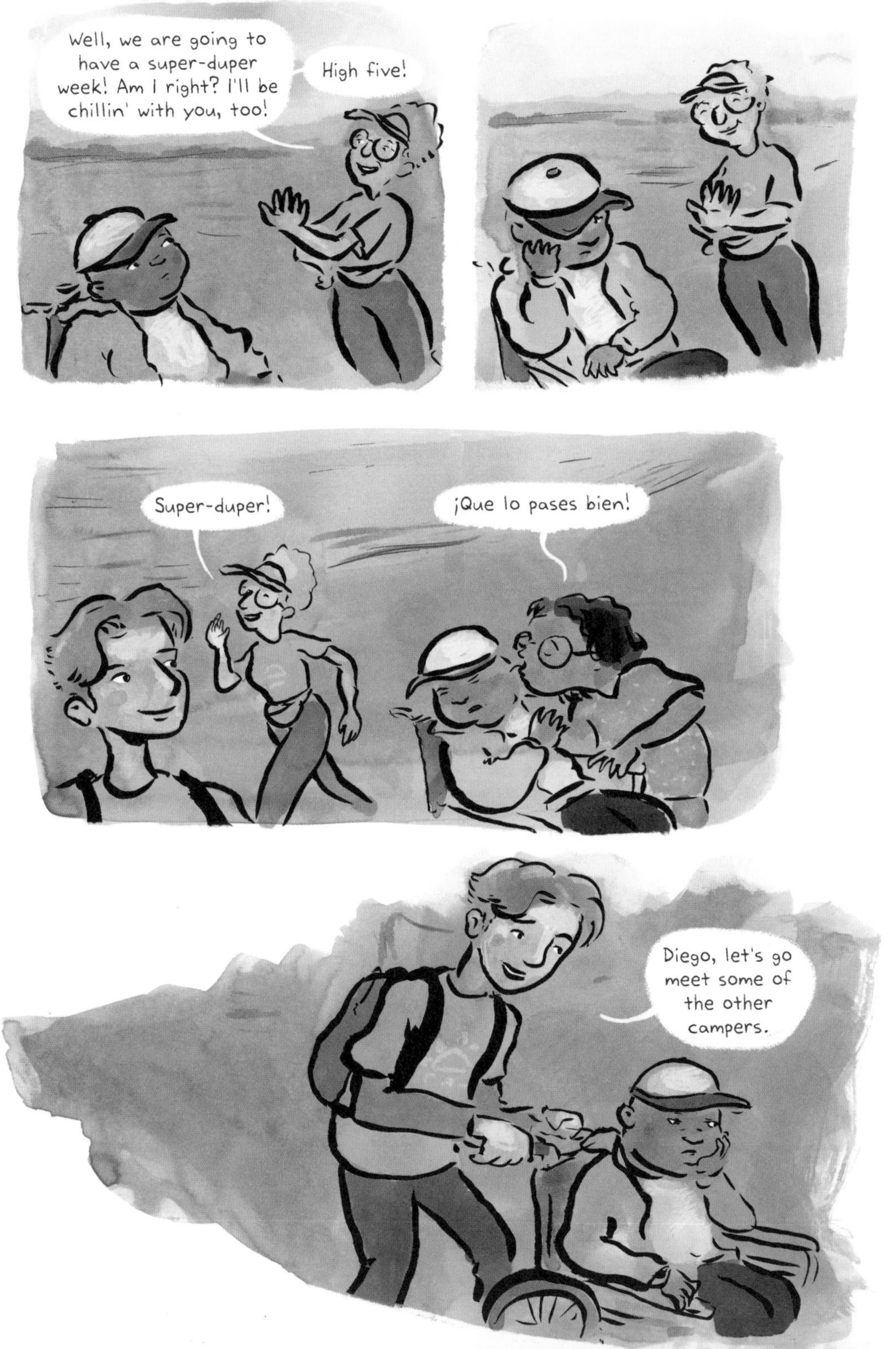
Well, we are going to have a super-duper week! Am I right? I'll be chillin' with you, too!
High five!
Super-duper!
¡Que lo pases bien!
Diego, let's go meet some of the other campers.

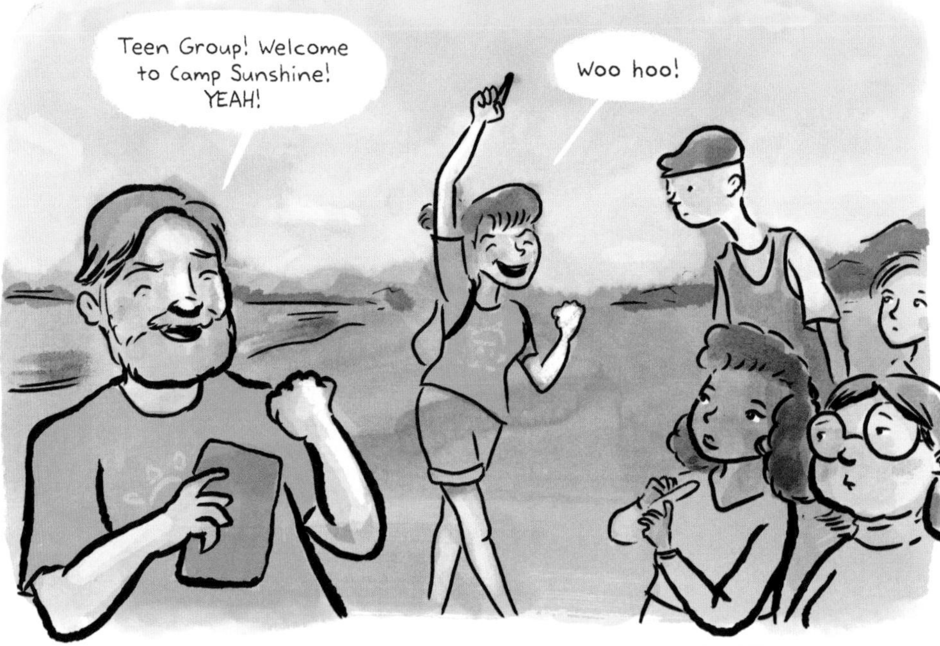
Teen Group! Welcome to Camp Sunshine! YEAH!
Woo hoo!

The Teen Group was small. And it seemed like Diego had more in common with his campmates than just cancer...

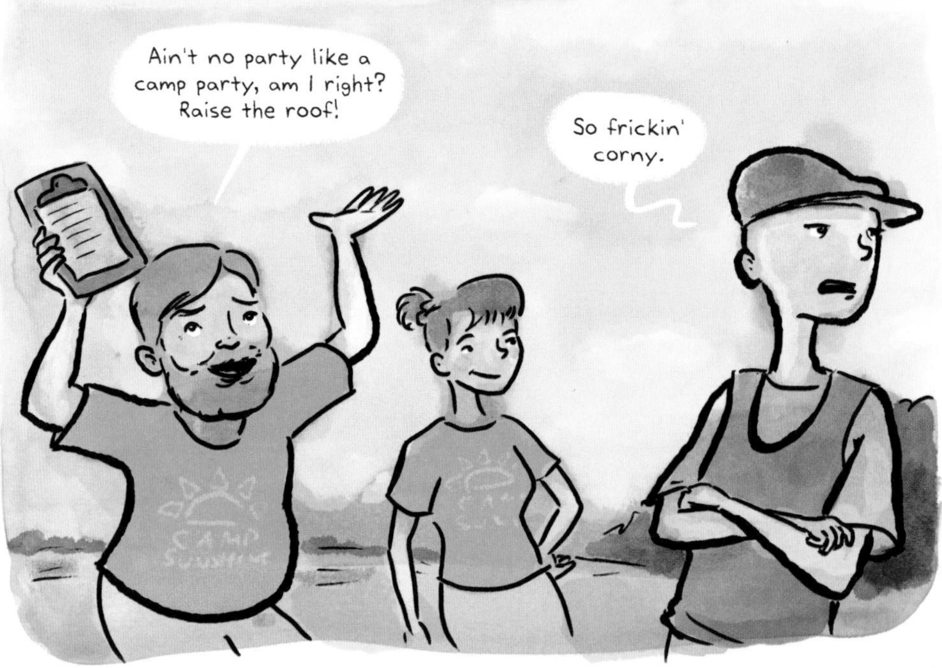
Ain't no party like a camp party, am I right? Raise the roof!
So frickin' corny.

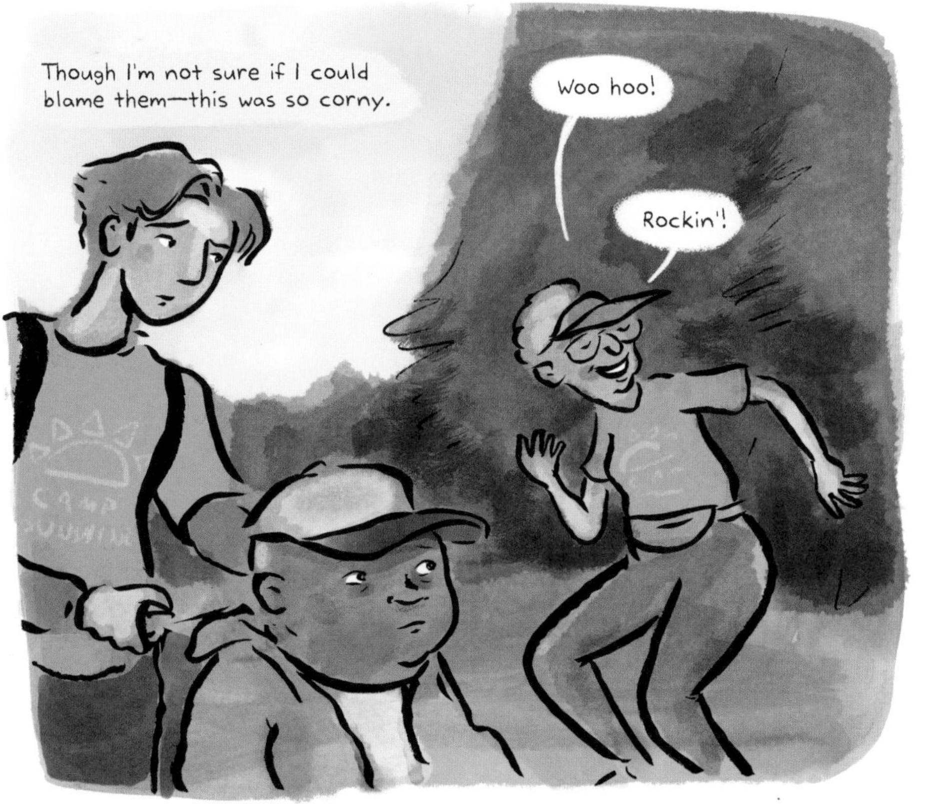
Though I'm not sure if I could blame them—this was so corny.
Woo hoo!
Rockin'!

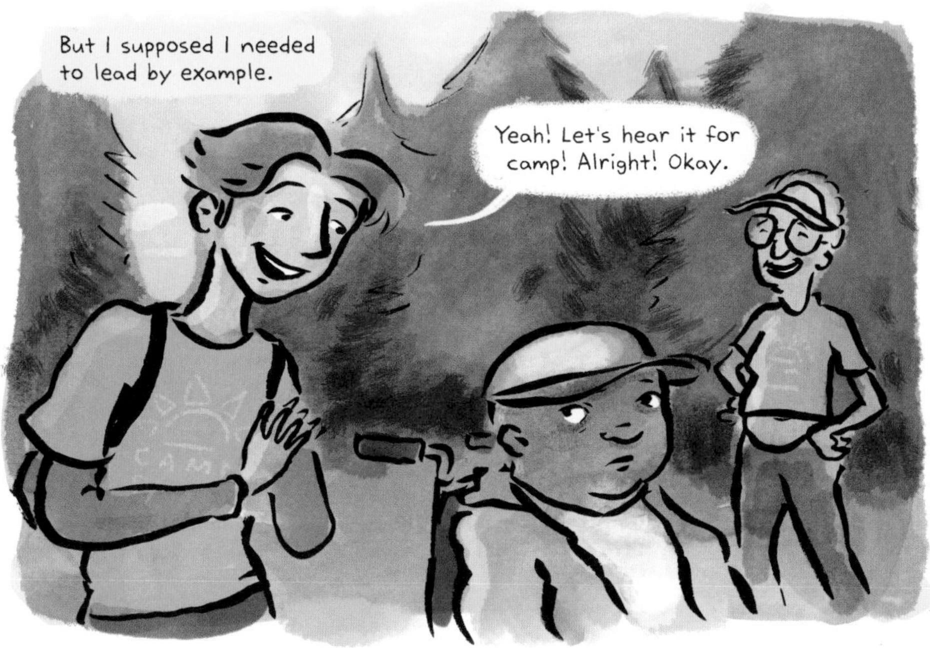
But I supposed I needed to lead by example.
Yeah! Let's hear it for camp! Alright! Okay.

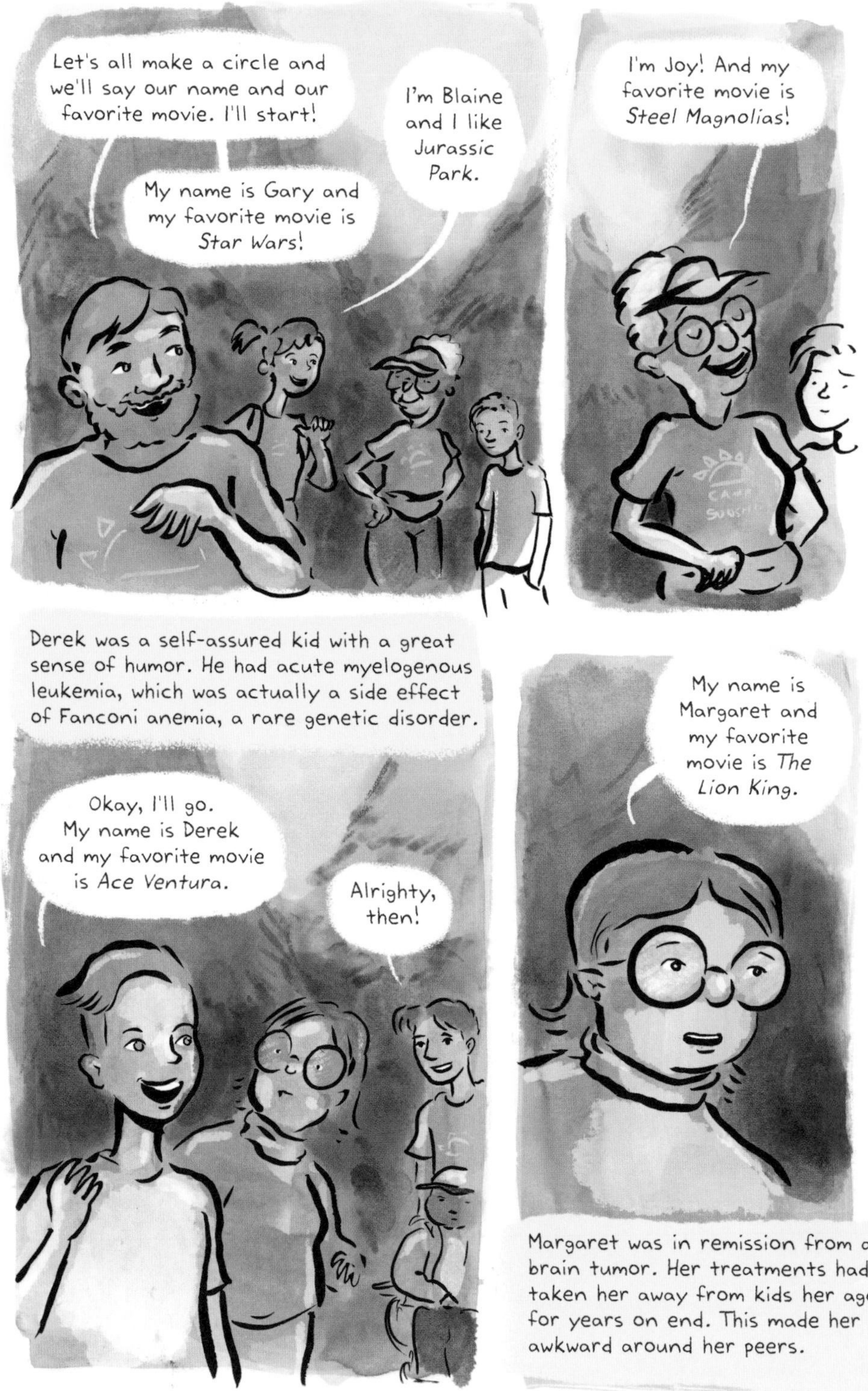
Let's all make a circle and we'll say our name and our favorite movie. I'll start!
My name is Gary and my favorite movie is *Star Wars*!
I'm Blaine and I like *Jurassic Park*.
I'm Joy! And my favorite movie is *Steel Magnolias*!
Derek was a self-assured kid with a great sense of humor. He had acute myelogenous leukemia, which was actually a side effect of Fanconi anemia, a rare genetic disorder.
Okay, I'll go. My name is Derek and my favorite movie is *Ace Ventura*.
Alrighty, then!
My name is Margaret and my favorite movie is *The Lion King*.
Margaret was in remission from a brain tumor. Her treatments had taken her away from kids her age for years on end. This made her awkward around her peers.

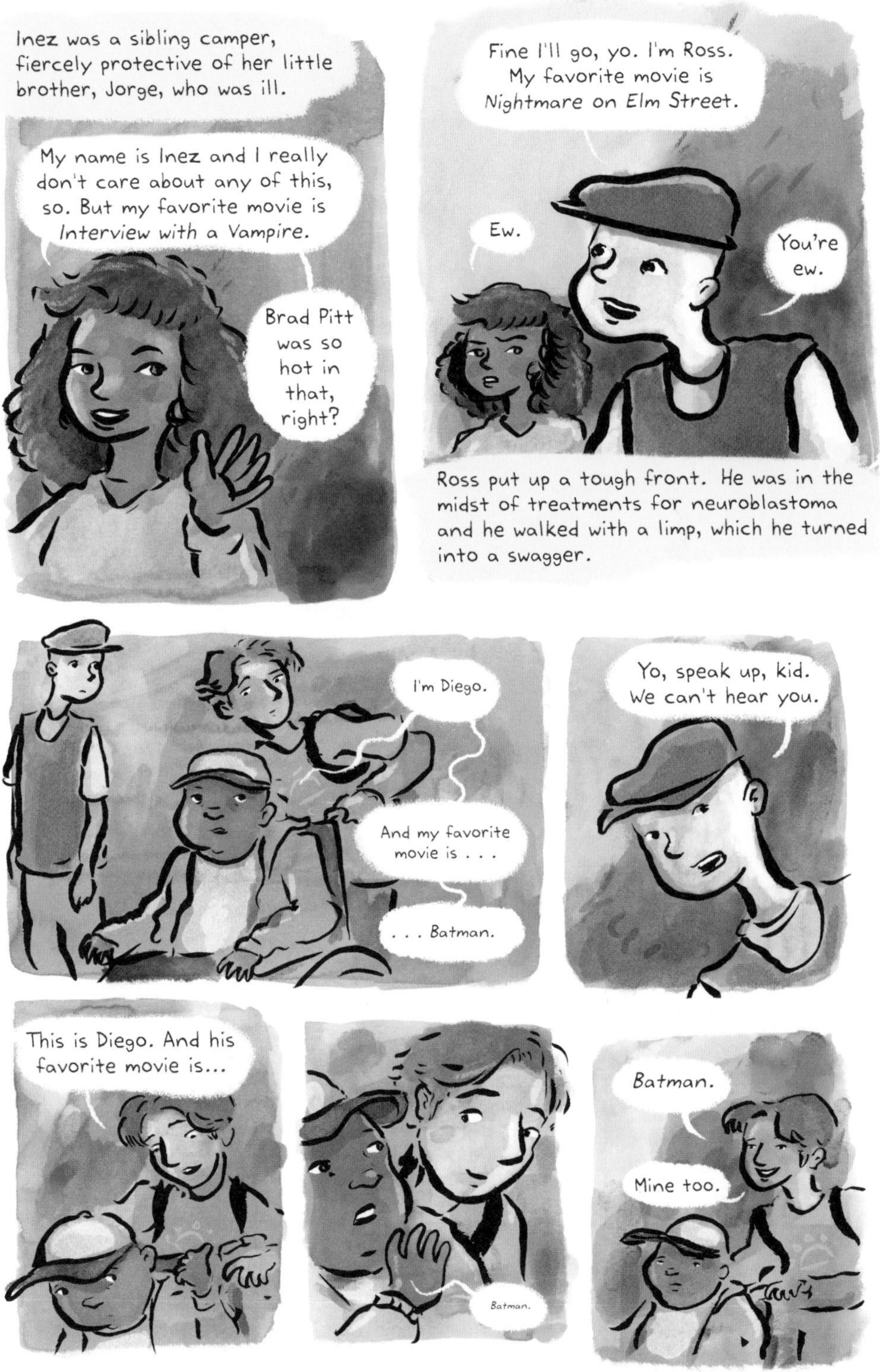
Inez was a sibling camper, fiercely protective of her little brother, Jorge, who was ill.
My name is Inez and I really don't care about any of this, so. But my favorite movie is *Interview with a Vampire.*
Brad Pitt was so hot in that, right?
Fine I'll go, yo. I'm Ross. My favorite movie is *Nightmare on Elm Street.*
Ew.
You're ew.
Ross put up a tough front. He was in the midst of treatments for neuroblastoma and he walked with a limp, which he turned into a swagger.
I'm Diego.
And my favorite movie is . . .
. . . Batman.
Yo, speak up, kid. We can't hear you.
This is Diego. And his favorite movie is...
Batman.
Batman.
Mine too.

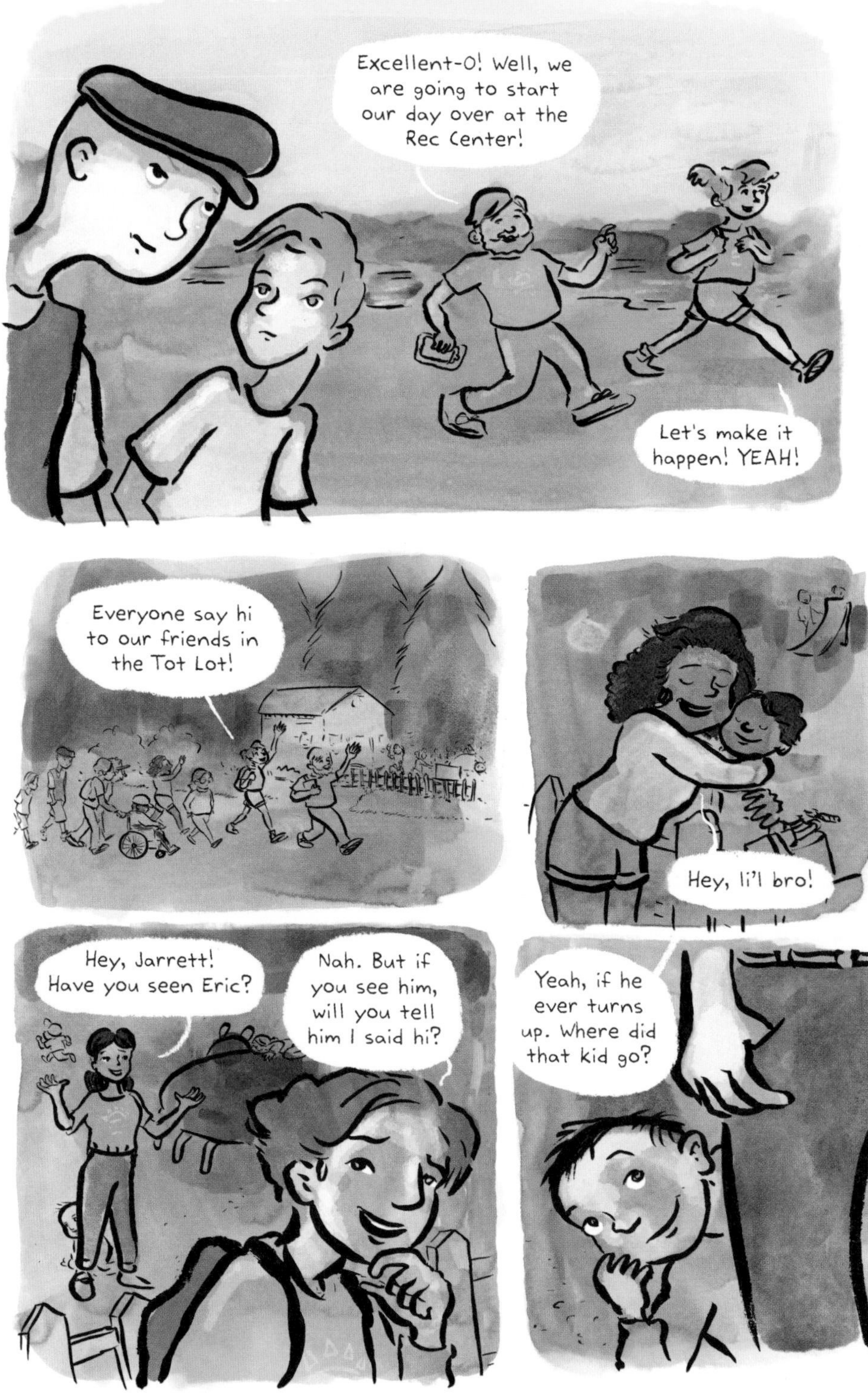
Excellent-O! Well, we are going to start our day over at the Rec Center!
Let's make it happen! YEAH!
Everyone say hi to our friends in the Tot Lot!
Hey, li'l bro!
Hey, Jarrett! Have you seen Eric?
Nah. But if you see him, will you tell him I said hi?
Yeah, if he ever turns up. Where did that kid go?

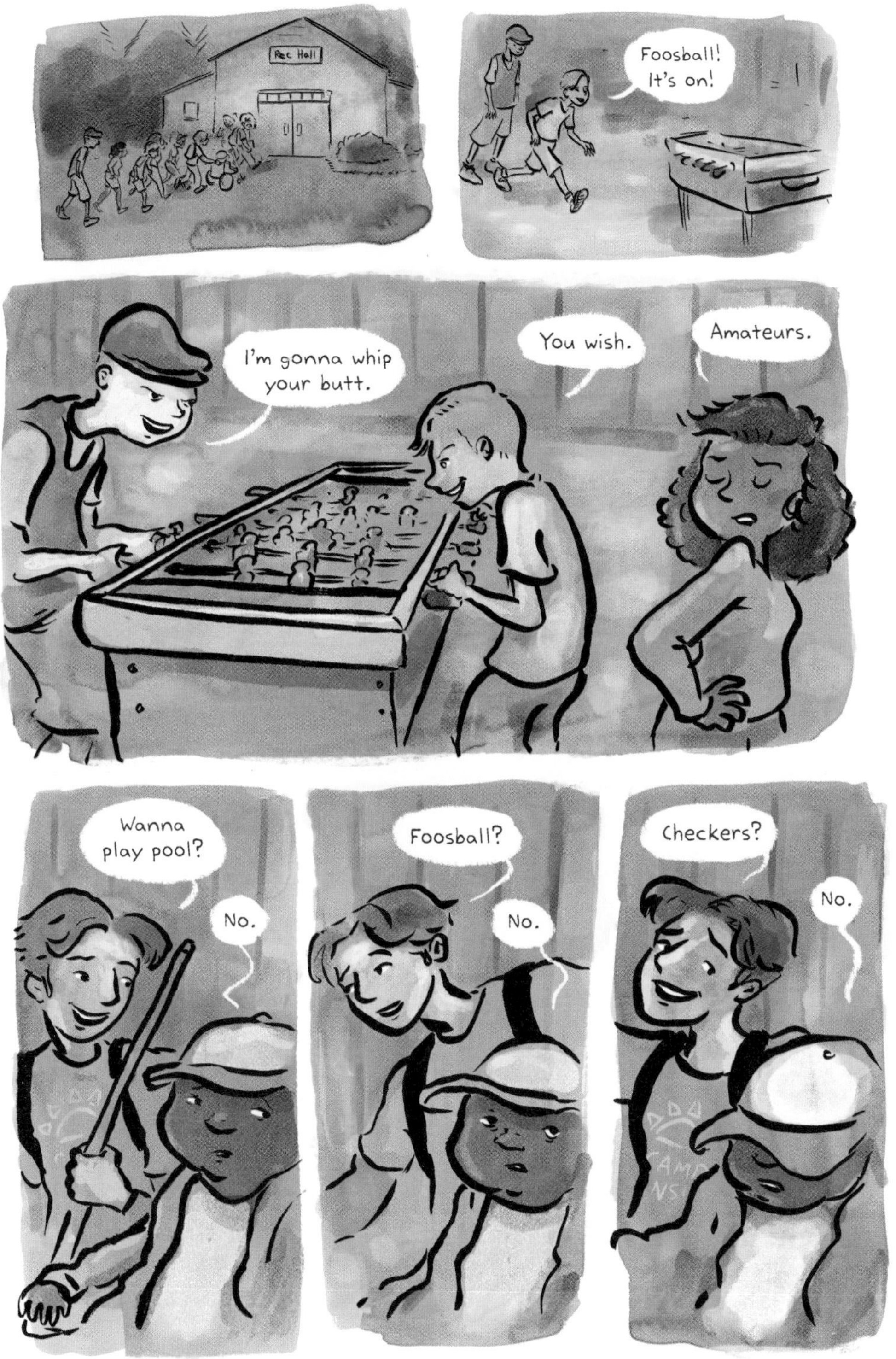
Rec Hall
Foosball! It's on!
I'm gonna whip your butt.
You wish.
Amateurs.
Wanna play pool?
No.
Foosball?
No.
Checkers?
No.

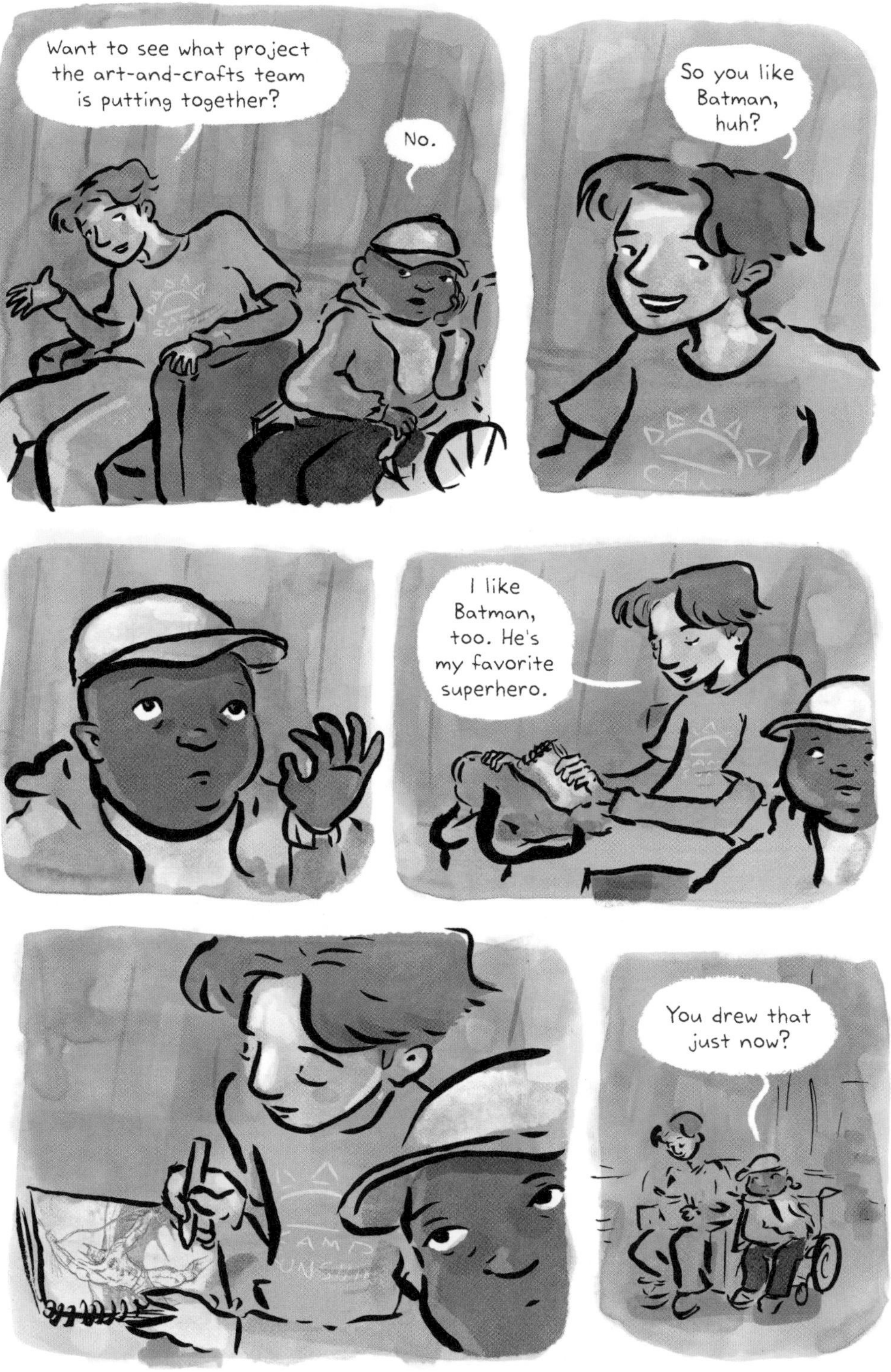
Want to see what project the art-and-crafts team is putting together?
No.
So you like Batman, huh?
I like Batman, too. He's my favorite superhero.
You drew that just now?

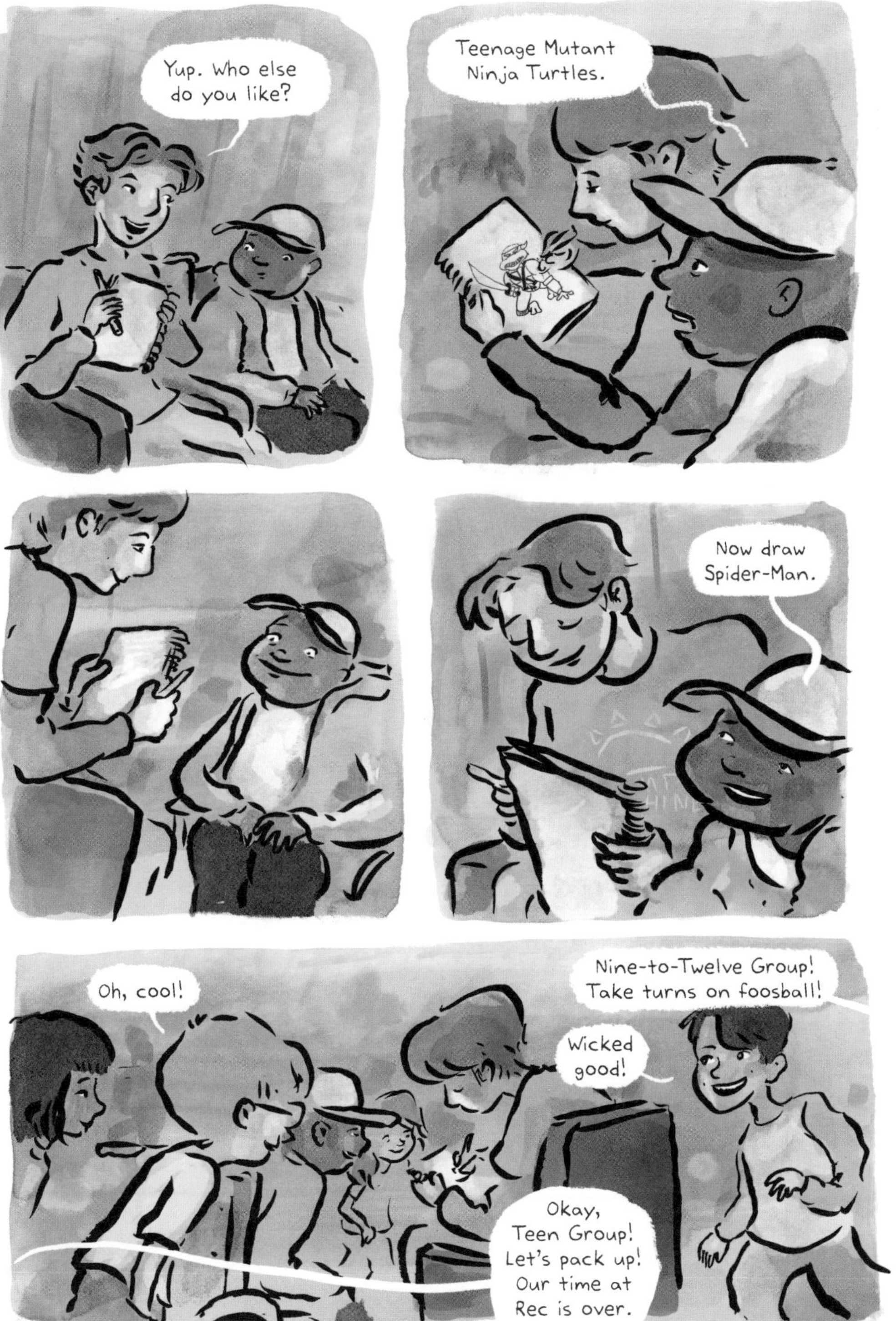

Yup. Who else do you like?
Teenage Mutant Ninja Turtles.
Now draw Spider-Man.
Oh, cool!
Nine-to-Twelve Group! Take turns on foosball!
Wicked good!
Okay, Teen Group! Let's pack up! Our time at Rec is over.

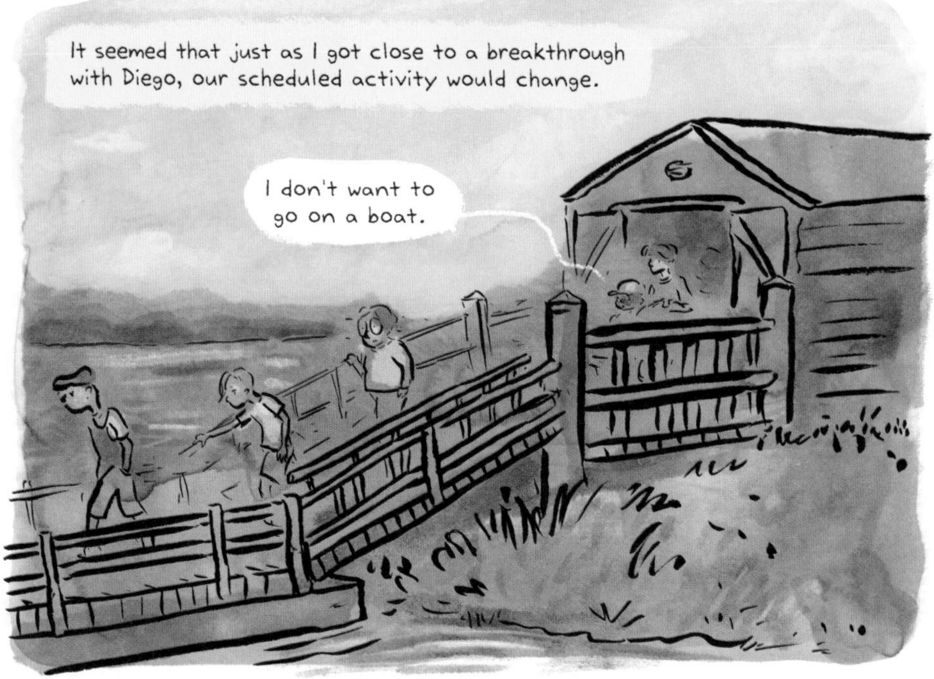
It seemed that just as I got close to a breakthrough with Diego, our scheduled activity would change.
I don't want to go on a boat.

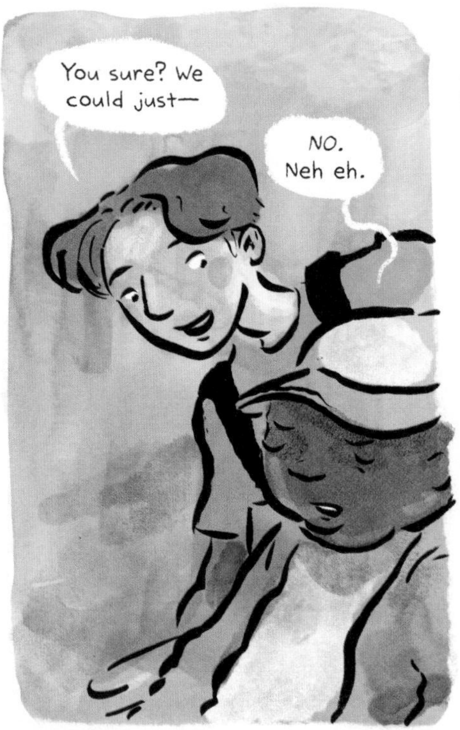
You sure? We could just—
NO. Neh eh.

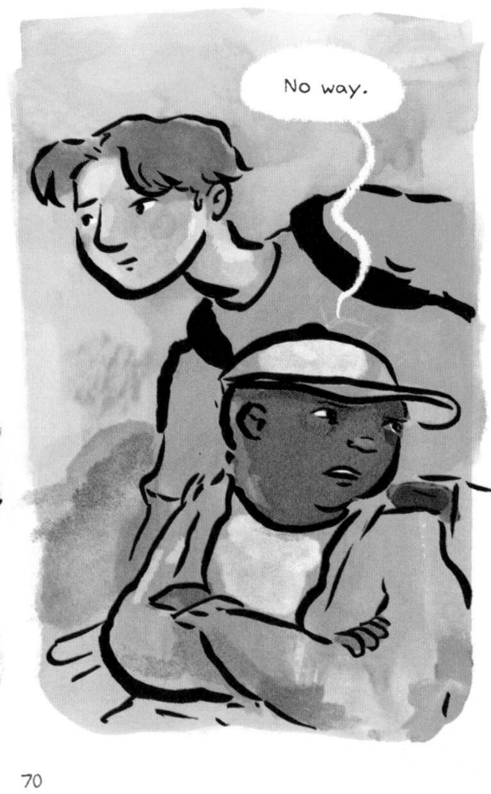
No way.

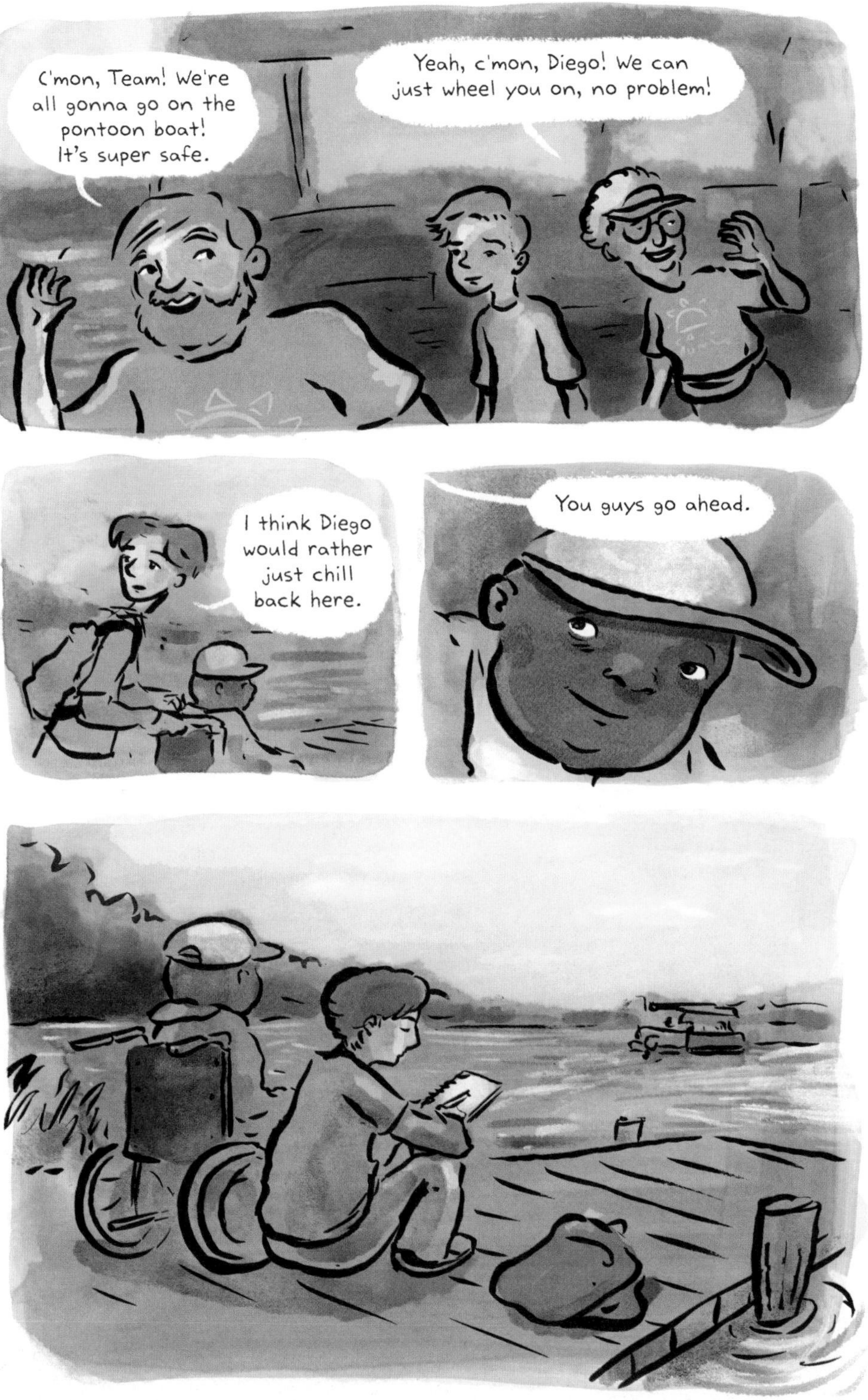
C'mon, Team! We're all gonna go on the pontoon boat! It's super safe.
Yeah, c'mon, Diego! We can just wheel you on, no problem!
I think Diego would rather just chill back here.
You guys go ahead.

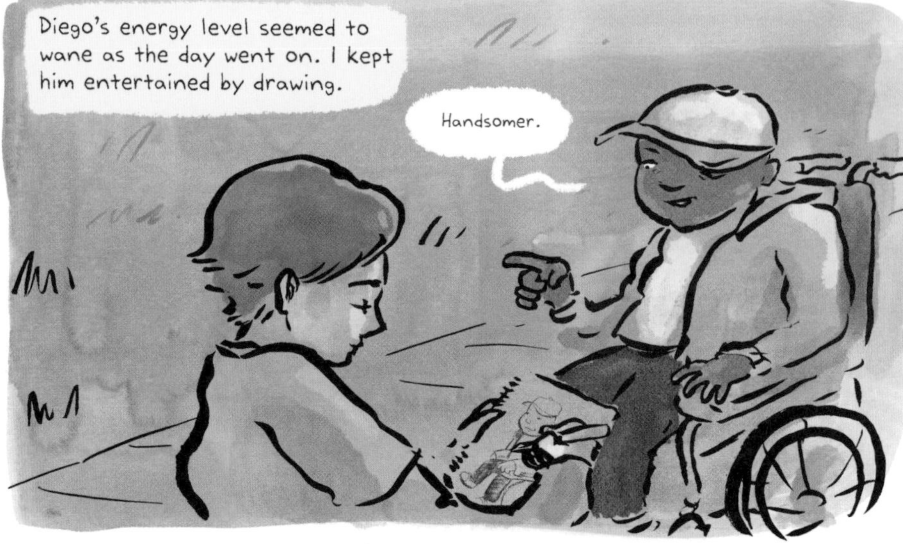
Diego's energy level seemed to wane as the day went on. I kept him entertained by drawing.
Handsomer.

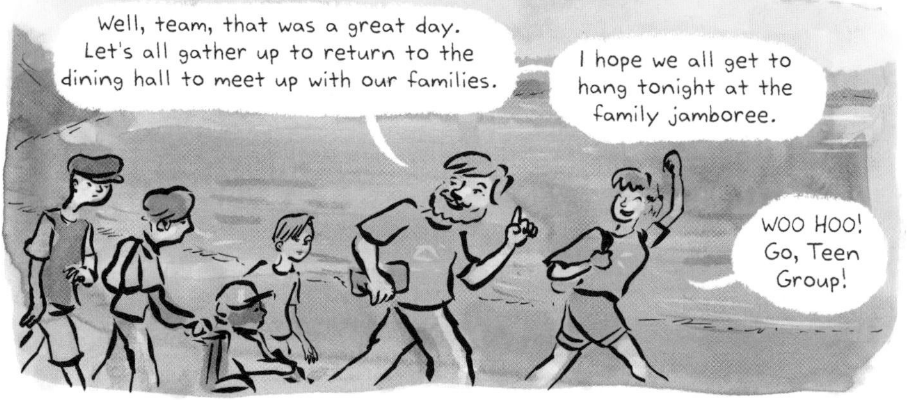
Well, team, that was a great day. Let's all gather up to return to the dining hall to meet up with our families.
I hope we all get to hang tonight at the family jamboree.
WOO HOO! Go, Teen Group!

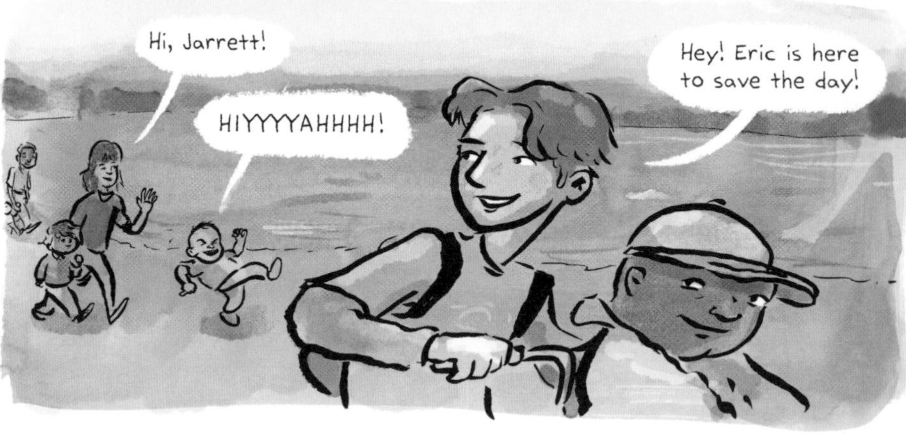
Hi, Jarrett!
HIYYYYAHHHH!
Hey! Eric is here to save the day!

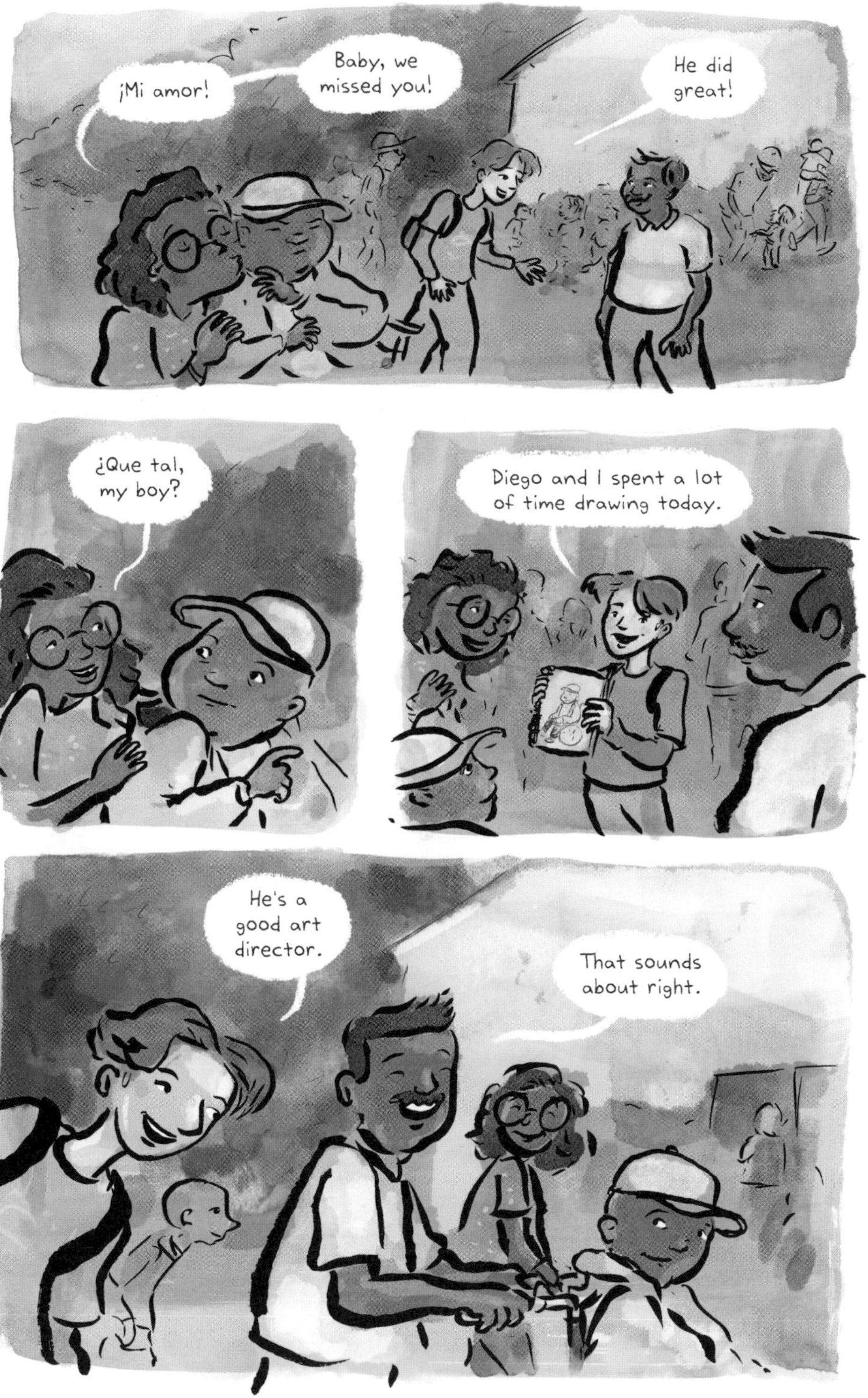
¡Mi amor!
Baby, we missed you!
He did great!
¿Que tal, my boy?
Diego and I spent a lot of time drawing today.
He's a good art director.
That sounds about right.

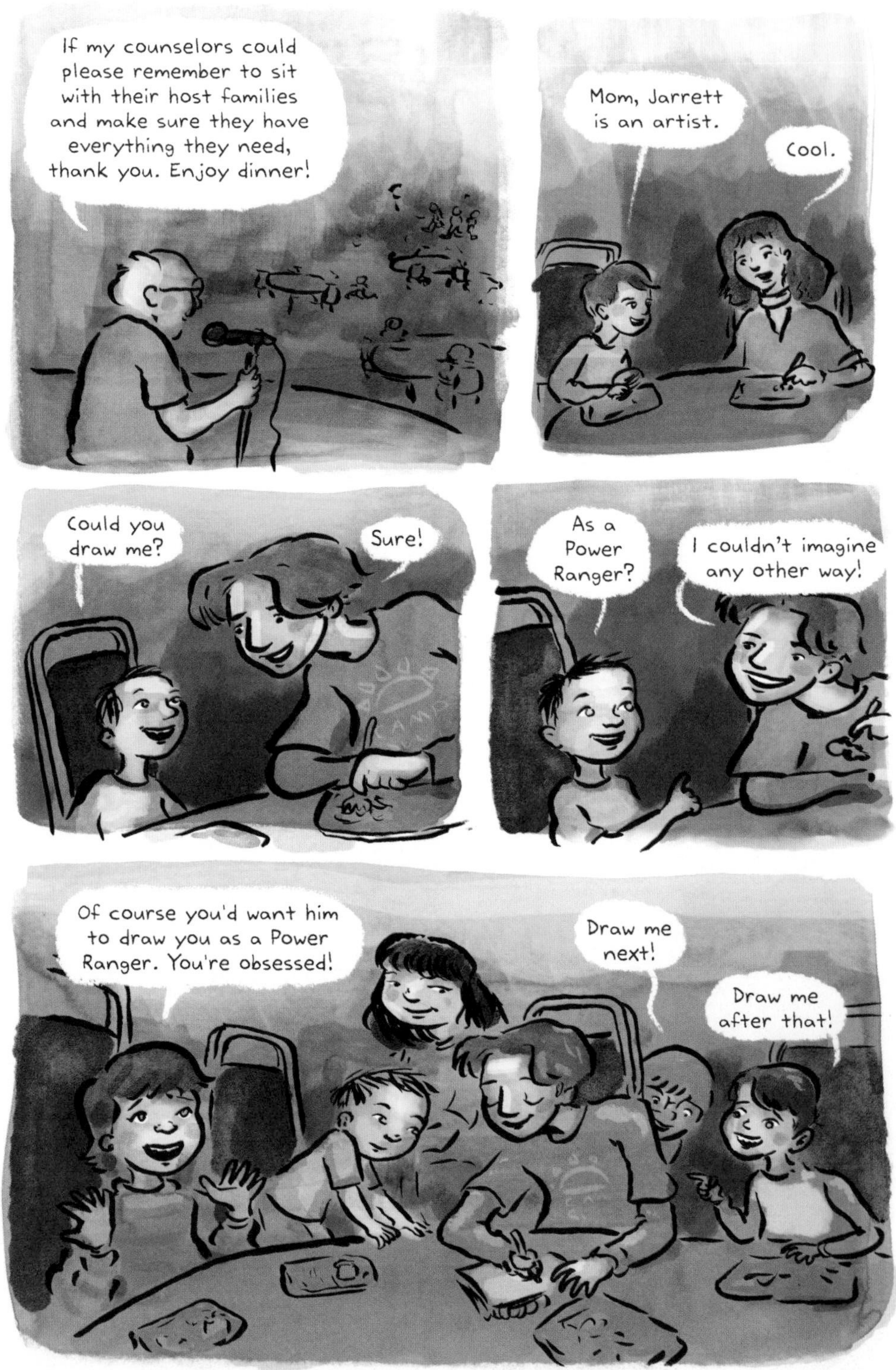
If my counselors could please remember to sit with their host families and make sure they have everything they need, thank you. Enjoy dinner!
Mom, Jarrett is an artist.
Cool.
Could you draw me?
Sure!
As a Power Ranger?
I couldn't imagine any other way!
Of course you'd want him to draw you as a Power Ranger. You're obsessed!
Draw me next!
Draw me after that!

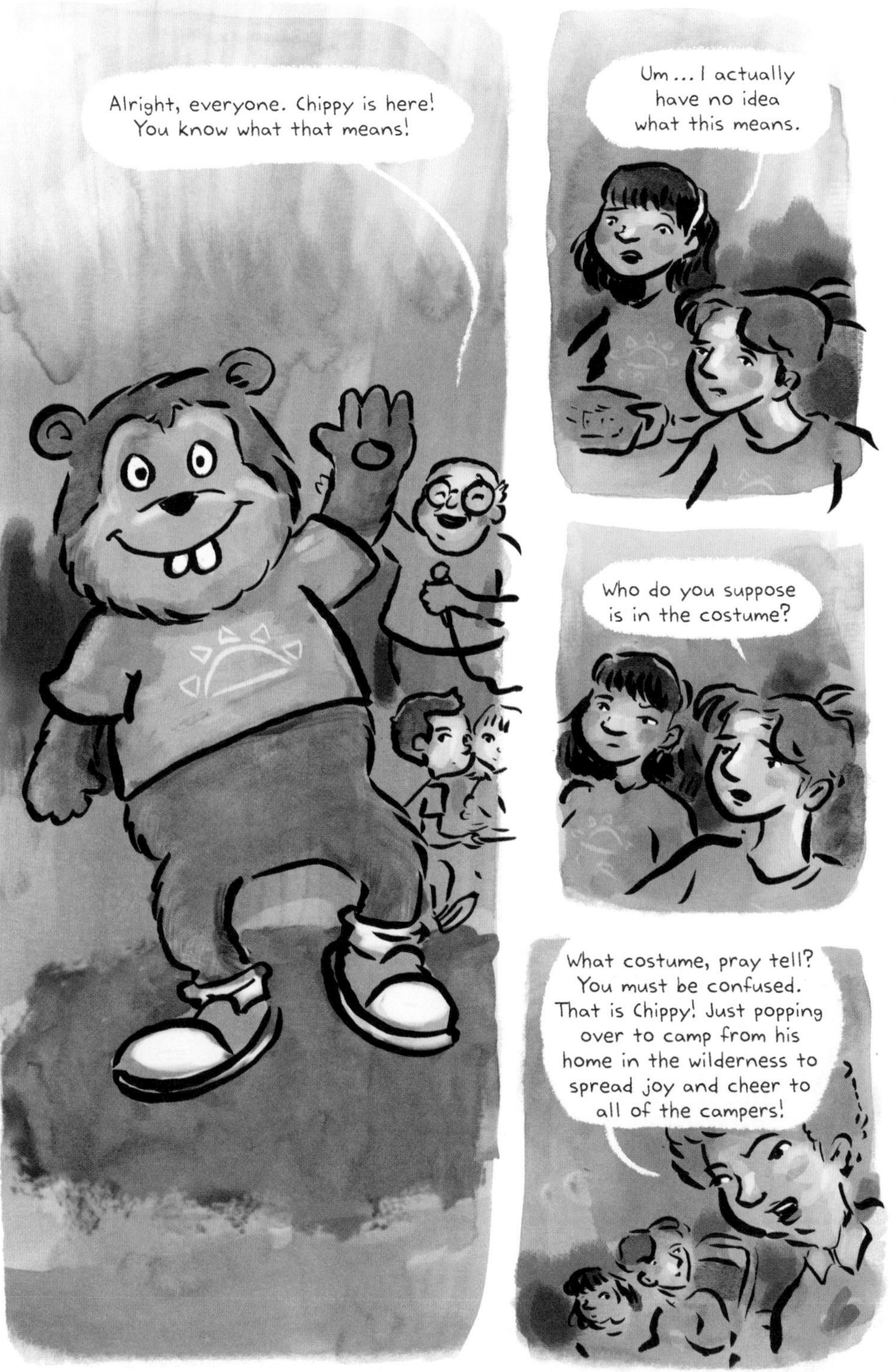
Alright, everyone. Chippy is here! You know what that means!
Um... I actually have no idea what this means.
Who do you suppose is in the costume?
What costume, pray tell? You must be confused. That is Chippy! Just popping over to camp from his home in the wilderness to spread joy and cheer to all of the campers!

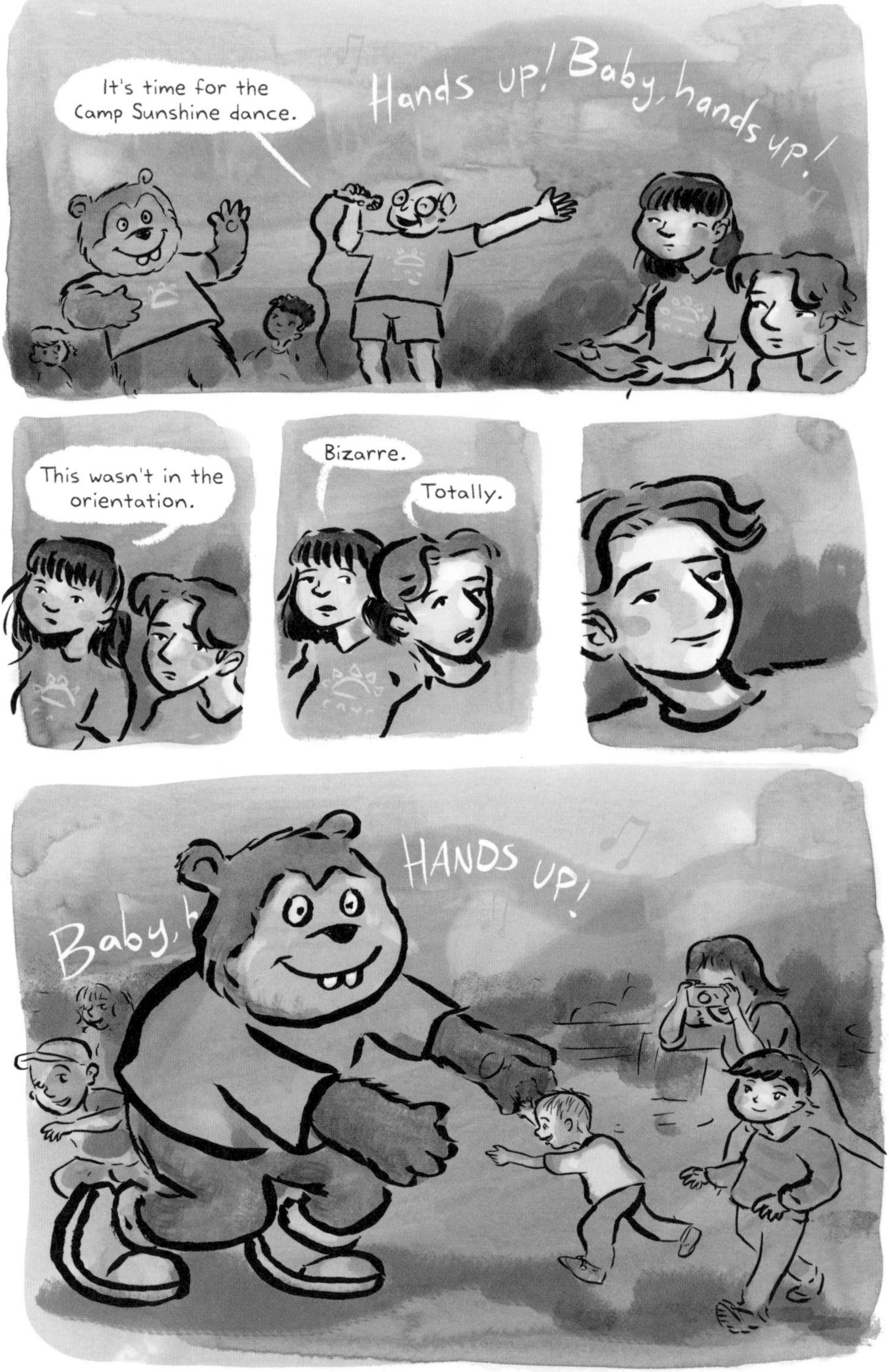
It's time for the Camp Sunshine dance.
Hands up! Baby, hands up!
This wasn't in the orientation.
Bizarre.
Totally.
HANDS UP!
Baby, h

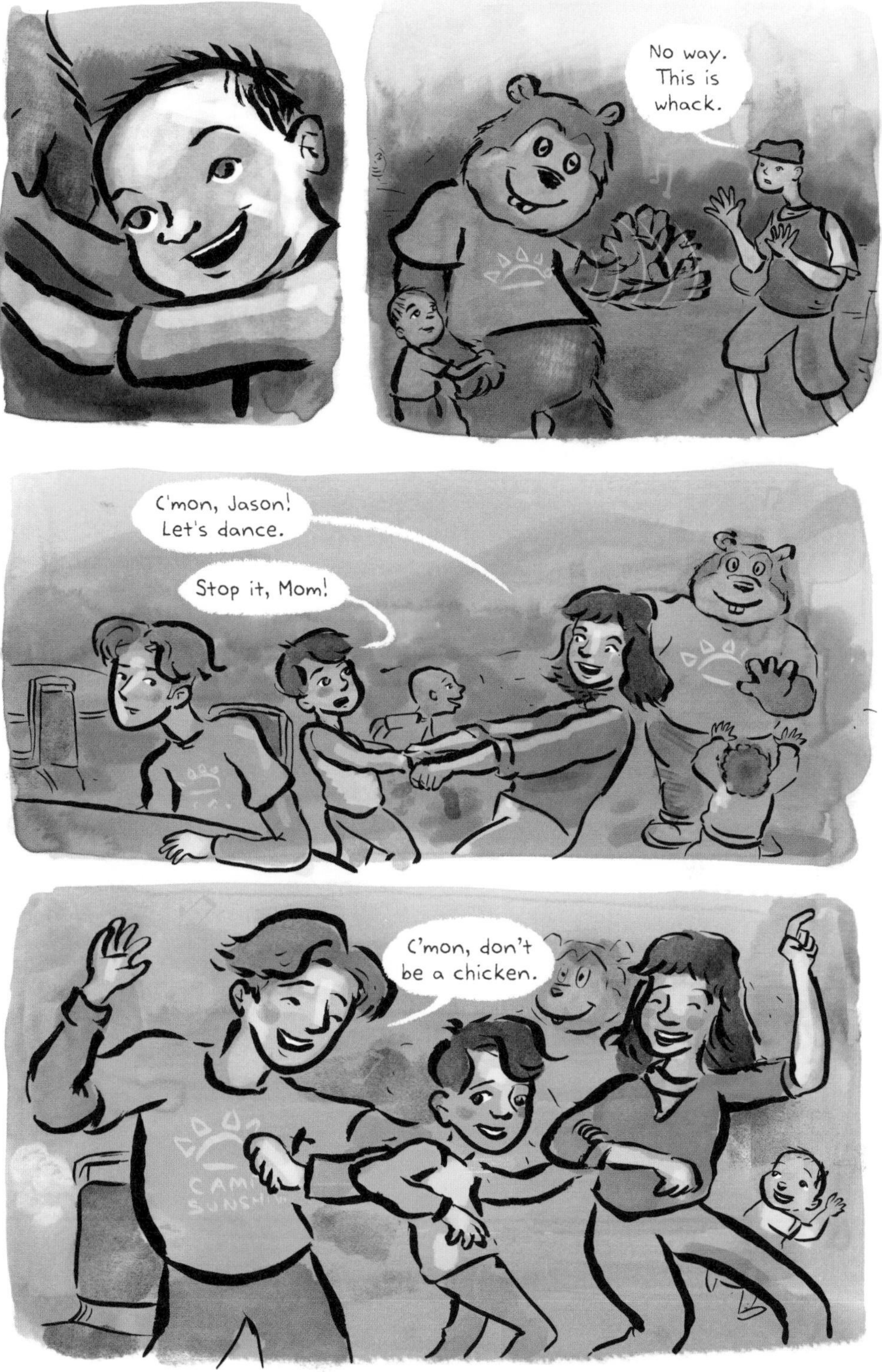
No way. This is whack.
C'mon, Jason! Let's dance.
Stop it, Mom!
C'mon, don't be a chicken.
CAMP SUNSHINE

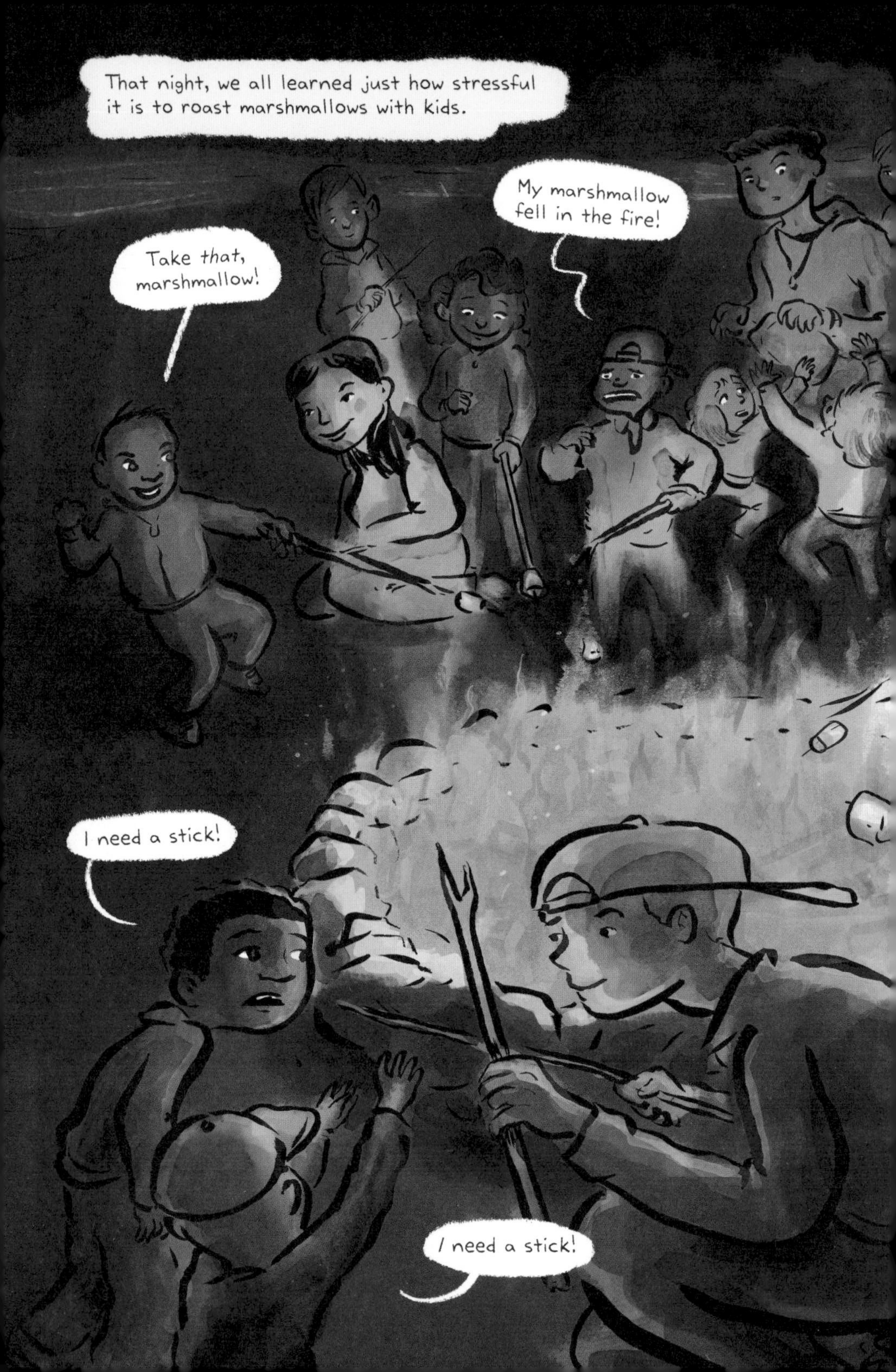
That night, we all learned just how stressful it is to roast marshmallows with kids.
Take *that*, marshmallow!
My marshmallow fell in the fire!
I need a stick!
I need a stick!

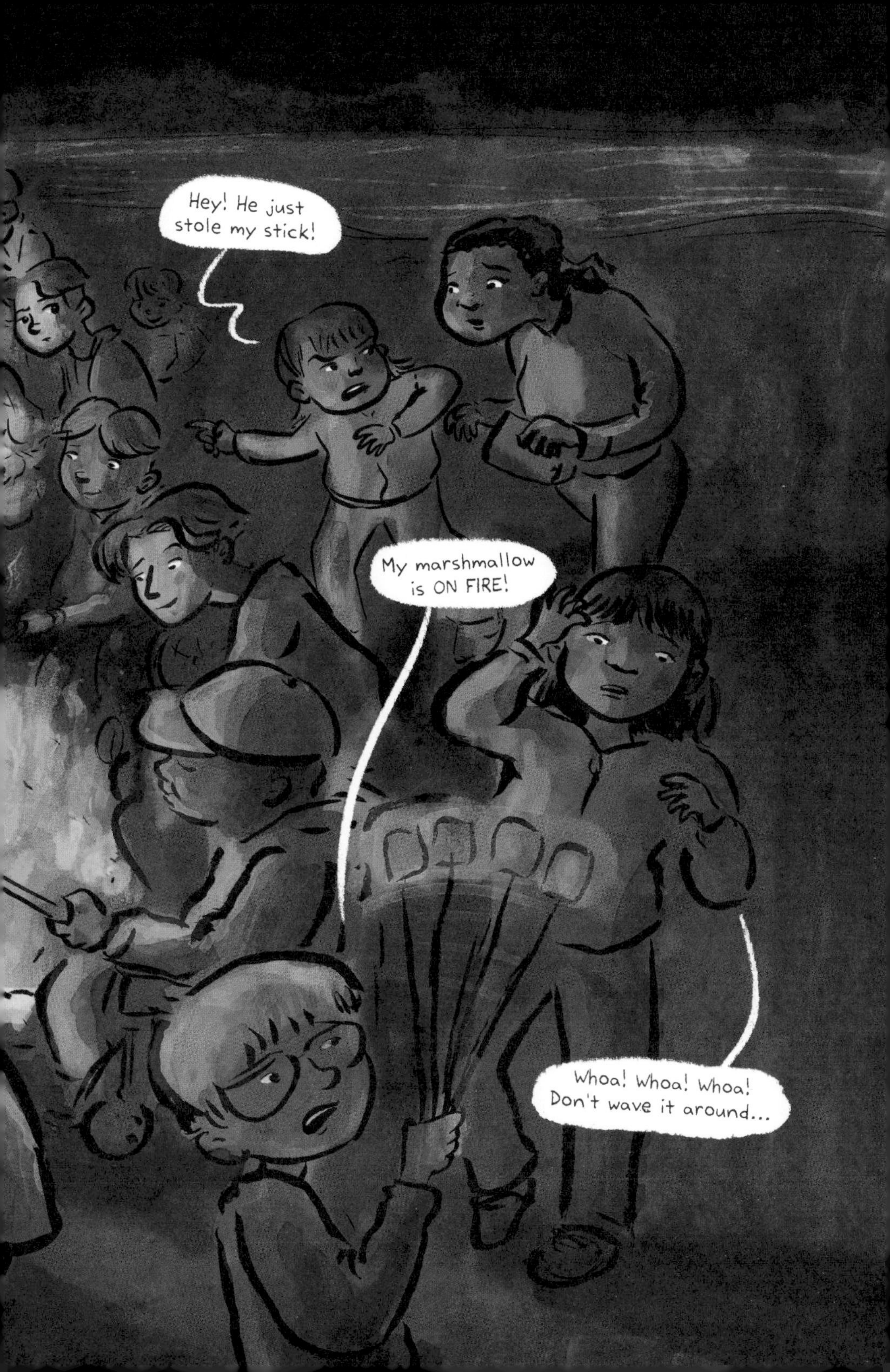
Hey! He just stole my stick!
My marshmallow is ON FIRE!
Whoa! Whoa! Whoa! Don't wave it around...

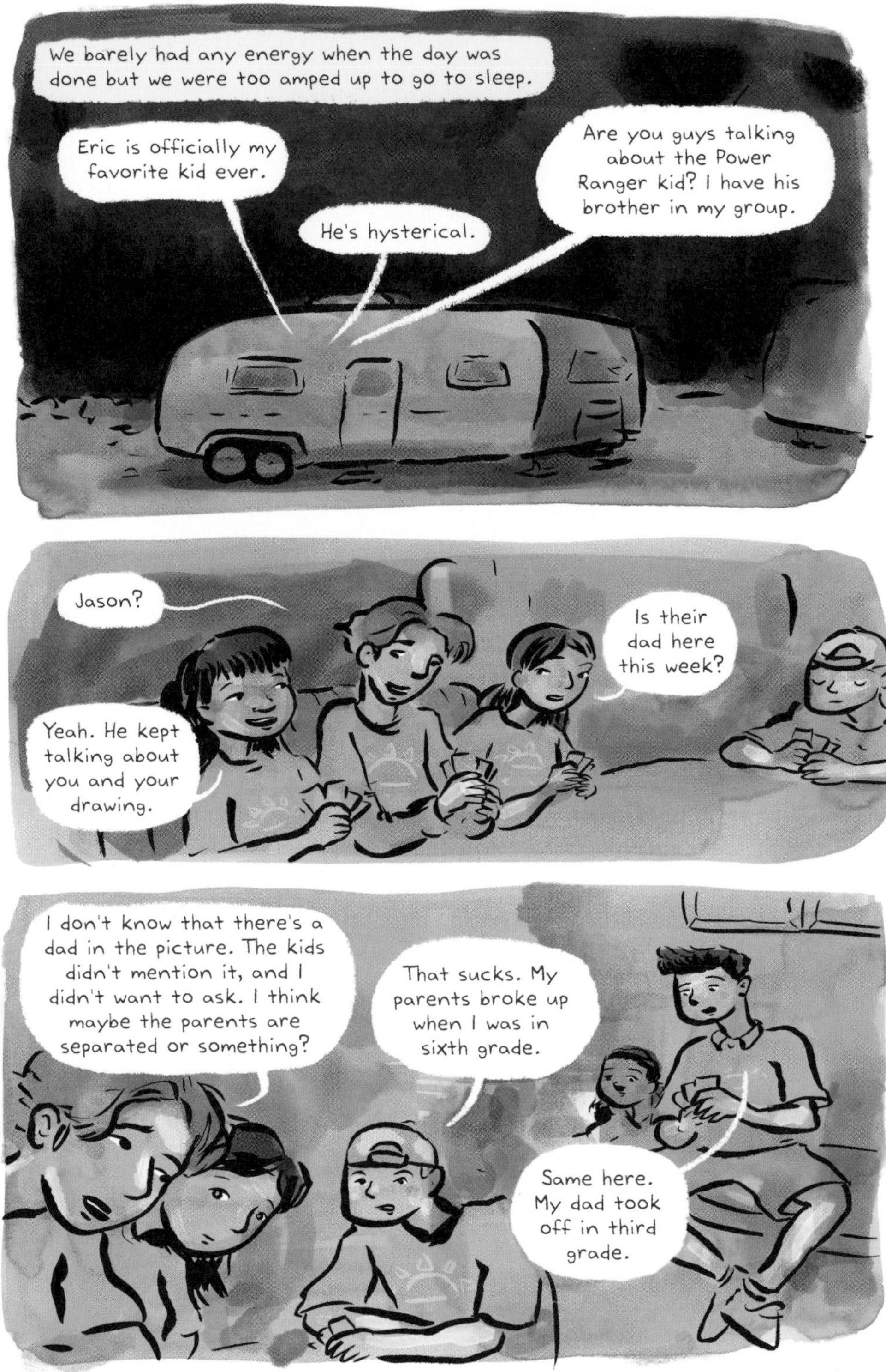
We barely had any energy when the day was done but we were too amped up to go to sleep.
Eric is officially my favorite kid ever.
He's hysterical.
Are you guys talking about the Power Ranger kid? I have his brother in my group.
Jason?
Yeah. He kept talking about you and your drawing.
Is their dad here this week?
I don't know that there's a dad in the picture. The kids didn't mention it, and I didn't want to ask. I think maybe the parents are separated or something?
That sucks. My parents broke up when I was in sixth grade.
Same here. My dad took off in third grade.

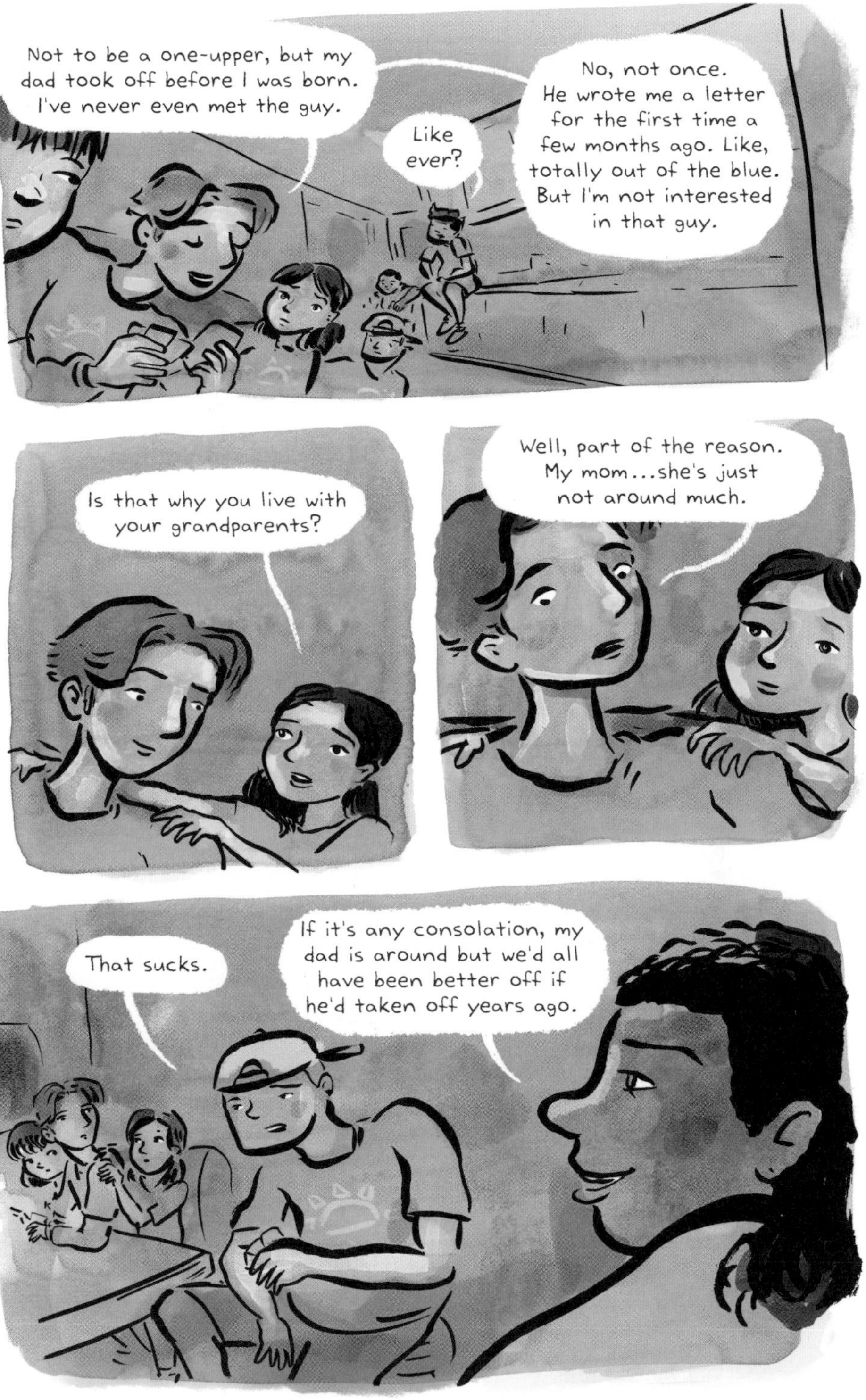
Not to be a one-upper, but my dad took off before I was born. I've never even met the guy.
Like ever?
No, not once. He wrote me a letter for the first time a few months ago. Like, totally out of the blue. But I'm not interested in that guy.
Is that why you live with your grandparents?
Well, part of the reason. My mom...she's just not around much.
That sucks.
If it's any consolation, my dad is around but we'd all have been better off if he'd taken off years ago.

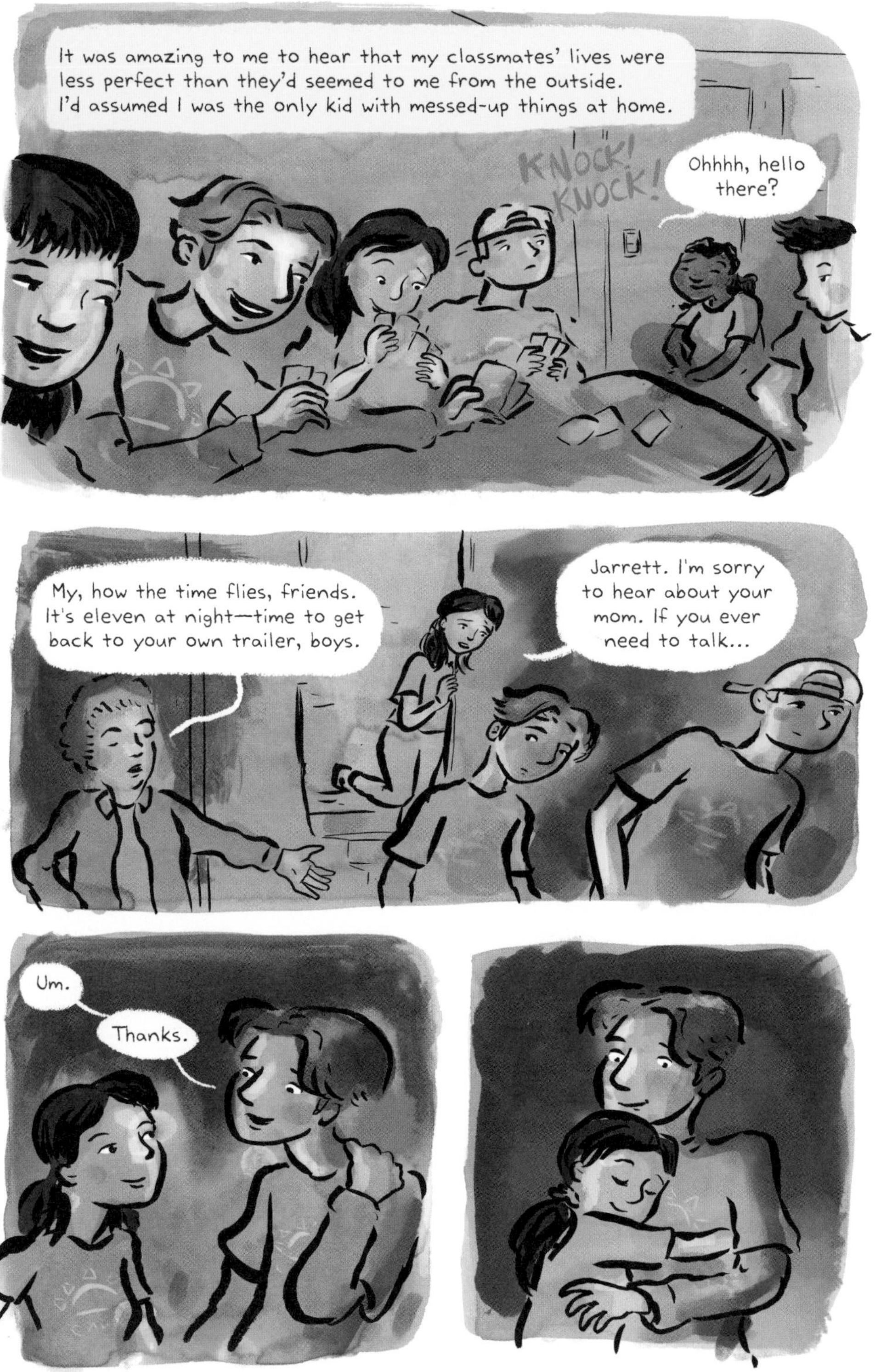
It was amazing to me to hear that my classmates' lives were less perfect than they'd seemed to me from the outside. I'd assumed I was the only kid with messed-up things at home.
KNOCK! KNOCK!
Ohhhh, hello there?
My, how the time flies, friends. It's eleven at night—time to get back to your own trailer, boys.
Jarrett. I'm sorry to hear about your mom. If you ever need to talk...
Um.
Thanks.

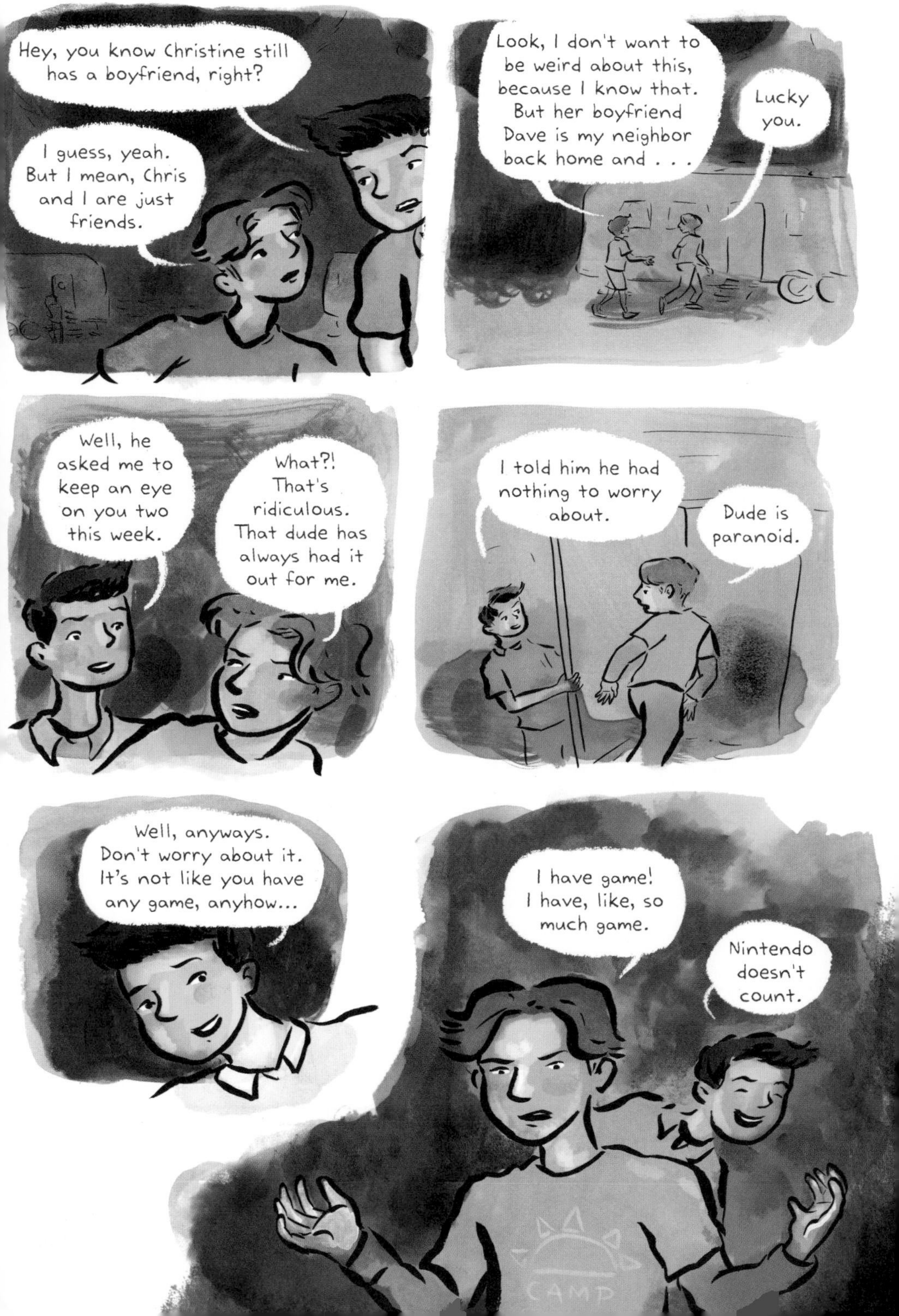
Hey, you know Christine still has a boyfriend, right?
I guess, yeah. But I mean, Chris and I are just friends.
Look, I don't want to be weird about this, because I know that. But her boyfriend Dave is my neighbor back home and . . .
Lucky you.
Well, he asked me to keep an eye on you two this week.
What?! That's ridiculous. That dude has always had it out for me.
I told him he had nothing to worry about.
Dude is paranoid.
Well, anyways. Don't worry about it. It's not like you have any game, anyhow...
I have game! I have, like, so much game.
Nintendo doesn't count.
CAMP

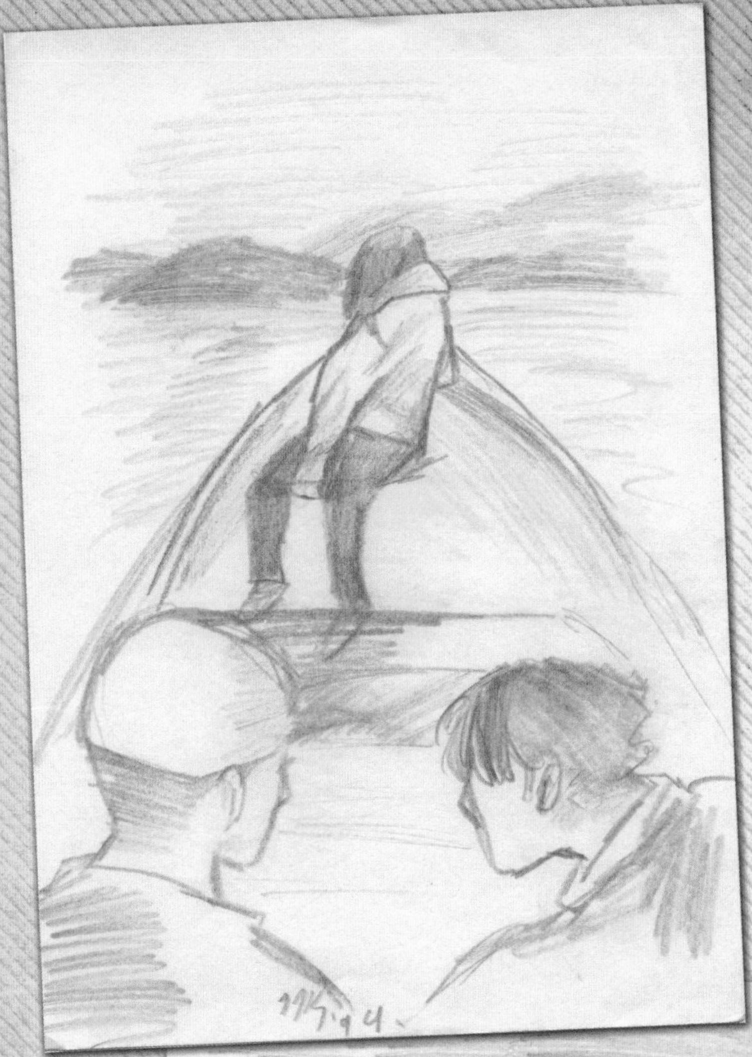

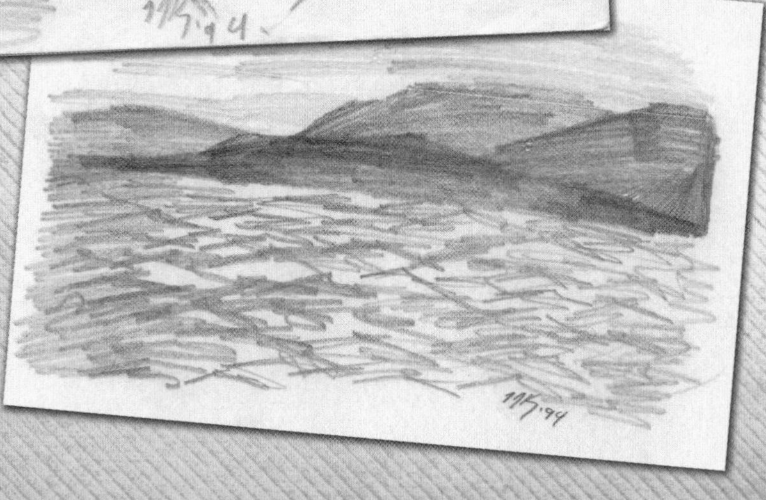

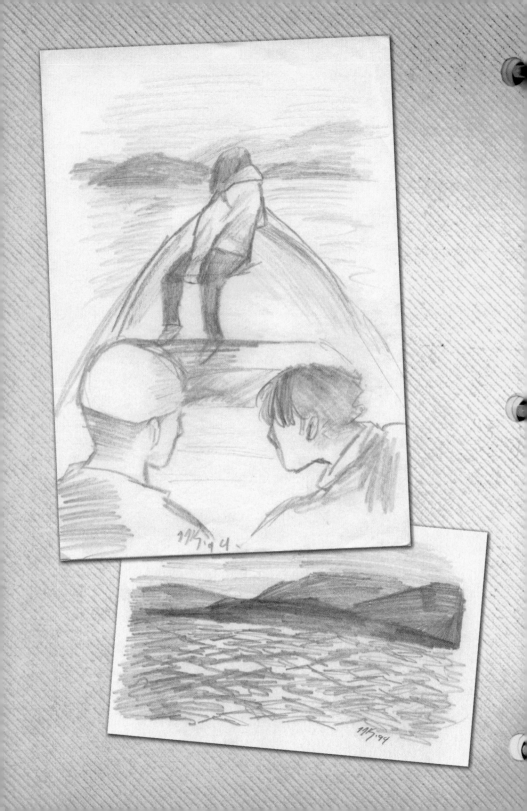

CHAPTER 3
TEAM BUILDING

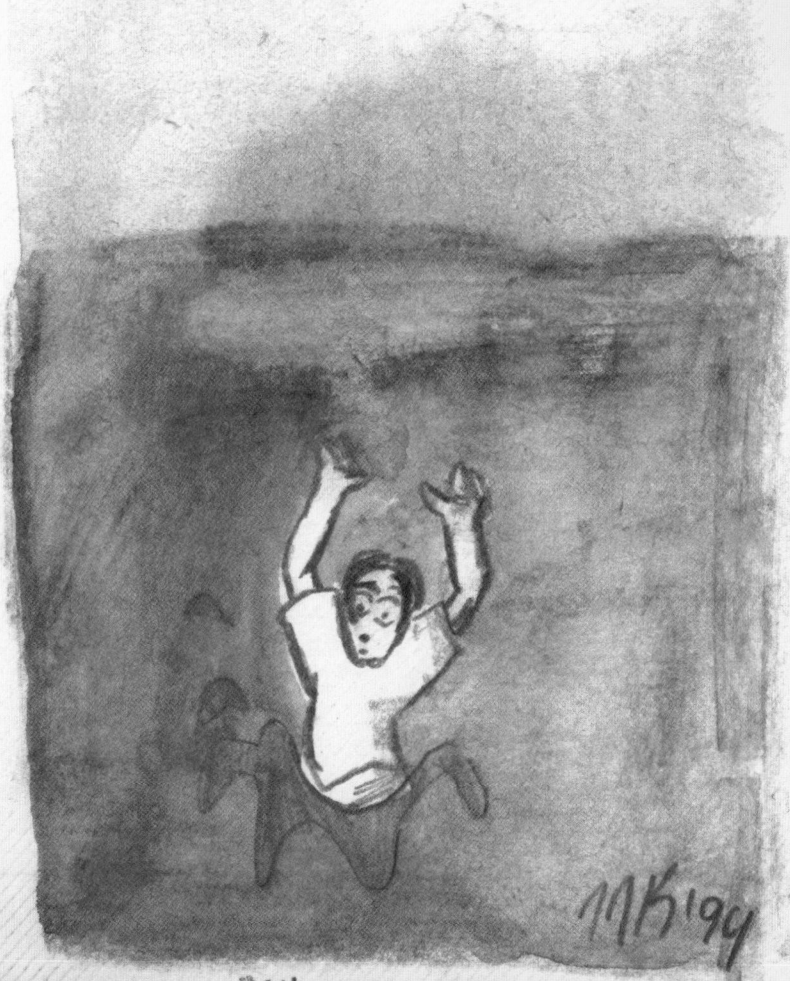
MK'99

"OH, WATER, WATER!!"

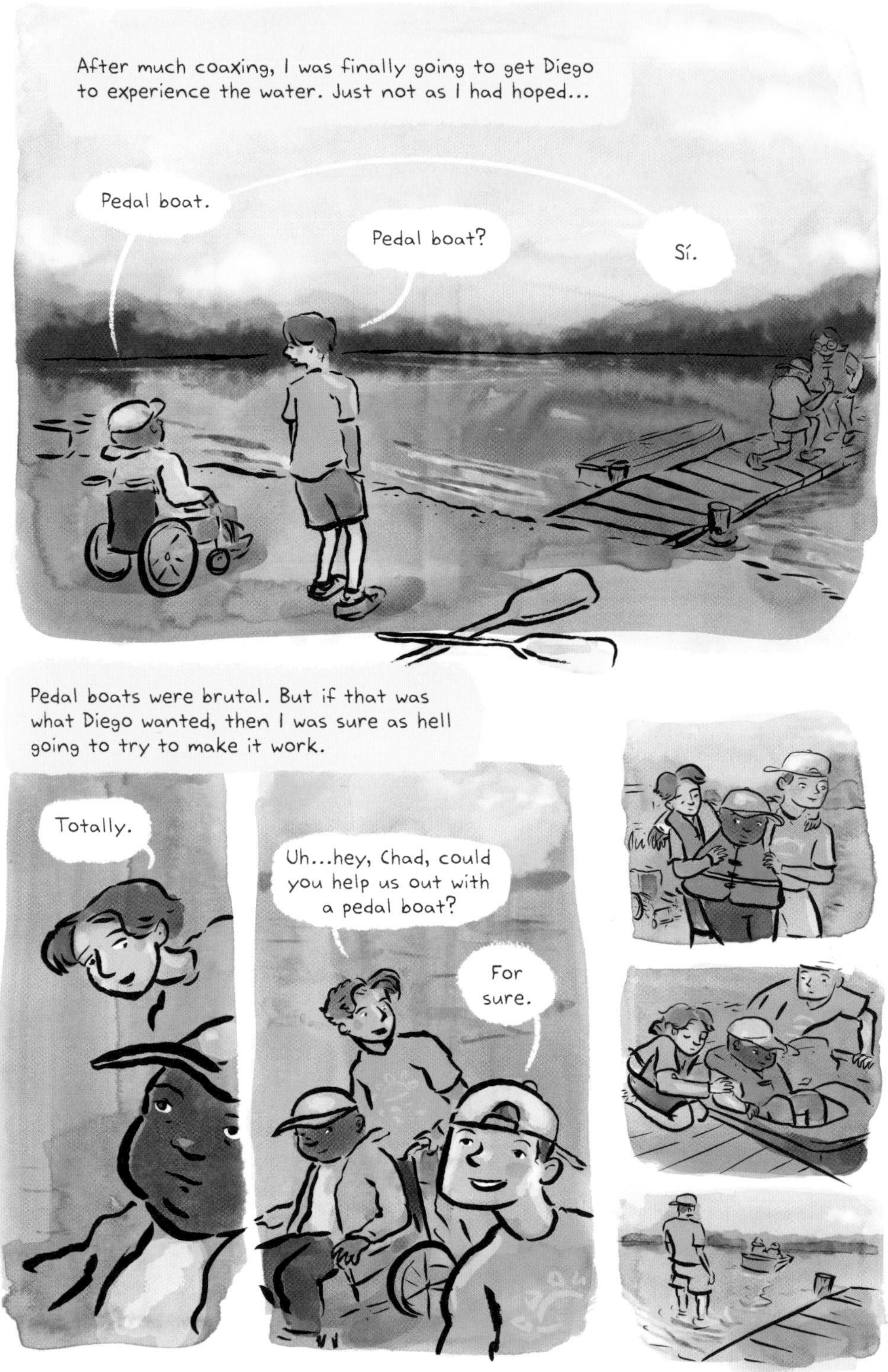
After much coaxing, I was finally going to get Diego to experience the water. Just not as I had hoped...
Pedal boat.
Pedal boat?
Sí.
Pedal boats were brutal. But if that was what Diego wanted, then I was sure as hell going to try to make it work.
Totally.
Uh...hey, Chad, could you help us out with a pedal boat?
For sure.

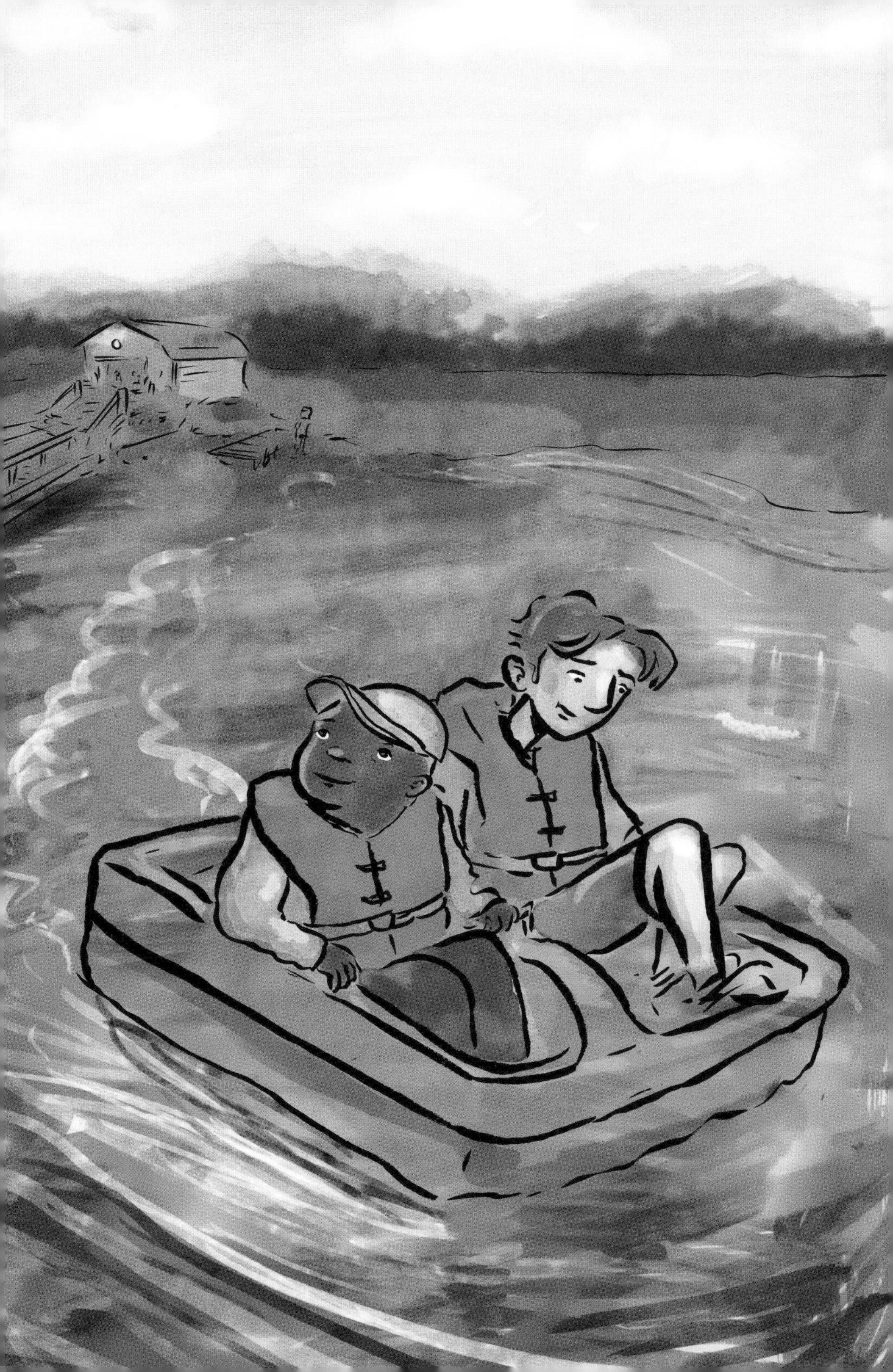

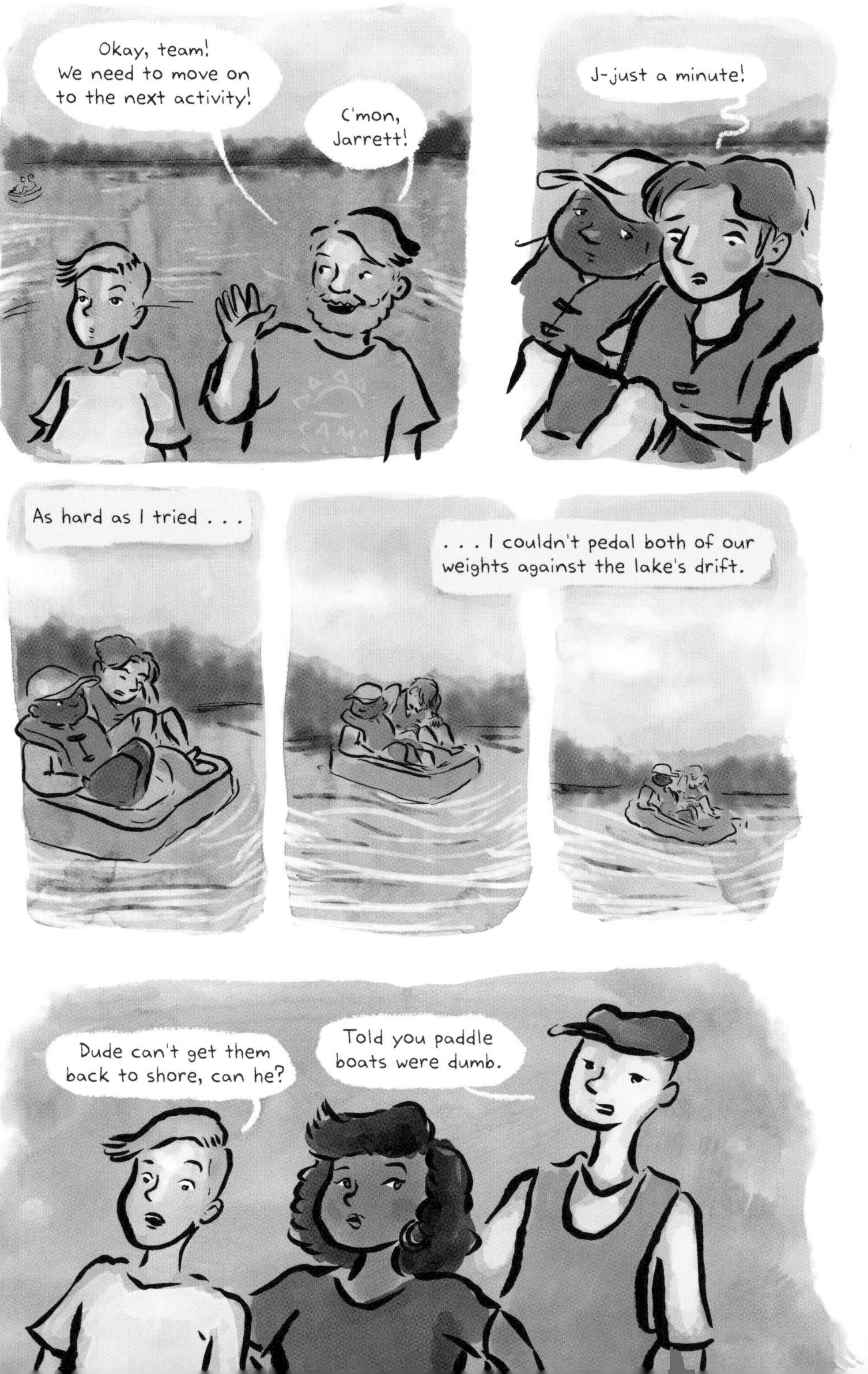
Okay, team! We need to move on to the next activity!
C'mon, Jarrett!
J-just a minute!
As hard as I tried . . .
. . . I couldn't pedal both of our weights against the lake's drift.
Dude can't get them back to shore, can he?
Told you paddle boats were dumb.

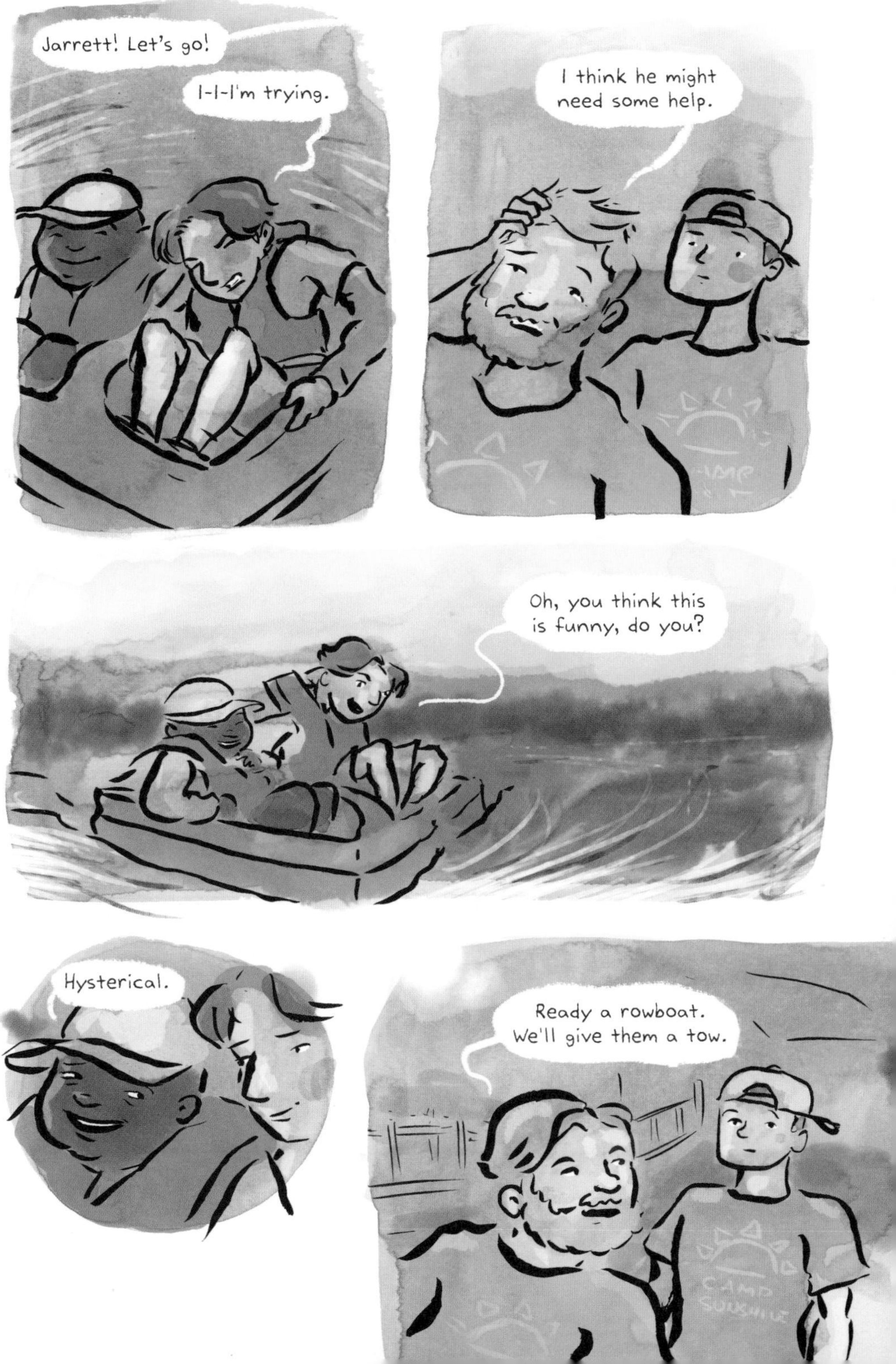
Jarrett! Let's go!
I-I-I'm trying.
I think he might need some help.
Oh, you think this is funny, do you?
Hysterical.
Ready a rowboat. We'll give them a tow.
CAMP SUNSHINE

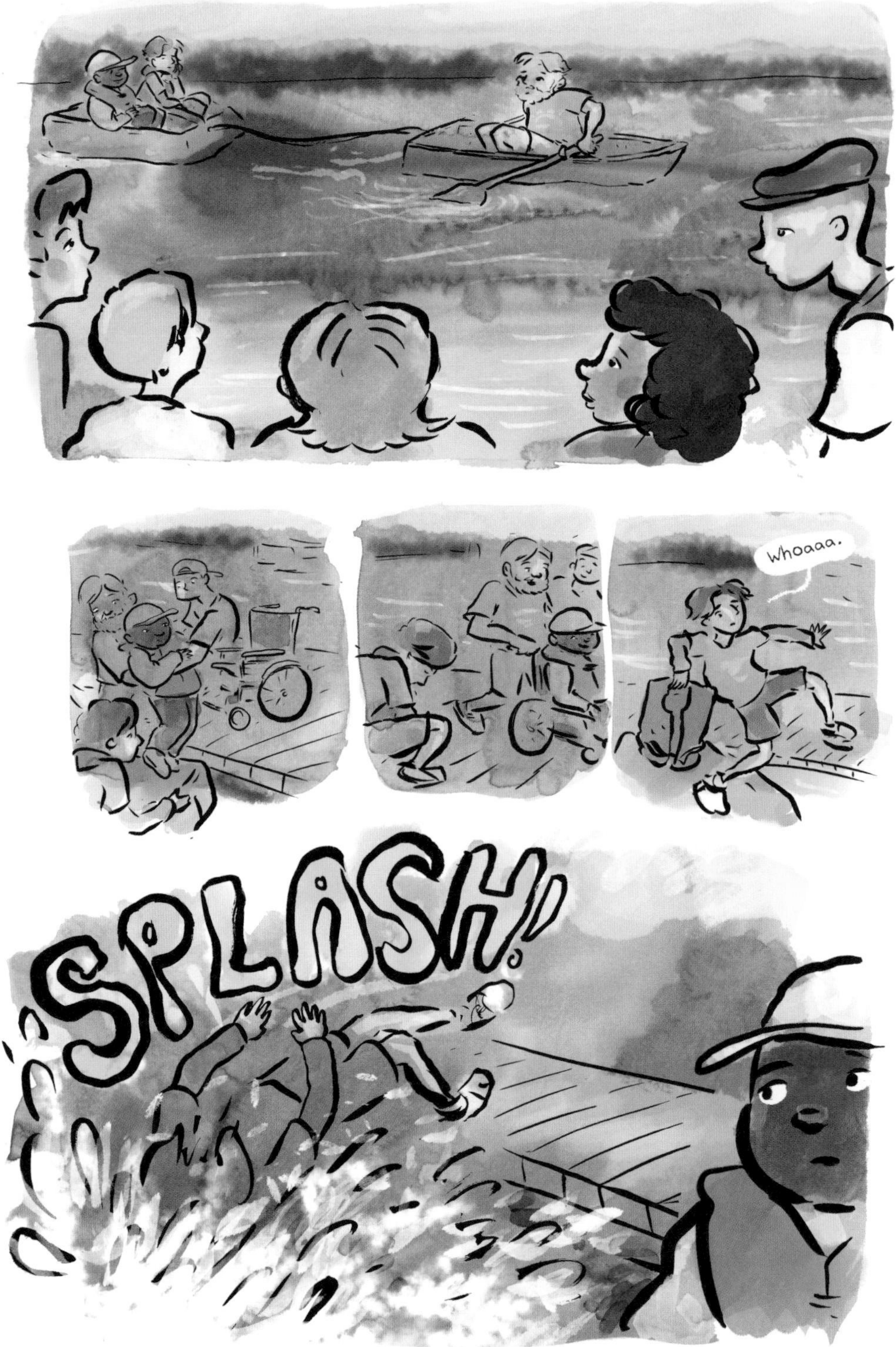
Whoaaa.
SPLASH!

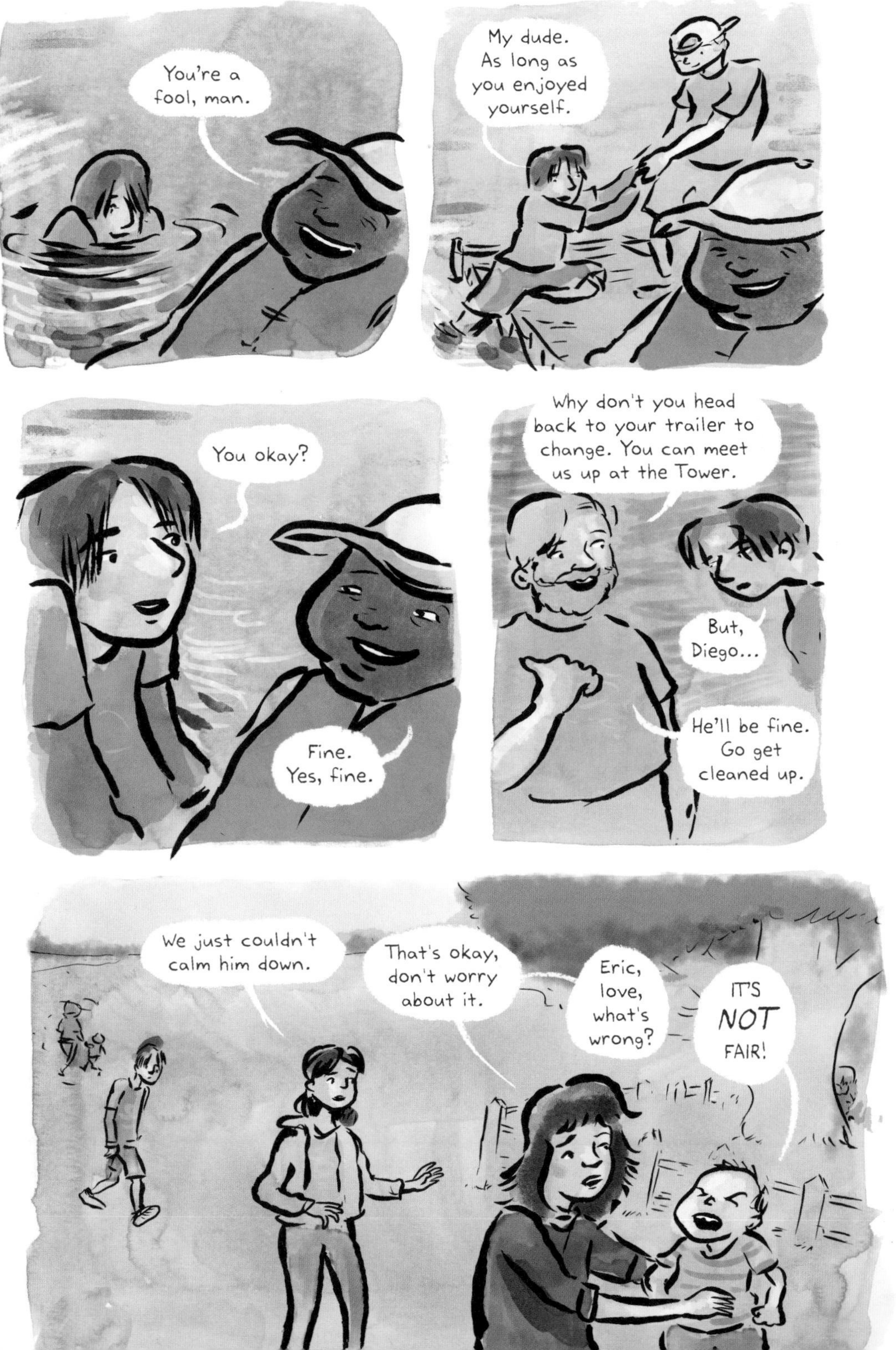
You're a fool, man.
My dude. As long as you enjoyed yourself.
You okay?
Fine. Yes, fine.
Why don't you head back to your trailer to change. You can meet us up at the Tower.
But, Diego...
He'll be fine. Go get cleaned up.
We just couldn't calm him down.
That's okay, don't worry about it.
Eric, love, what's wrong?
IT'S NOT FAIR!

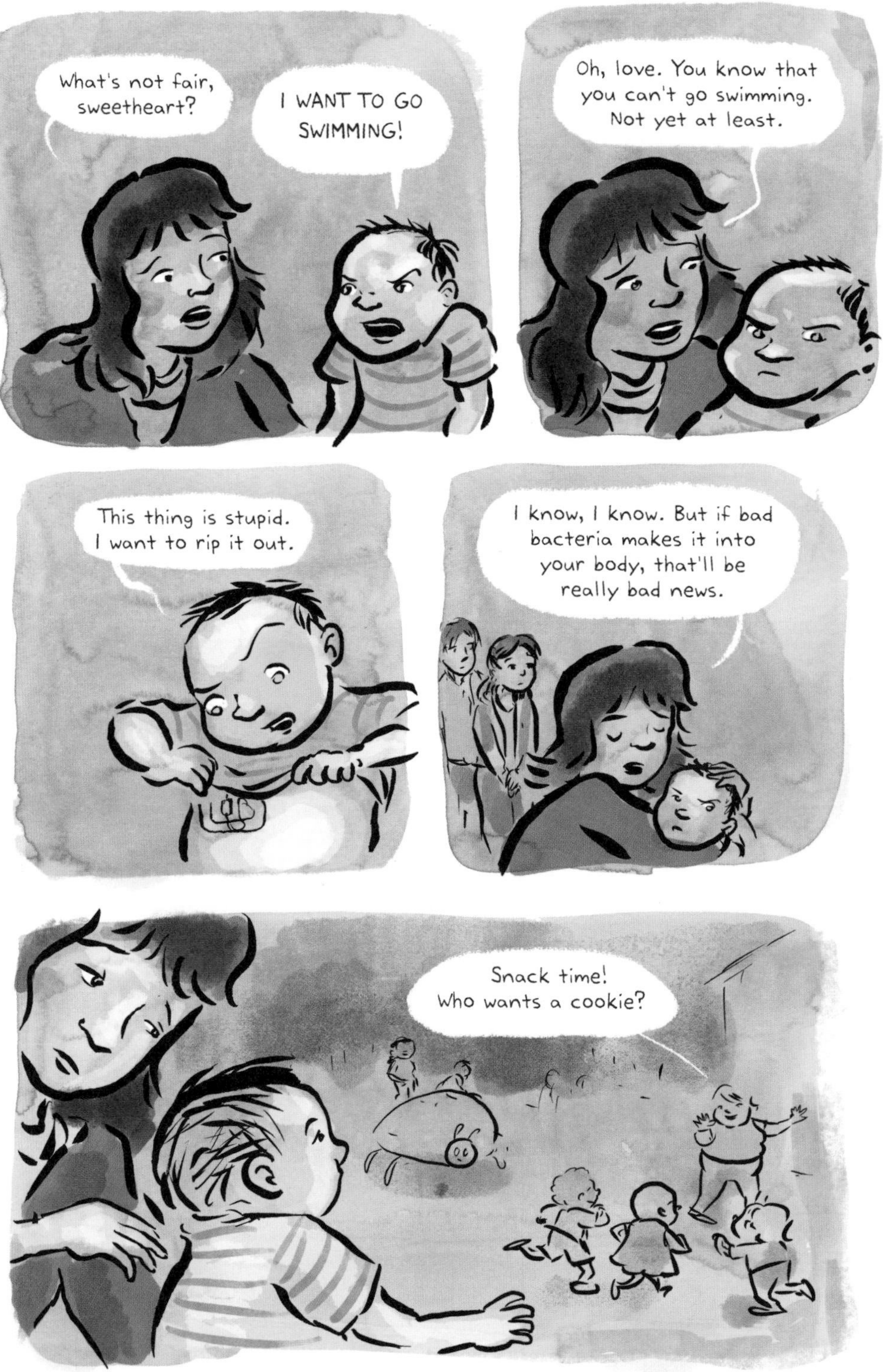
What's not fair, sweetheart?
I WANT TO GO SWIMMING!
Oh, love. You know that you can't go swimming. Not yet at least.
This thing is stupid. I want to rip it out.
I know, I know. But if bad bacteria makes it into your body, that'll be really bad news.
Snack time! Who wants a cookie?

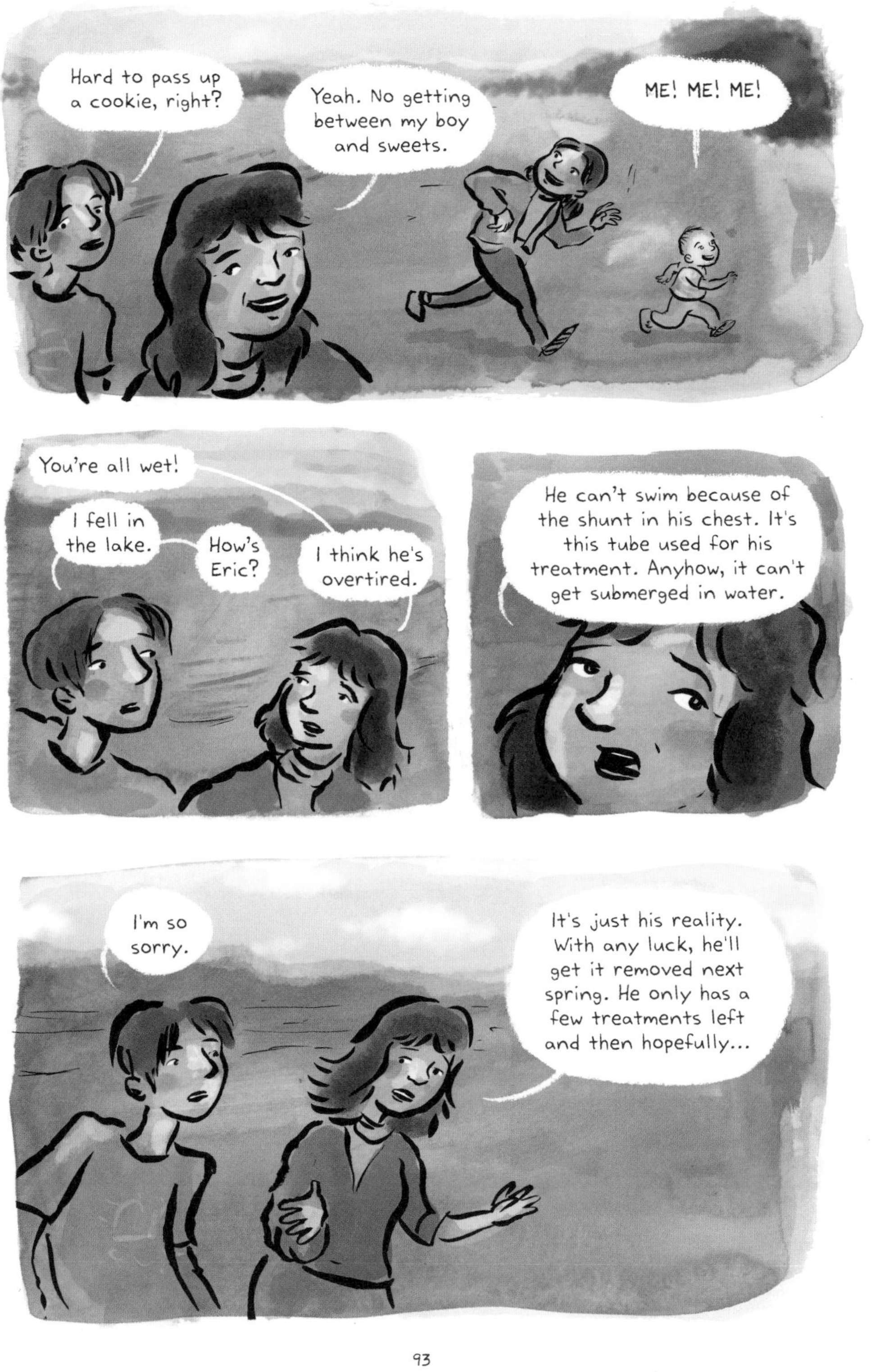
Hard to pass up a cookie, right?
Yeah. No getting between my boy and sweets.
ME! ME! ME!
You're all wet!
I fell in the lake.
How's Eric?
I think he's overtired.
He can't swim because of the shunt in his chest. It's this tube used for his treatment. Anyhow, it can't get submerged in water.
I'm so sorry.
It's just his reality. With any luck, he'll get it removed next spring. He only has a few treatments left and then hopefully...

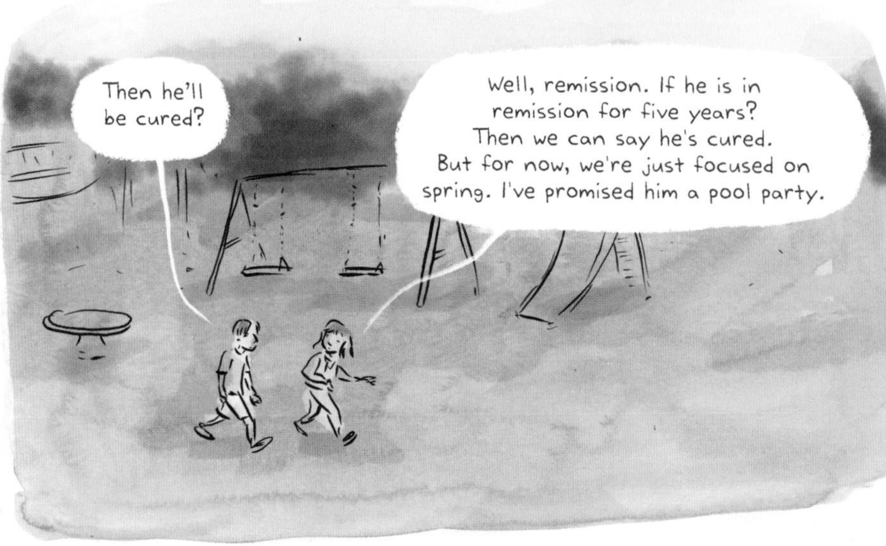
Then he'll be cured?
Well, remission. If he is in remission for five years? Then we can say he's cured. But for now, we're just focused on spring. I've promised him a pool party.

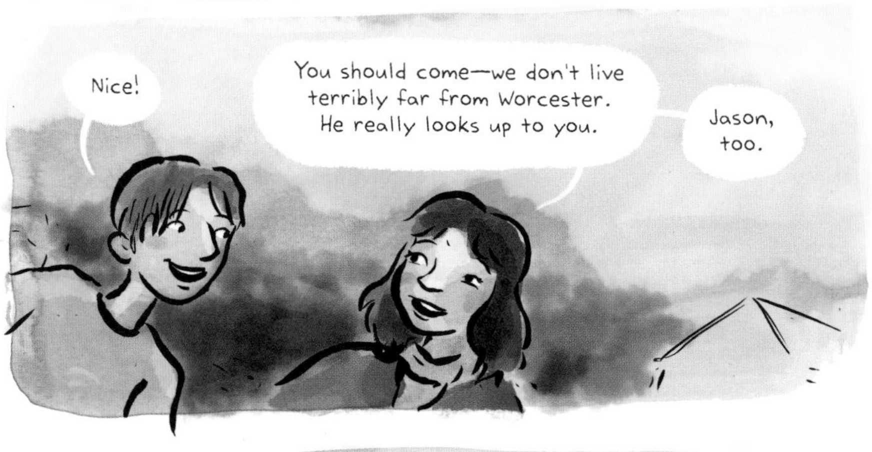
Nice!
You should come—we don't live terribly far from Worcester. He really looks up to you.
Jason, too.

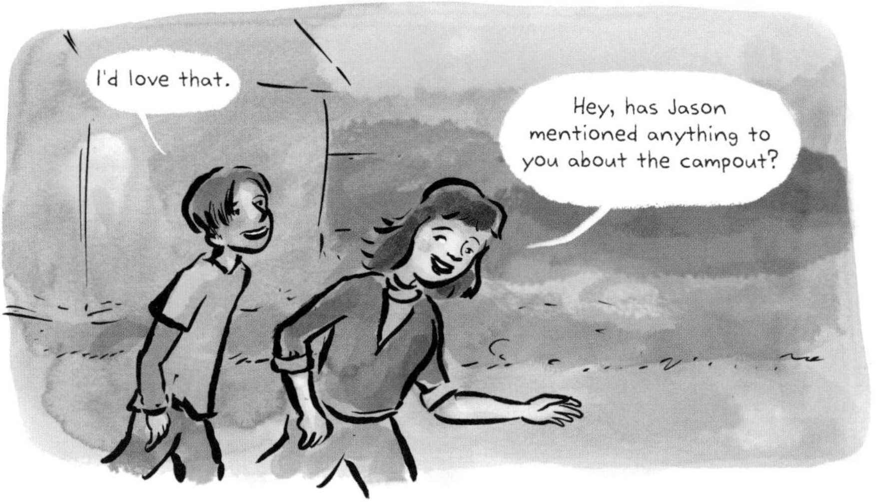
I'd love that.
Hey, has Jason mentioned anything to you about the campout?

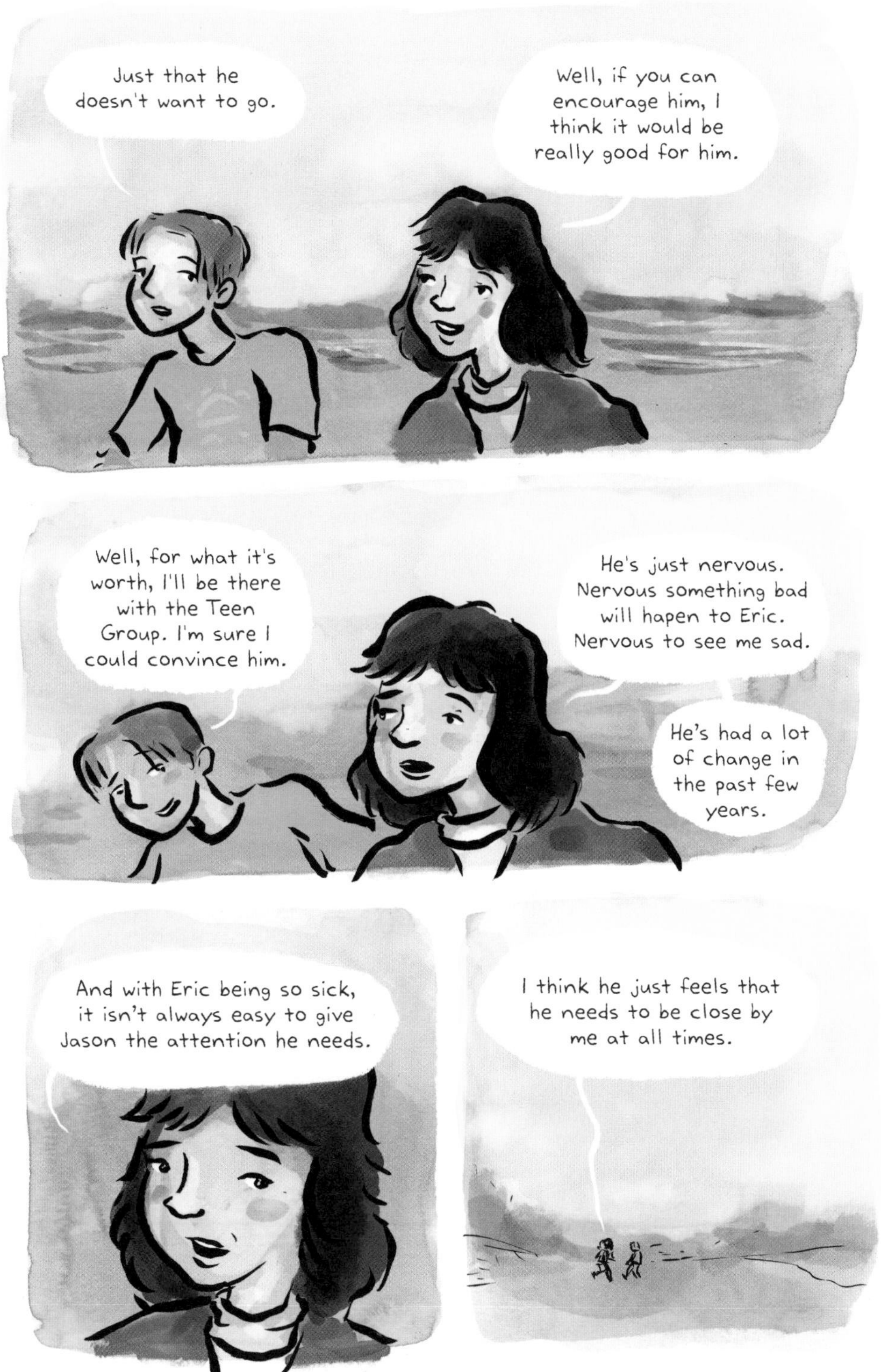
Just that he doesn't want to go.
Well, if you can encourage him, I think it would be really good for him.
Well, for what it's worth, I'll be there with the Teen Group. I'm sure I could convince him.
He's just nervous. Nervous something bad will hapen to Eric. Nervous to see me sad.
He's had a lot of change in the past few years.
And with Eric being so sick, it isn't always easy to give Jason the attention he needs.
I think he just feels that he needs to be close by me at all times.

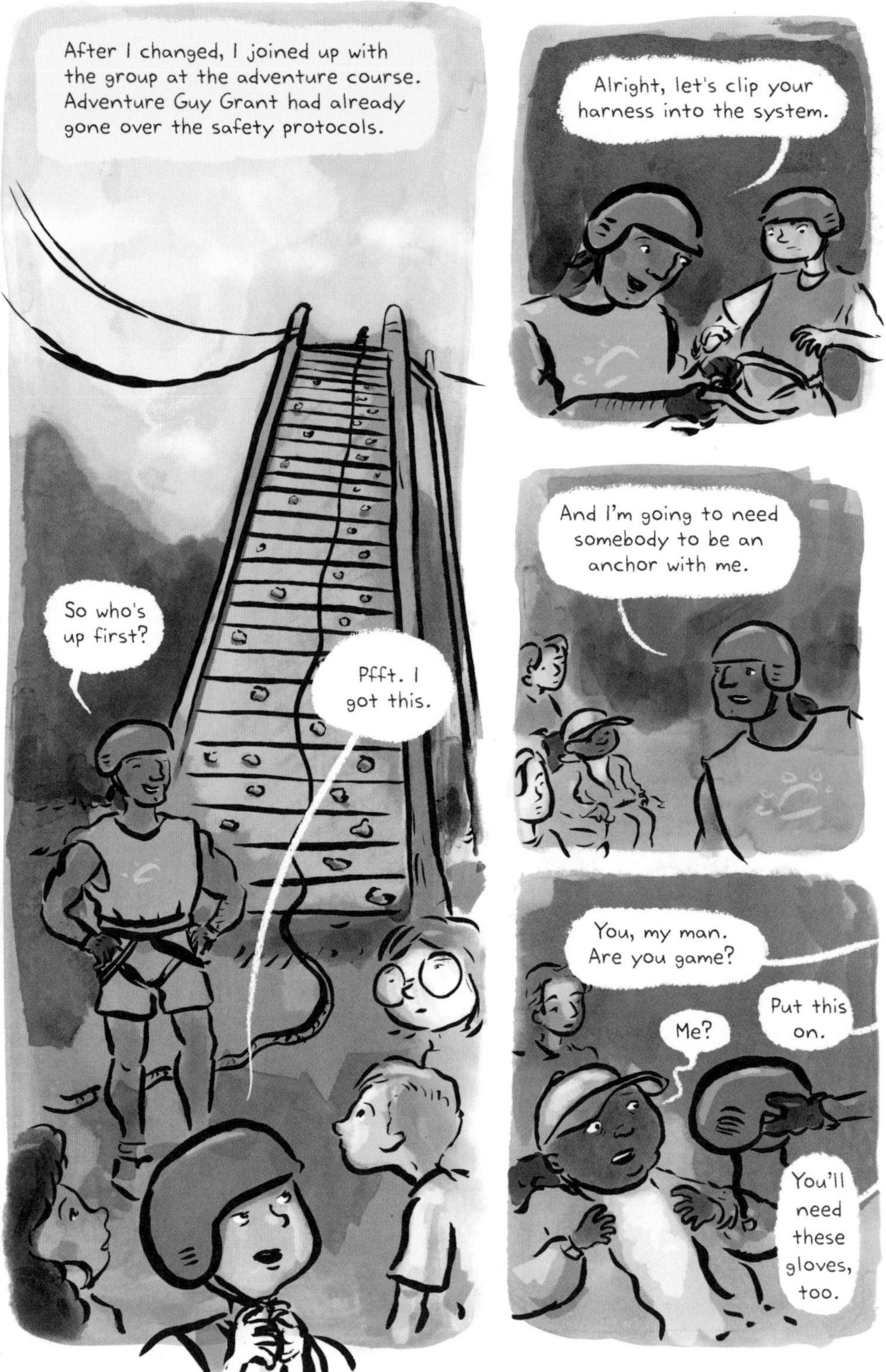
After I changed, I joined up with the group at the adventure course. Adventure Guy Grant had already gone over the safety protocols.
So who's up first?
Pfft. I got this.
Alright, let's clip your harness into the system.
And I'm going to need somebody to be an anchor with me.
You, my man. Are you game?
Me?
Put this on.
You'll need these gloves, too.

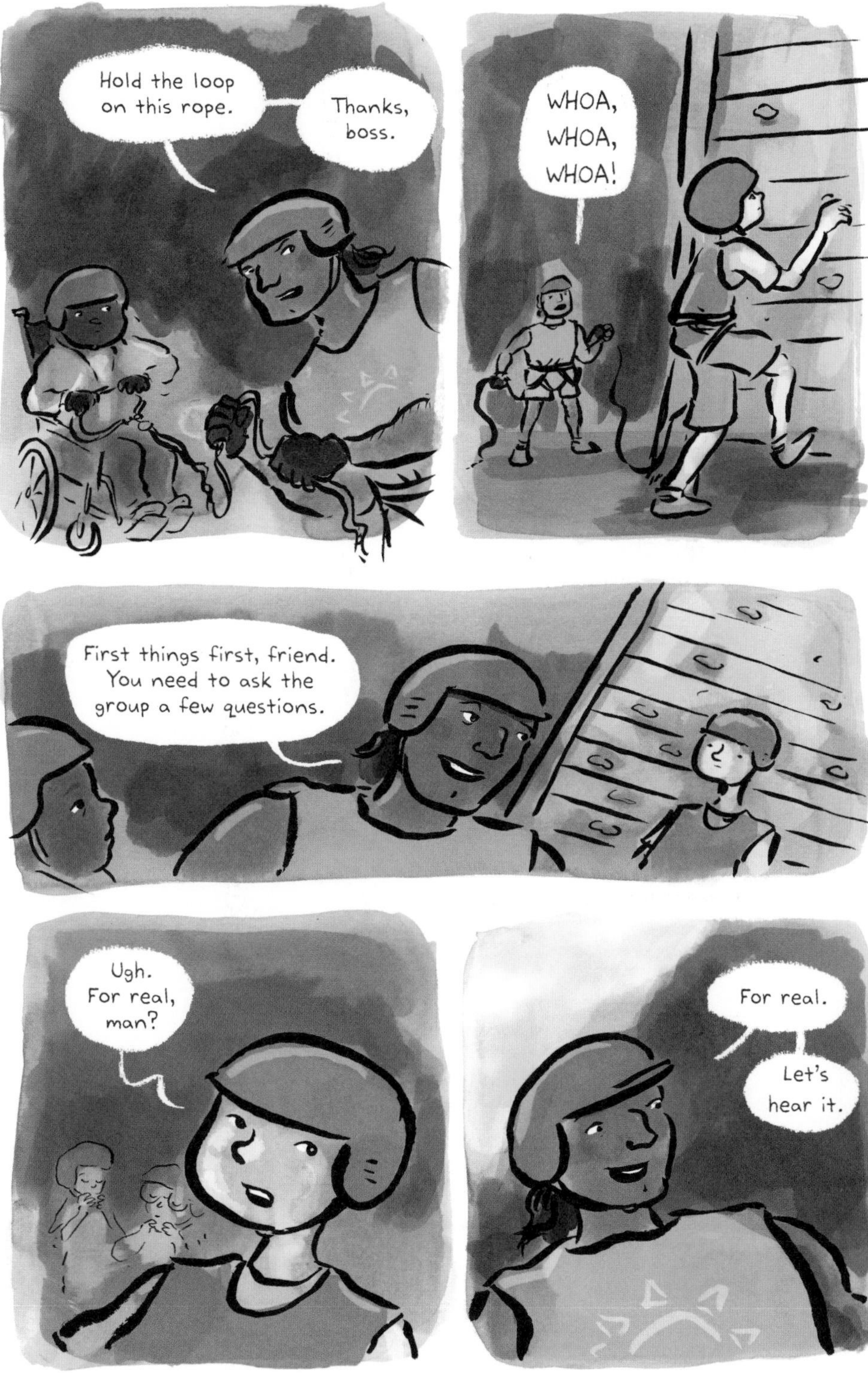
Hold the loop on this rope.
Thanks, boss.
WHOA, WHOA, WHOA!
First things first, friend. You need to ask the group a few questions.
Ugh. For real, man?
For real.
Let's hear it.

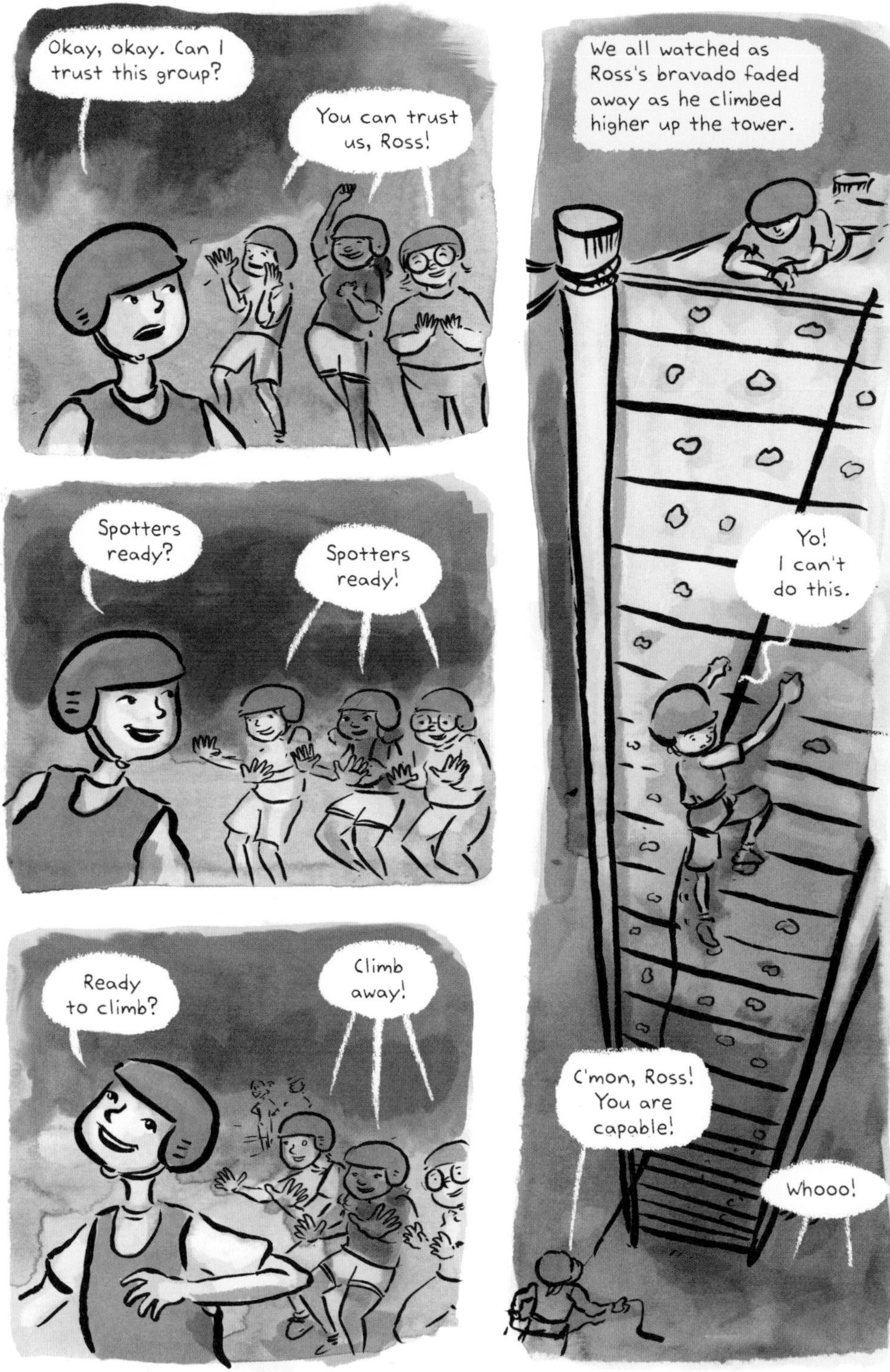

Okay, okay. Can I trust this group?
You can trust us, Ross!
Spotters ready?
Spotters ready!
Ready to climb?
Climb away!
We all watched as Ross's bravado faded away as he climbed higher up the tower.
Yo! I can't do this.
C'mon, Ross! You are capable!
Whooo!

Ross reached within himself . . .

Look at his knees wobbling!

Let's just focus on support, Derek.

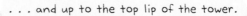
. . . and up to the top lip of the tower.

Here ya go, kid!

I DID IT!!!

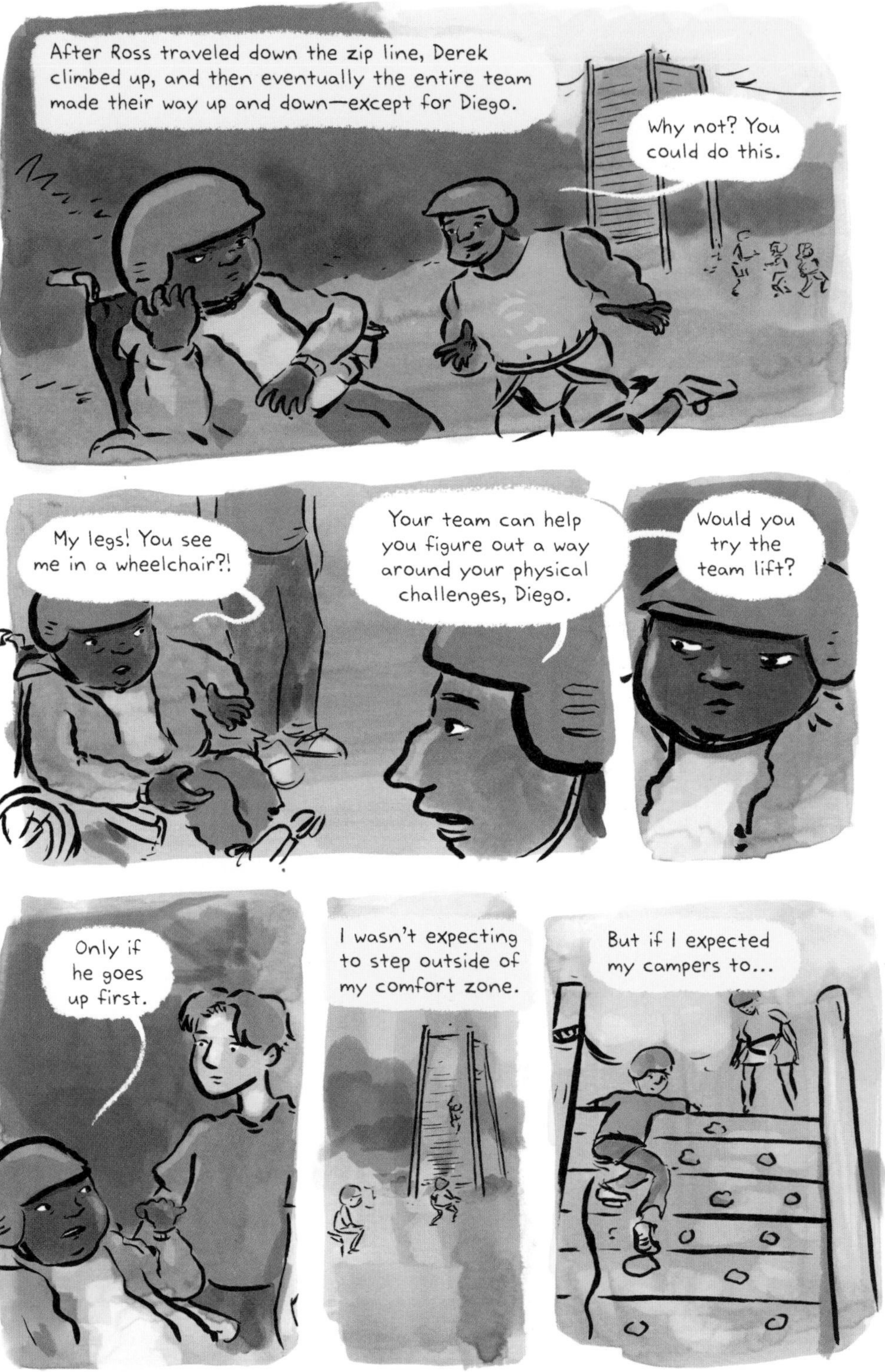
After Ross traveled down the zip line, Derek climbed up, and then eventually the entire team made their way up and down—except for Diego.
Why not? You could do this.
My legs! You see me in a wheelchair?!
Your team can help you figure out a way around your physical challenges, Diego.
Would you try the team lift?
Only if he goes up first.
I wasn't expecting to step outside of my comfort zone.
But if I expected my campers to...

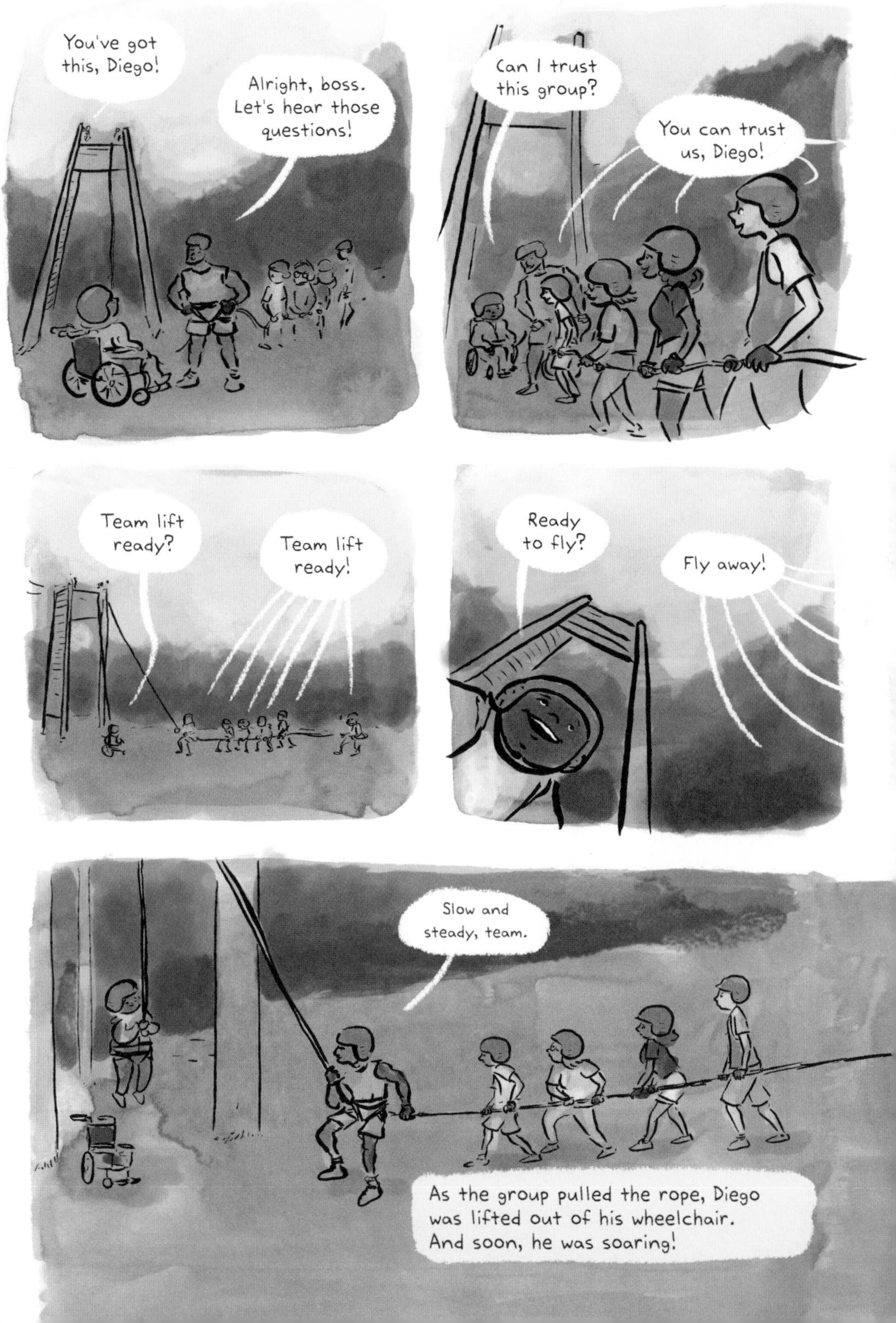

You've got this, Diego!
Alright, boss. Let's hear those questions!
Can I trust this group?
You can trust us, Diego!
Team lift ready?
Team lift ready!
Ready to fly?
Fly away!
Slow and steady, team.
As the group pulled the rope, Diego was lifted out of his wheelchair. And soon, he was soaring!

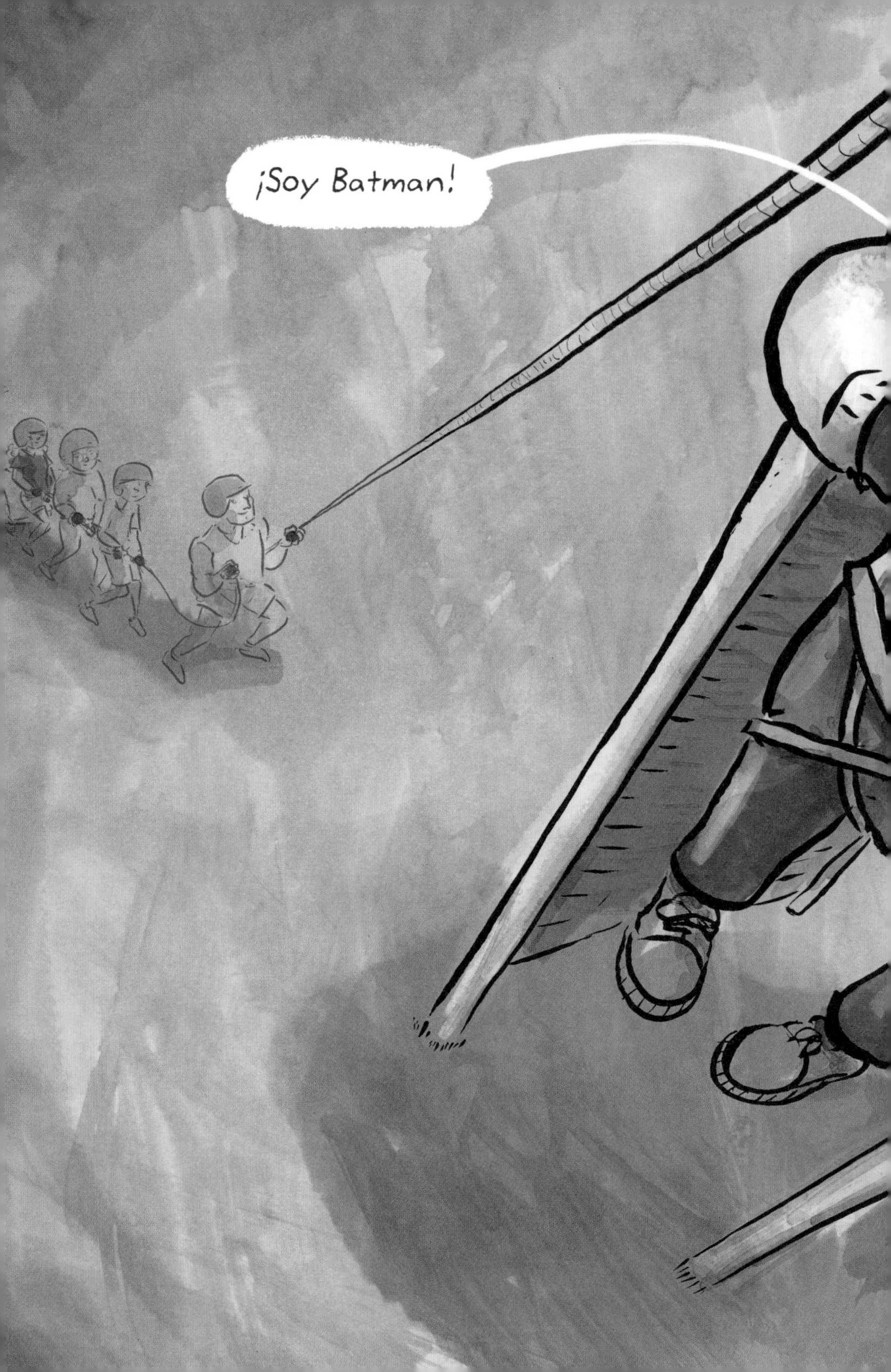
¡Soy Batman!

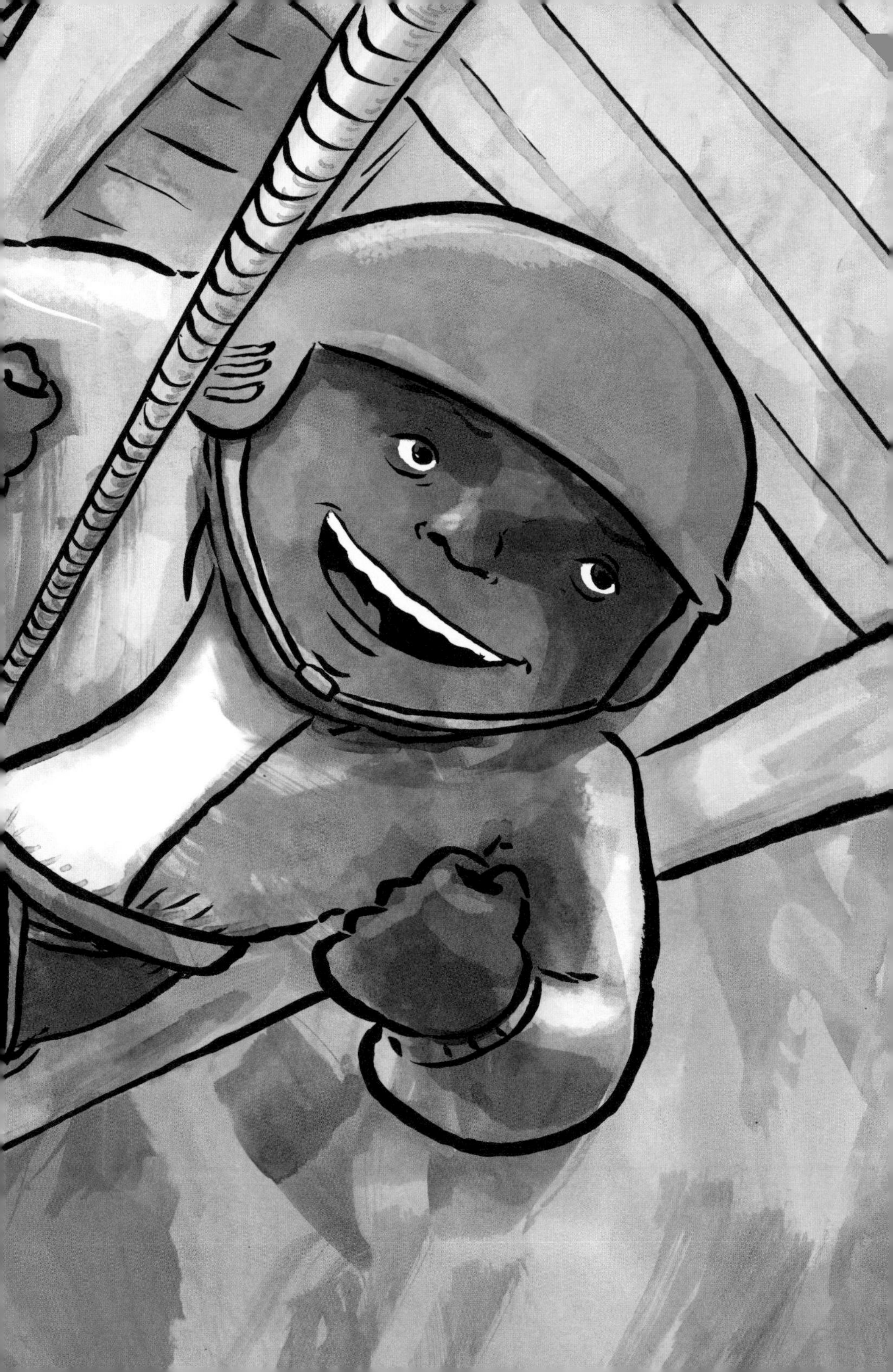

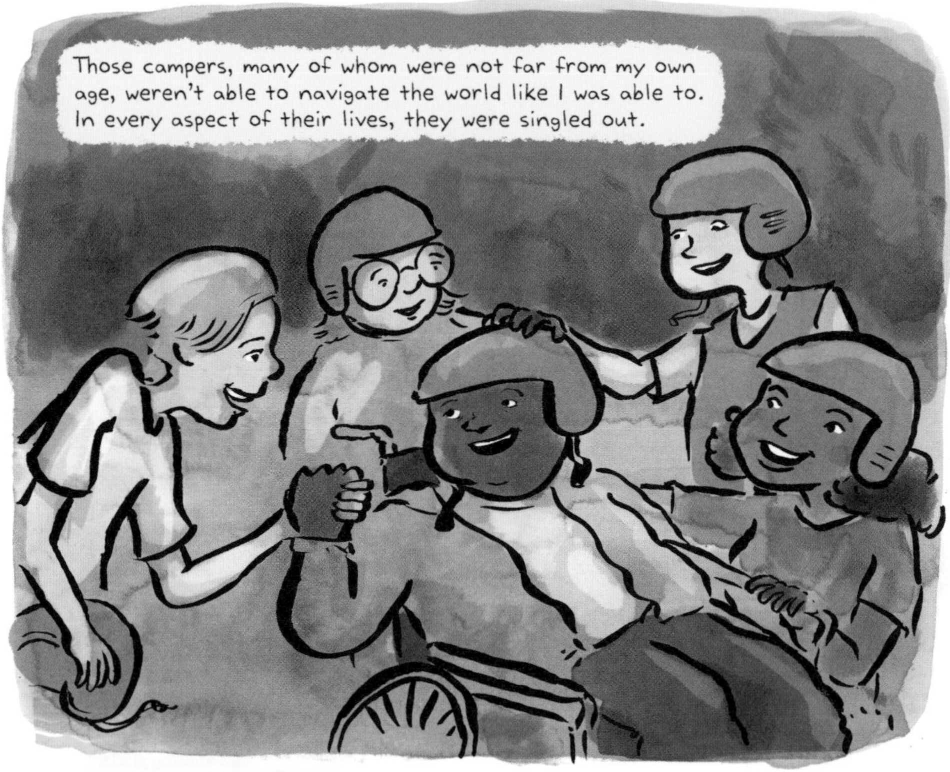
Those campers, many of whom were not far from my own age, weren't able to navigate the world like I was able to. In every aspect of their lives, they were singled out.

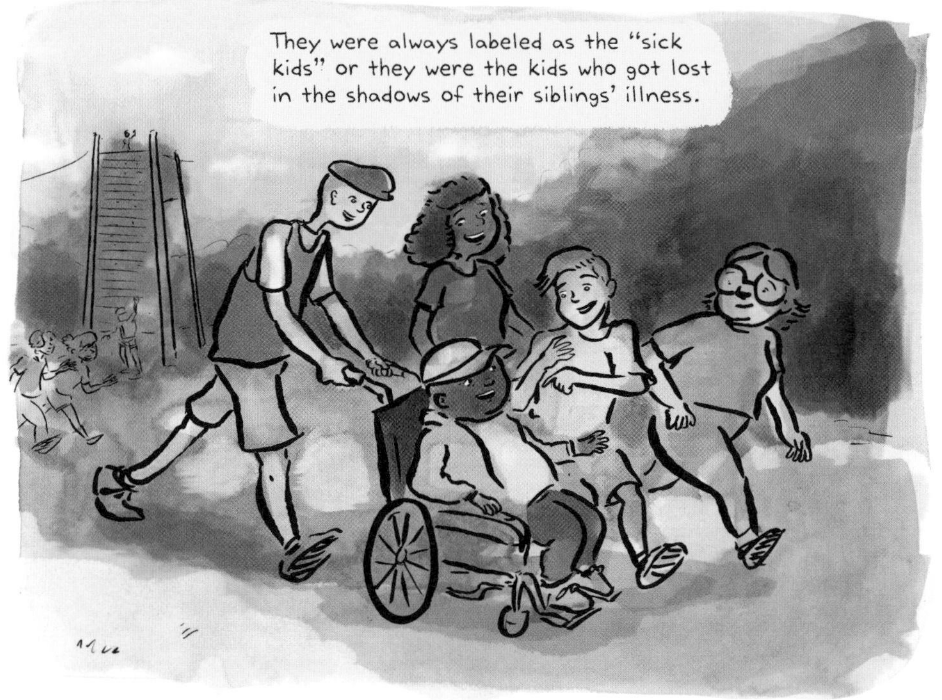
They were always labeled as the "sick kids" or they were the kids who got lost in the shadows of their siblings' illness.

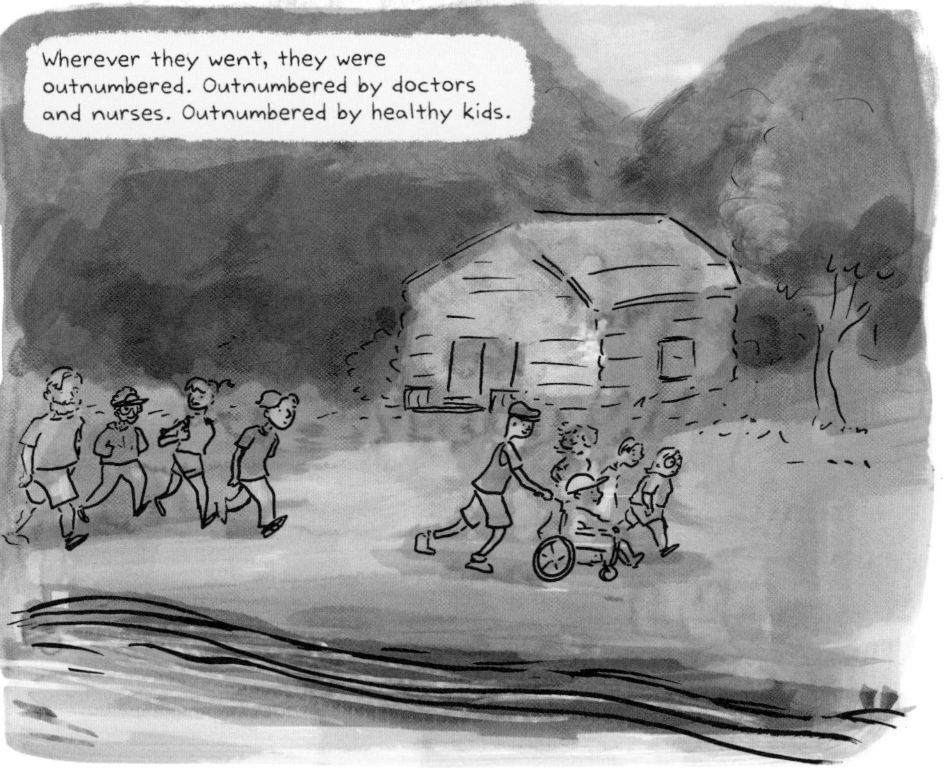
Wherever they went, they were outnumbered. Outnumbered by doctors and nurses. Outnumbered by healthy kids.

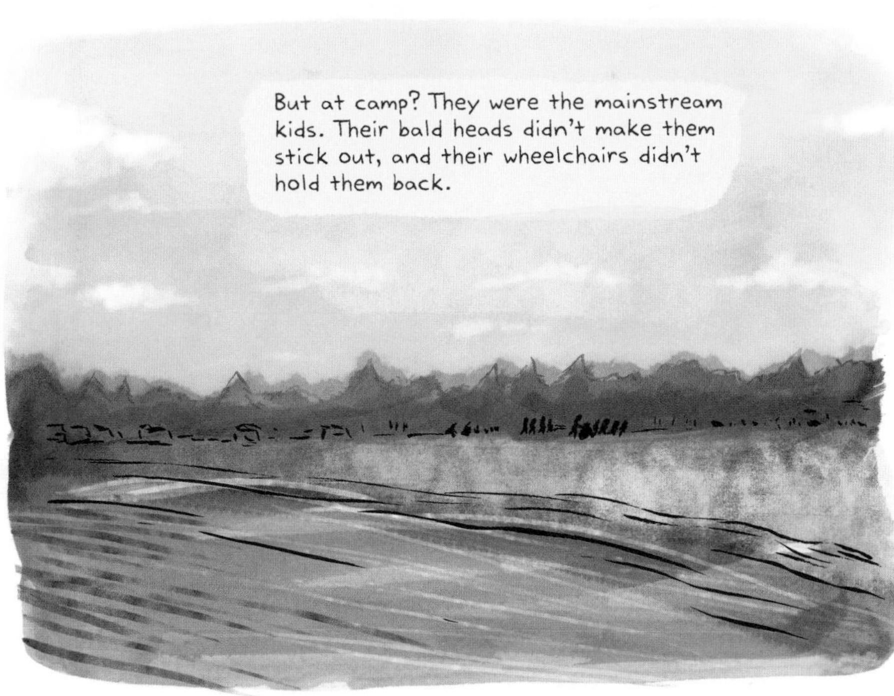
But at camp? They were the mainstream kids. Their bald heads didn't make them stick out, and their wheelchairs didn't hold them back.

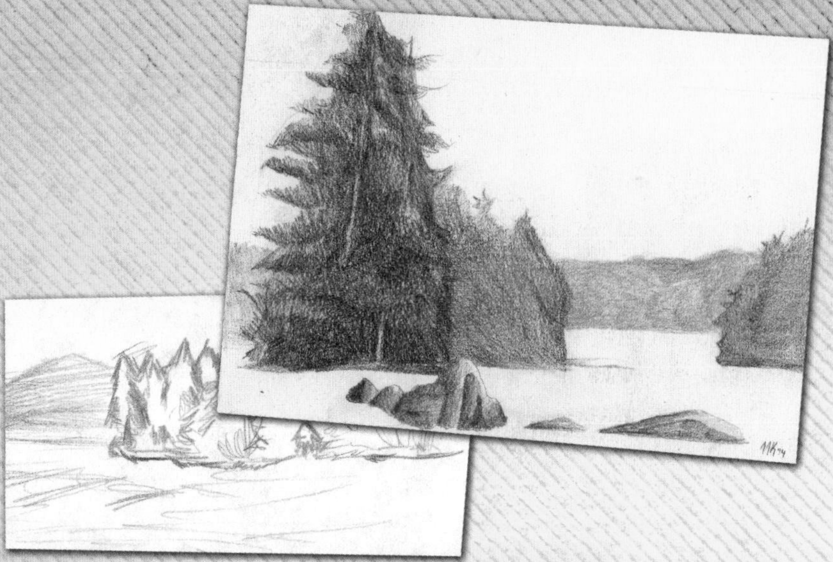

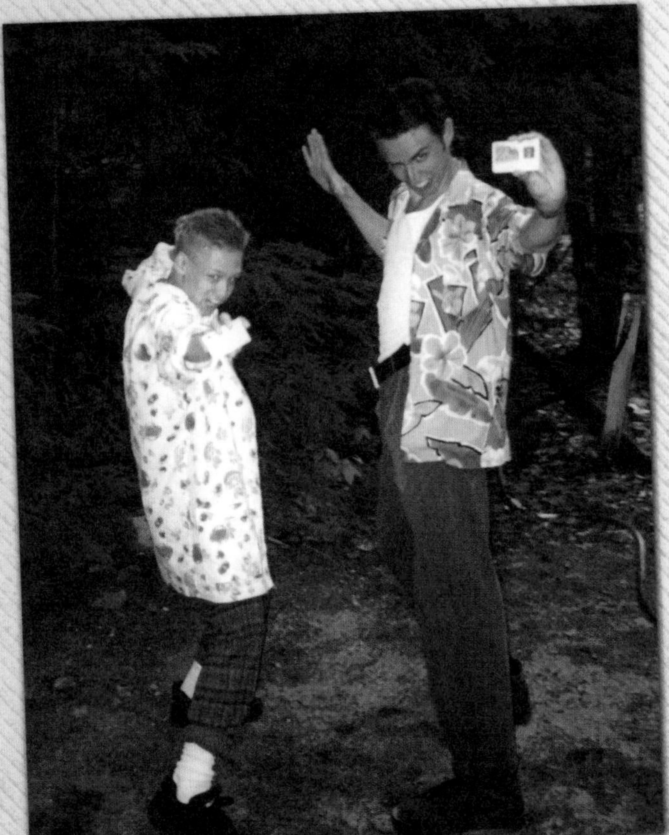

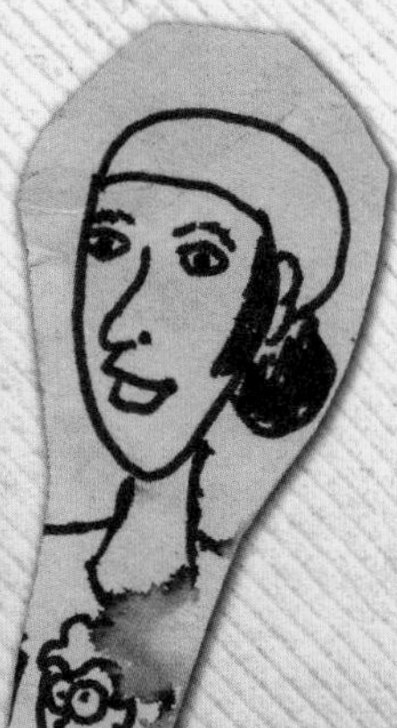

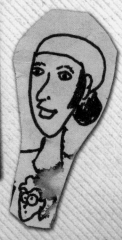

CHAPTER 4
CAMP OUT

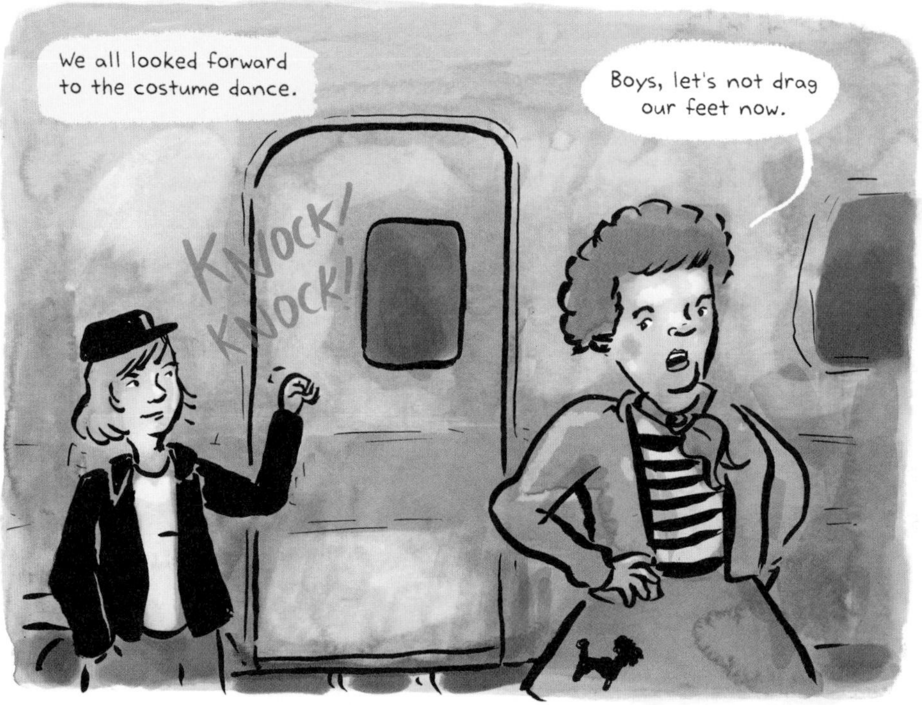
We all looked forward to the costume dance.
Boys, let's not drag our feet now.
KNOCK! KNOCK!

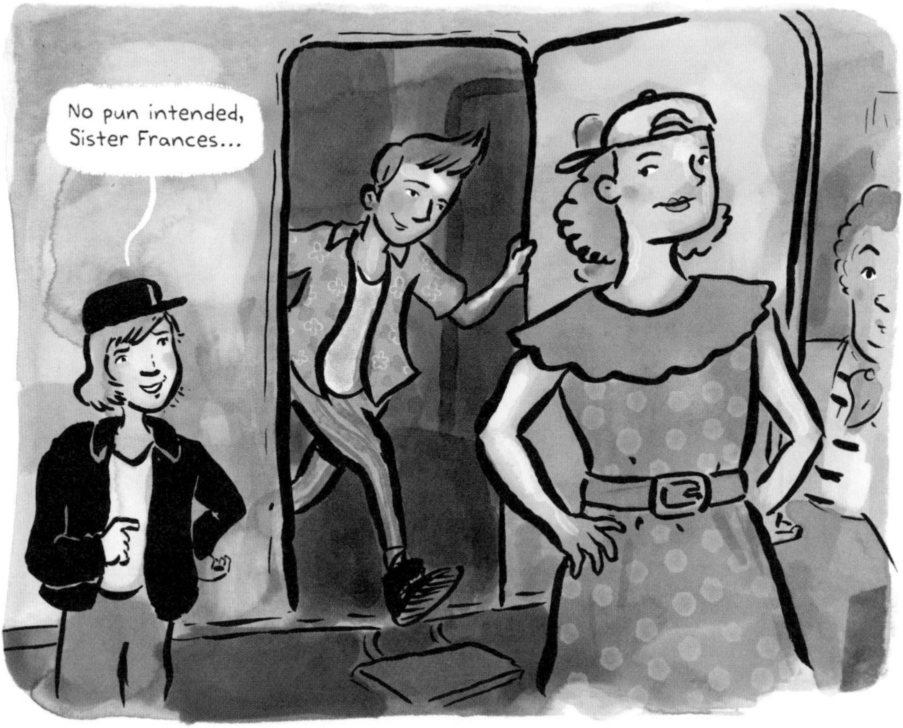
No pun intended, Sister Frances...

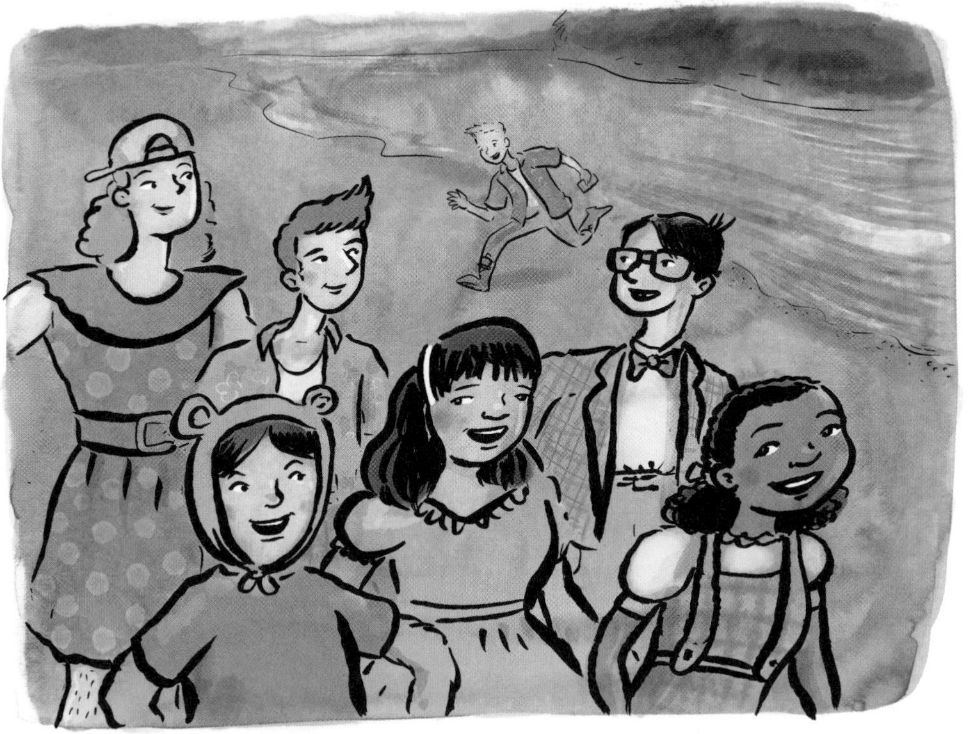

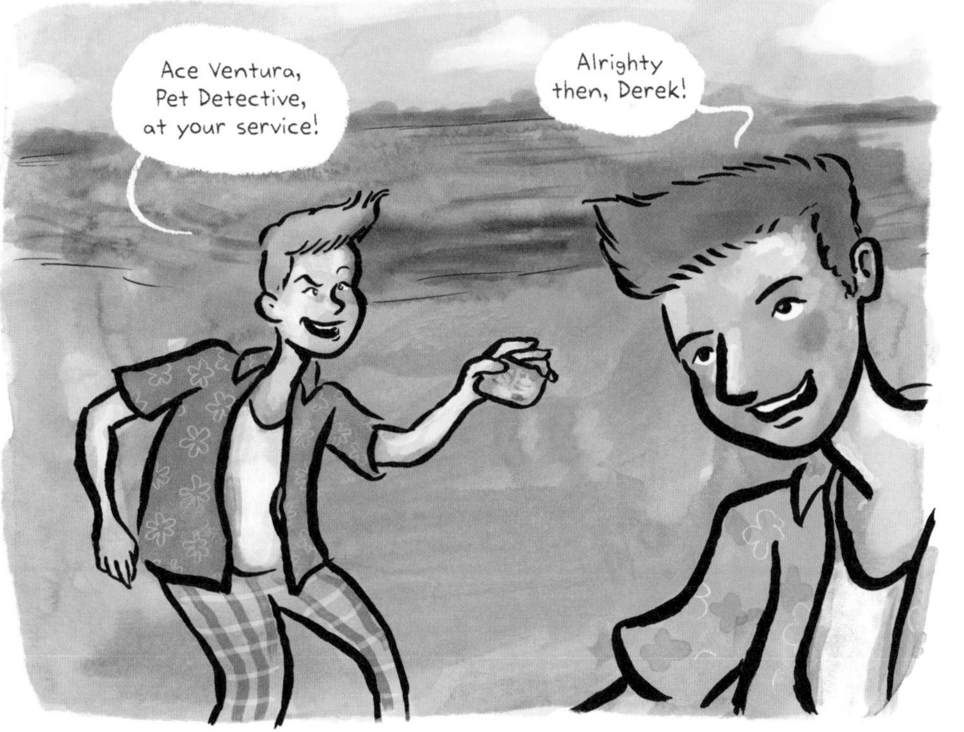
Ace Ventura,
Pet Detective,
at your service!
Alrighty
then, Derek!

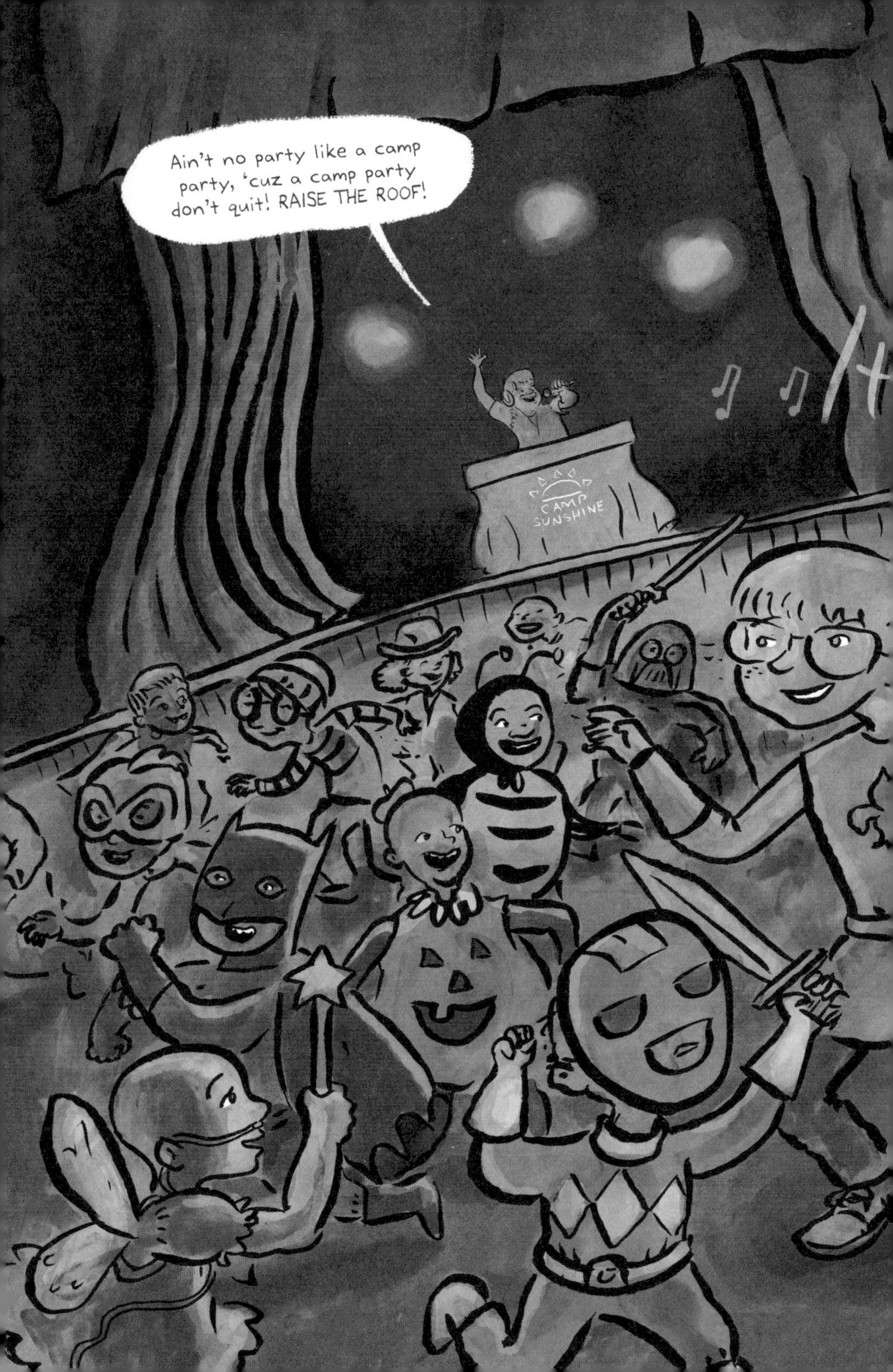
Ain't no party like a camp party, 'cuz a camp party don't quit! RAISE THE ROOF!
CAMP SUNSHINE

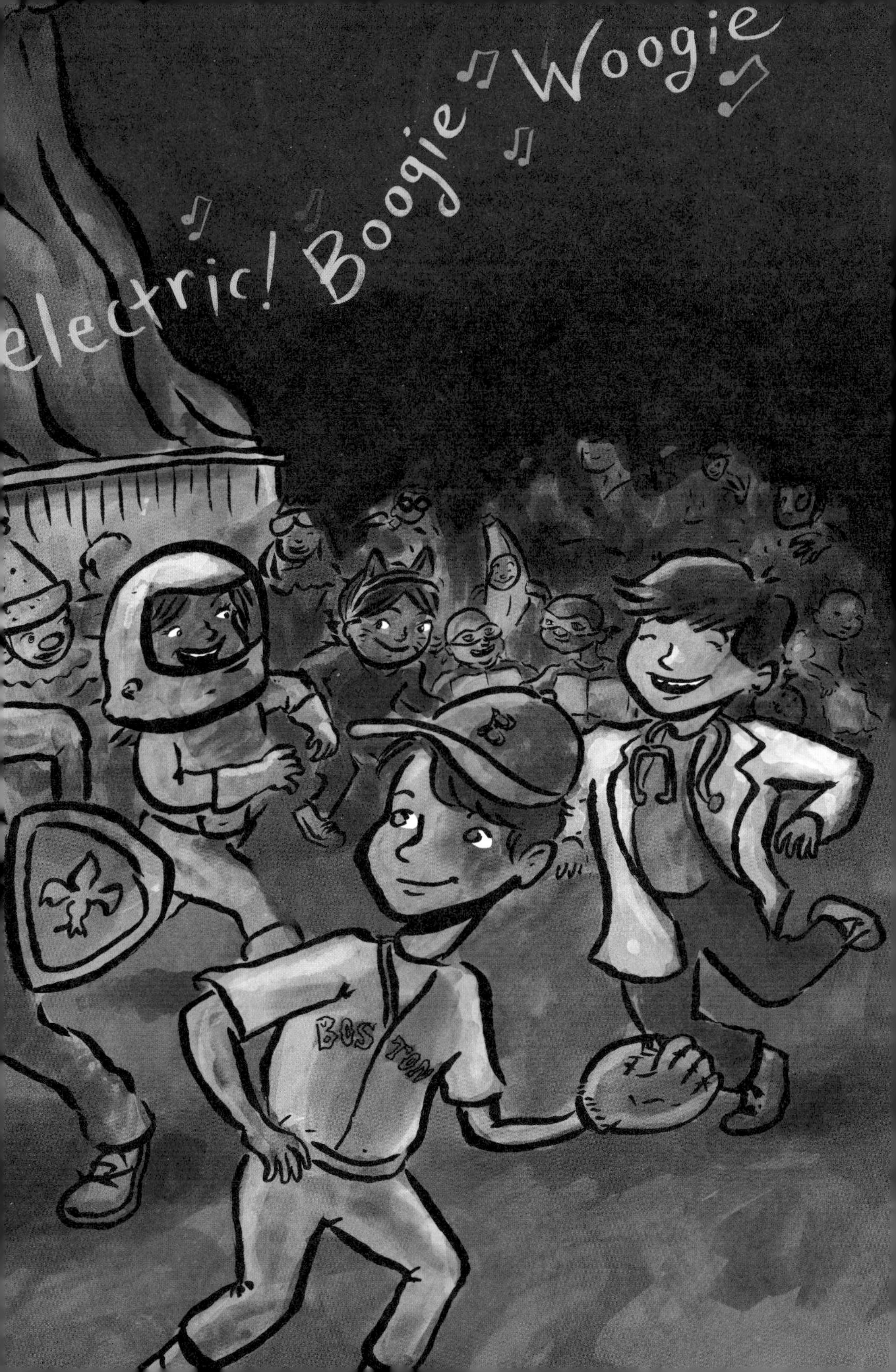
electric! Boogie Woogie
BOSTON

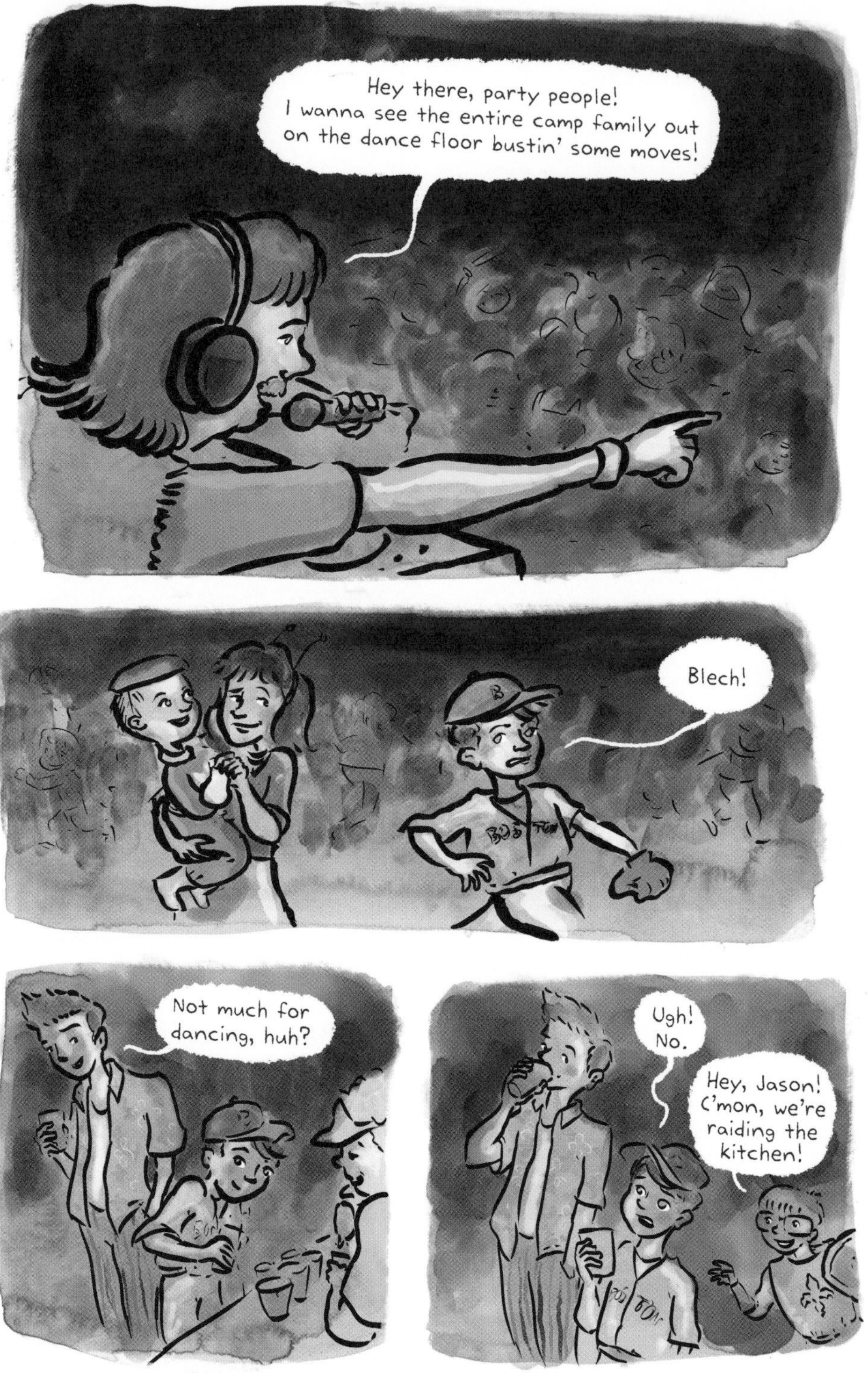
Hey there, party people! I wanna see the entire camp family out on the dance floor bustin' some moves!
Blech!
Not much for dancing, huh?
Ugh! No.
Hey, Jason! C'mon, we're raiding the kitchen!

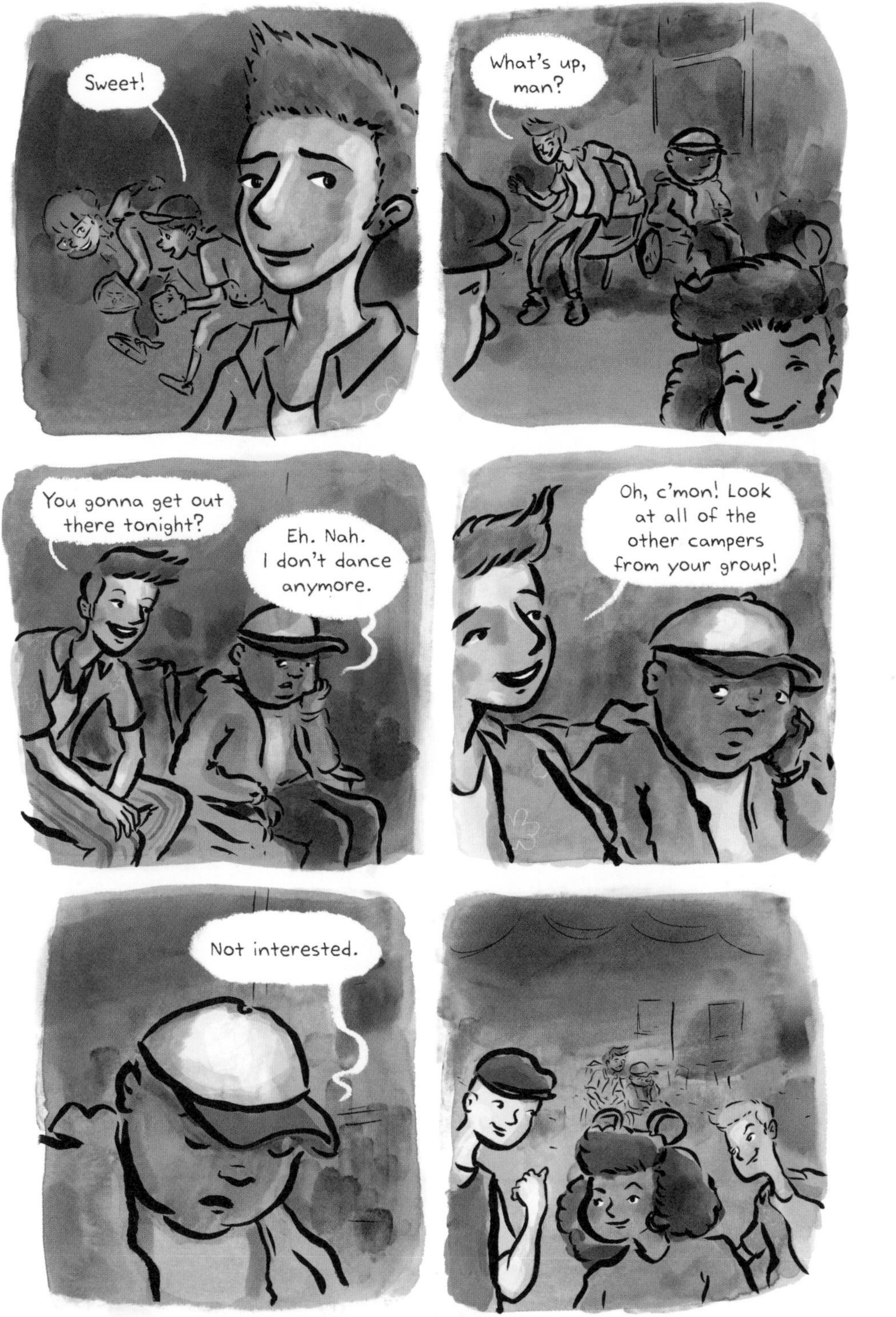

Sweet!
What's up, man?
You gonna get out there tonight?
Eh. Nah. I don't dance anymore.
Oh, c'mon! Look at all of the other campers from your group!
Not interested.

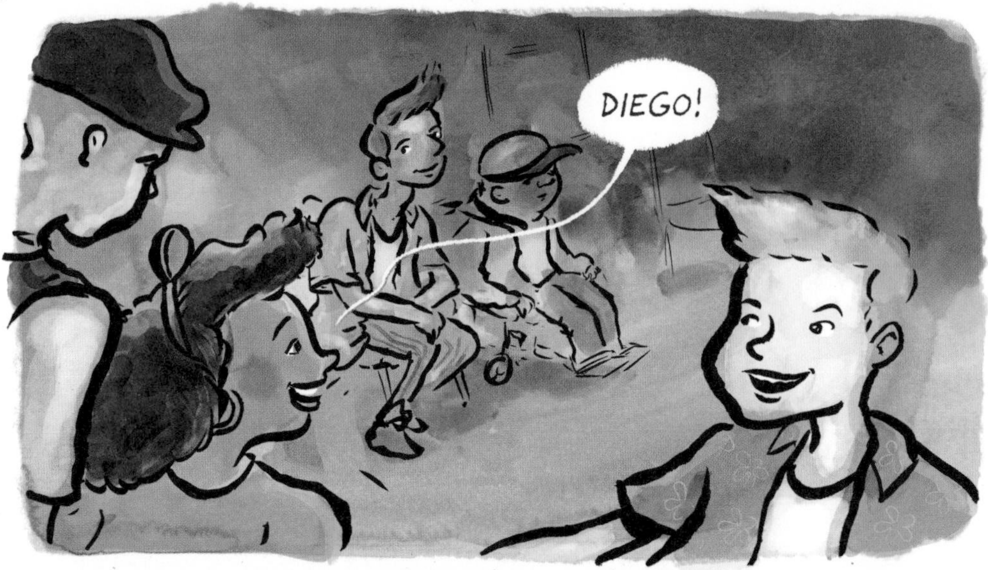
DIEGO!

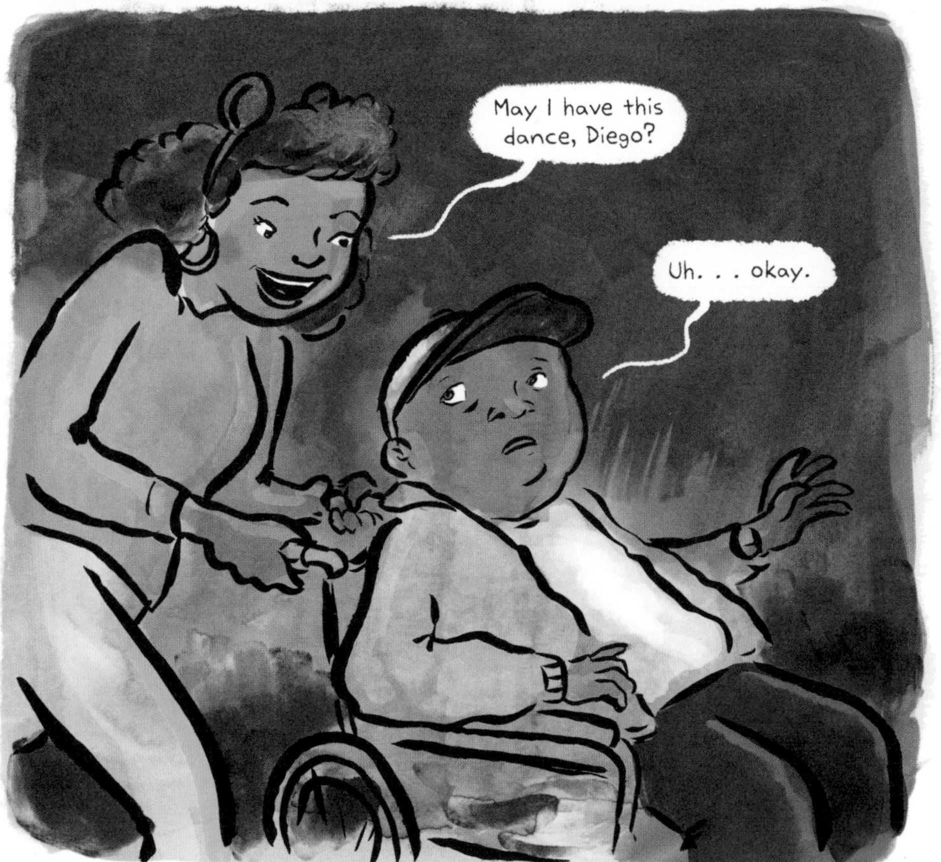
May I have this dance, Diego?
Uh. . . okay.

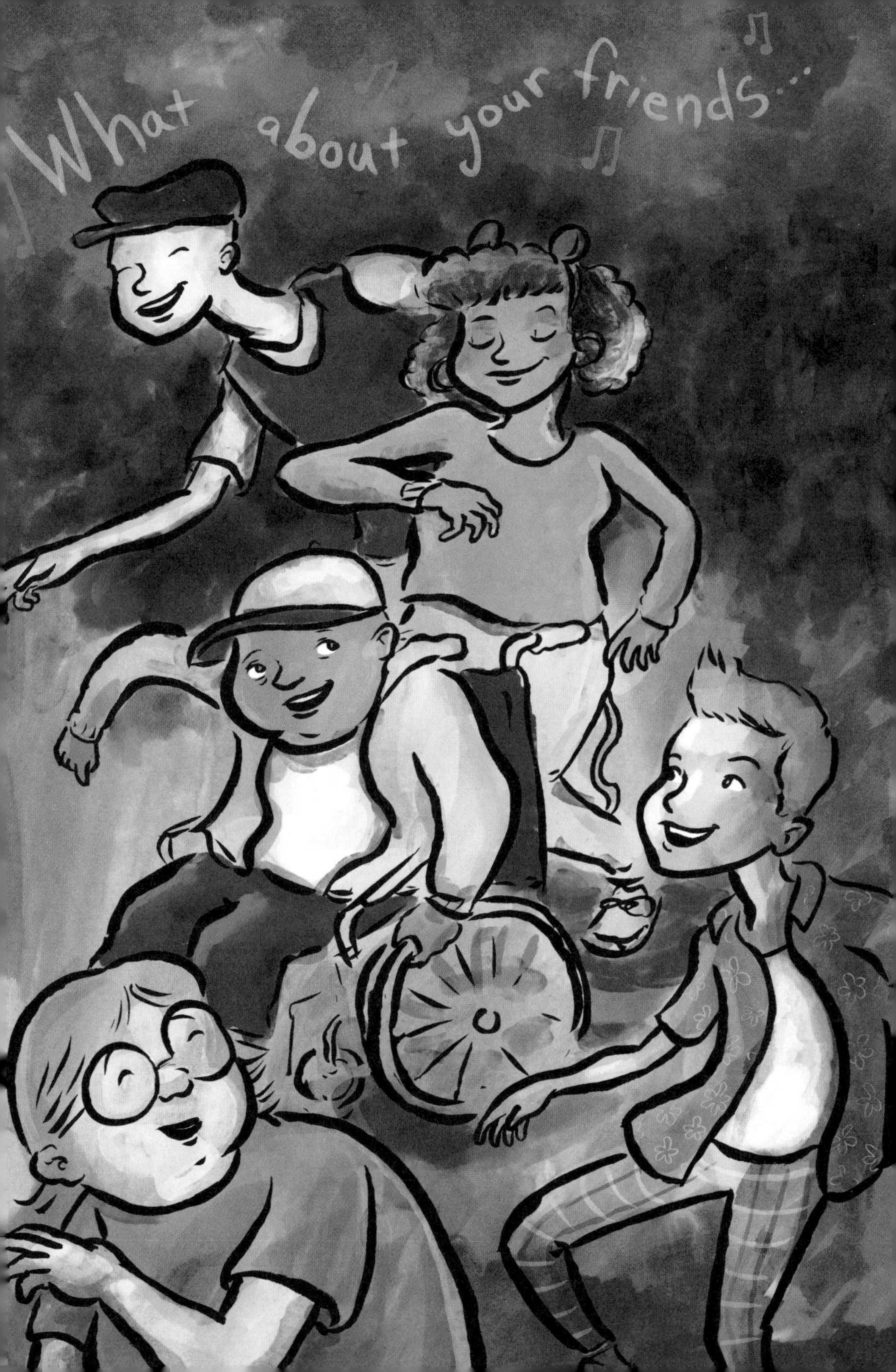
What about your friends...

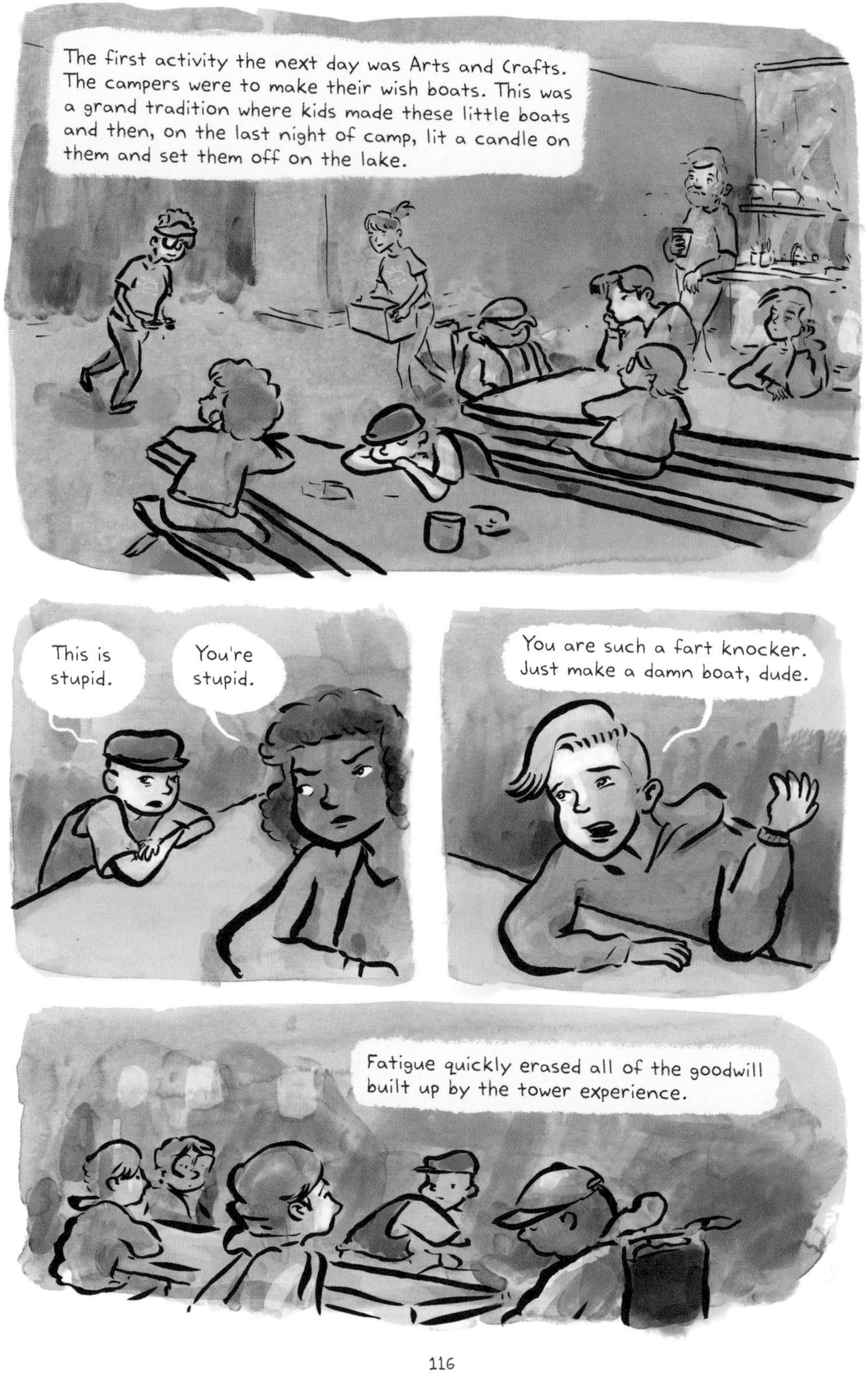
The first activity the next day was Arts and Crafts. The campers were to make their wish boats. This was a grand tradition where kids made these little boats and then, on the last night of camp, lit a candle on them and set them off on the lake.
This is stupid.
You're stupid.
You are such a fart knocker. Just make a damn boat, dude.
Fatigue quickly erased all of the goodwill built up by the tower experience.

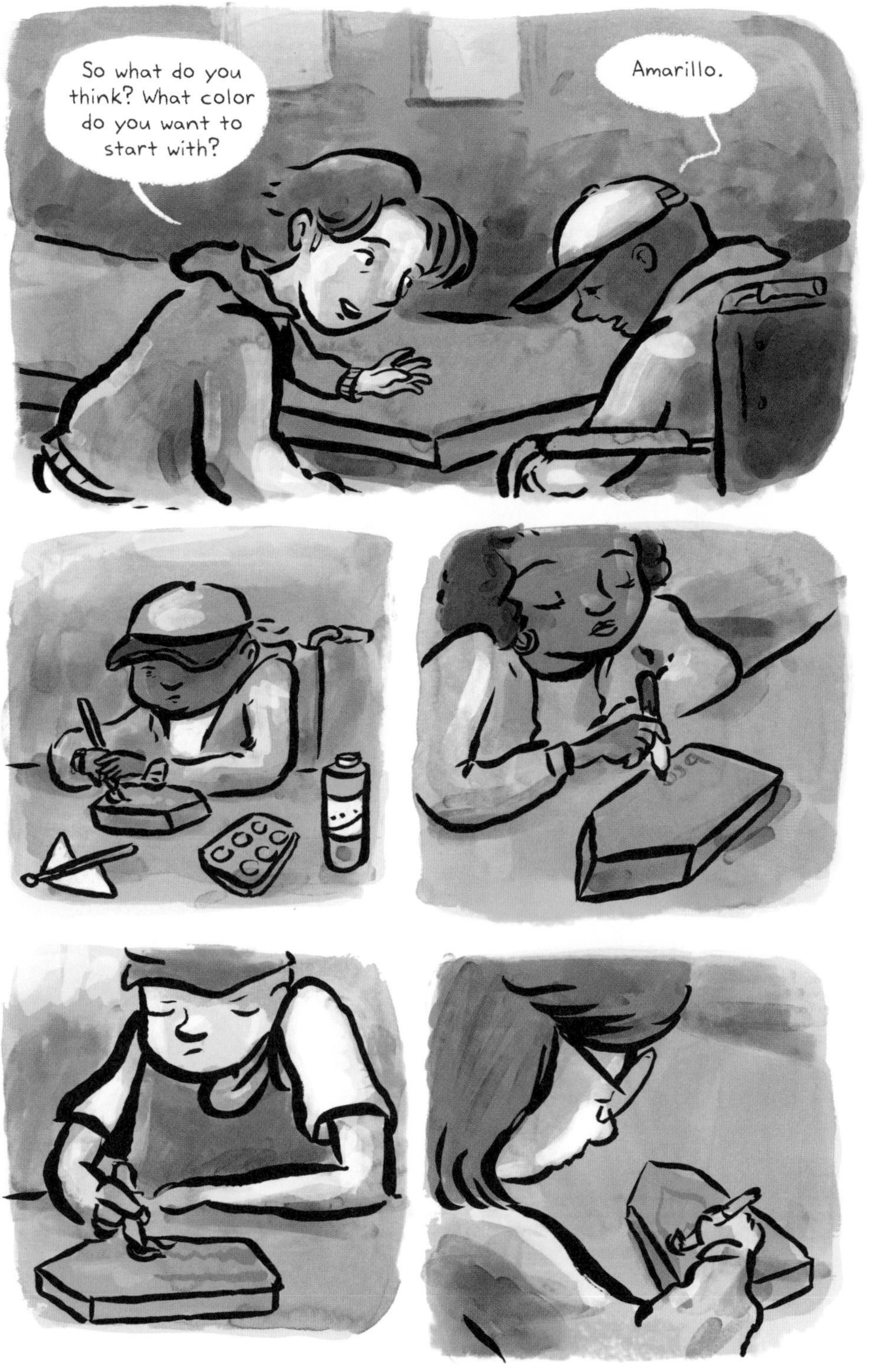
So what do you think? What color do you want to start with?
Amarillo.

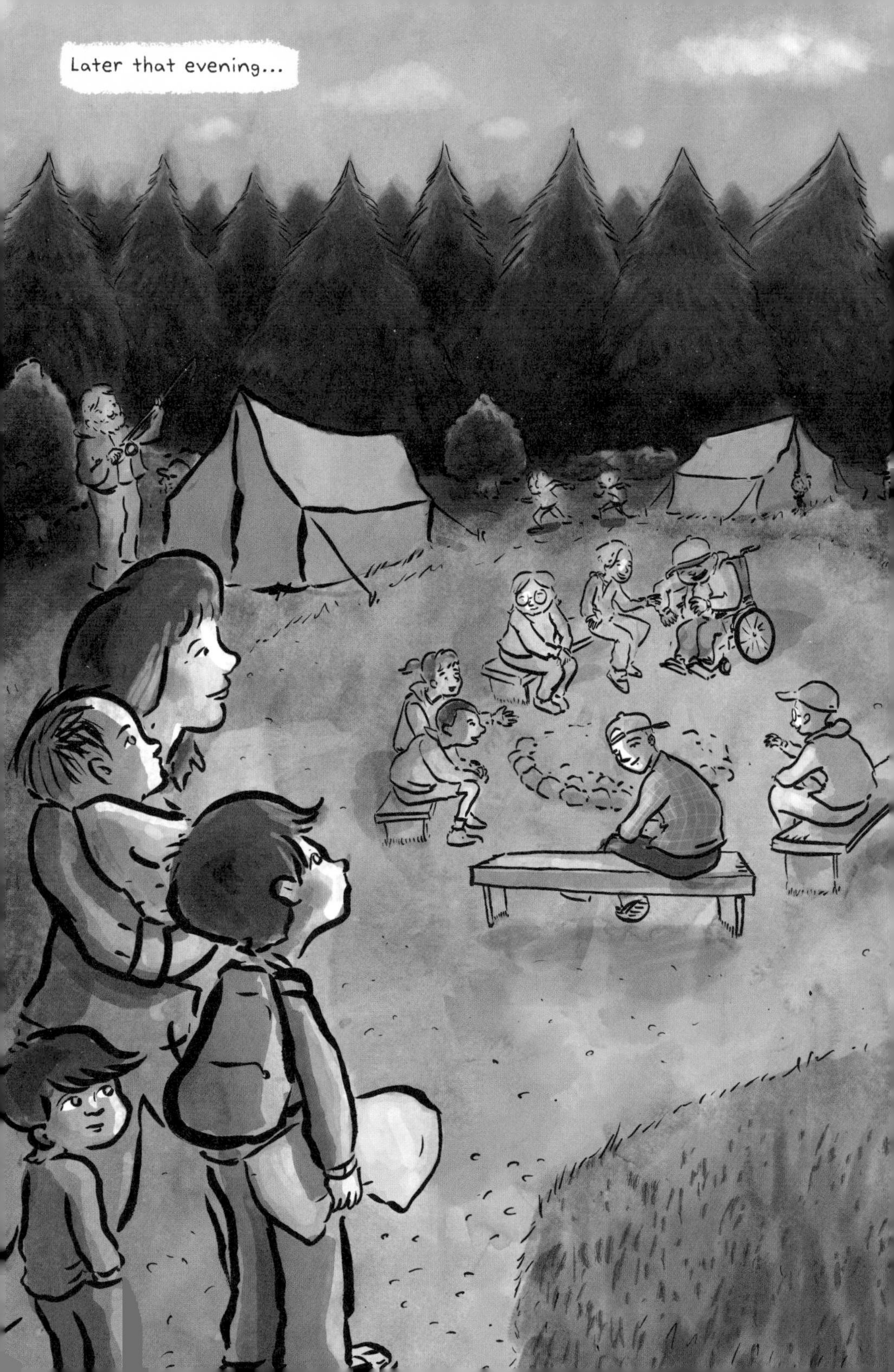
Later that evening...

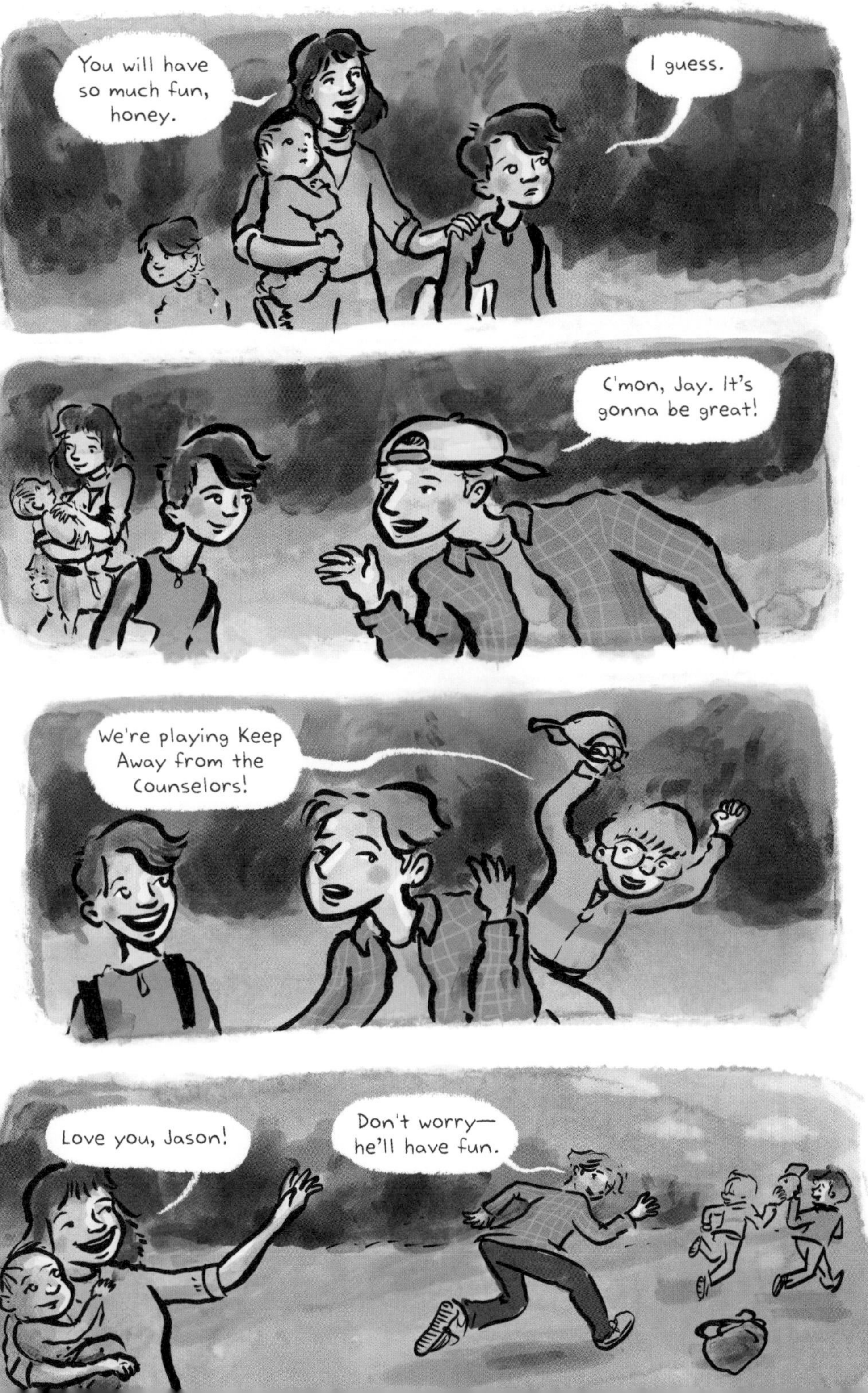
You will have so much fun, honey.
I guess.
C'mon, Jay. It's gonna be great!
We're playing Keep Away from the Counselors!
Love you, Jason!
Don't worry— he'll have fun.

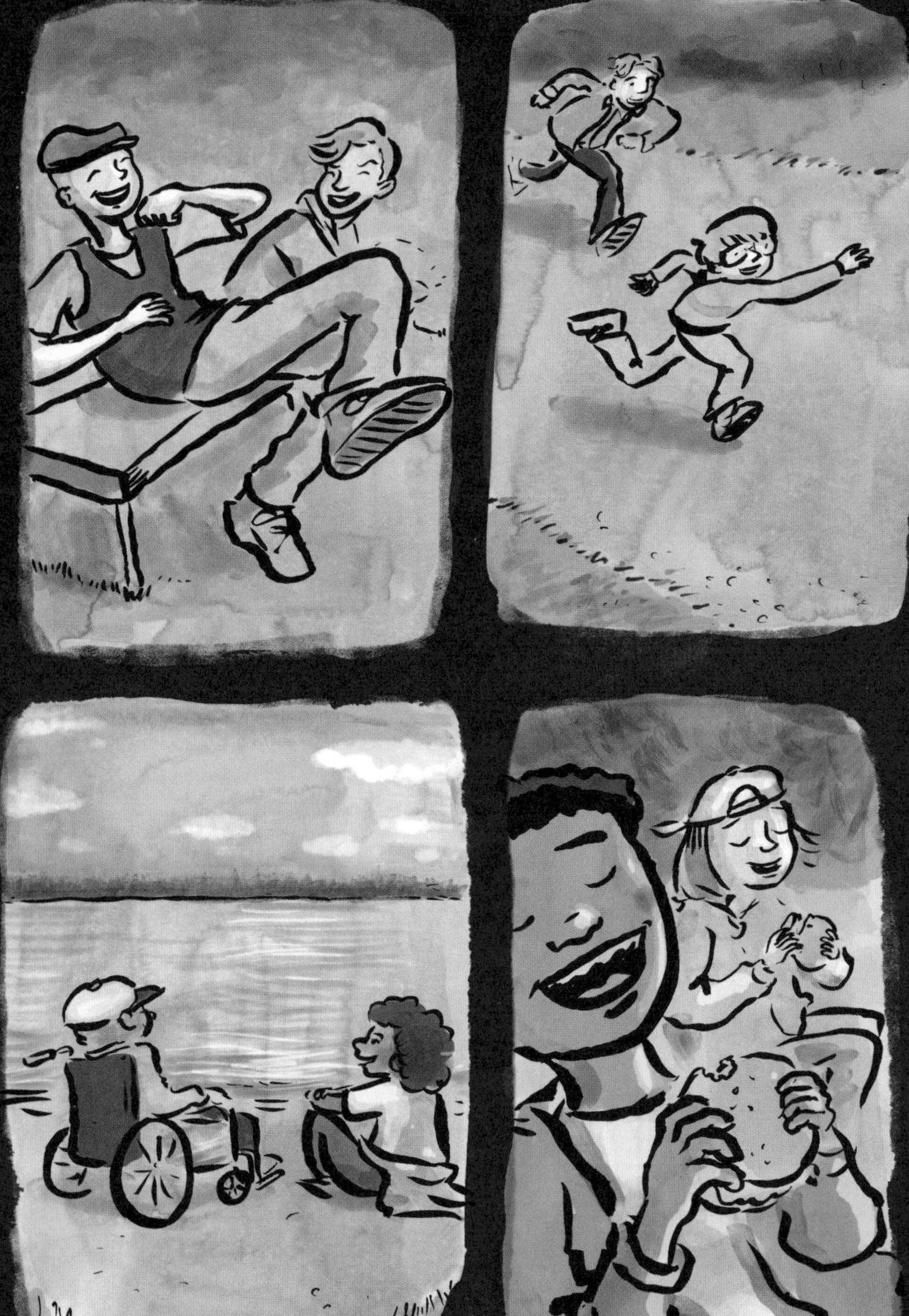

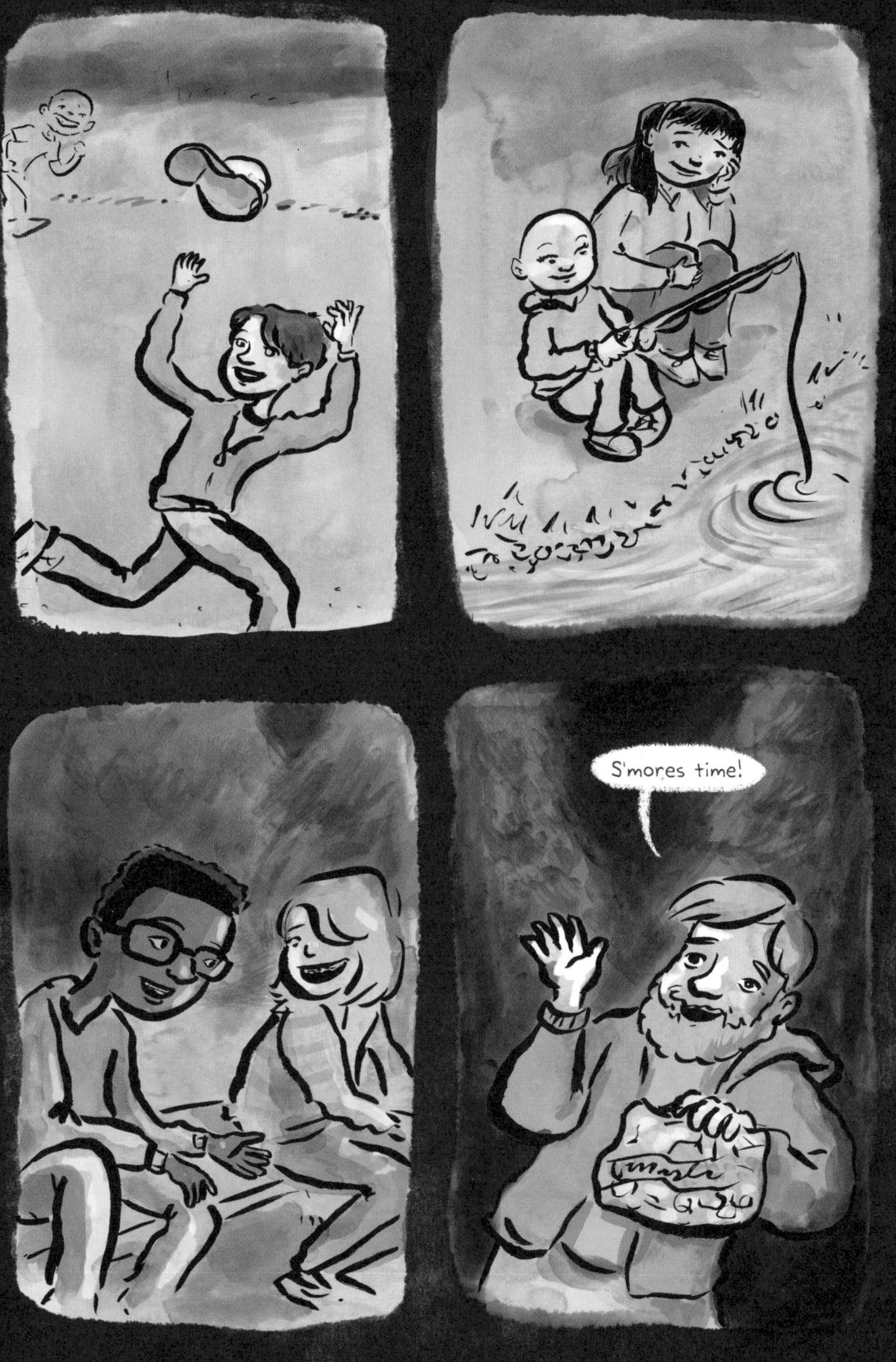
S'mores time!

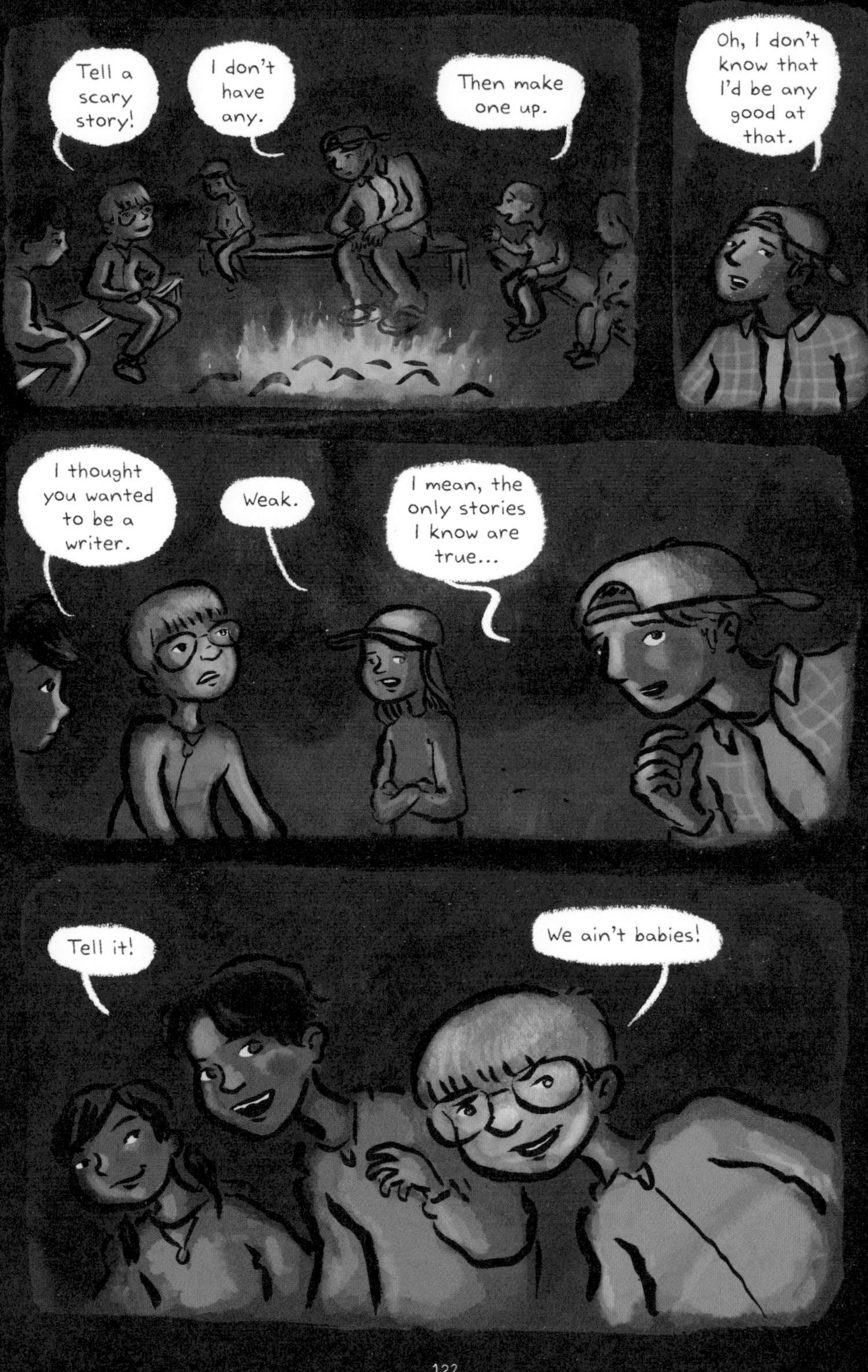
Tell a scary story!
I don't have any.
Then make one up.
Oh, I don't know that I'd be any good at that.
I thought you wanted to be a writer.
Weak.
I mean, the only stories I know are true...
Tell it!
We ain't babies!

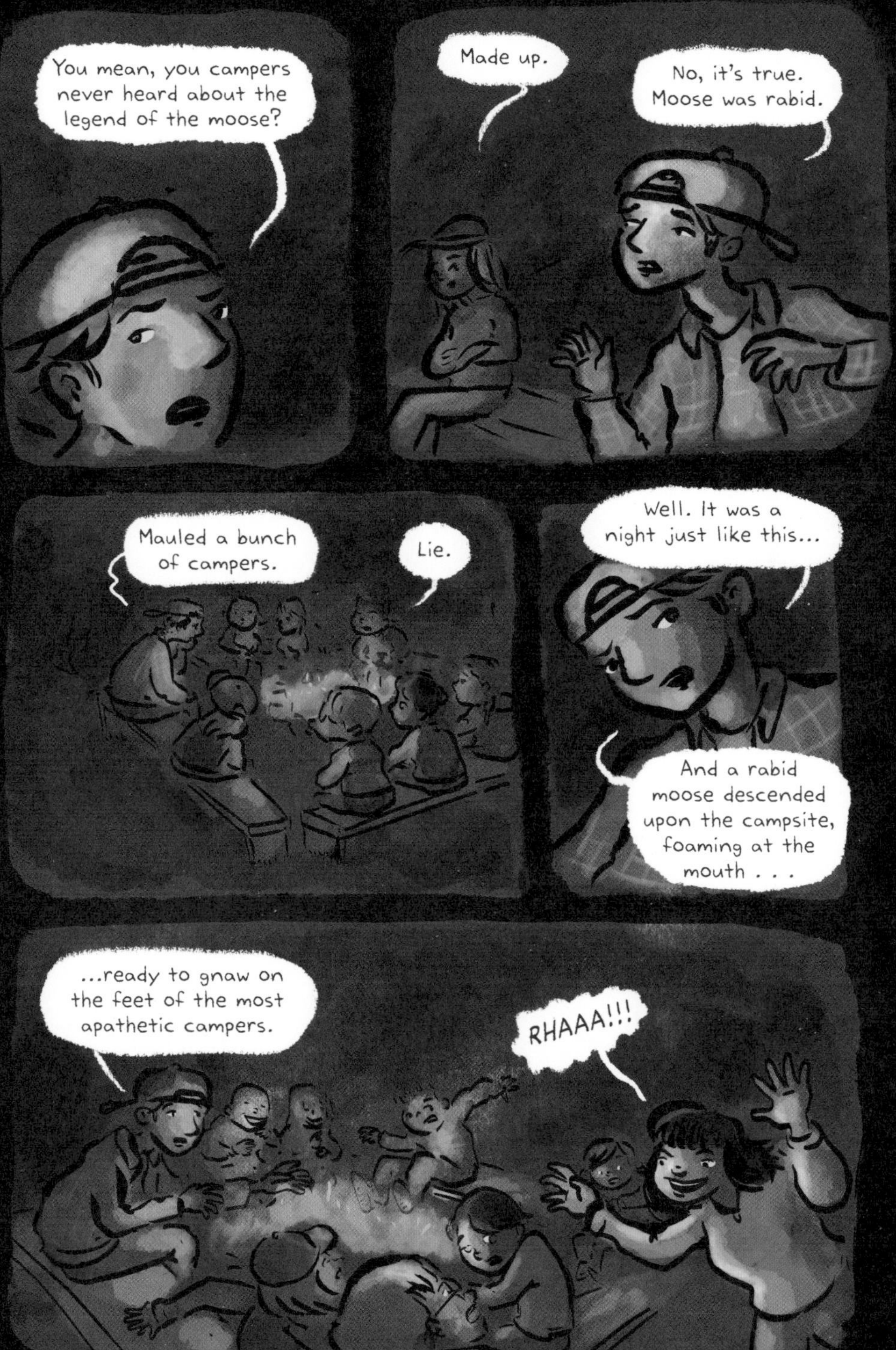
You mean, you campers never heard about the legend of the moose?
Made up.
No, it's true. Moose was rabid.
Mauled a bunch of campers.
Lie.
Well. It was a night just like this...
And a rabid moose descended upon the campsite, foaming at the mouth . . .
...ready to gnaw on the feet of the most apathetic campers.
RHAAA!!!

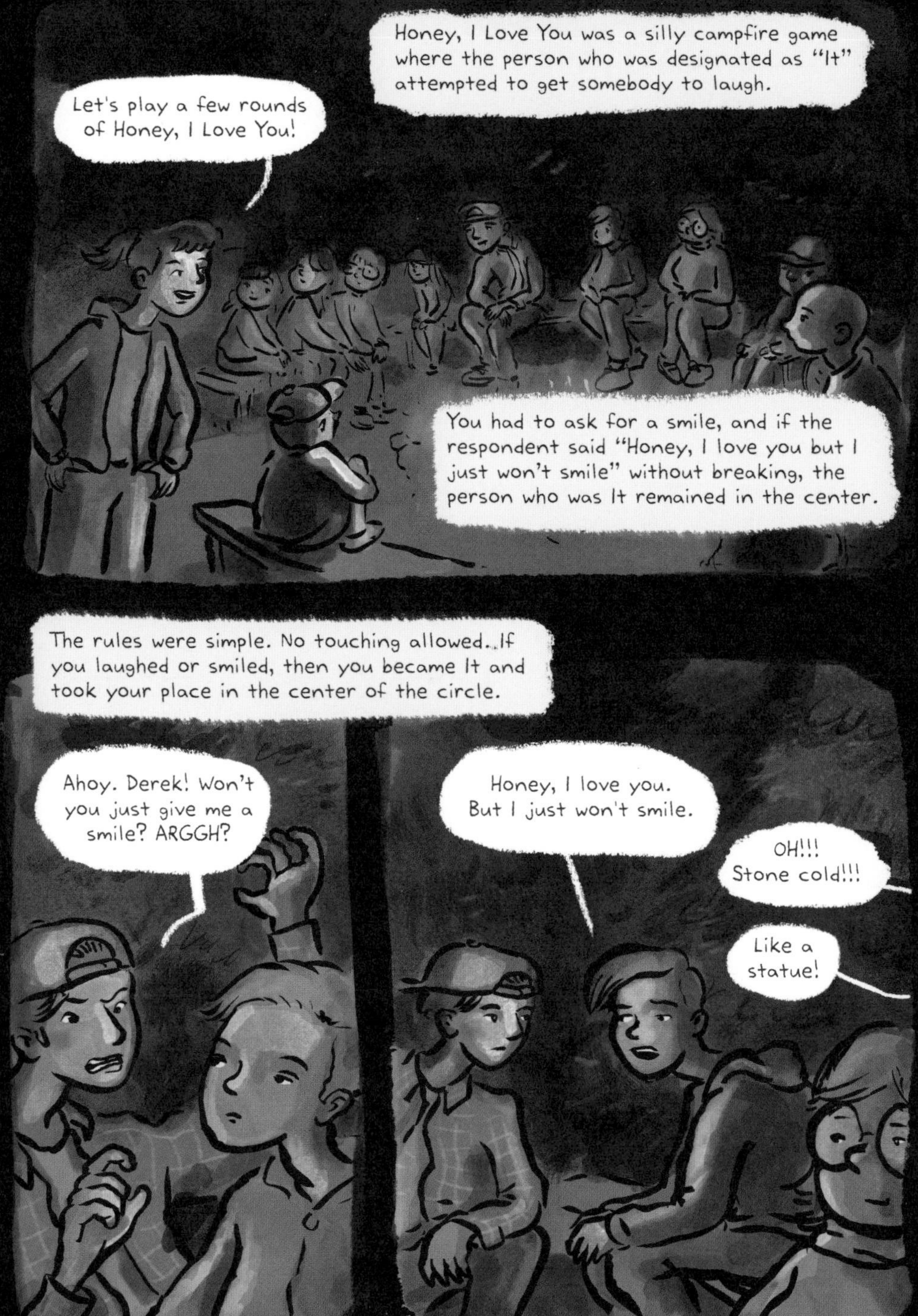
Honey, I Love You was a silly campfire game where the person who was designated as "It" attempted to get somebody to laugh.
Let's play a few rounds of Honey, I Love You!
You had to ask for a smile, and if the respondent said "Honey, I love you but I just won't smile" without breaking, the person who was It remained in the center.
The rules were simple. No touching allowed...If you laughed or smiled, then you became It and took your place in the center of the circle.
Ahoy. Derek! Won't you just give me a smile? ARGGH?
Honey, I love you. But I just won't smile.
OH!!! Stone cold!!!
Like a statue!

Alright, alright.

Jason. Jason! My dude, Jason! Won't yoouuuuu just give meeeeee a smile?

Honey. I. I-I love...

You. But I just won't...

And when you saw an opportunity for somebody to break, you turned up the volume on the silliness. . .

Oh pweeeeease, oh pweeeeeeease?

Won't you smiiile?

Okay, Jason. In the middle!

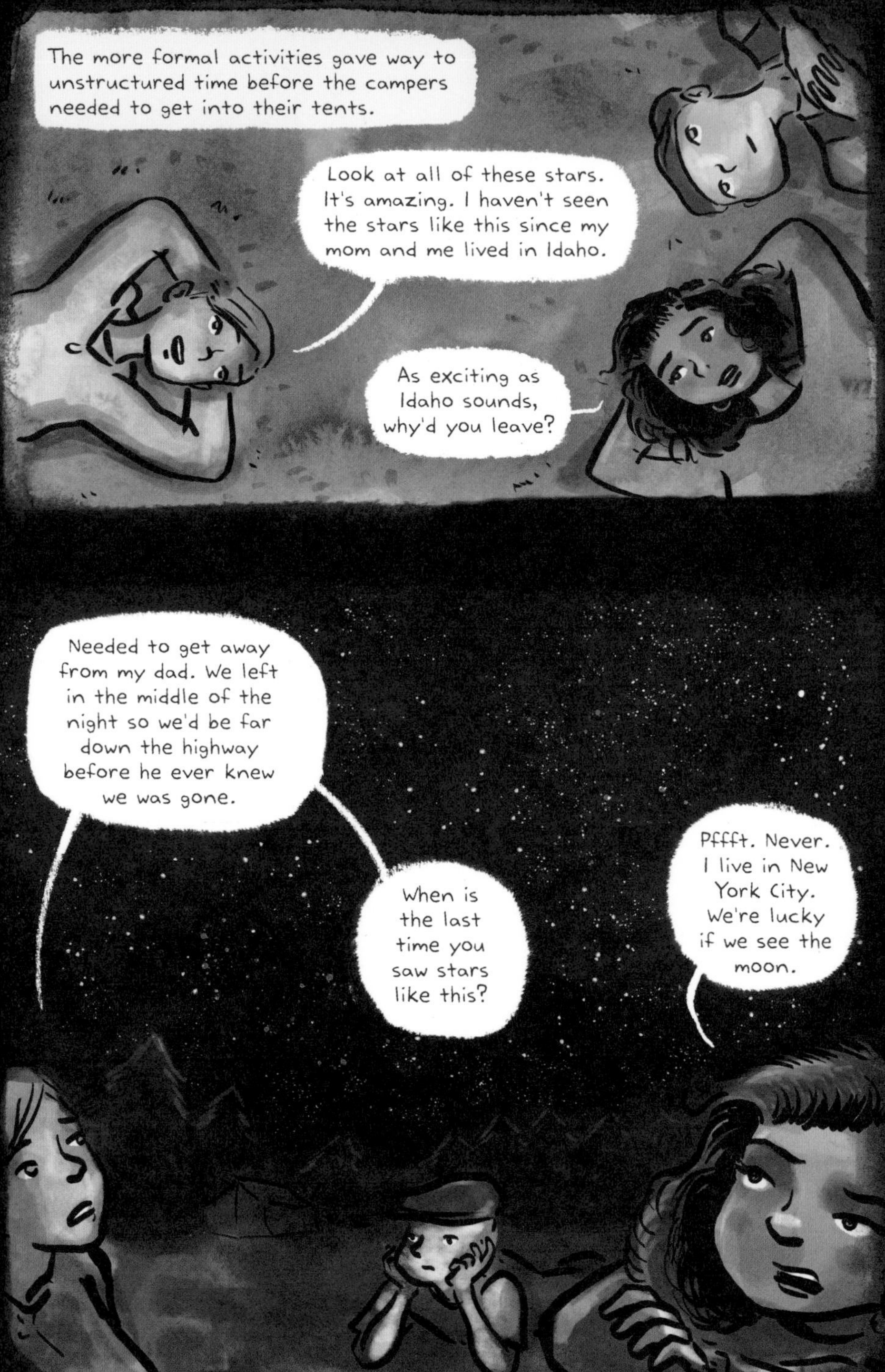
The more formal activities gave way to unstructured time before the campers needed to get into their tents.
Look at all of these stars. It's amazing. I haven't seen the stars like this since my mom and me lived in Idaho.
As exciting as Idaho sounds, why'd you leave?
Needed to get away from my dad. We left in the middle of the night so we'd be far down the highway before he ever knew we was gone.
When is the last time you saw stars like this?
Pffft. Never. I live in New York City. We're lucky if we see the moon.

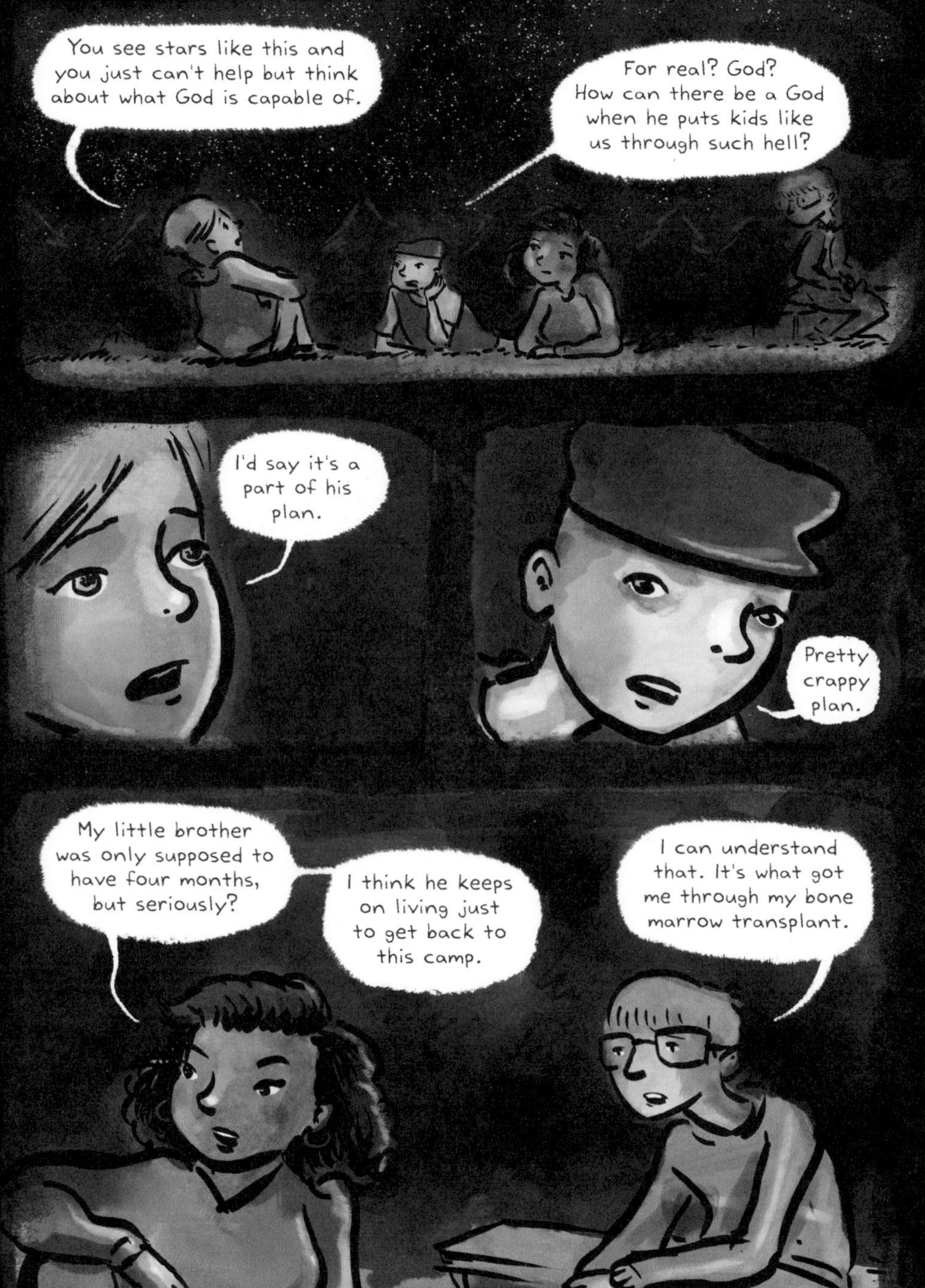
You see stars like this and you just can't help but think about what God is capable of.
For real? God? How can there be a God when he puts kids like us through such hell?
I'd say it's a part of his plan.
Pretty crappy plan.
My little brother was only supposed to have four months, but seriously?
I think he keeps on living just to get back to this camp.
I can understand that. It's what got me through my bone marrow transplant.

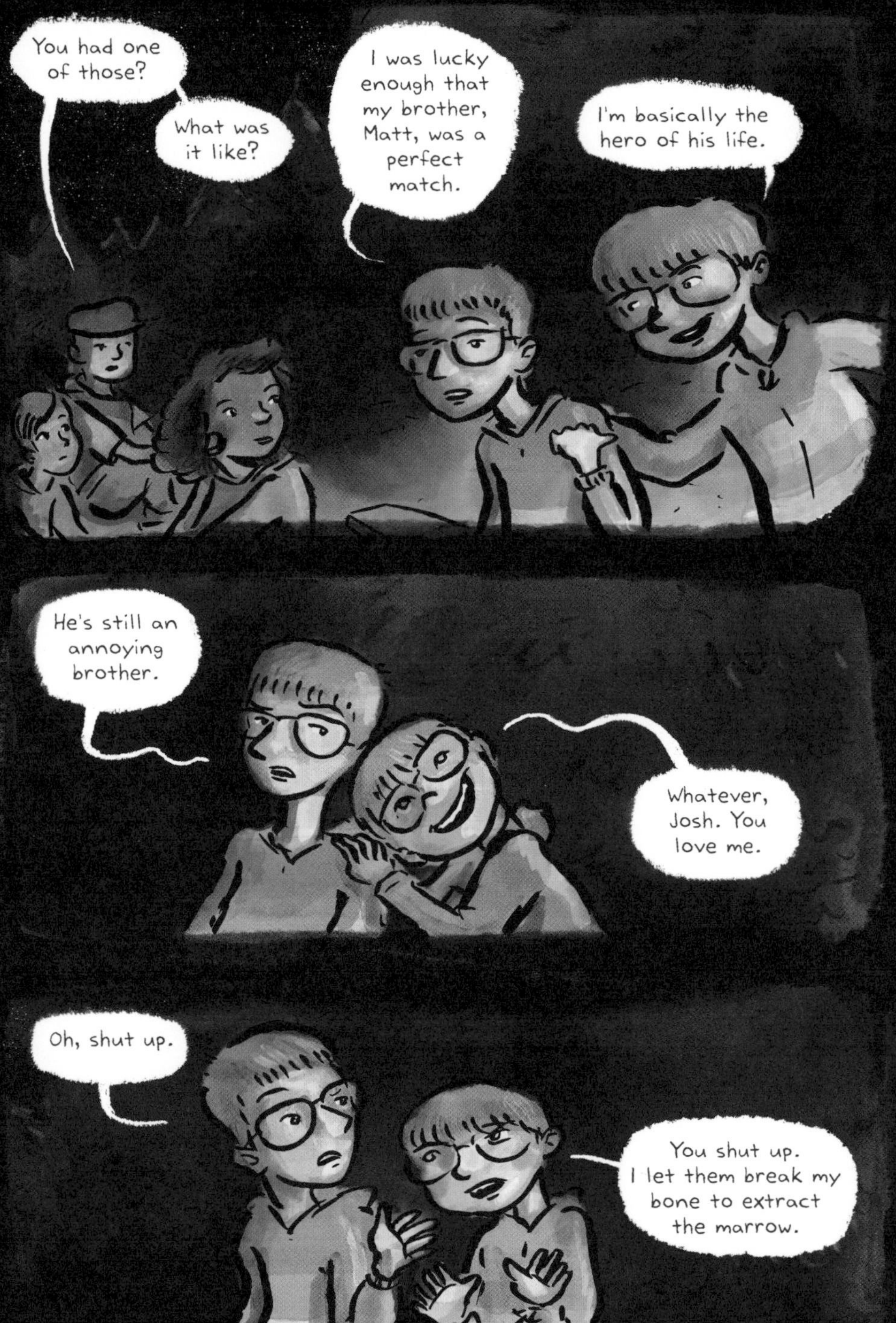
You had one of those?
What was it like?
I was lucky enough that my brother, Matt, was a perfect match.
I'm basically the hero of his life.
He's still an annoying brother.
Whatever, Josh. You love me.
Oh, shut up.
You shut up. I let them break my bone to extract the marrow.

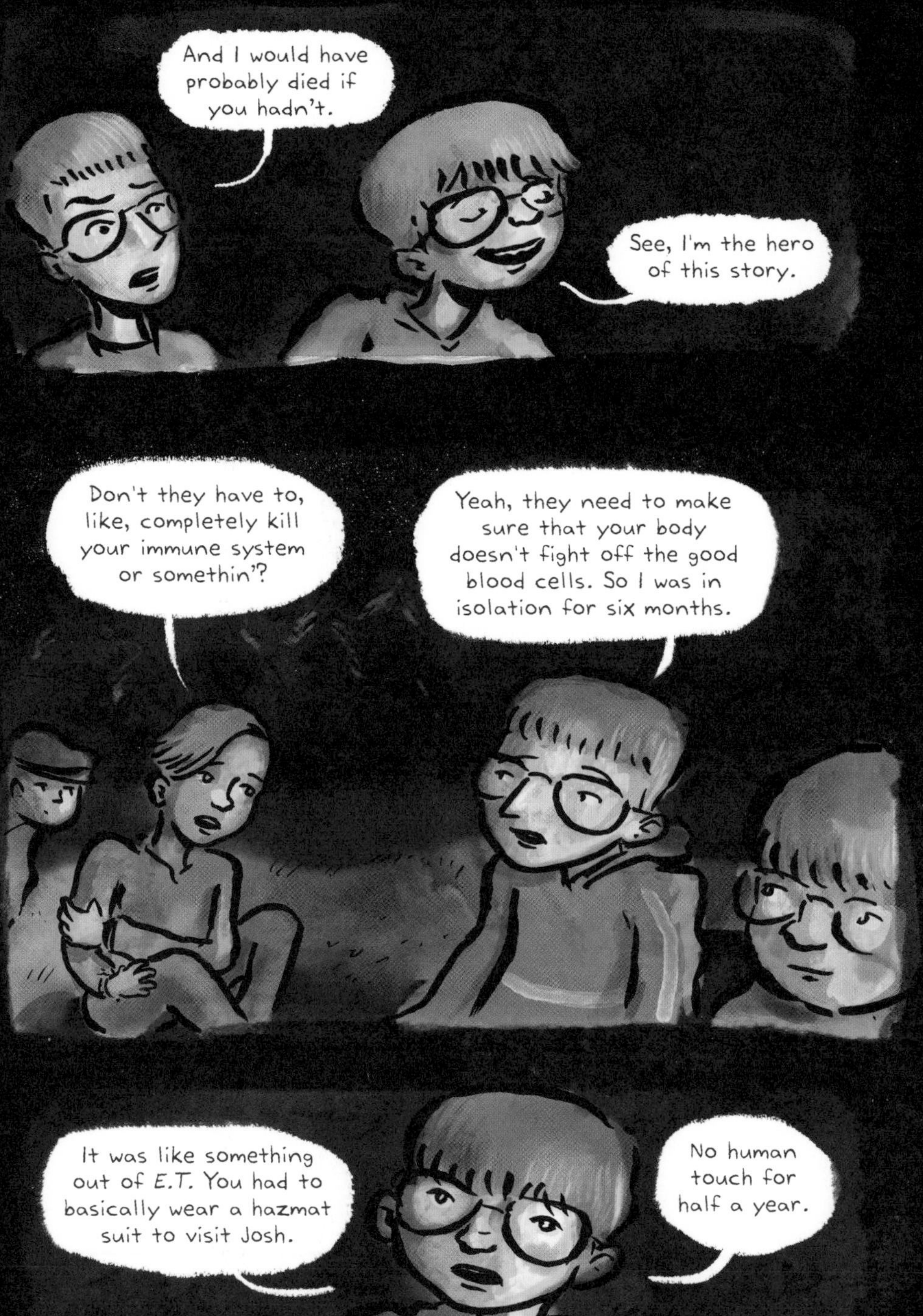

And I would have probably died if you hadn't.
See, I'm the hero of this story.
Don't they have to, like, completely kill your immune system or somethin'?
Yeah, they need to make sure that your body doesn't fight off the good blood cells. So I was in isolation for six months.
It was like something out of *E.T.* You had to basically wear a hazmat suit to visit Josh.
No human touch for half a year.

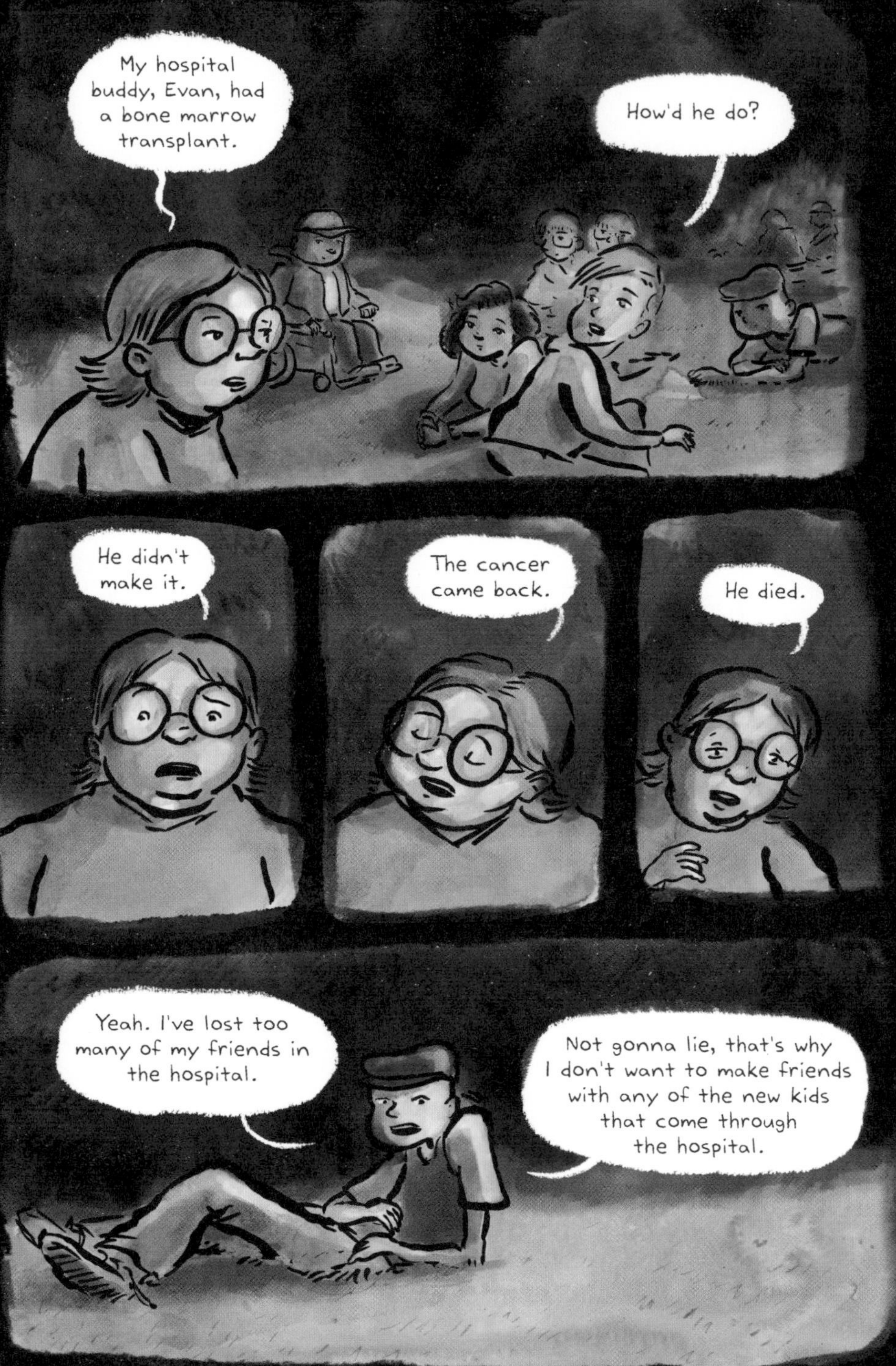
My hospital buddy, Evan, had a bone marrow transplant.
How'd he do?
He didn't make it.
The cancer came back.
He died.
Yeah. I've lost too many of my friends in the hospital.
Not gonna lie, that's why I don't want to make friends with any of the new kids that come through the hospital.

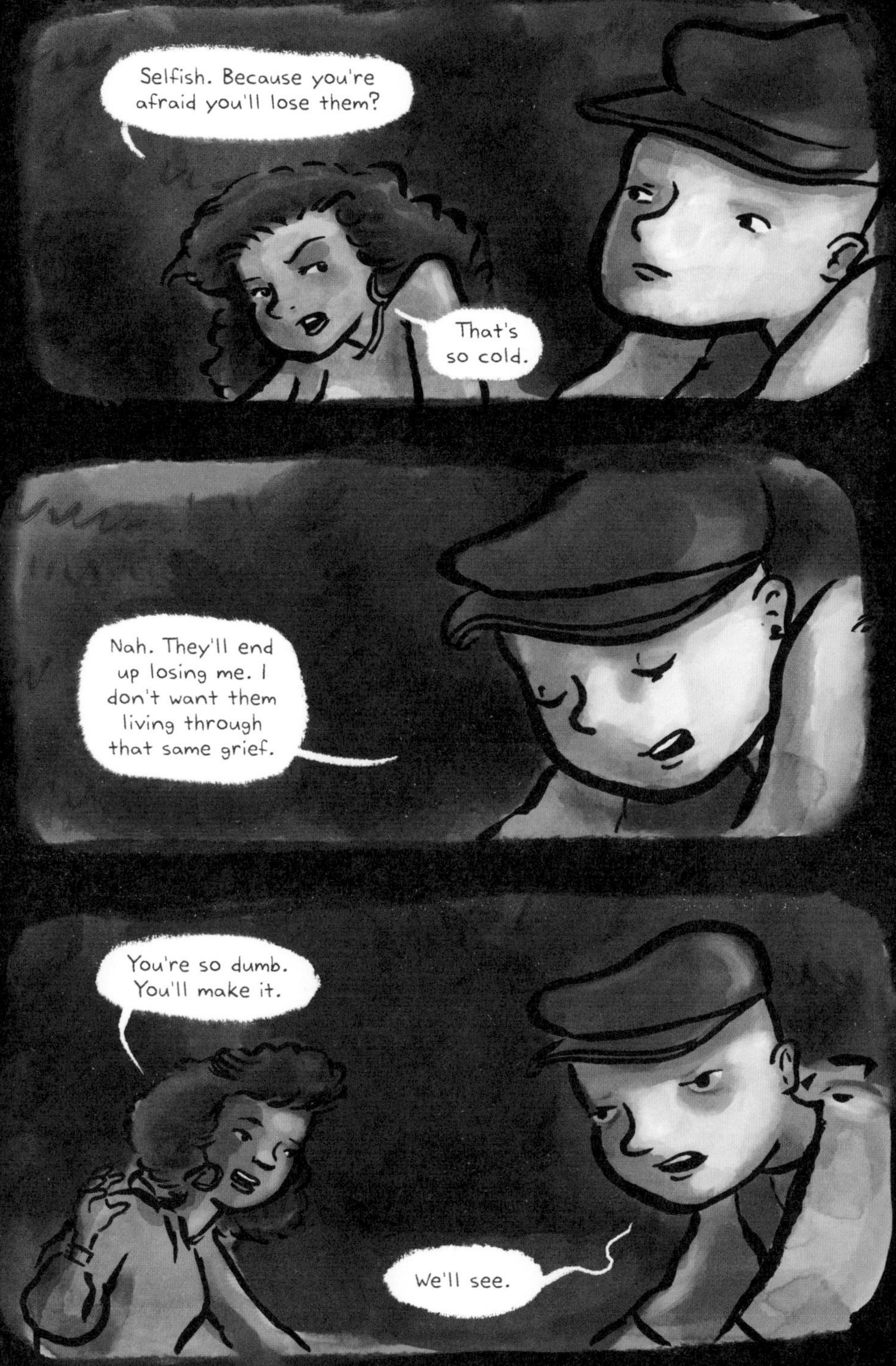

Selfish. Because you're afraid you'll lose them?
That's so cold.
Nah. They'll end up losing me. I don't want them living through that same grief.
You're so dumb. You'll make it.
We'll see.

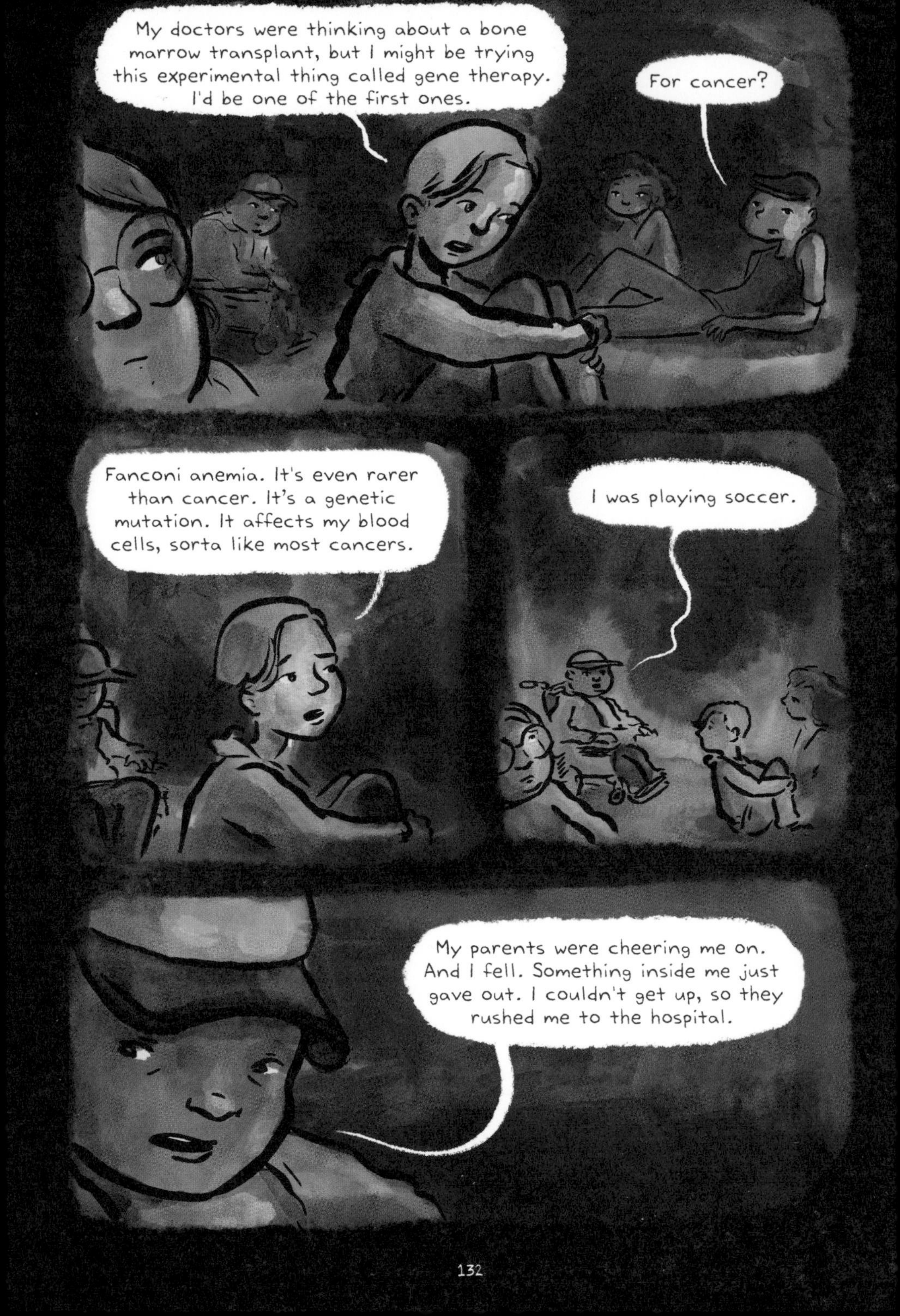
My doctors were thinking about a bone marrow transplant, but I might be trying this experimental thing called gene therapy. I'd be one of the first ones.
For cancer?
Fanconi anemia. It's even rarer than cancer. It's a genetic mutation. It affects my blood cells, sorta like most cancers.
I was playing soccer.
My parents were cheering me on. And I fell. Something inside me just gave out. I couldn't get up, so they rushed me to the hospital.

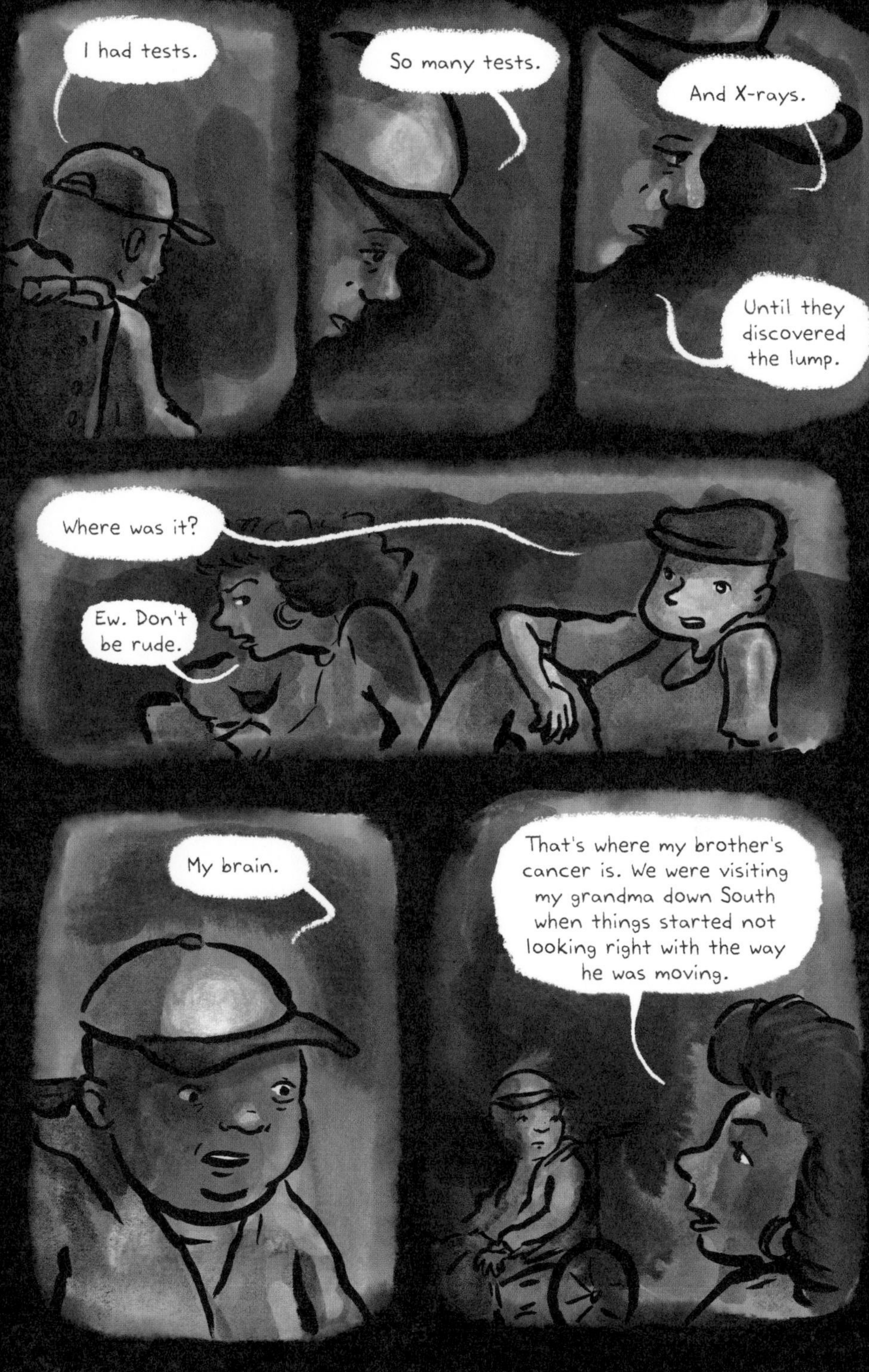
I had tests.
So many tests.
And X-rays.
Until they discovered the lump.
Where was it?
Ew. Don't be rude.
My brain.
That's where my brother's cancer is. We were visiting my grandma down South when things started not looking right with the way he was moving.

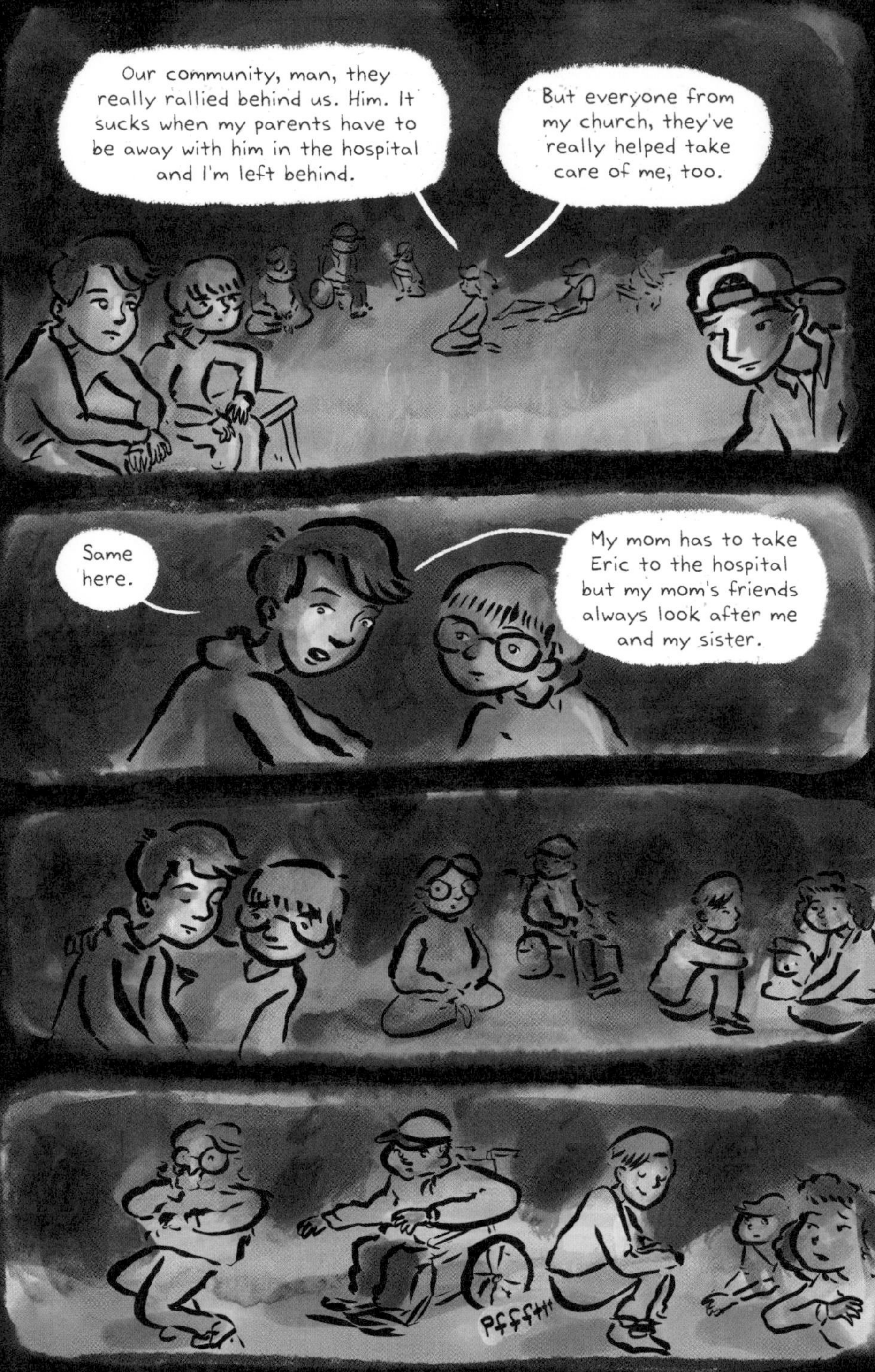
Our community, man, they really rallied behind us. Him. It sucks when my parents have to be away with him in the hospital and I'm left behind.
But everyone from my church, they've really helped take care of me, too.
Same here.
My mom has to take Eric to the hospital but my mom's friends always look after me and my sister.
Pfffttt

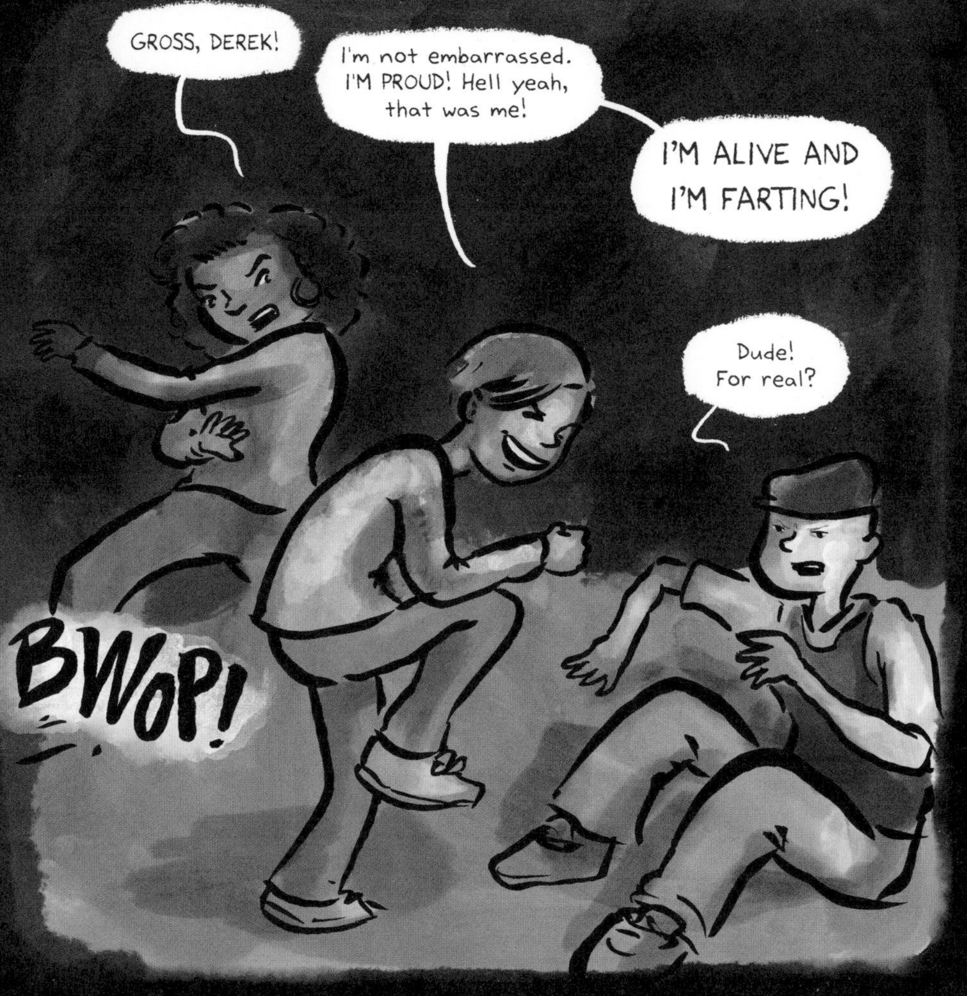
GROSS, DEREK!
I'm not embarrassed. I'M PROUD! Hell yeah, that was me!
I'M ALIVE AND I'M FARTING!
Dude! For real?
BWOP!

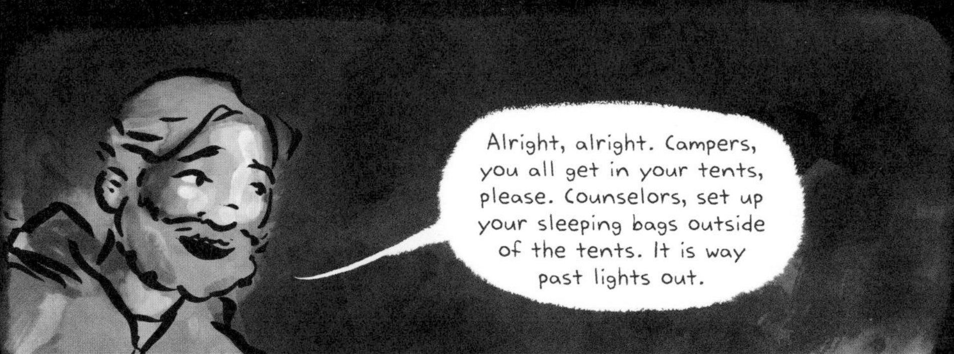
Alright, alright. Campers, you all get in your tents, please. Counselors, set up your sleeping bags outside of the tents. It is way past lights out.

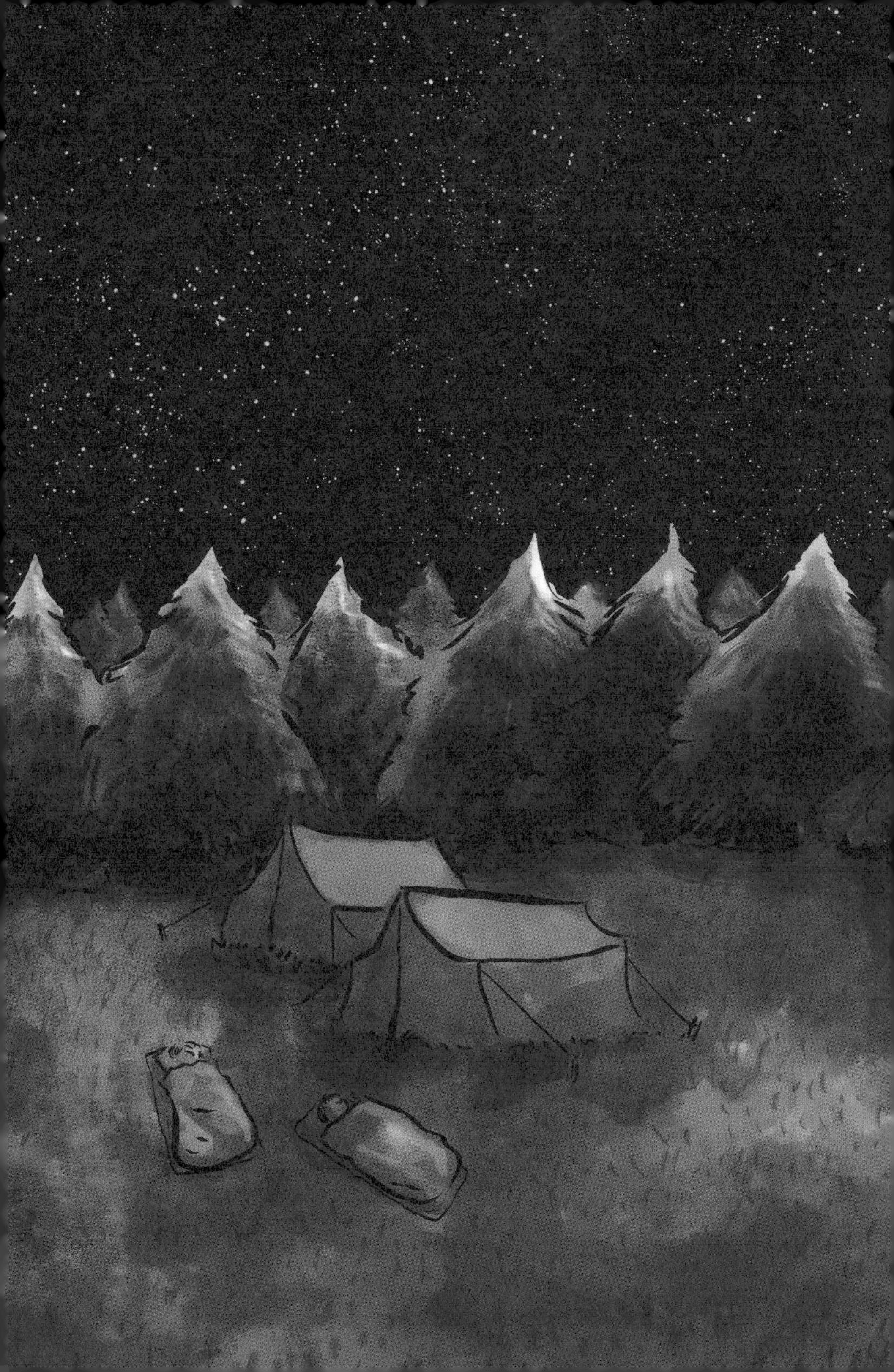

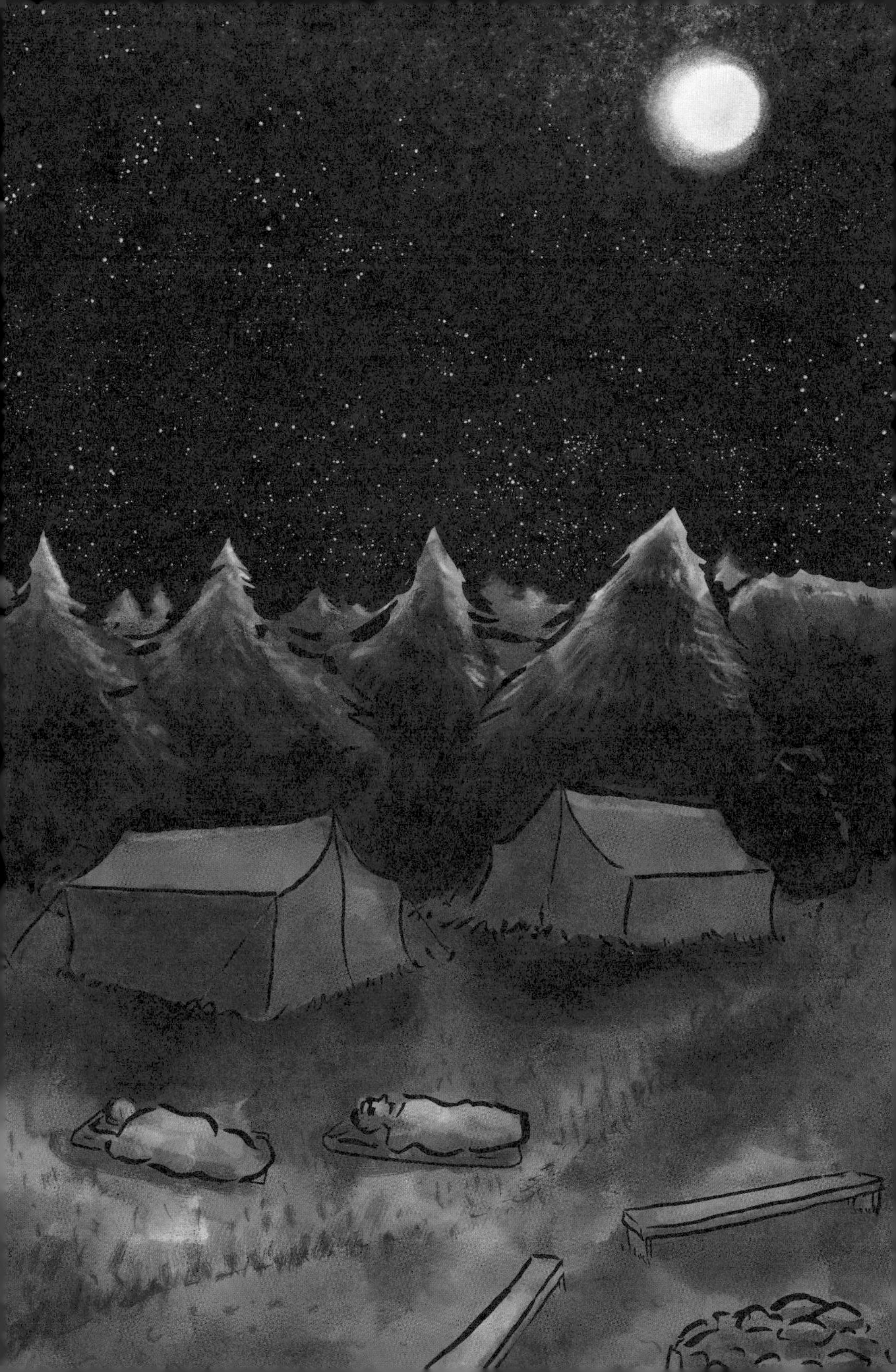

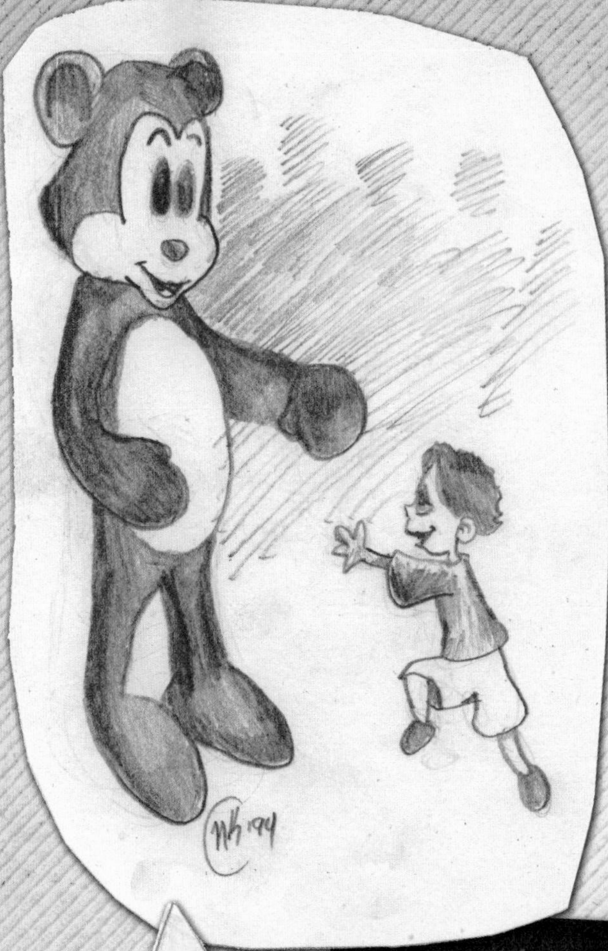

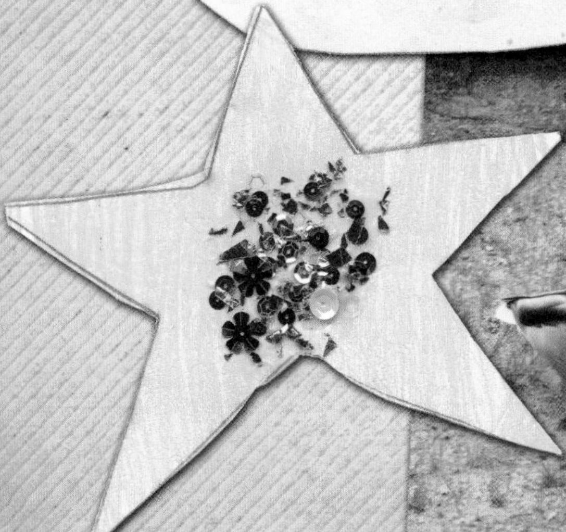

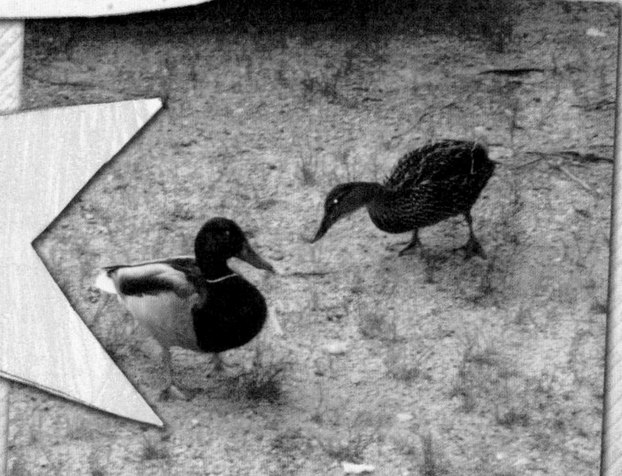

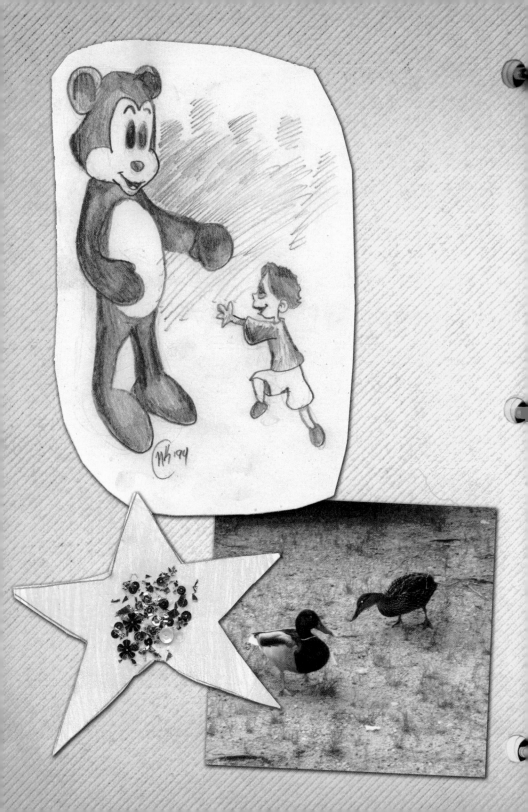

CHAPTER 5
THE HERE AND NOW

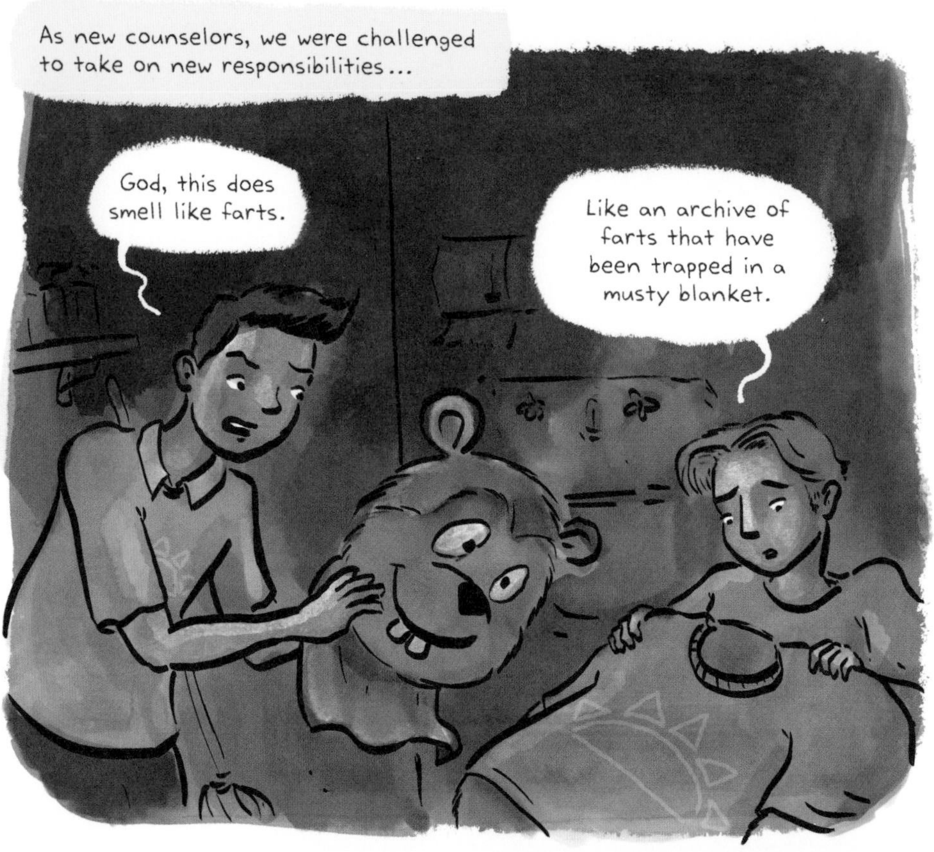
As new counselors, we were challenged to take on new responsibilities...
God, this does smell like farts.
Like an archive of farts that have been trapped in a musty blanket.

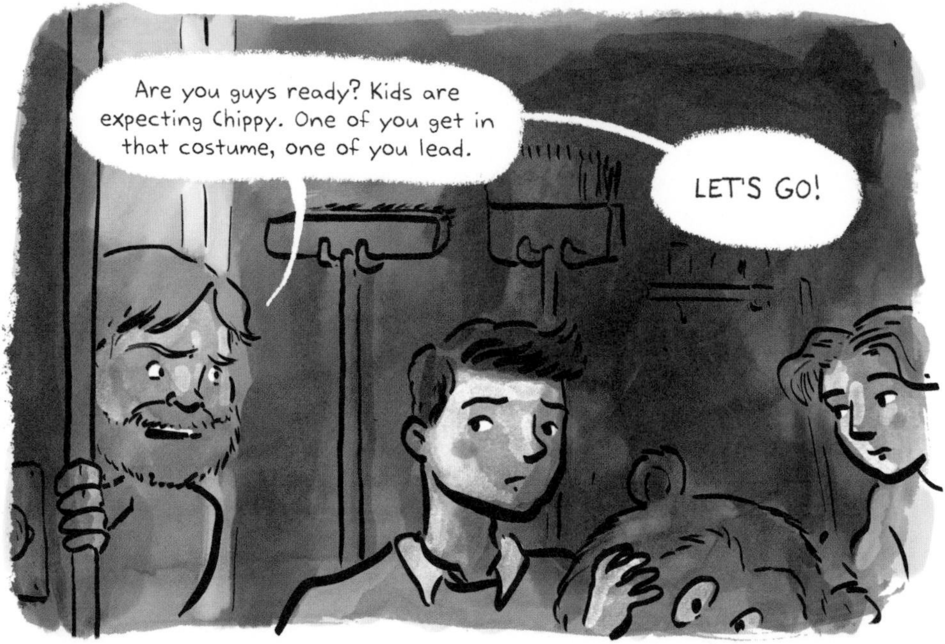
Are you guys ready? Kids are expecting Chippy. One of you get in that costume, one of you lead.
LET'S GO!

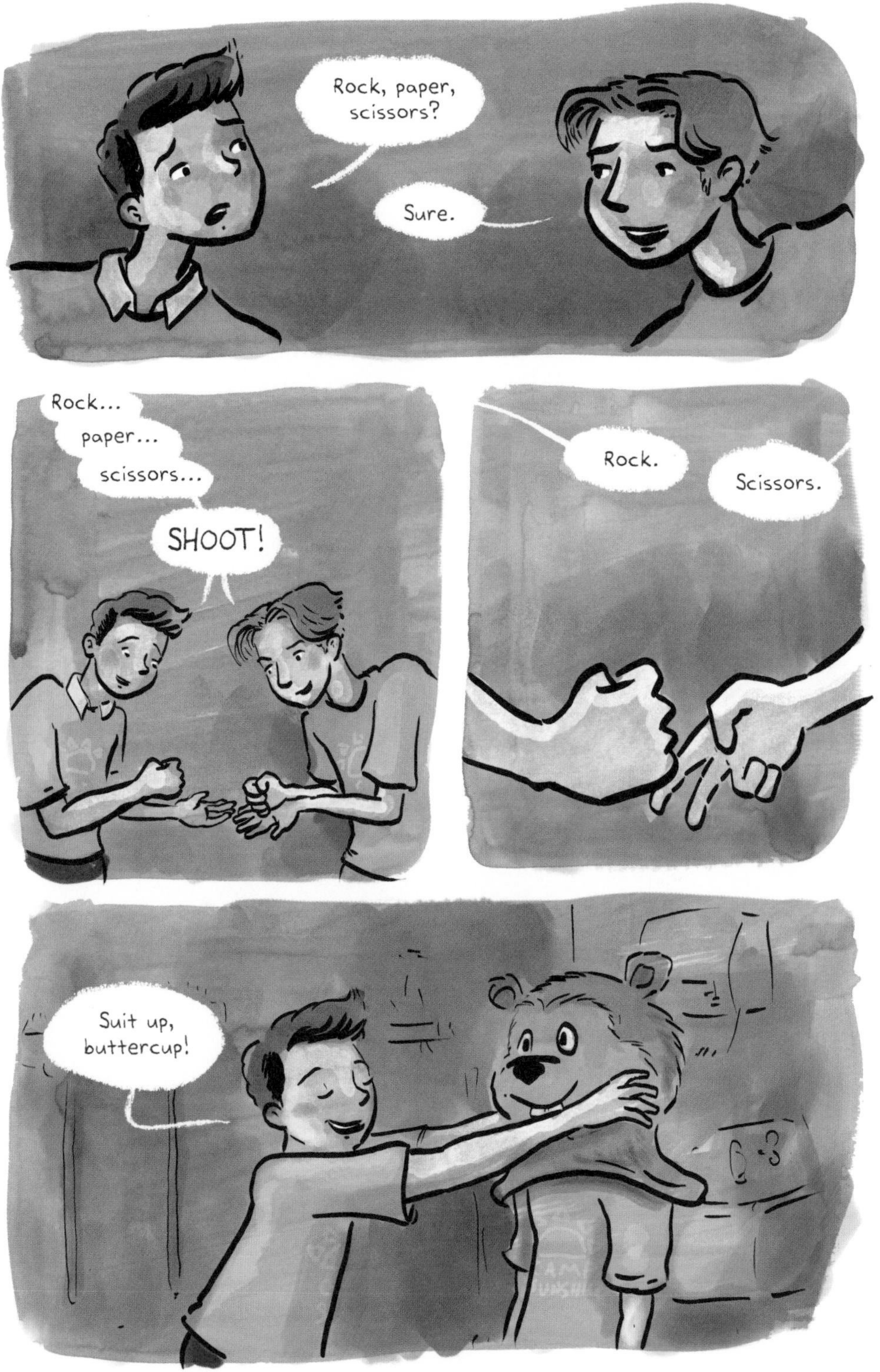
Rock, paper, scissors?
Sure.
Rock...
paper...
scissors...
SHOOT!
Rock.
Scissors.
Suit up, buttercup!

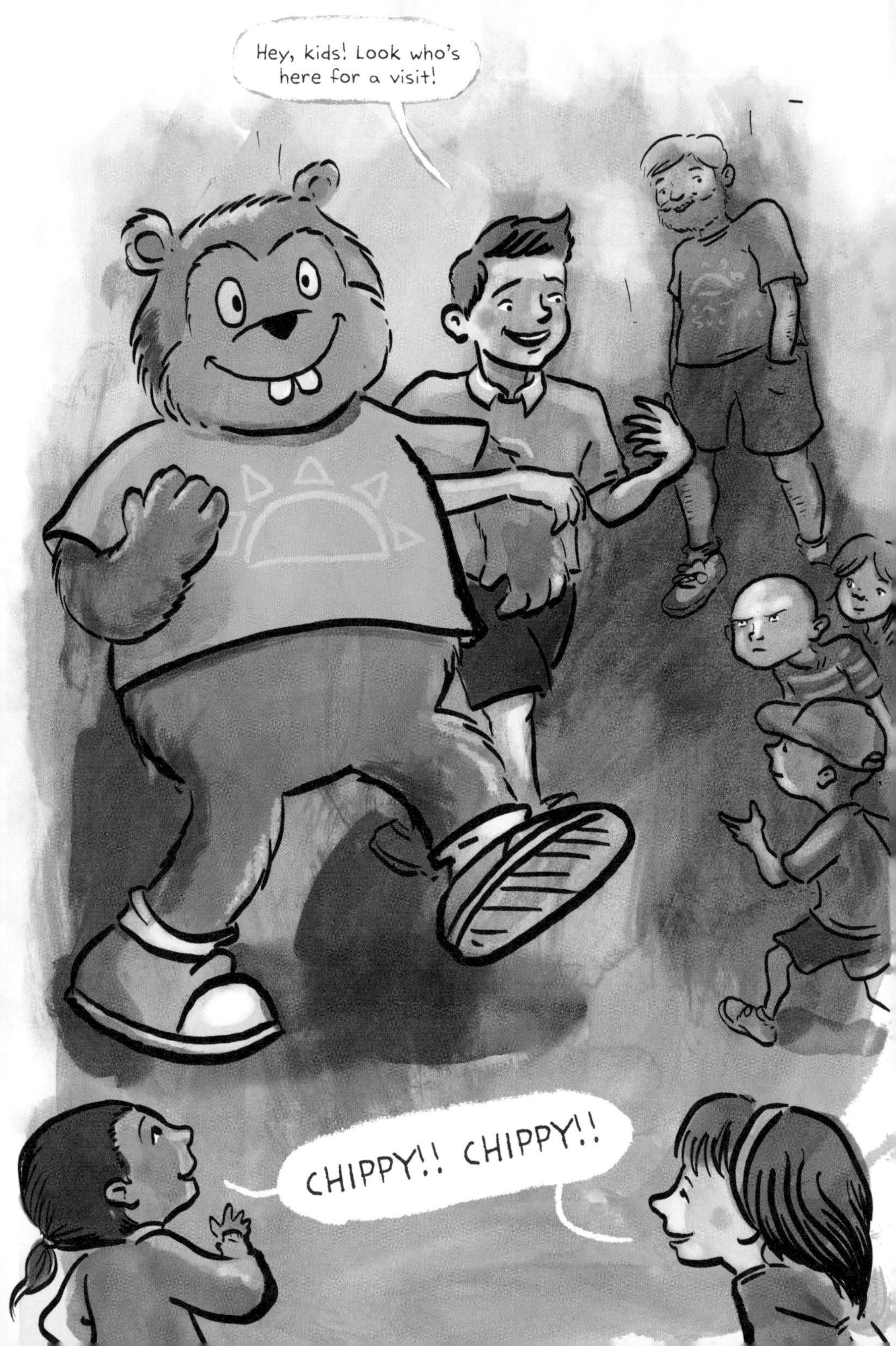
Hey, kids! Look who's here for a visit!
CHIPPY!! CHIPPY!!

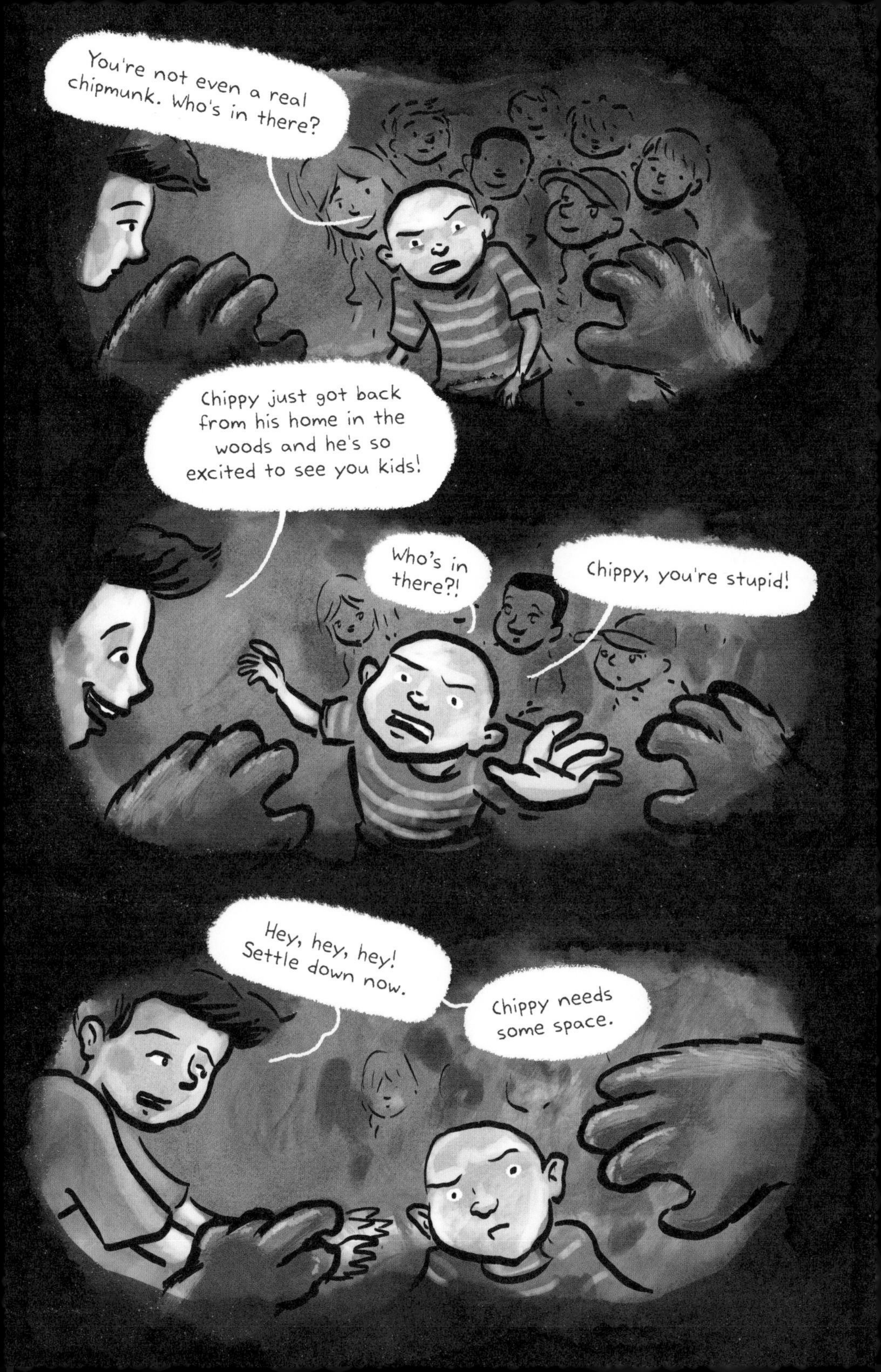
You're not even a real chipmunk. Who's in there?
Chippy just got back from his home in the woods and he's so excited to see you kids!
Who's in there?!
Chippy, you're stupid!
Hey, hey, hey! Settle down now.
Chippy needs some space.

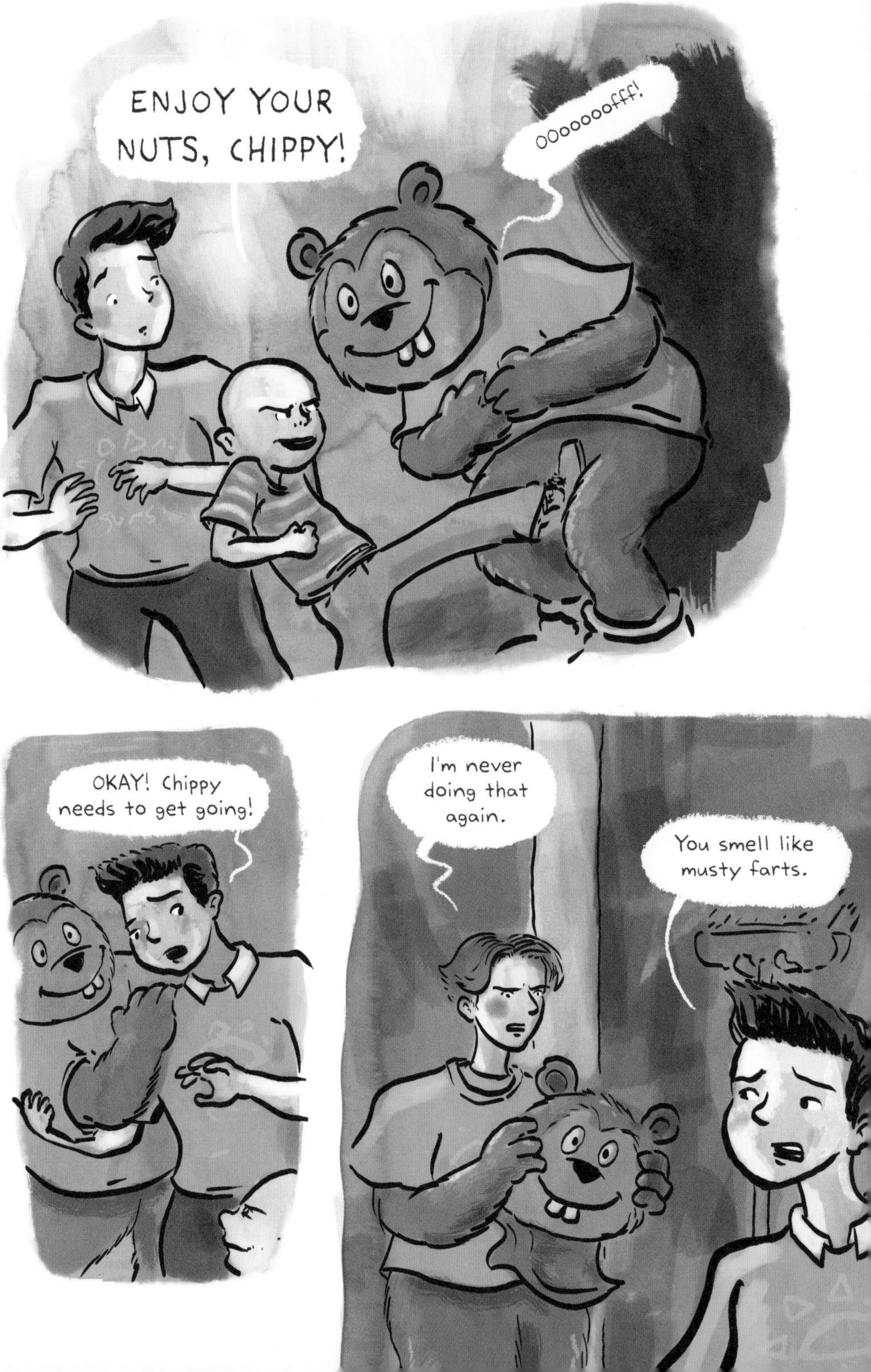
ENJOY YOUR NUTS, CHIPPY!
OOooooofff!
OKAY! Chippy needs to get going!
I'm never doing that again.
You smell like musty farts.

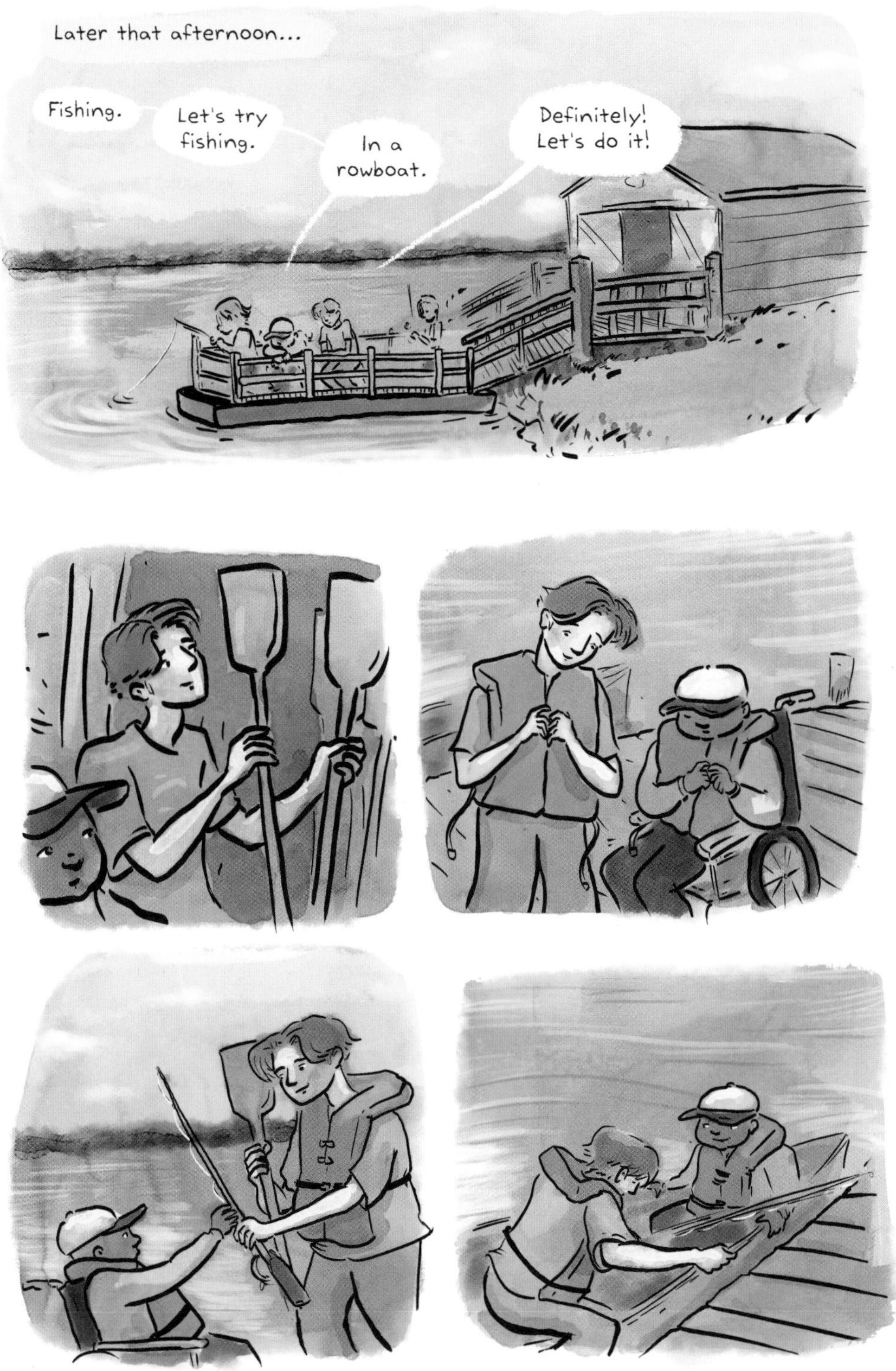
Later that afternoon...
Fishing.
Let's try fishing.
In a rowboat.
Definitely! Let's do it!

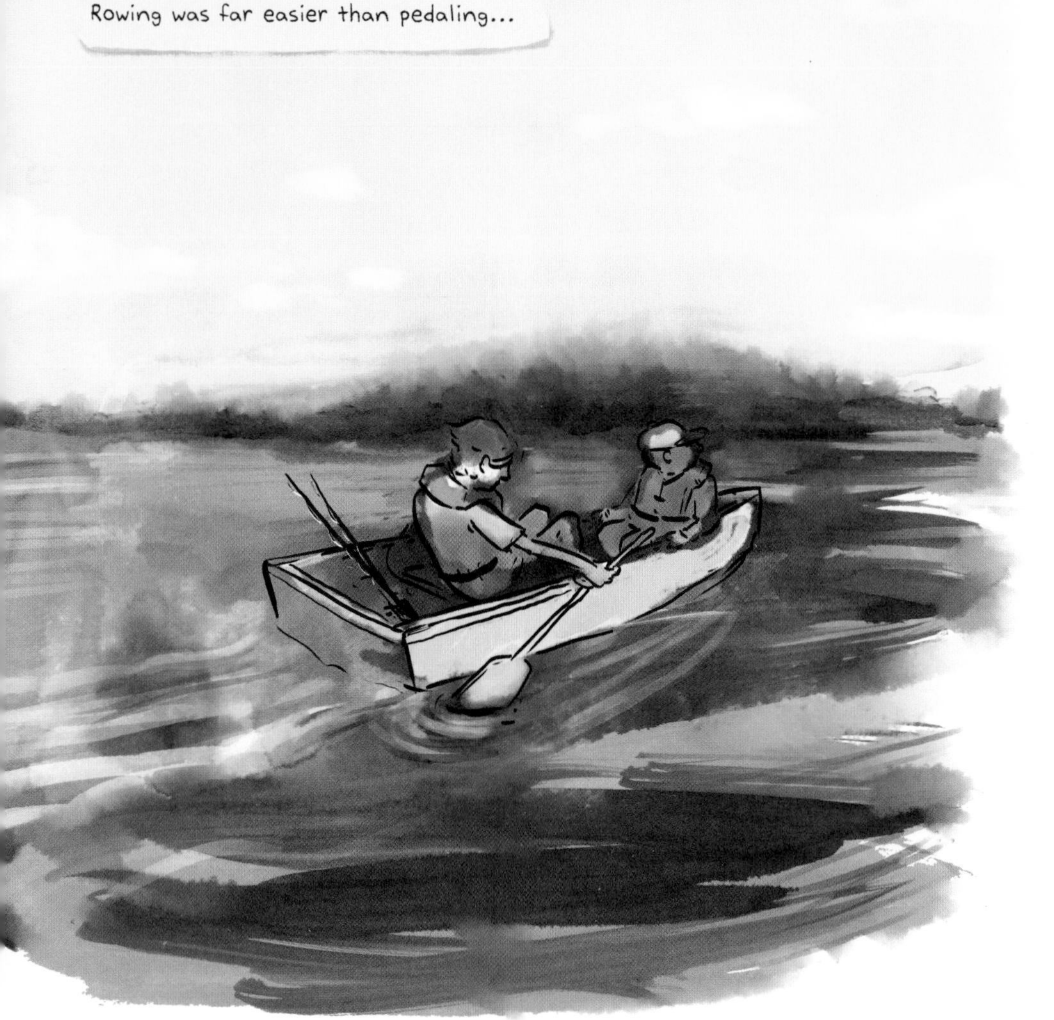
Rowing was far easier than pedaling...

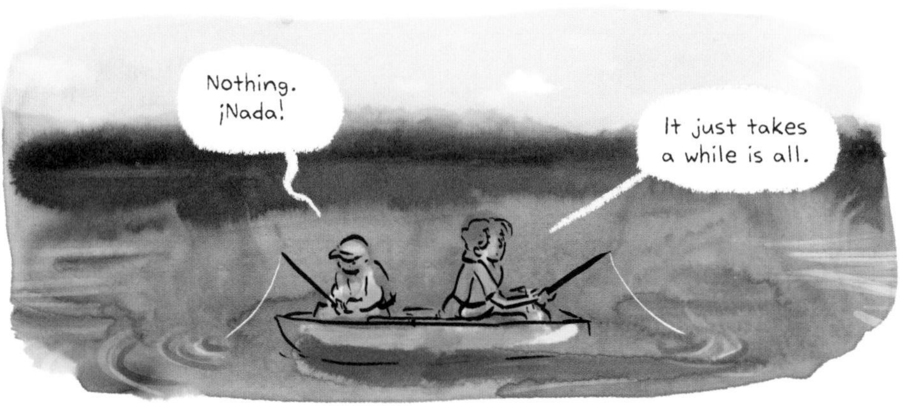
Nothing.
¡Nada!
It just takes
a while is all.

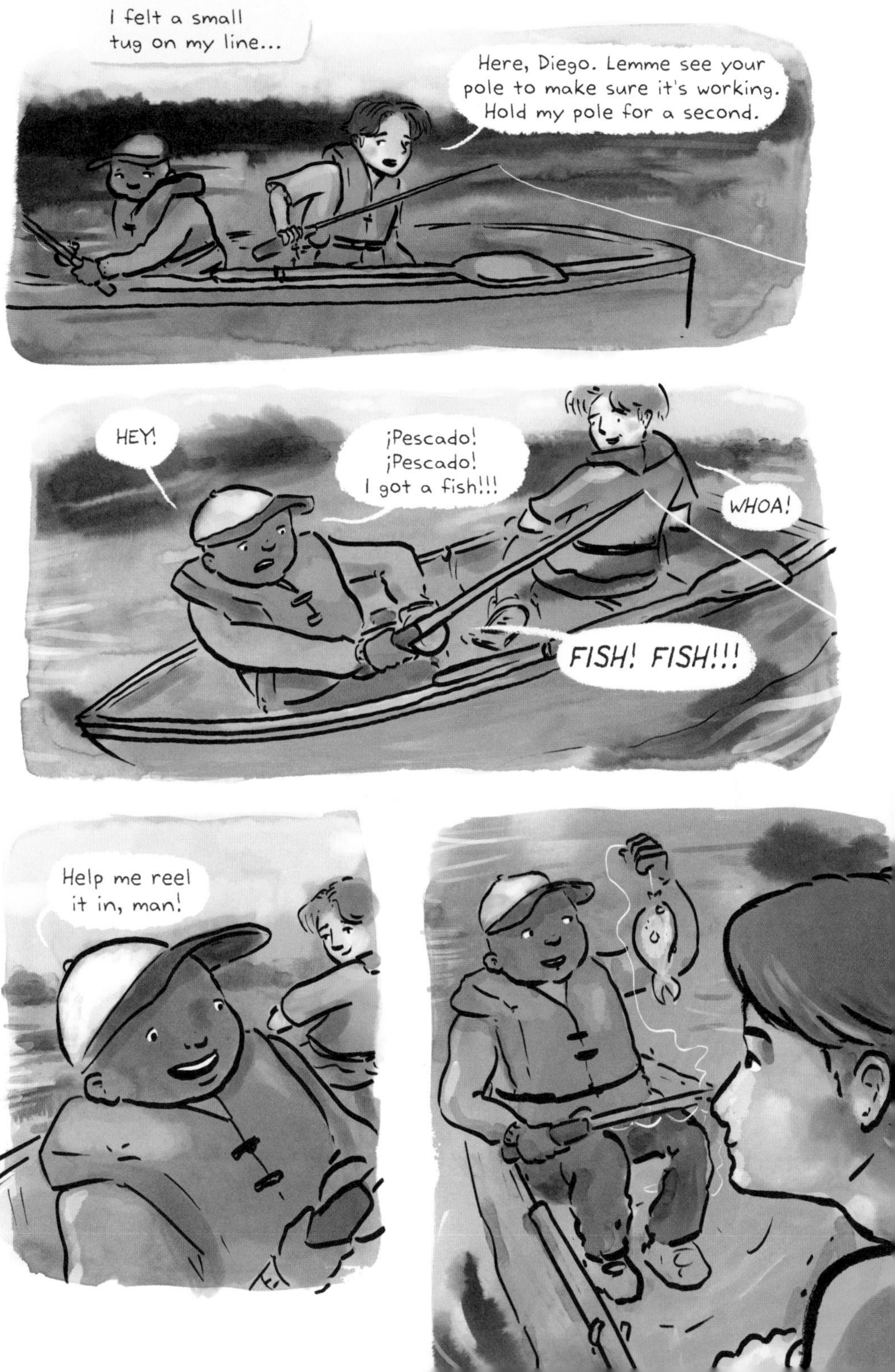
I felt a small tug on my line...
Here, Diego. Lemme see your pole to make sure it's working. Hold my pole for a second.
HEY!
¡Pescado! ¡Pescado! I got a fish!!!
WHOA!
FISH! FISH!!!
Help me reel it in, man!

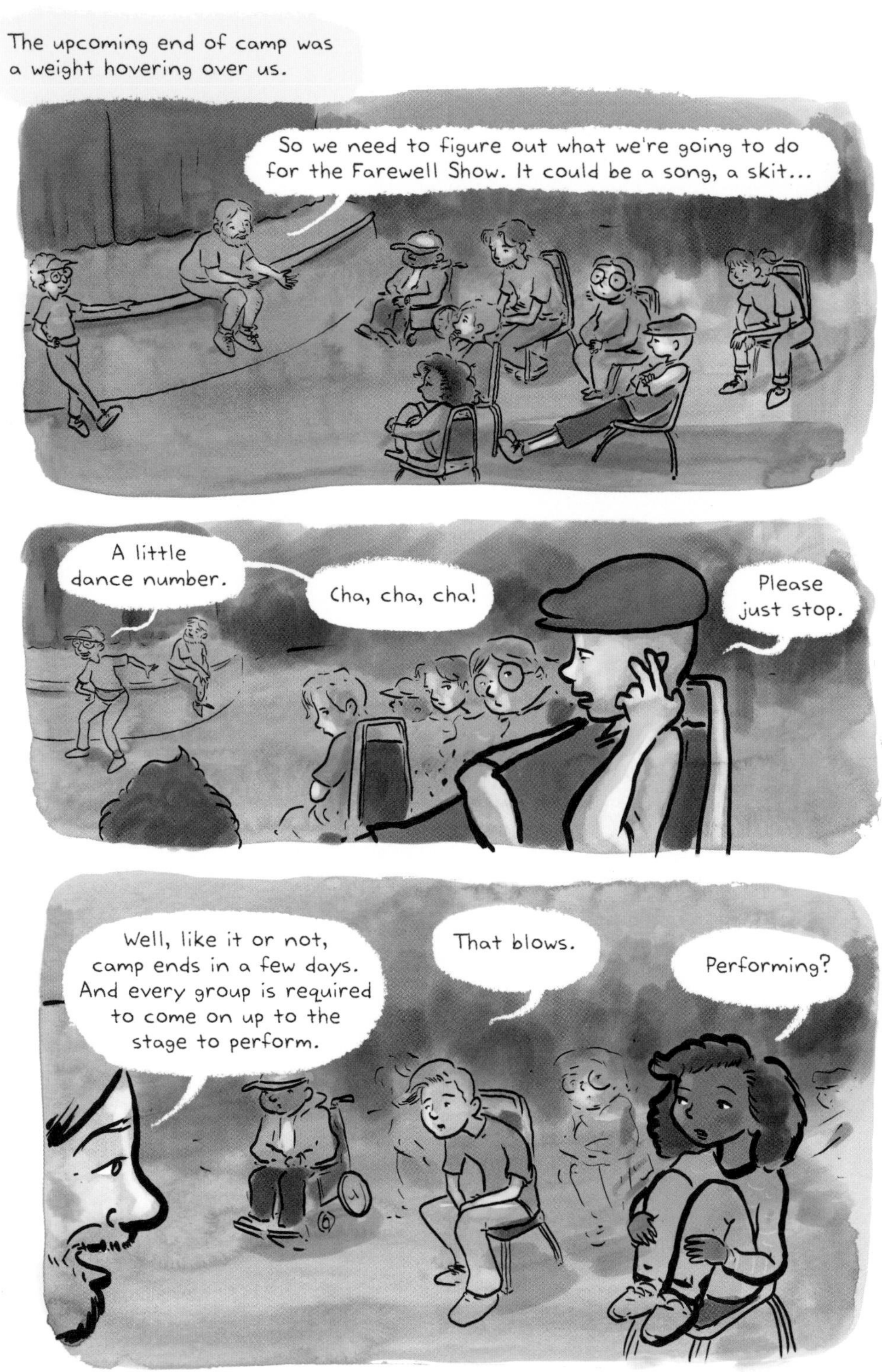
The upcoming end of camp was a weight hovering over us.
So we need to figure out what we're going to do for the Farewell Show. It could be a song, a skit...
A little dance number.
Cha, cha, cha!
Please just stop.
Well, like it or not, camp ends in a few days. And every group is required to come on up to the stage to perform.
That blows.
Performing?

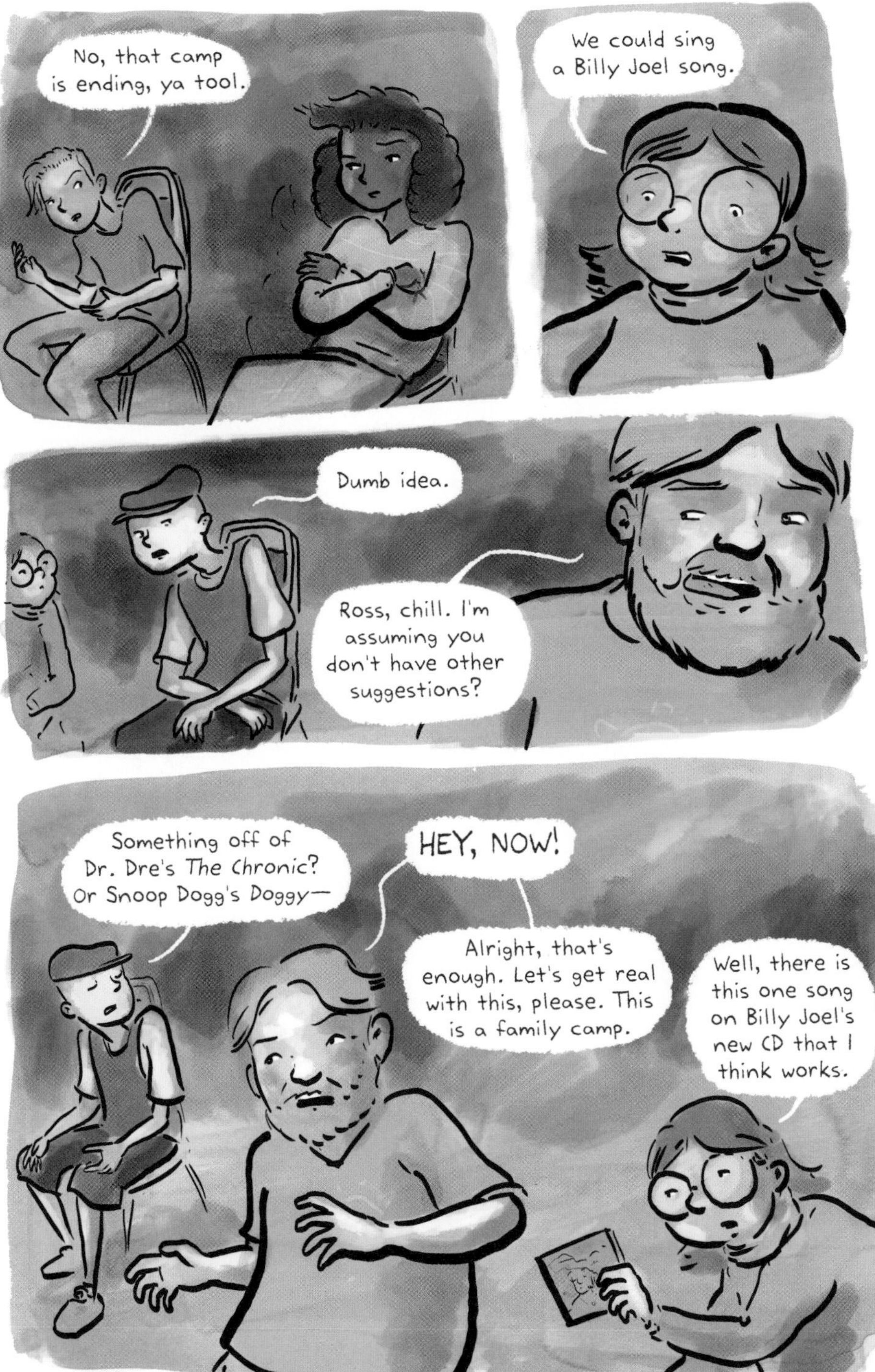
No, that camp is ending, ya tool.
We could sing a Billy Joel song.
Dumb idea.
Ross, chill. I'm assuming you don't have other suggestions?
Something off of Dr. Dre's The Chronic? Or Snoop Dogg's Doggy—
HEY, NOW!
Alright, that's enough. Let's get real with this, please. This is a family camp.
Well, there is this one song on Billy Joel's new CD that I think works.

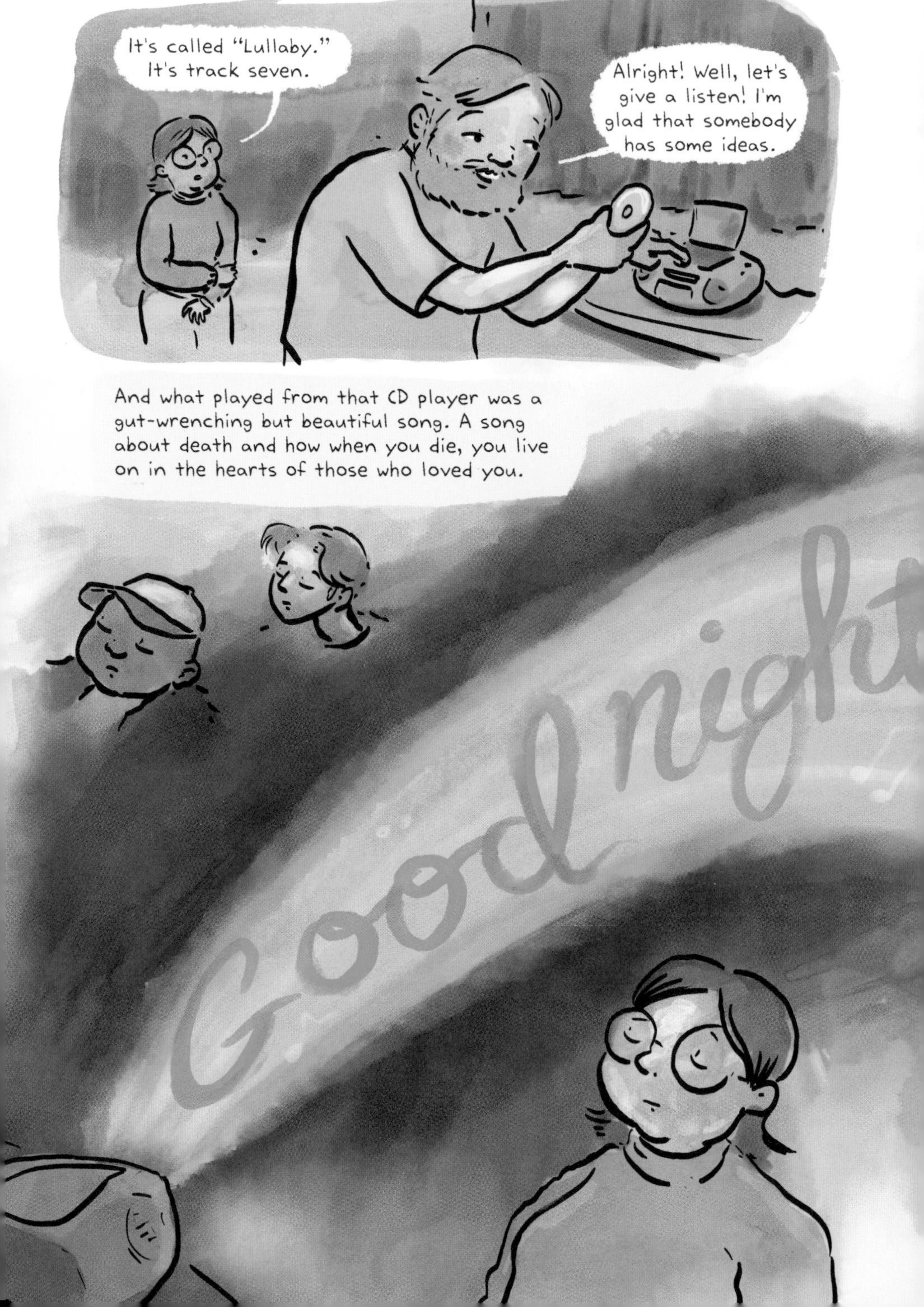
It's called "Lullaby." It's track seven.
Alright! Well, let's give a listen! I'm glad that somebody has some ideas.
And what played from that CD player was a gut-wrenching but beautiful song. A song about death and how when you die, you live on in the hearts of those who loved you.
Good night

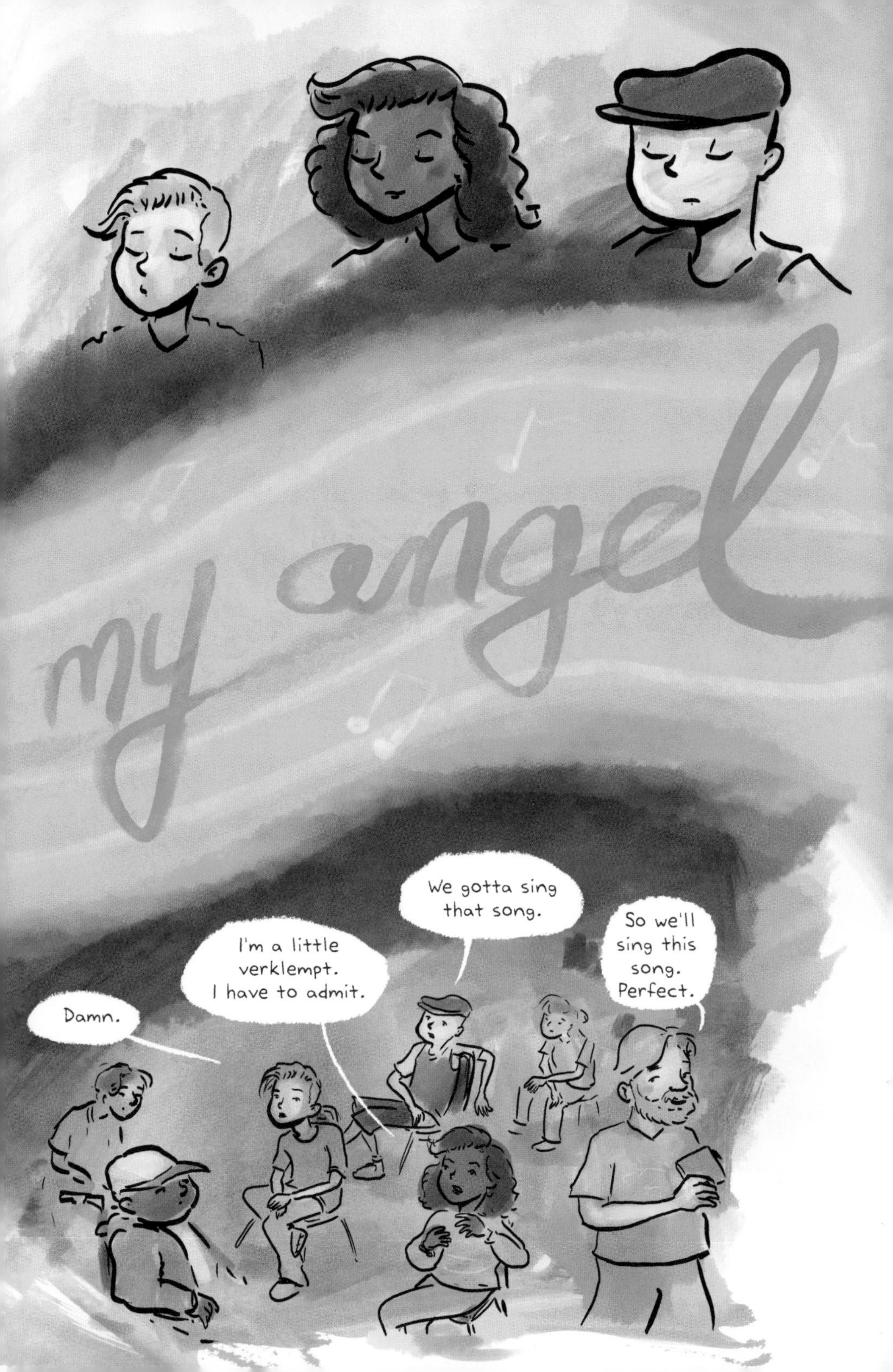
my angel
Damn.
I'm a little verklempt. I have to admit.
We gotta sing that song.
So we'll sing this song. Perfect.

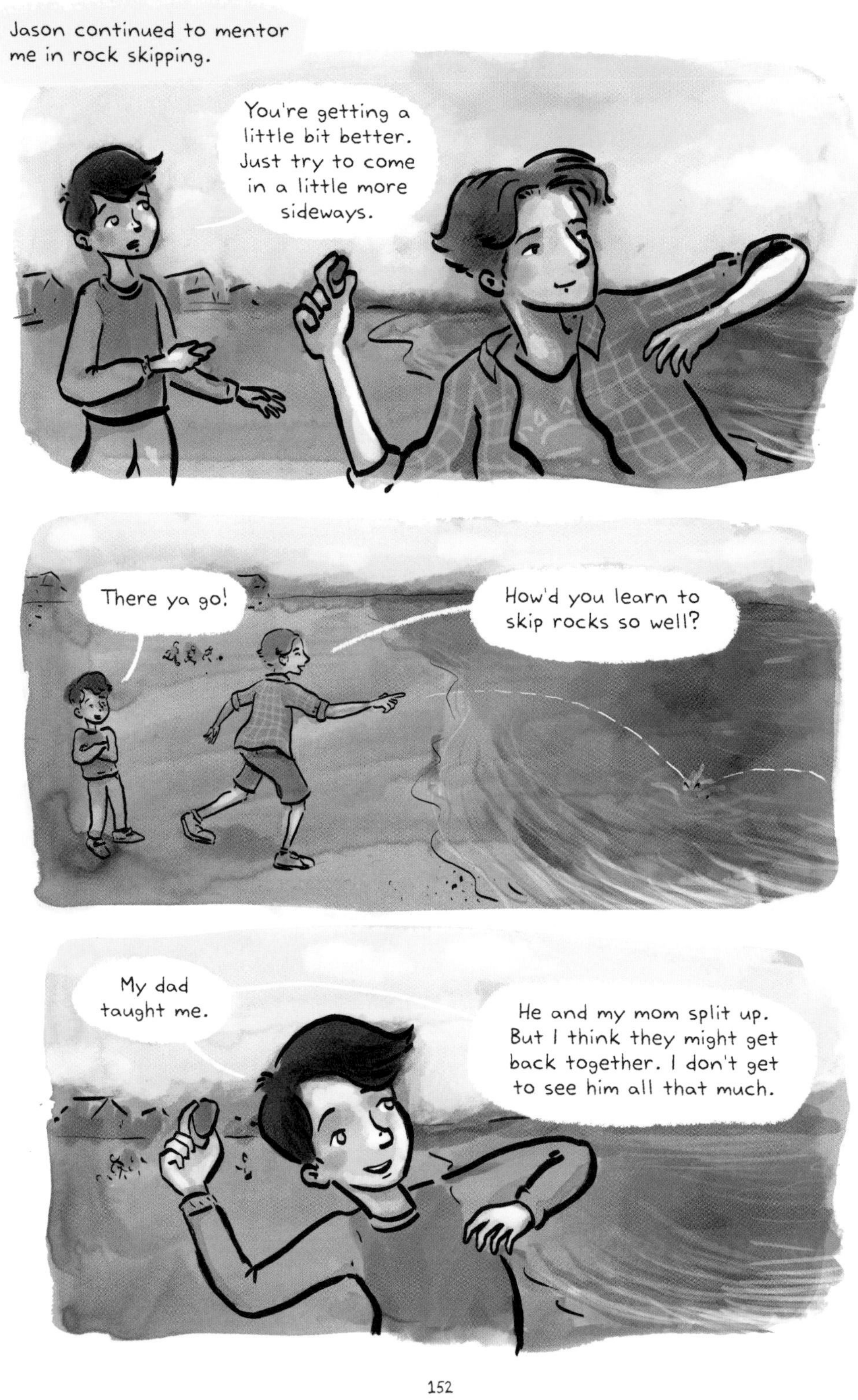
Jason continued to mentor me in rock skipping.
You're getting a little bit better. Just try to come in a little more sideways.
There ya go!
How'd you learn to skip rocks so well?
My dad taught me.
He and my mom split up. But I think they might get back together. I don't get to see him all that much.

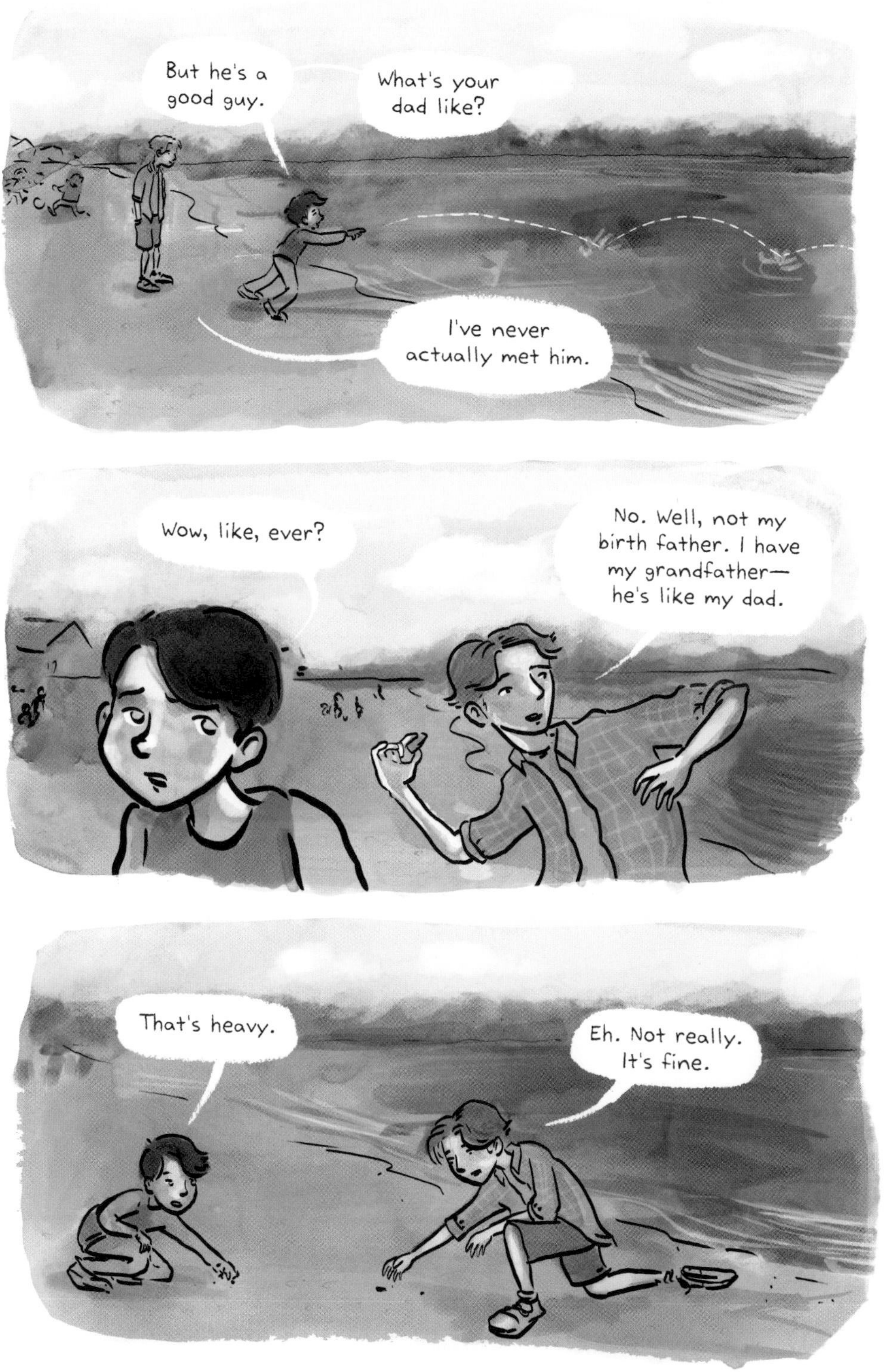
But he's a good guy.
What's your dad like?
I've never actually met him.
Wow, like, ever?
No. Well, not my birth father. I have my grandfather—he's like my dad.
That's heavy.
Eh. Not really. It's fine.

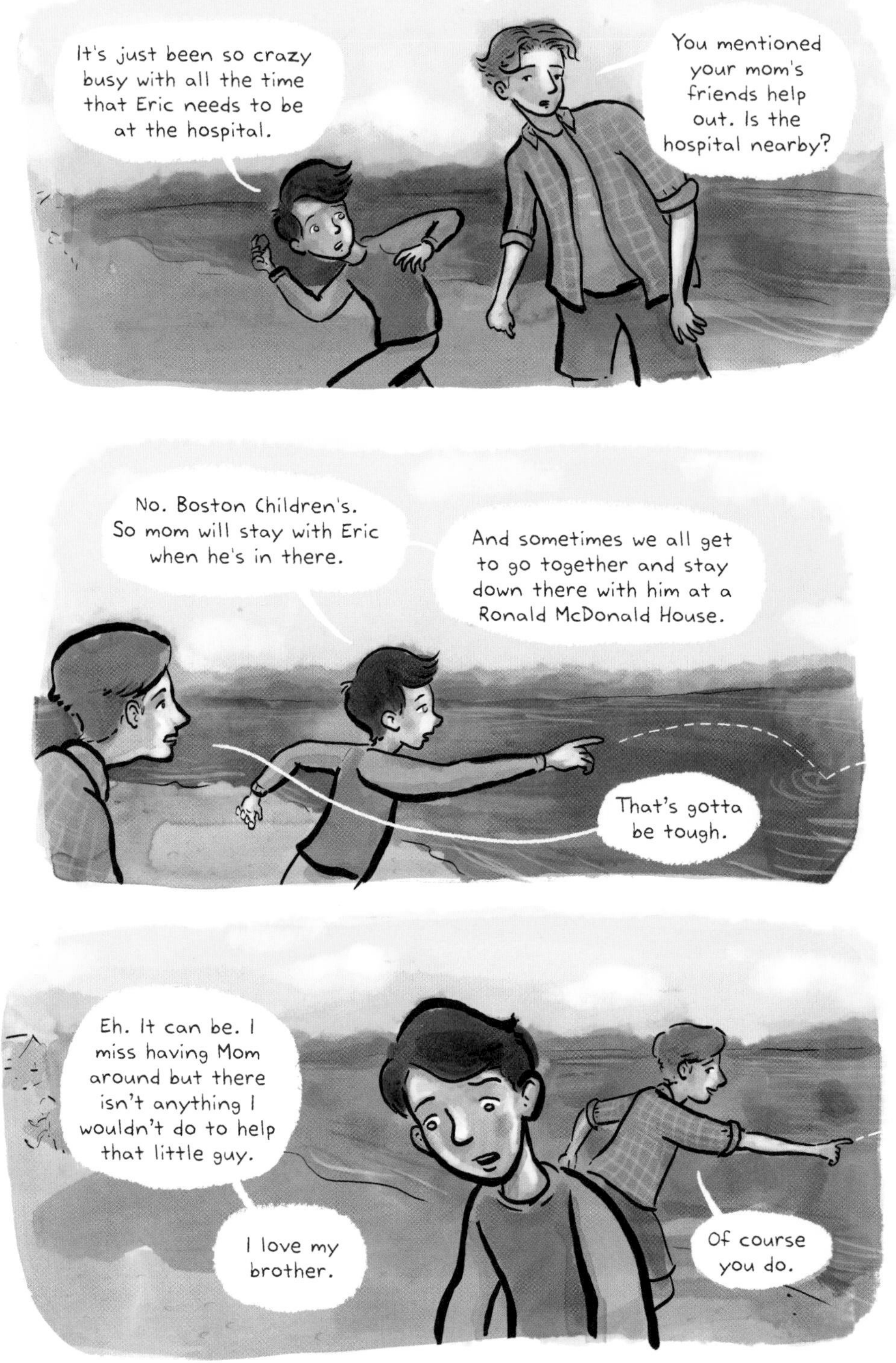
It's just been so crazy busy with all the time that Eric needs to be at the hospital.
You mentioned your mom's friends help out. Is the hospital nearby?
No. Boston Children's. So mom will stay with Eric when he's in there.
And sometimes we all get to go together and stay down there with him at a Ronald McDonald House.
That's gotta be tough.
Eh. It can be. I miss having Mom around but there isn't anything I wouldn't do to help that little guy.
I love my brother.
Of course you do.

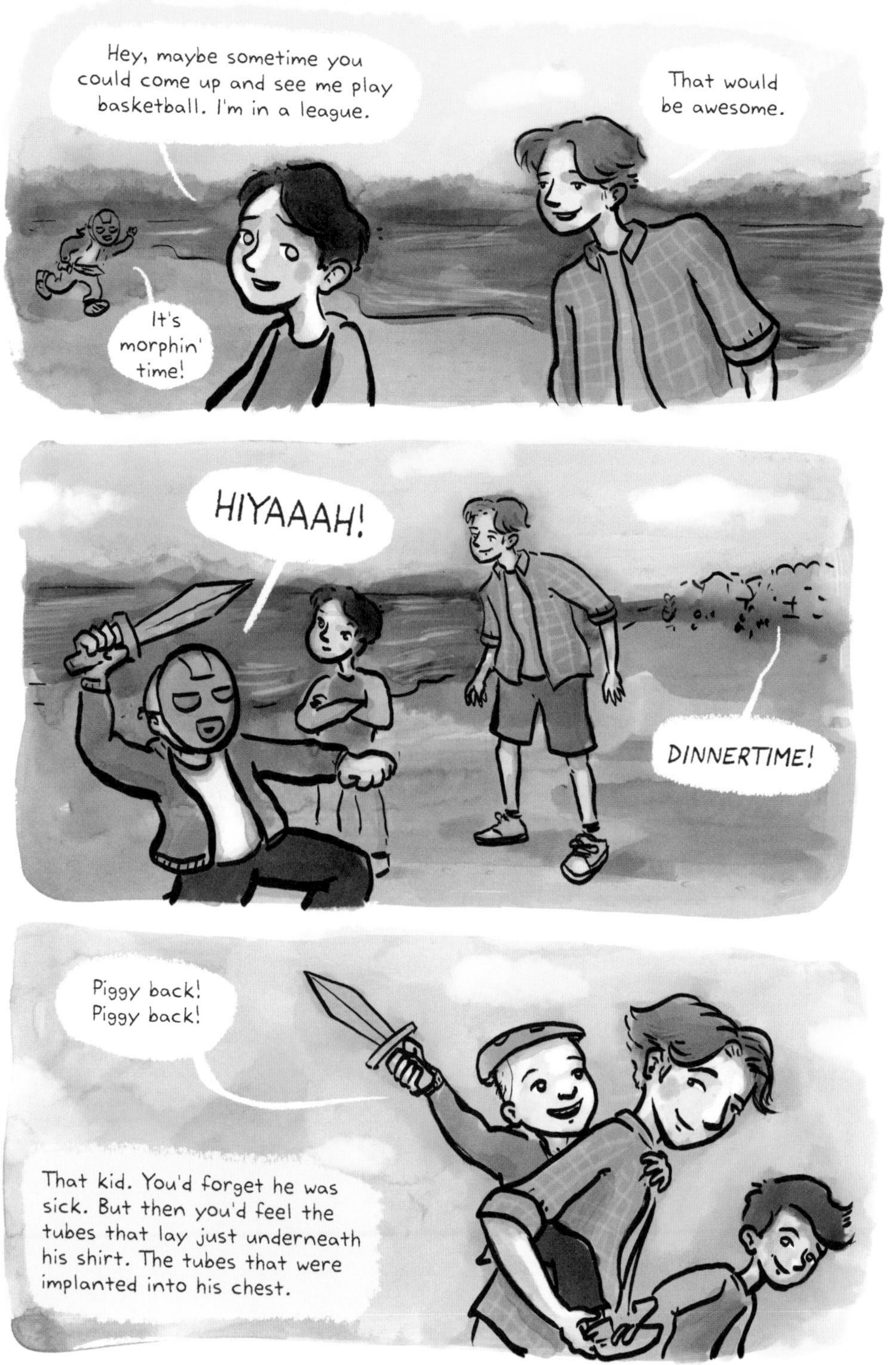
Hey, maybe sometime you could come up and see me play basketball. I'm in a league.
It's morphin' time!
That would be awesome.
HIYAAAH!
DINNERTIME!
Piggy back! Piggy back!
That kid. You'd forget he was sick. But then you'd feel the tubes that lay just underneath his shirt. The tubes that were implanted into his chest.

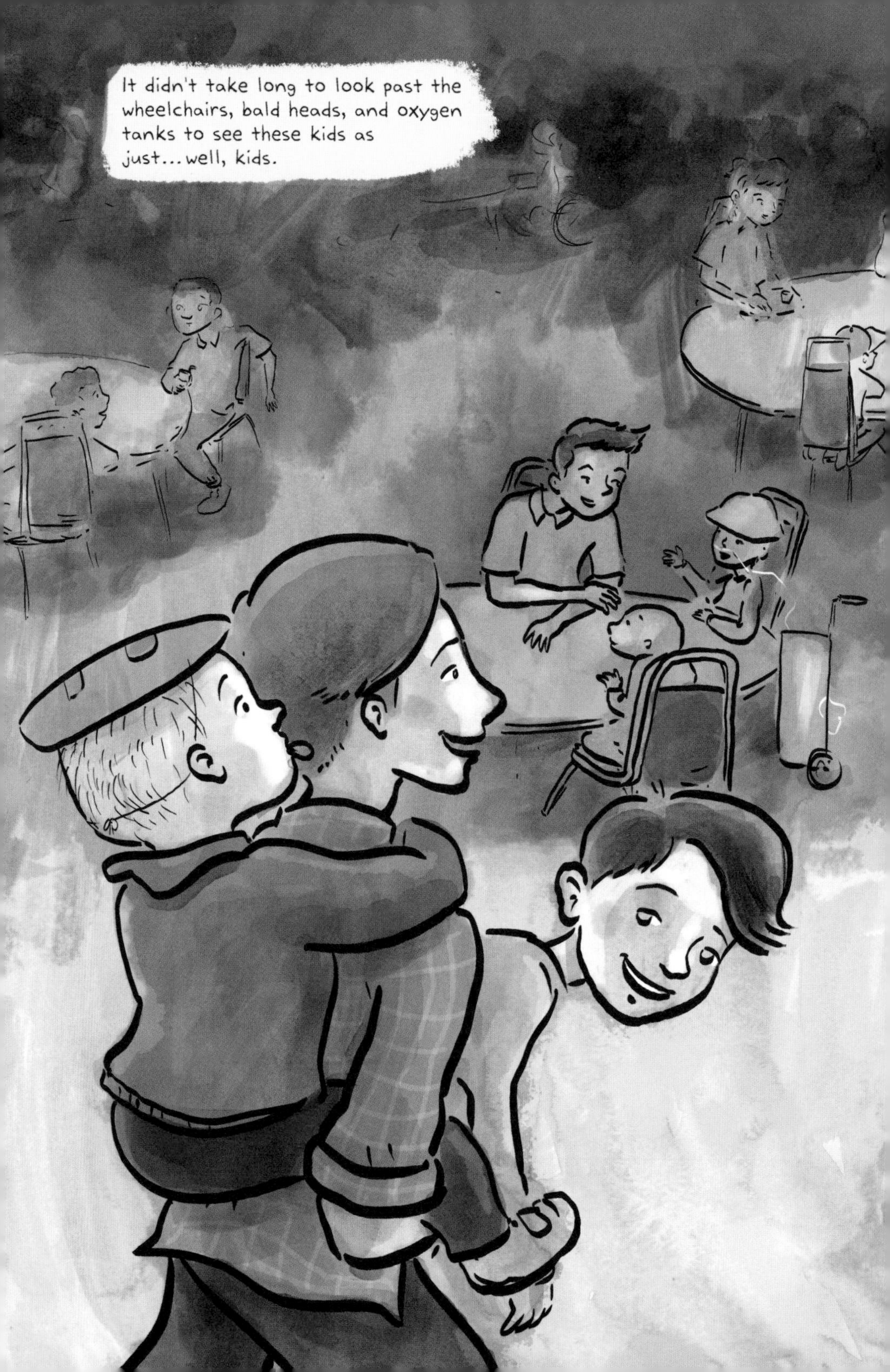
It didn't take long to look past the wheelchairs, bald heads, and oxygen tanks to see these kids as just... well, kids.

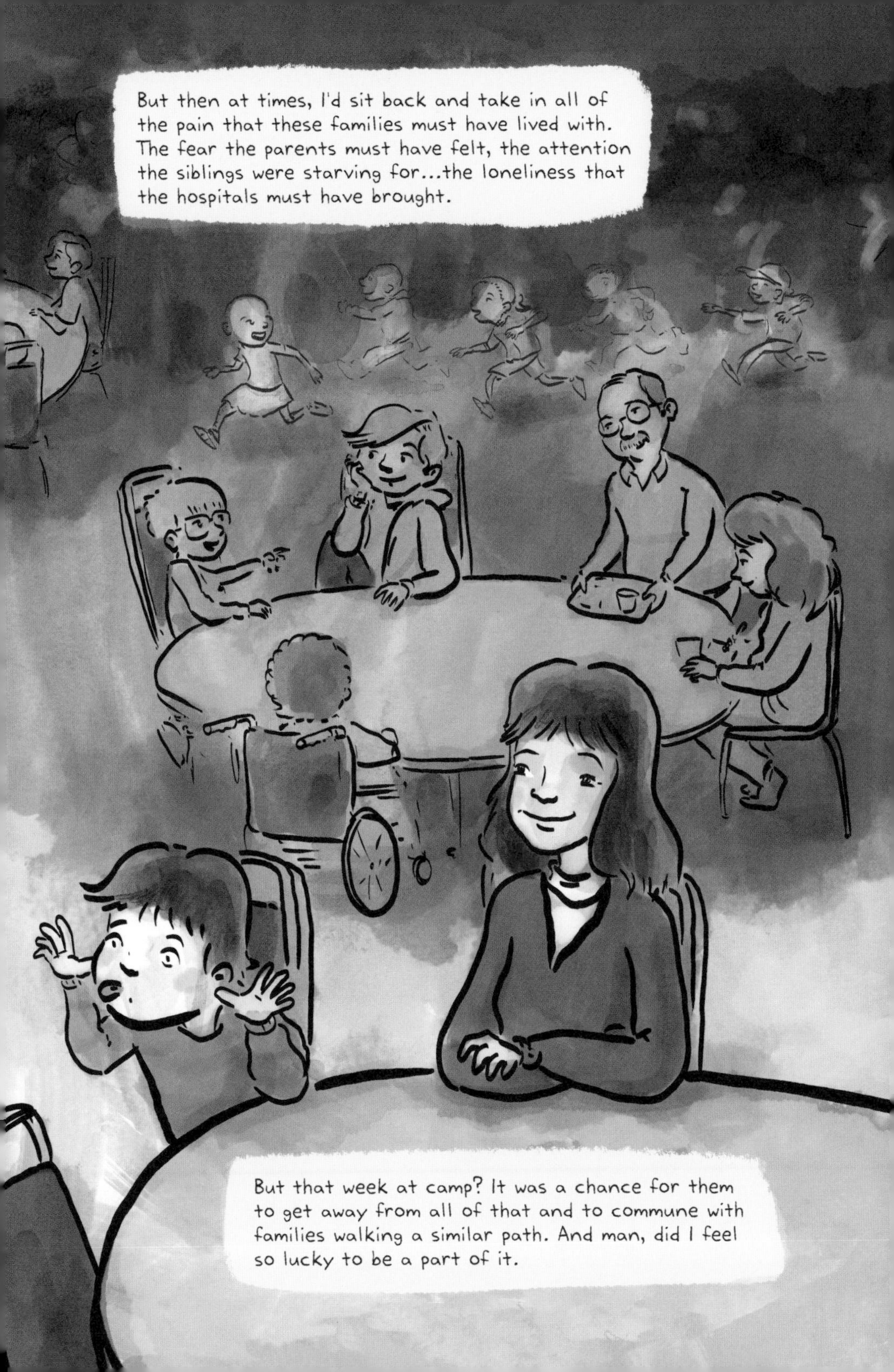
But then at times, I'd sit back and take in all of the pain that these families must have lived with. The fear the parents must have felt, the attention the siblings were starving for...the loneliness that the hospitals must have brought.
But that week at camp? It was a chance for them to get away from all of that and to commune with families walking a similar path. And man, did I feel so lucky to be a part of it.

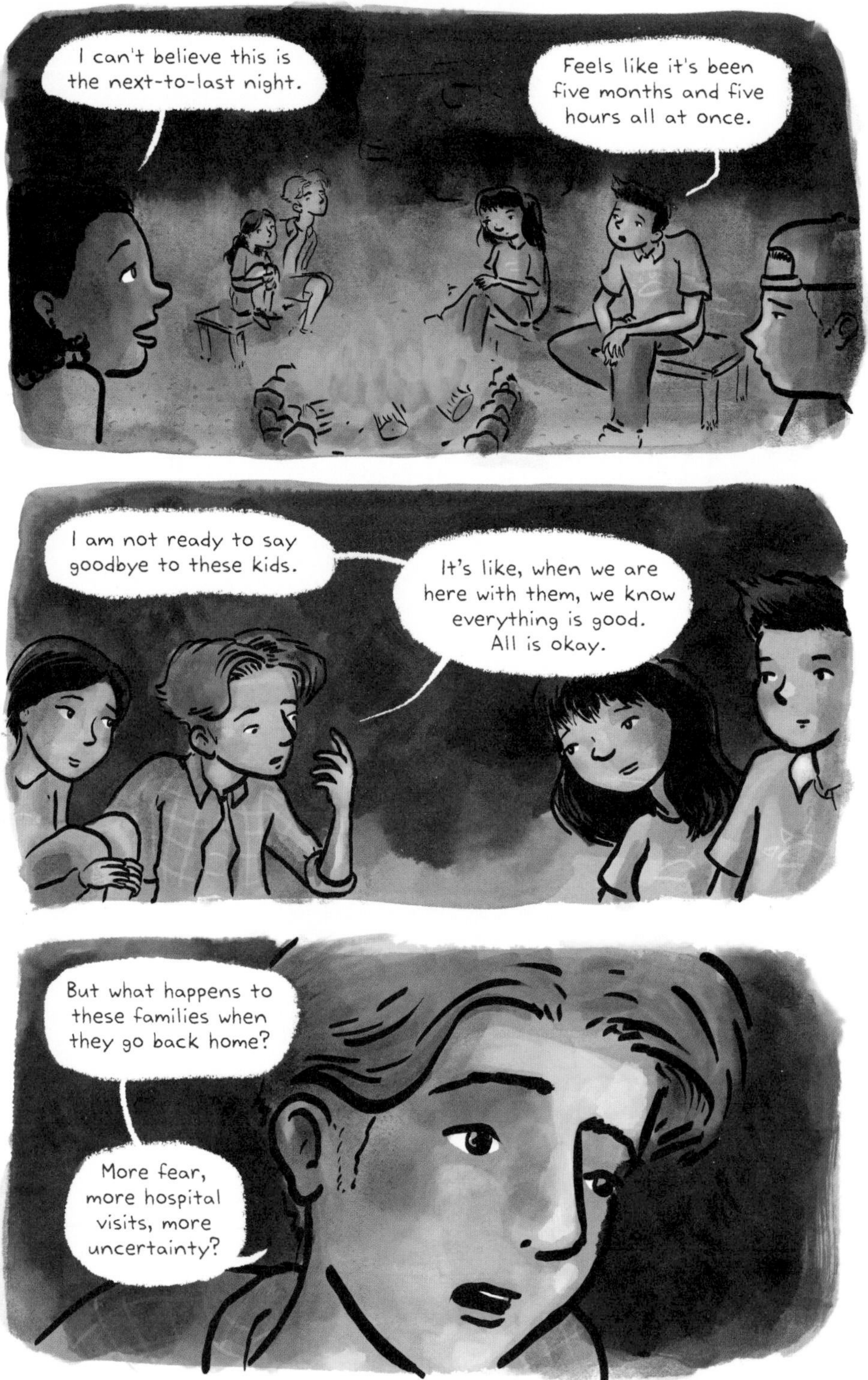
I can't believe this is the next-to-last night.
Feels like it's been five months and five hours all at once.
I am not ready to say goodbye to these kids.
It's like, when we are here with them, we know everything is good. All is okay.
But what happens to these families when they go back home?
More fear, more hospital visits, more uncertainty?

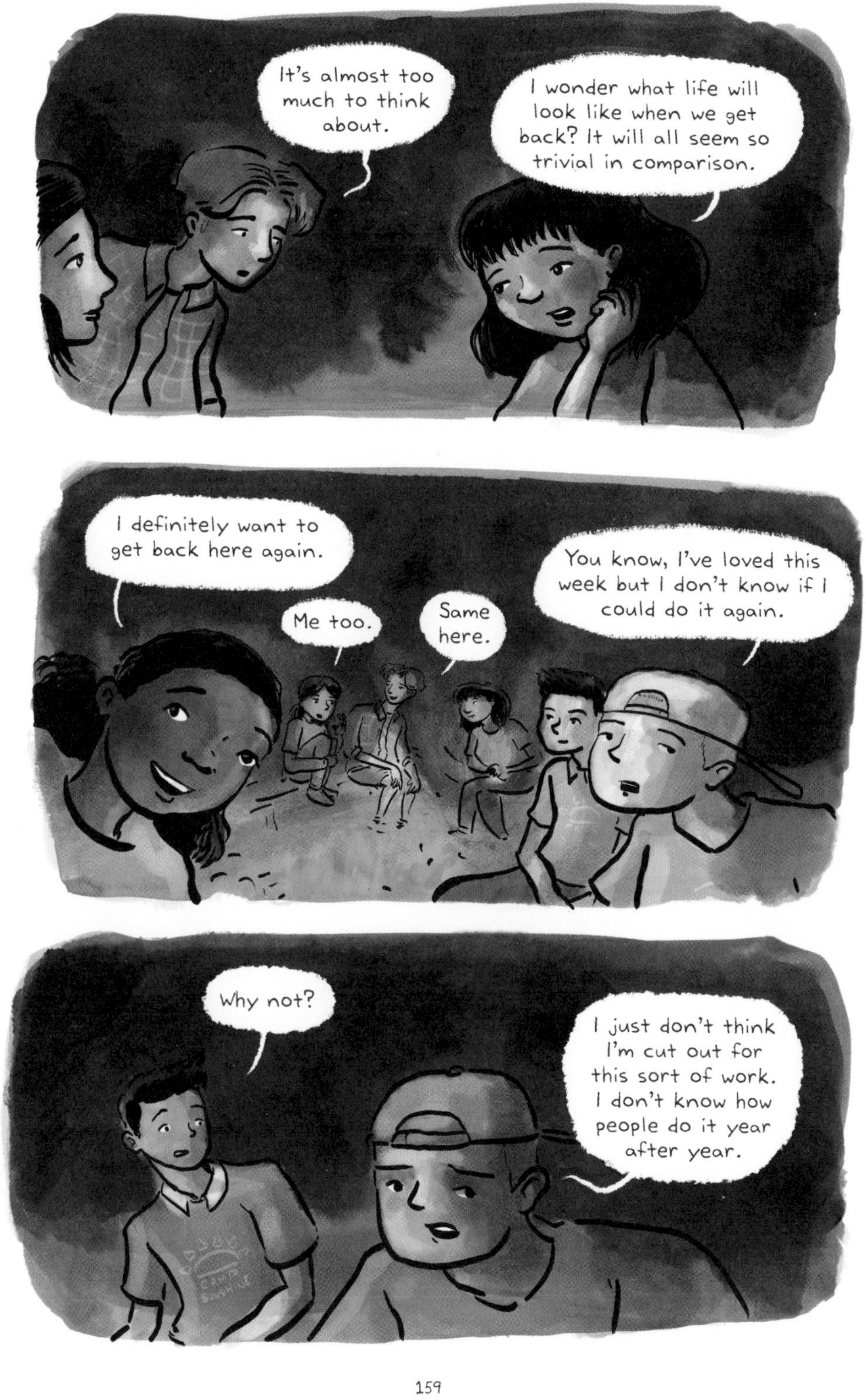
It's almost too much to think about.
I wonder what life will look like when we get back? It will all seem so trivial in comparison.
I definitely want to get back here again.
Me too.
Same here.
You know, I've loved this week but I don't know if I could do it again.
Why not?
I just don't think I'm cut out for this sort of work. I don't know how people do it year after year.

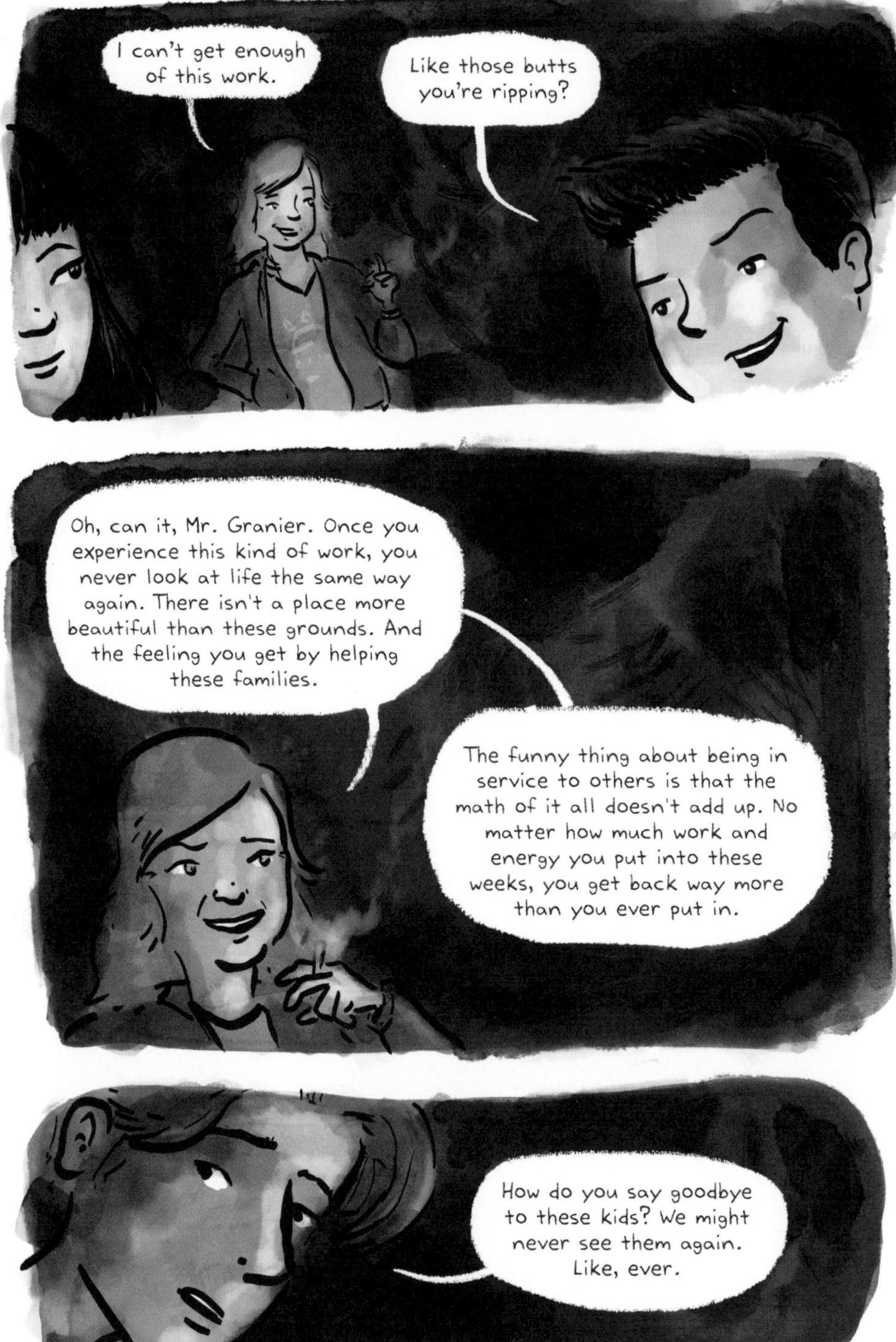
I can't get enough of this work.
Like those butts you're ripping?
Oh, can it, Mr. Granier. Once you experience this kind of work, you never look at life the same way again. There isn't a place more beautiful than these grounds. And the feeling you get by helping these families.
The funny thing about being in service to others is that the math of it all doesn't add up. No matter how much work and energy you put into these weeks, you get back way more than you ever put in.
How do you say goodbye to these kids? We might never see them again. Like, ever.

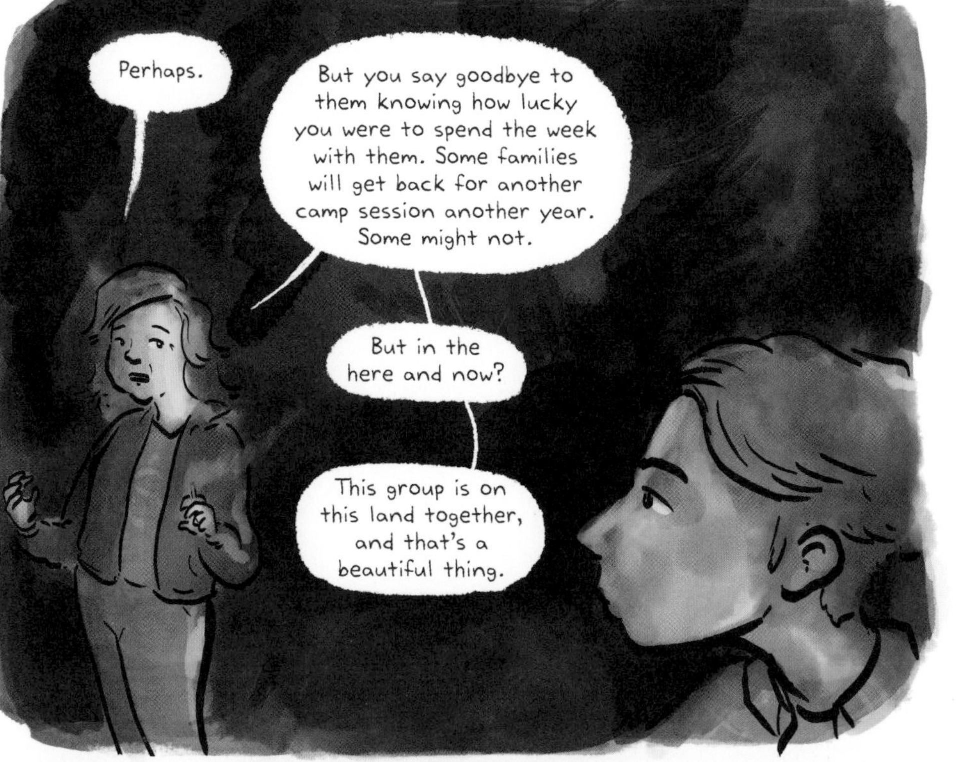
Perhaps.
But you say goodbye to them knowing how lucky you were to spend the week with them. Some families will get back for another camp session another year. Some might not.
But in the here and now?
This group is on this land together, and that's a beautiful thing.

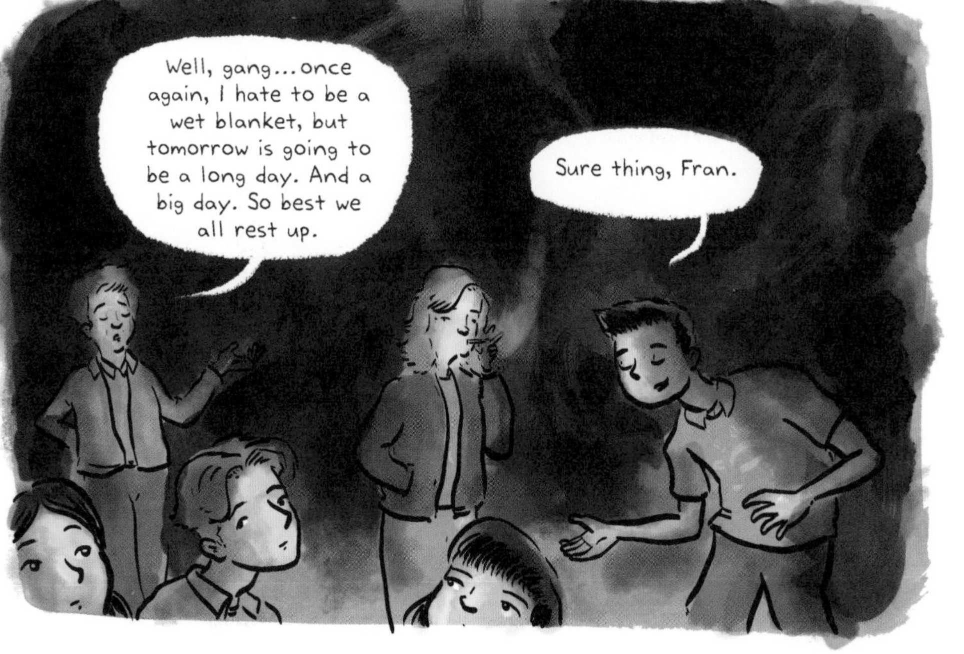
Well, gang...once again, I hate to be a wet blanket, but tomorrow is going to be a long day. And a big day. So best we all rest up.
Sure thing, Fran.

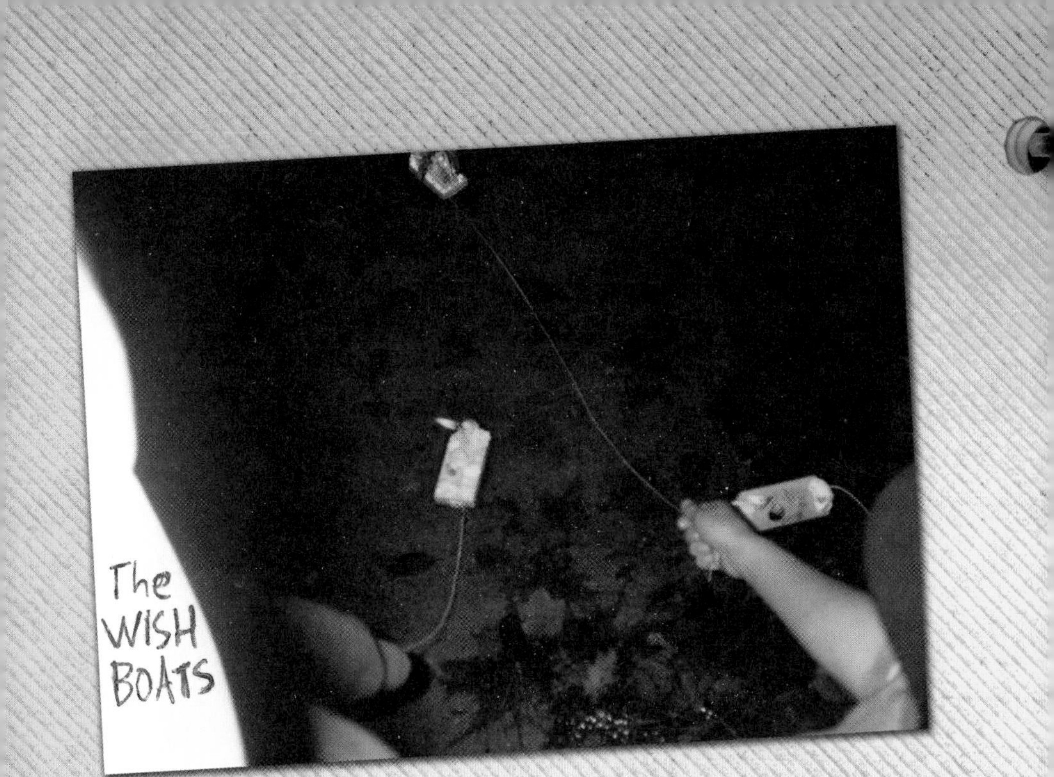
The WISH BOATS

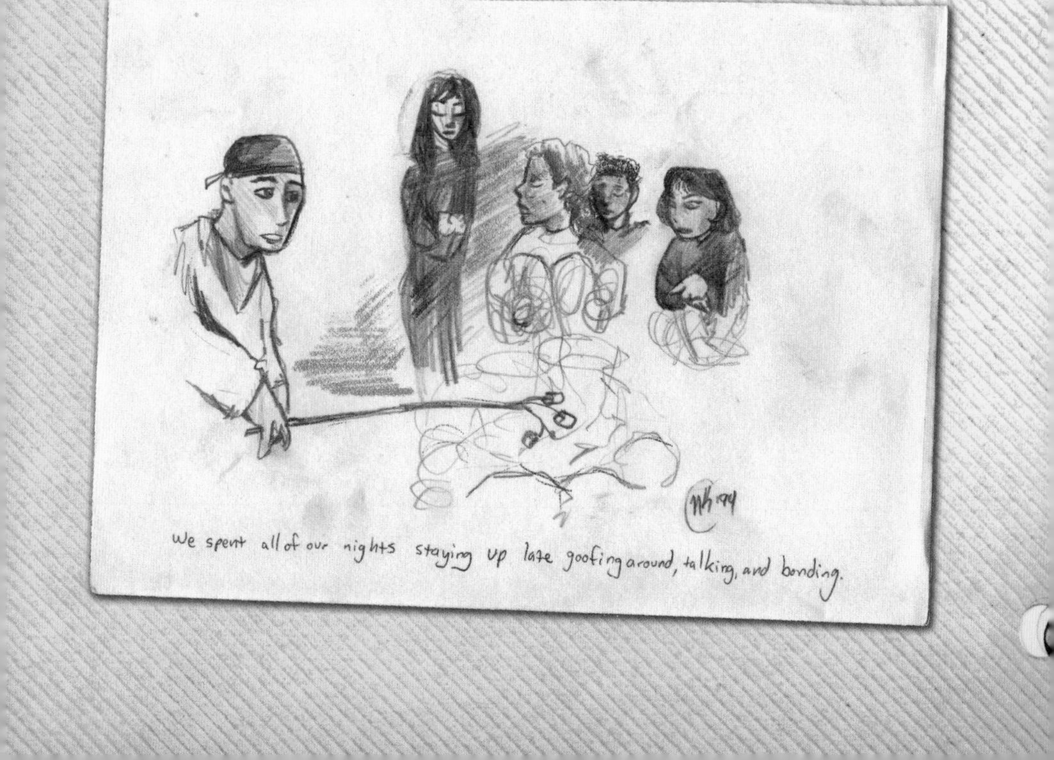
MK '94
we spent all of our nights staying up late goofing around, talking, and bonding.

CHAPTER 6
CURTAIN CALL

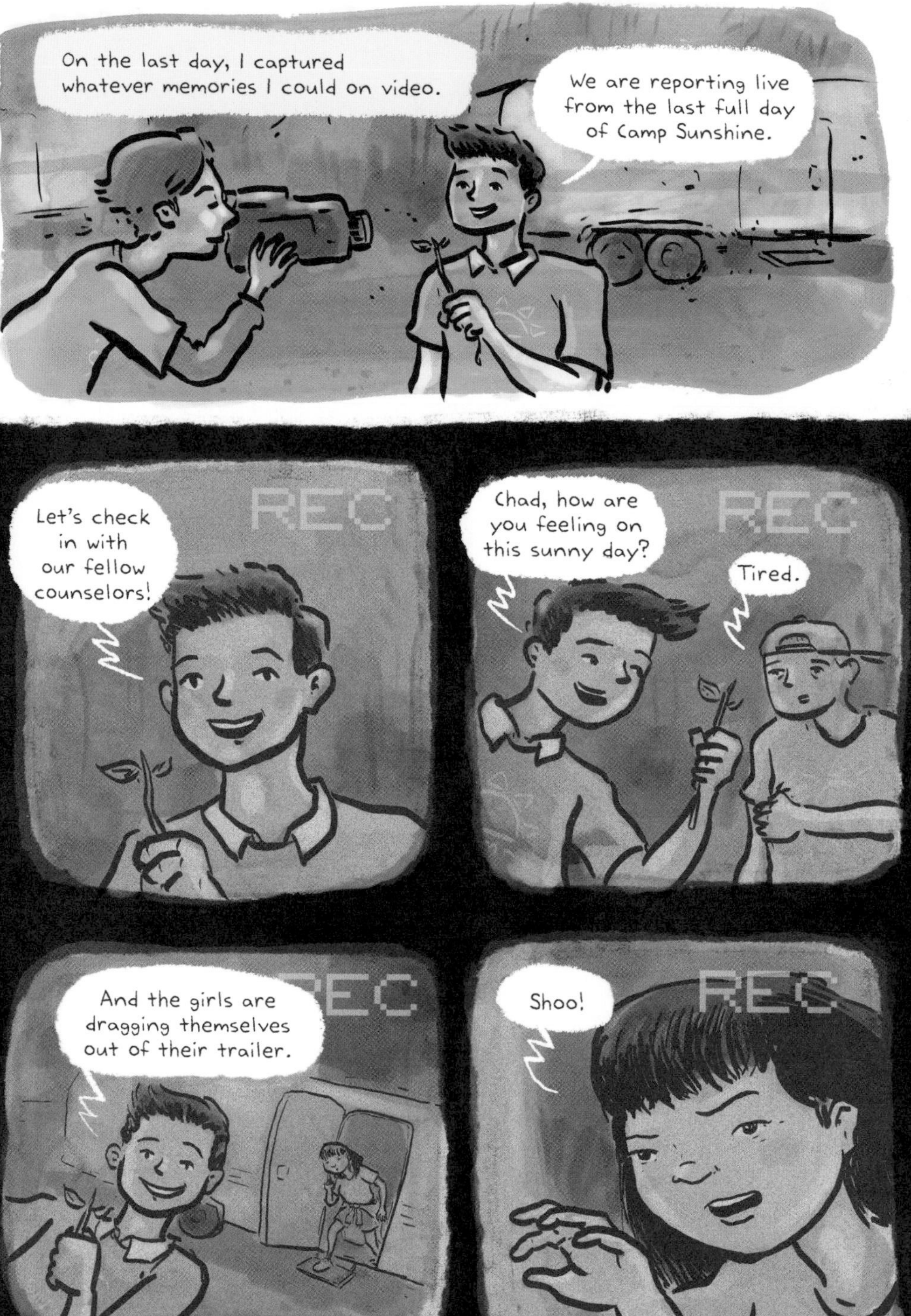
On the last day, I captured whatever memories I could on video.
We are reporting live from the last full day of Camp Sunshine.
REC
Let's check in with our fellow counselors!
REC
Chad, how are you feeling on this sunny day?
Tired.
REC
And the girls are dragging themselves out of their trailer.
REC
Shoo!

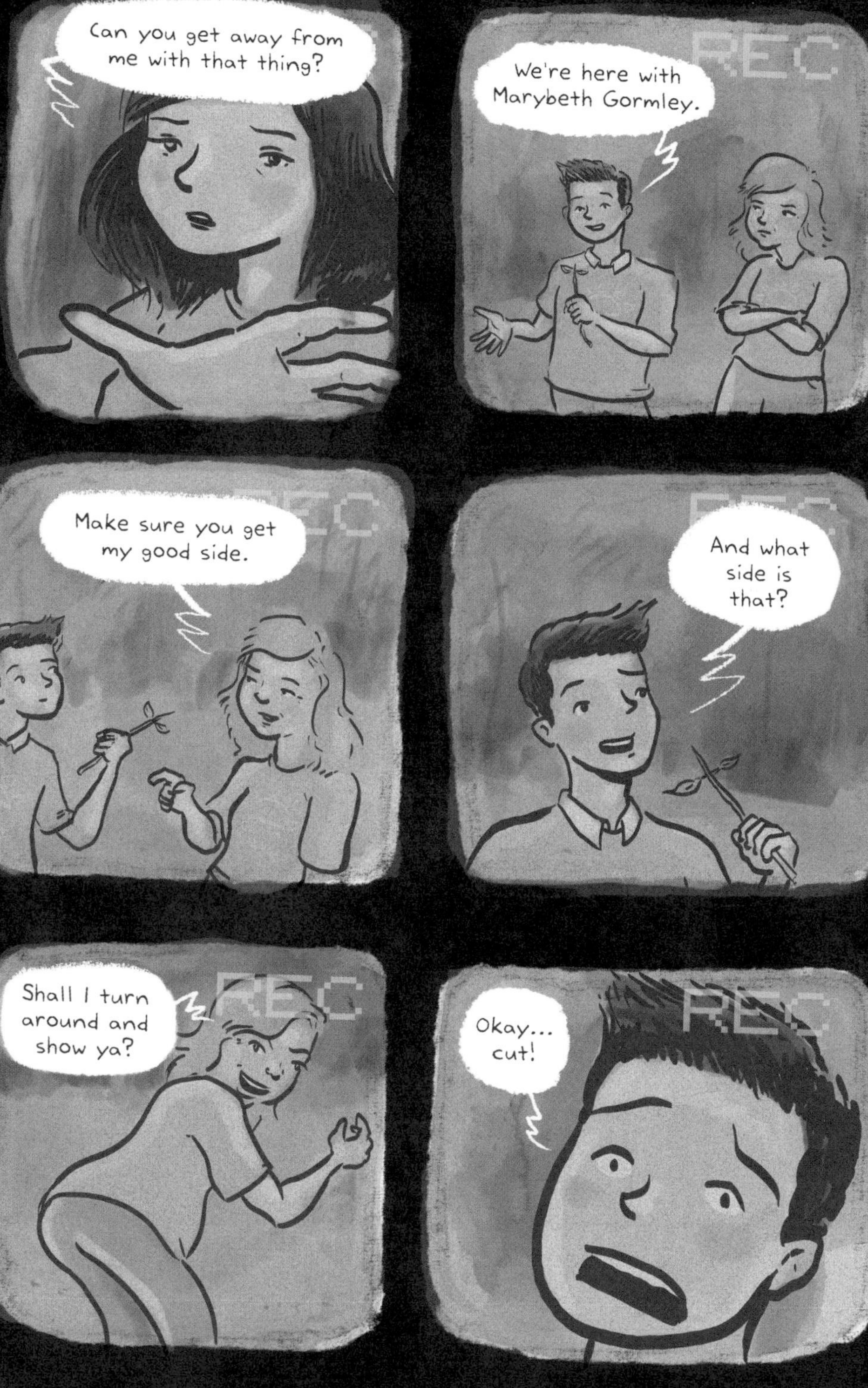
Can you get away from me with that thing?
REC
We're here with Marybeth Gormley.
REC
Make sure you get my good side.
REC
And what side is that?
REC
Shall I turn around and show ya?
REC
Okay... cut!

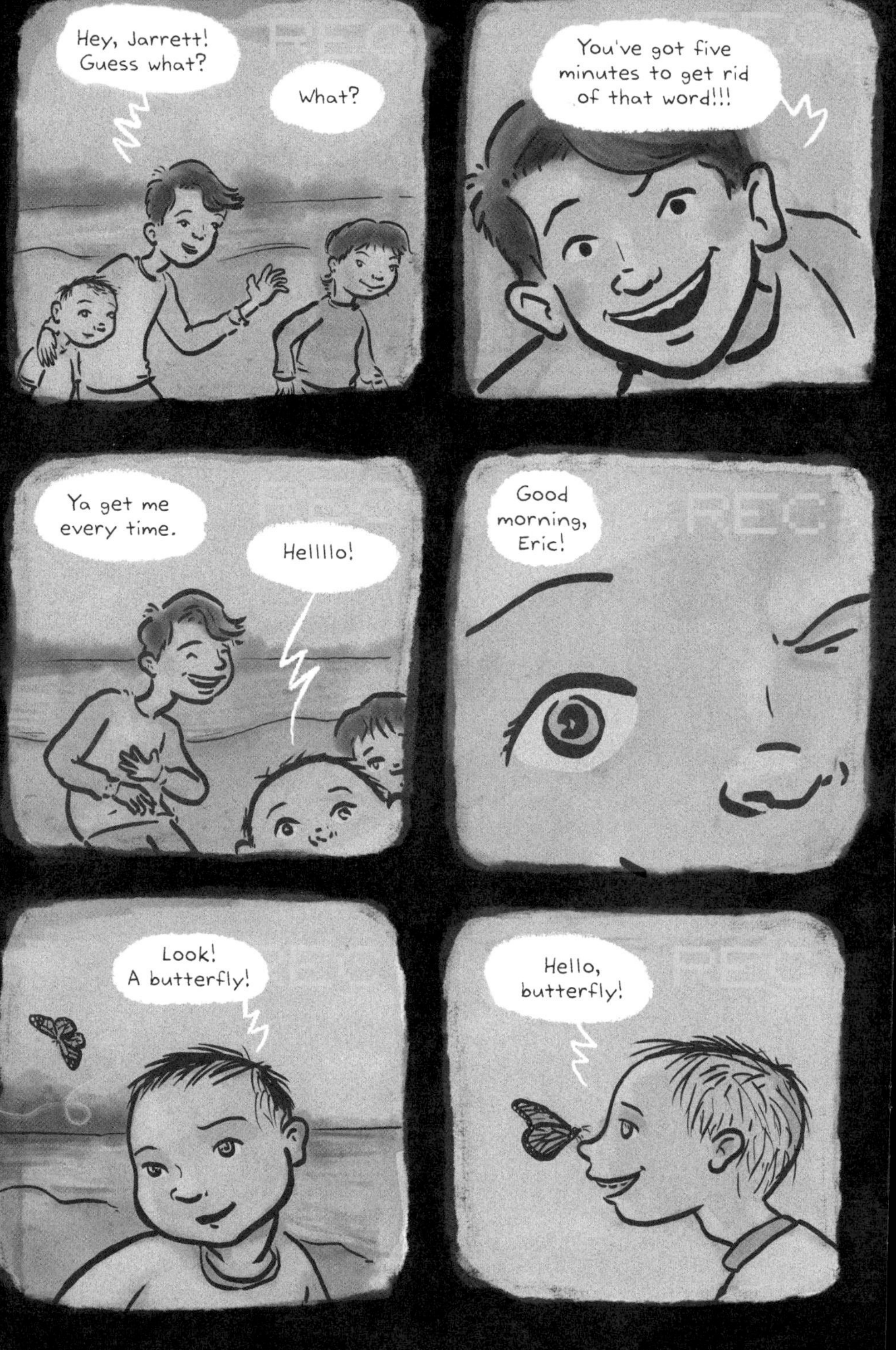
Hey, Jarrett! Guess what?
What?
You've got five minutes to get rid of that word!!!
Ya get me every time.
Hellllo!
Good morning, Eric!
REC
Look! A butterfly!
Hello, butterfly!

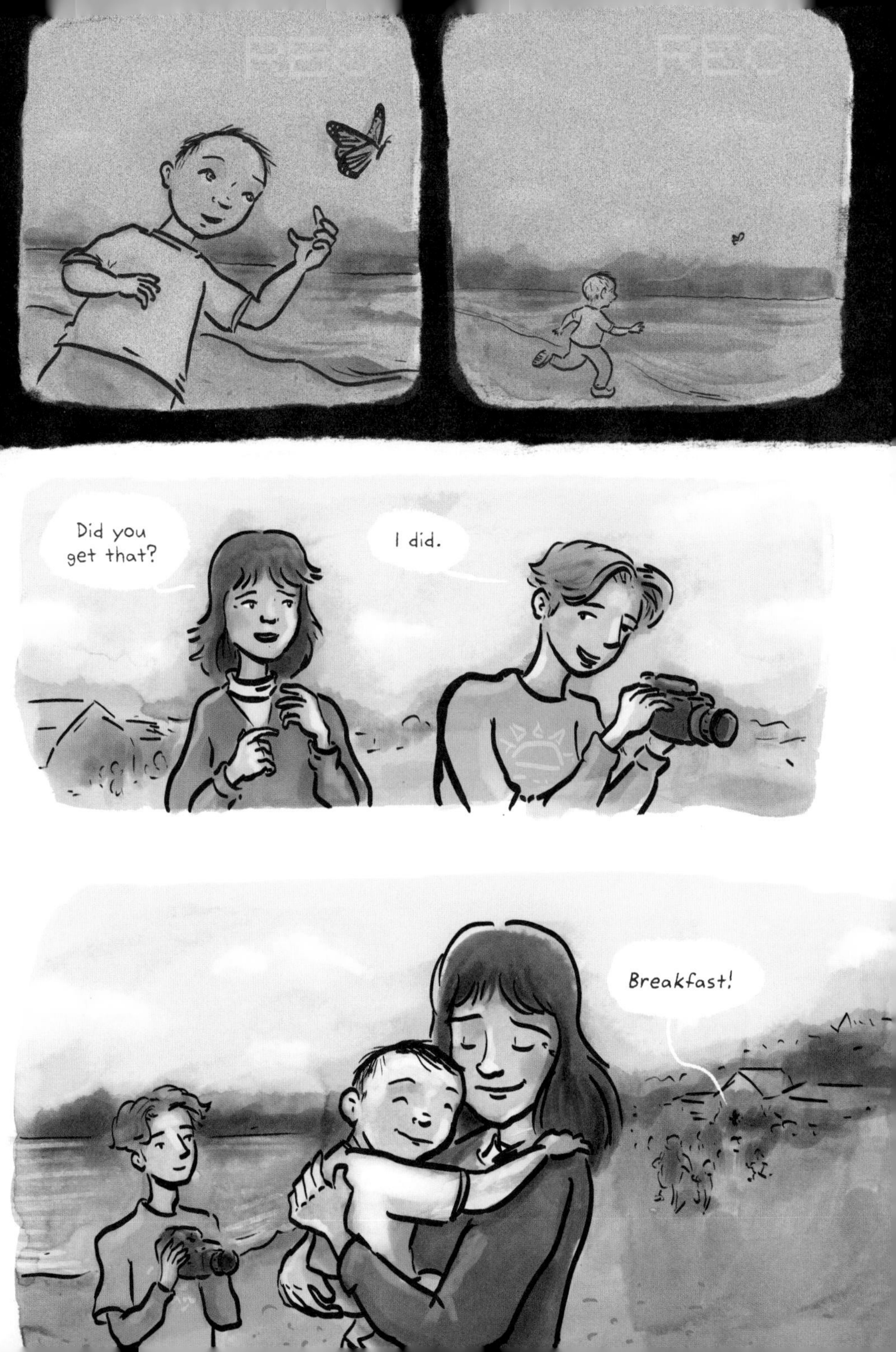
Did you get that?
I did.
Breakfast!

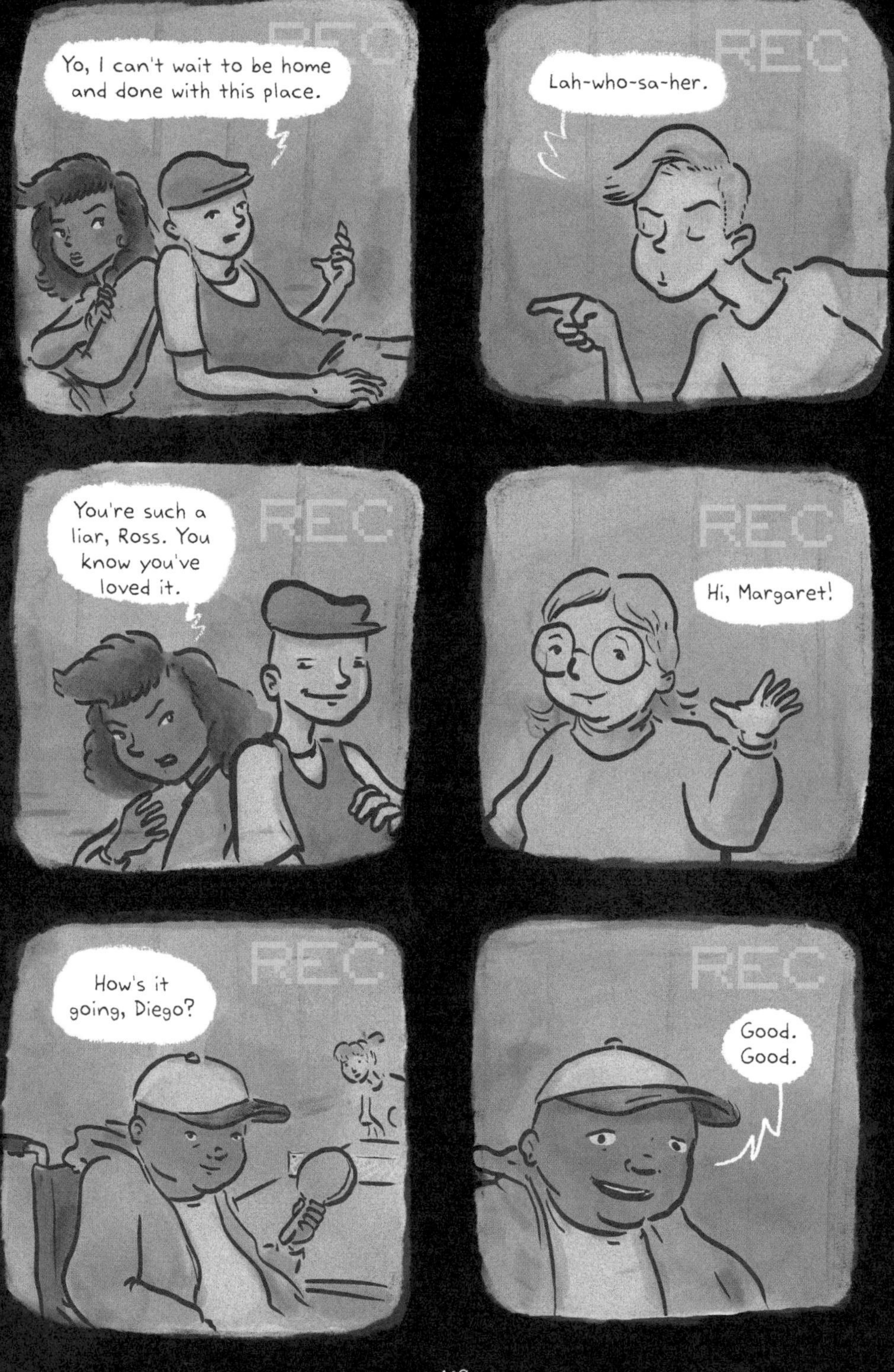
REC
Yo, I can't wait to be home and done with this place.
REC
Lah-who-sa-her.
You're such a liar, Ross. You know you've loved it.
REC
REC
Hi, Margaret!
How's it going, Diego?
REC
REC
Good. Good.

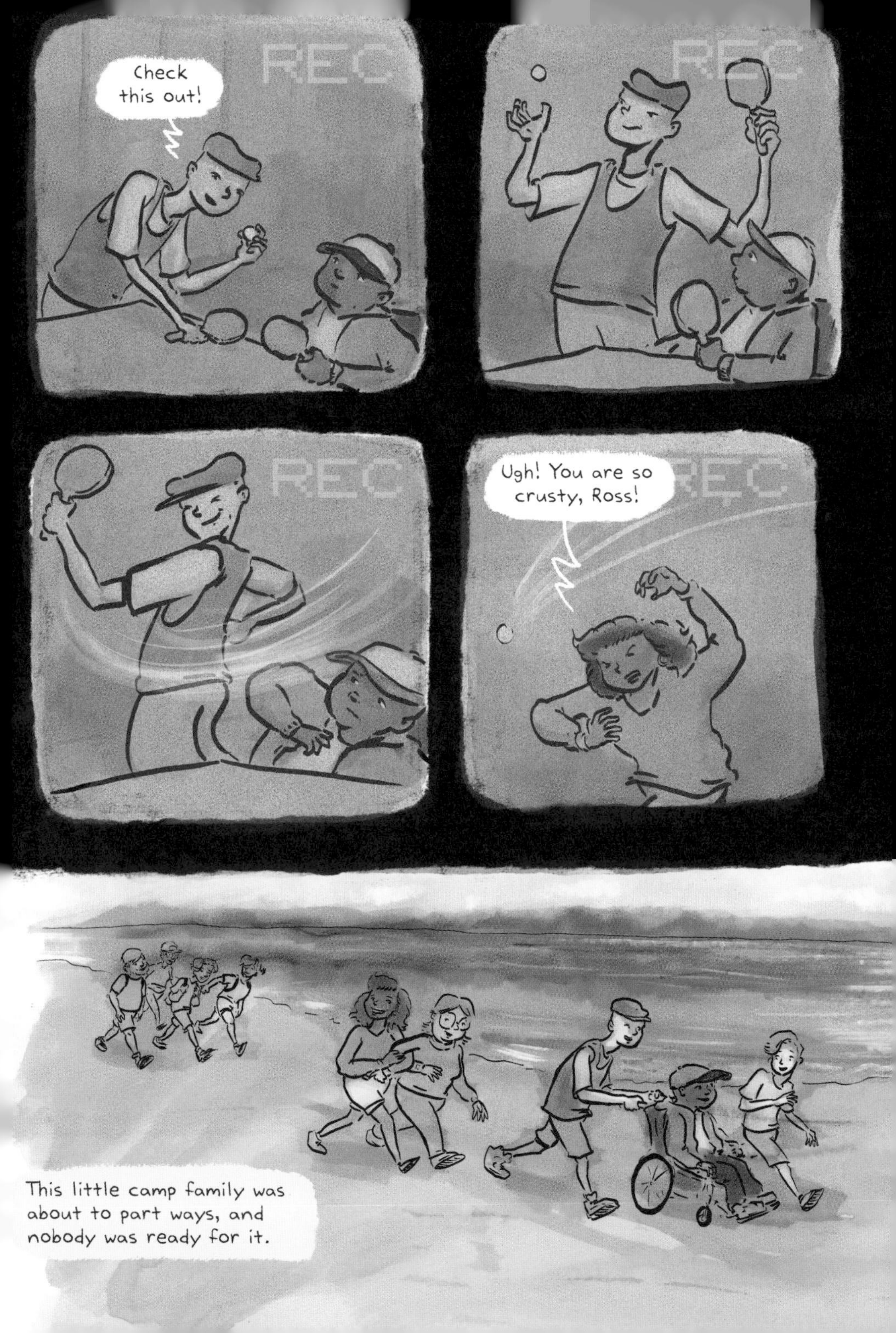
REC
Check this out!
REC
REC
REC
Ugh! You are so crusty, Ross!
This little camp family was about to part ways, and nobody was ready for it.

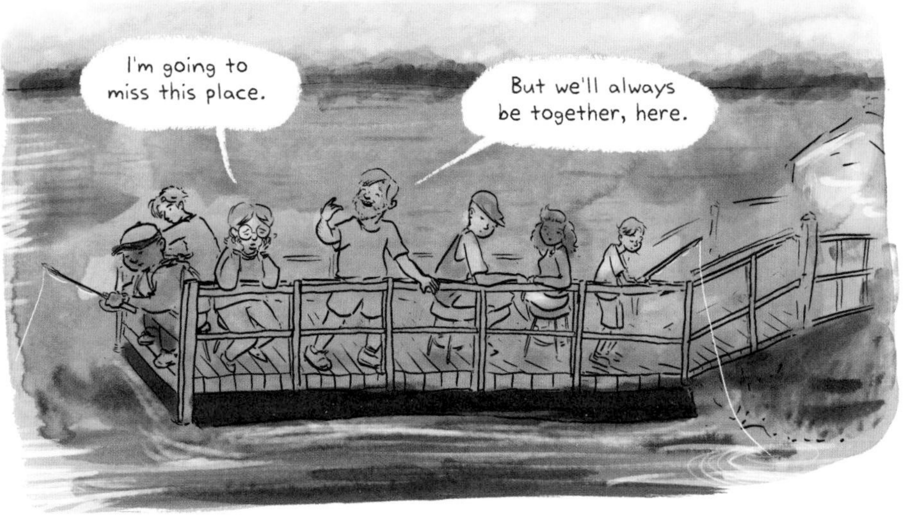
I'm going to miss this place.
But we'll always be together, here.

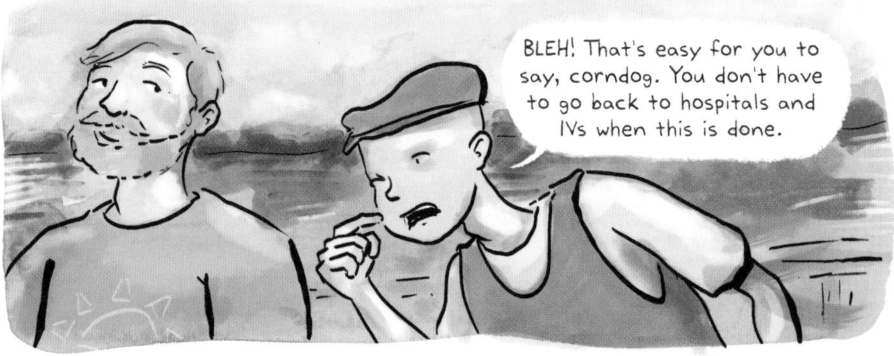
BLEH! That's easy for you to say, corndog. You don't have to go back to hospitals and IVs when this is done.

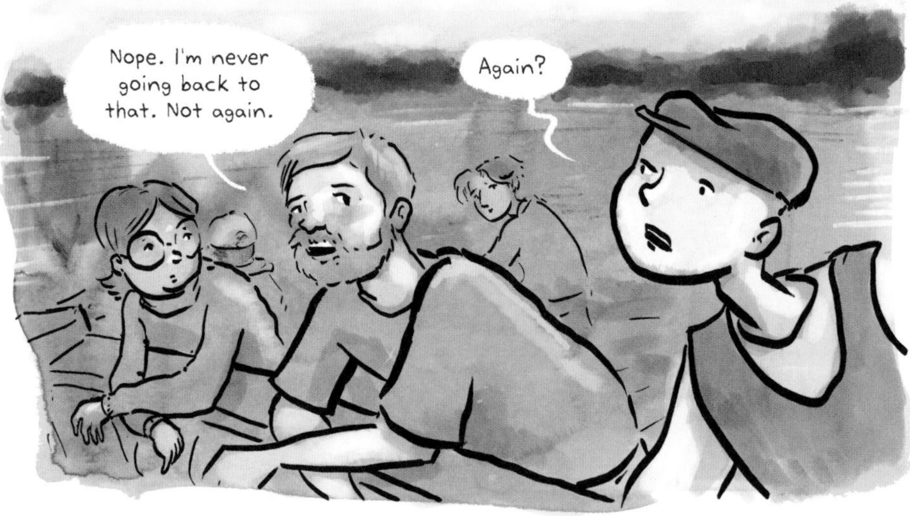
Nope. I'm never going back to that. Not again.
Again?

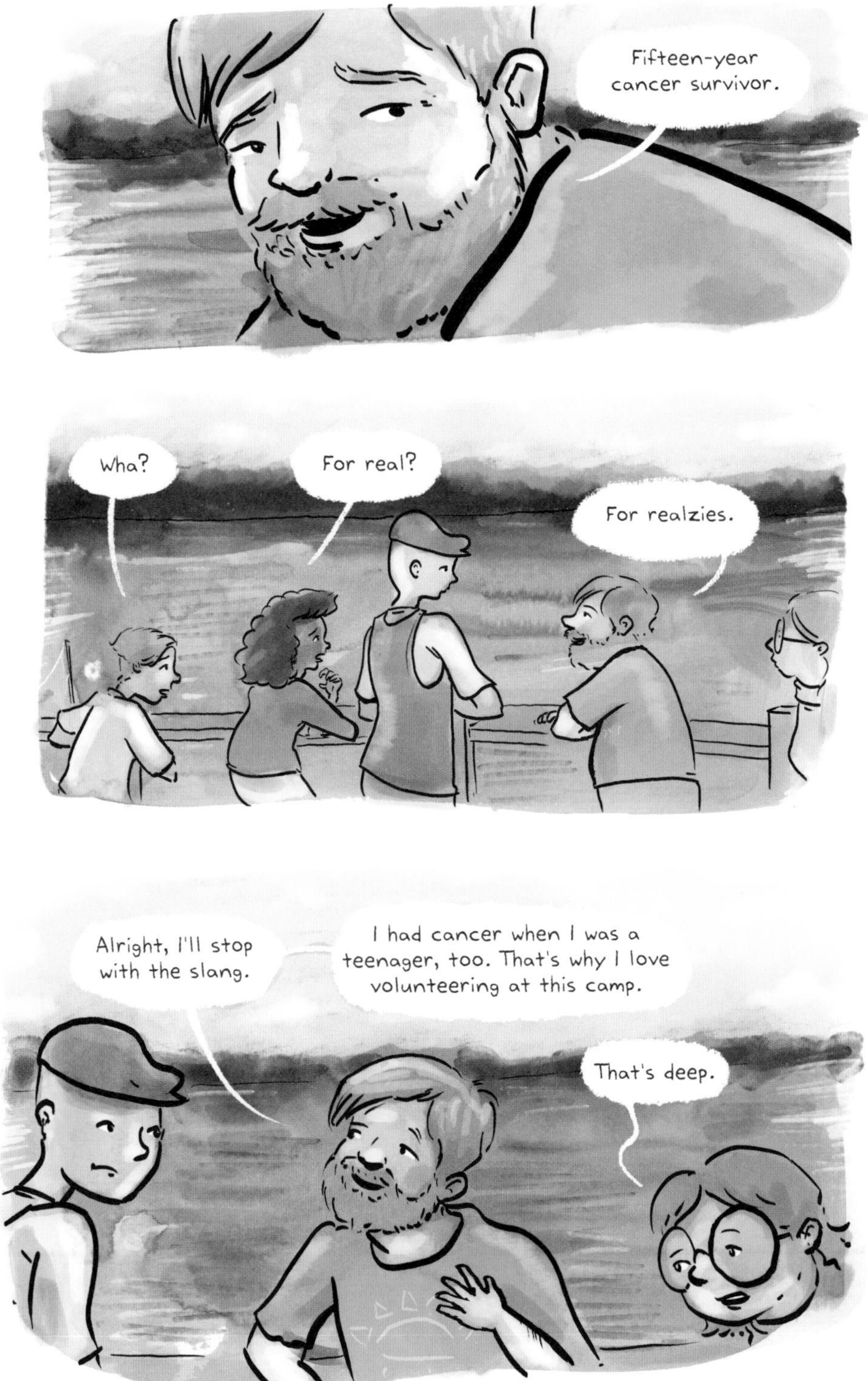
Fifteen-year cancer survivor.
Wha?
For real?
For realzies.
Alright, I'll stop with the slang.
I had cancer when I was a teenager, too. That's why I love volunteering at this camp.
That's deep.

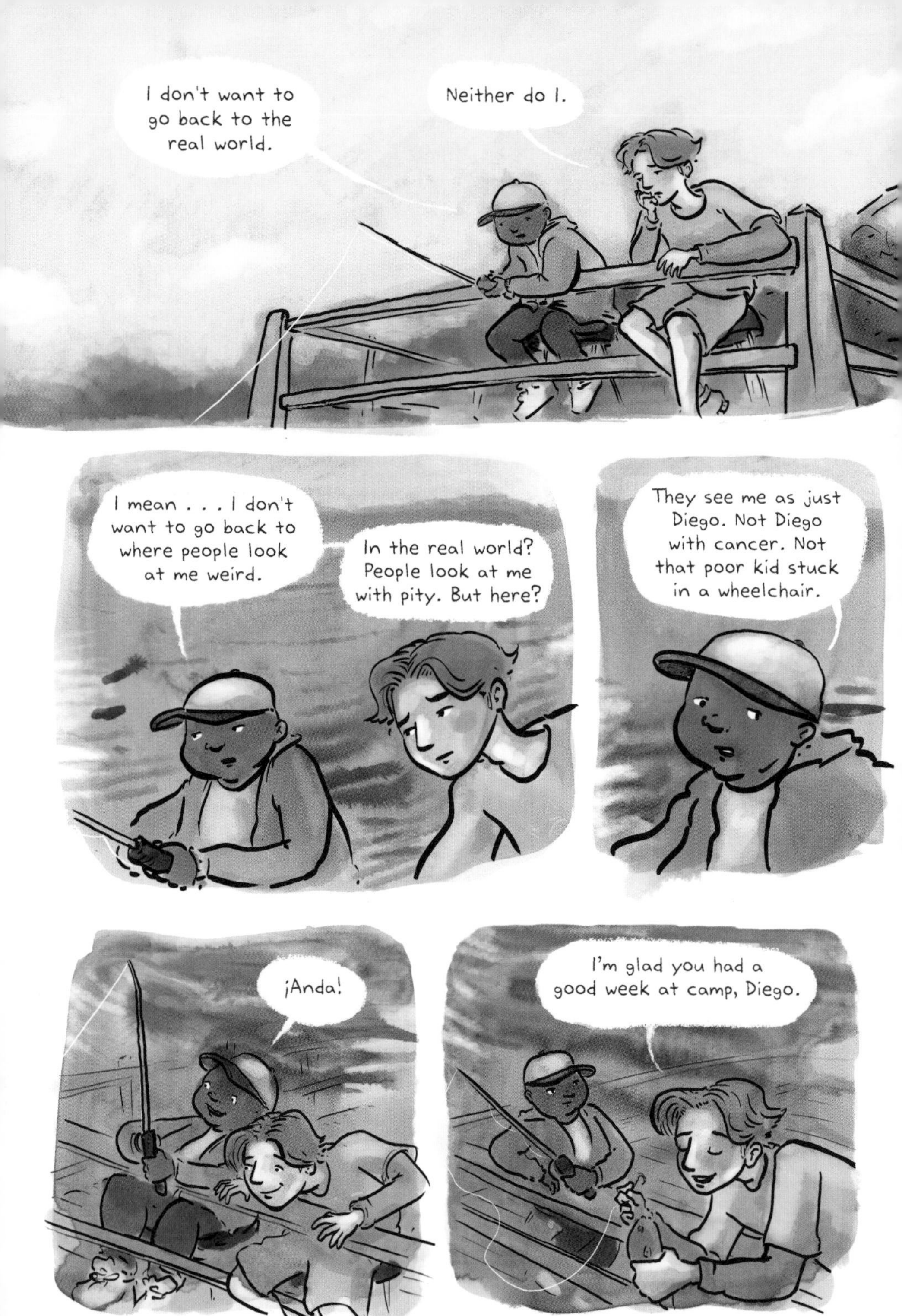
I don't want to go back to the real world.
Neither do I.
I mean . . . I don't want to go back to where people look at me weird.
In the real world? People look at me with pity. But here?
They see me as just Diego. Not Diego with cancer. Not that poor kid stuck in a wheelchair.
¡Anda!
I'm glad you had a good week at camp, Diego.

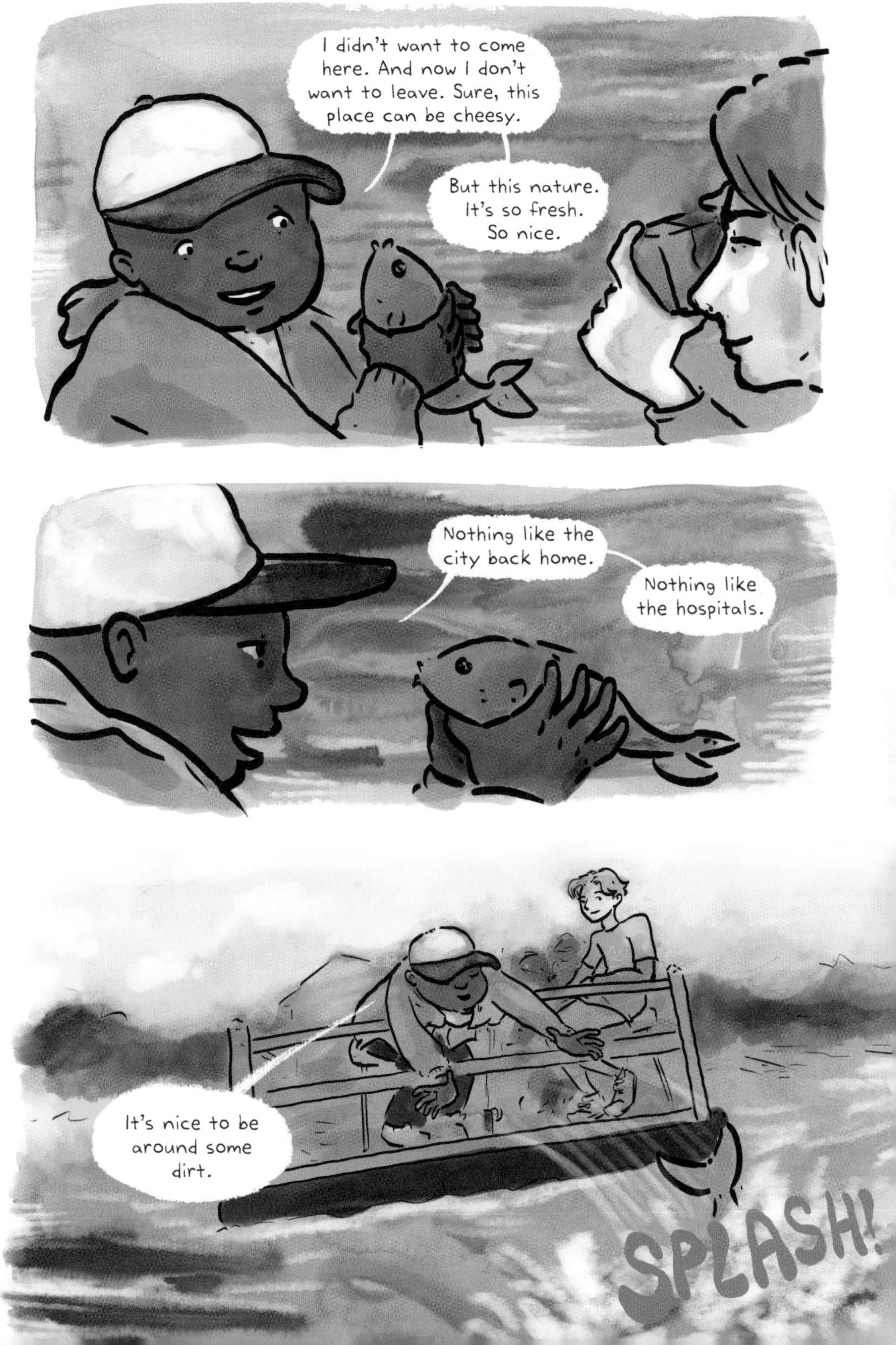
I didn't want to come here. And now I don't want to leave. Sure, this place can be cheesy.
But this nature. It's so fresh. So nice.
Nothing like the city back home.
Nothing like the hospitals.
It's nice to be around some dirt.
SPLASH!

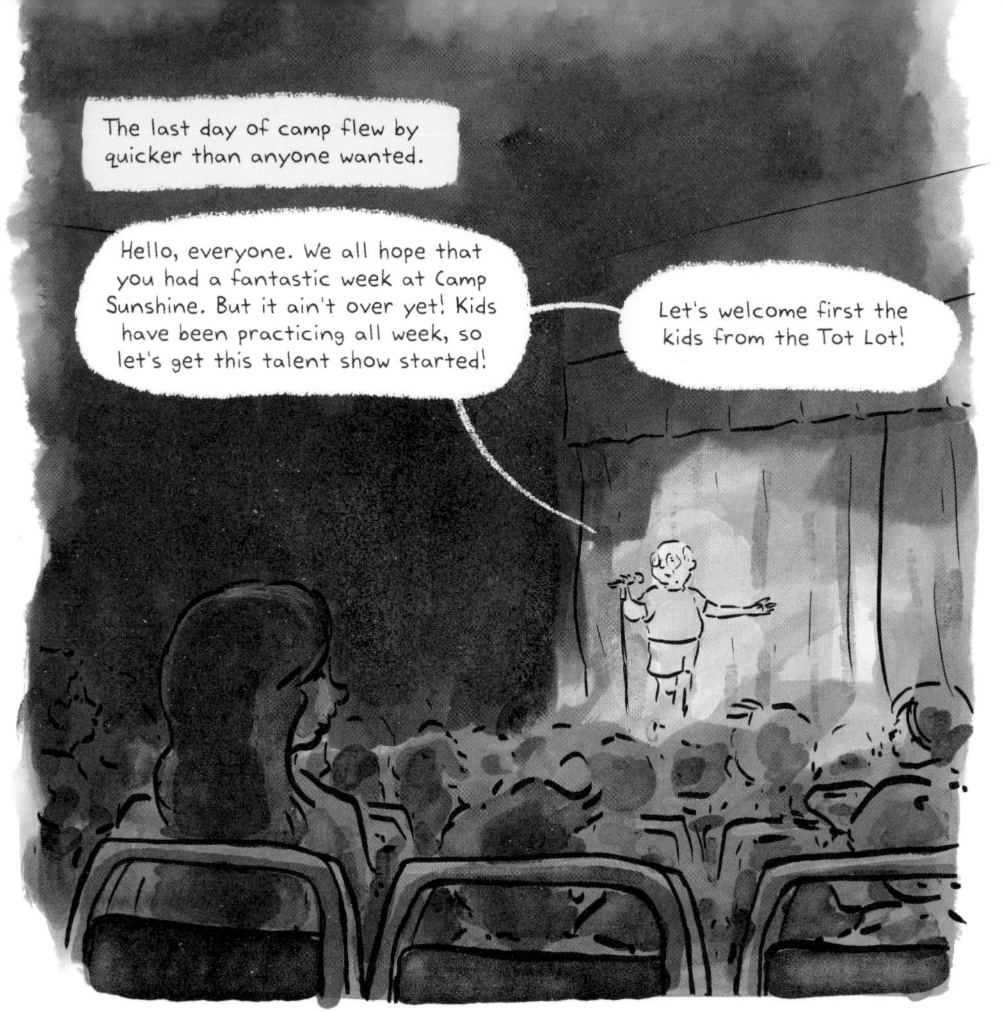
The last day of camp flew by quicker than anyone wanted.
Hello, everyone. We all hope that you had a fantastic week at Camp Sunshine. But it ain't over yet! Kids have been practicing all week, so let's get this talent show started!
Let's welcome first the kids from the Tot Lot!

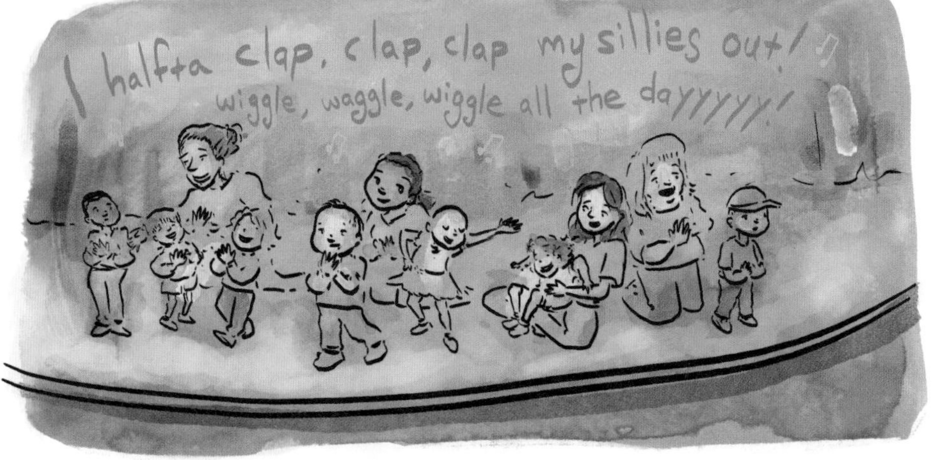
I halfta clap, clap, clap my sillies out!
wiggle, waggle, wiggle all the dayyyyy!

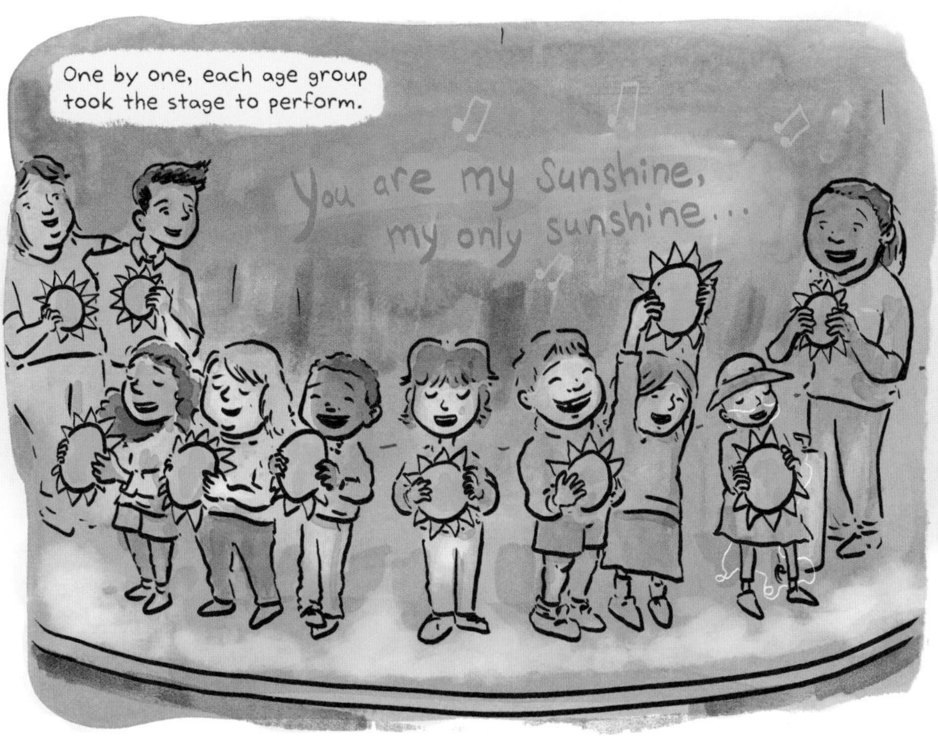
One by one, each age group took the stage to perform.
You are my sunshine, my only sunshine...

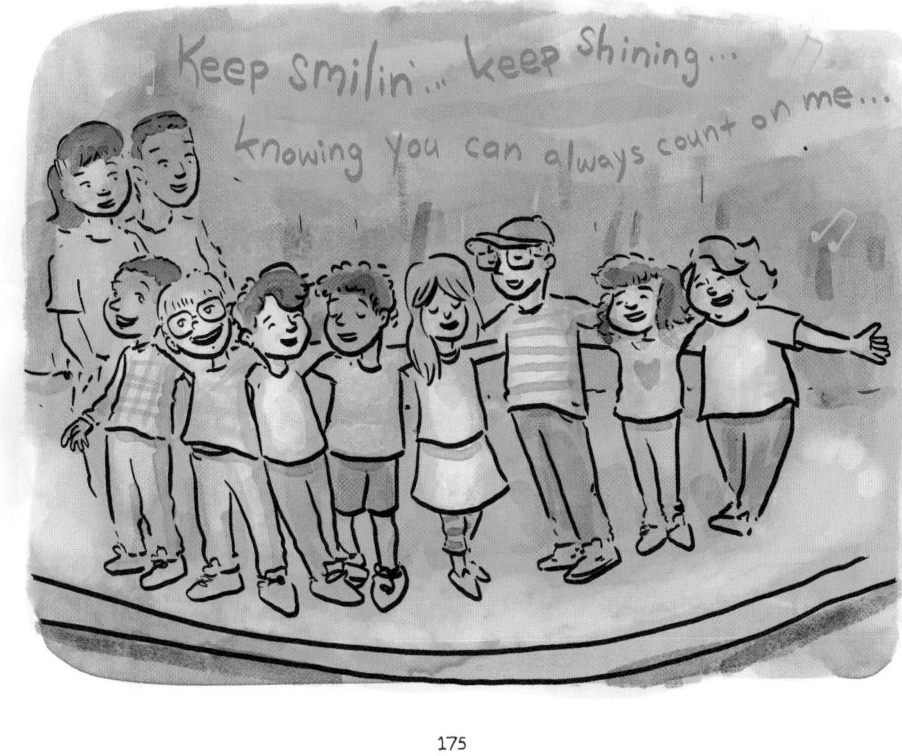
Keep smilin'... keep shining...
knowing you can always count on me...

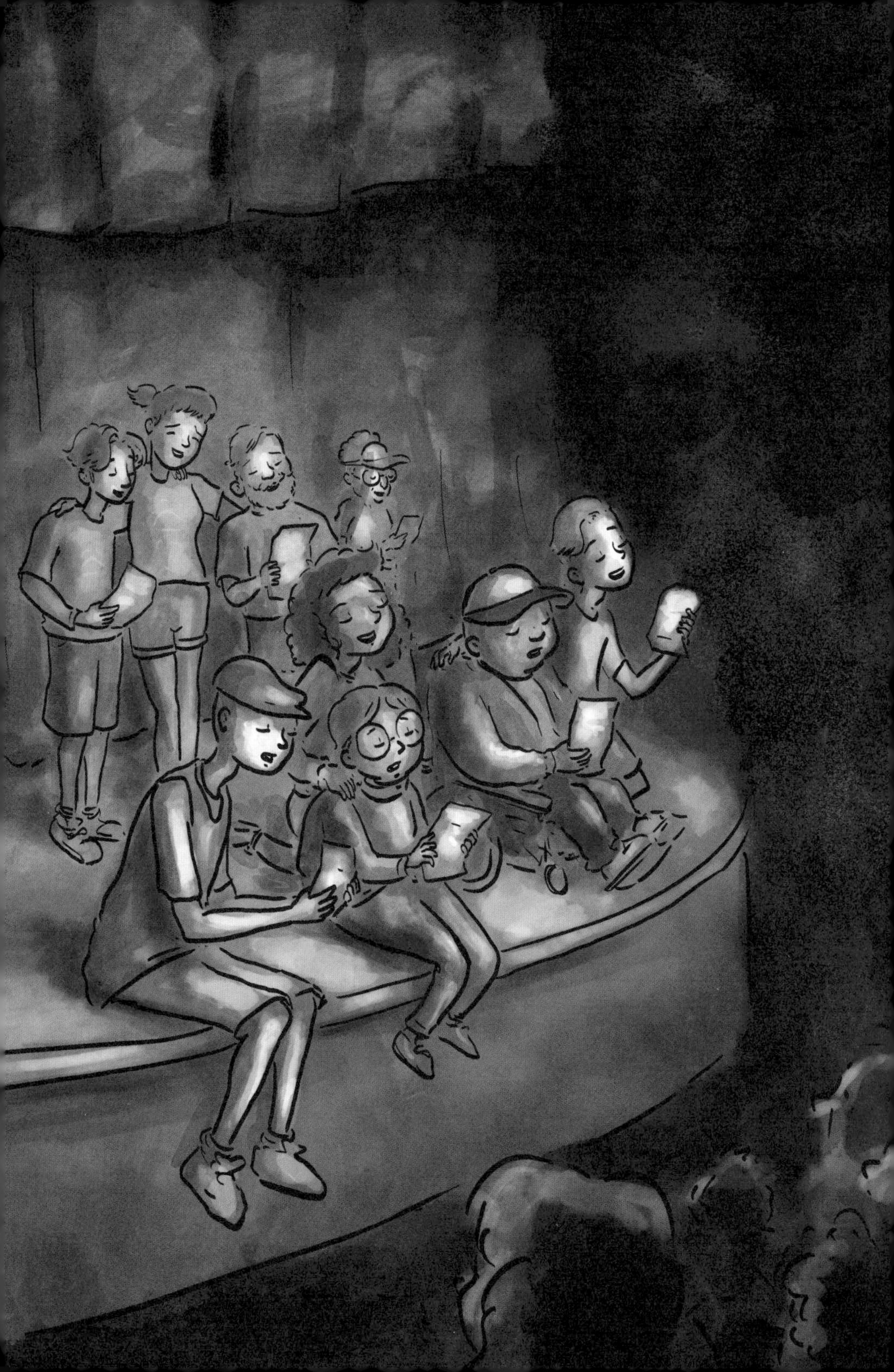

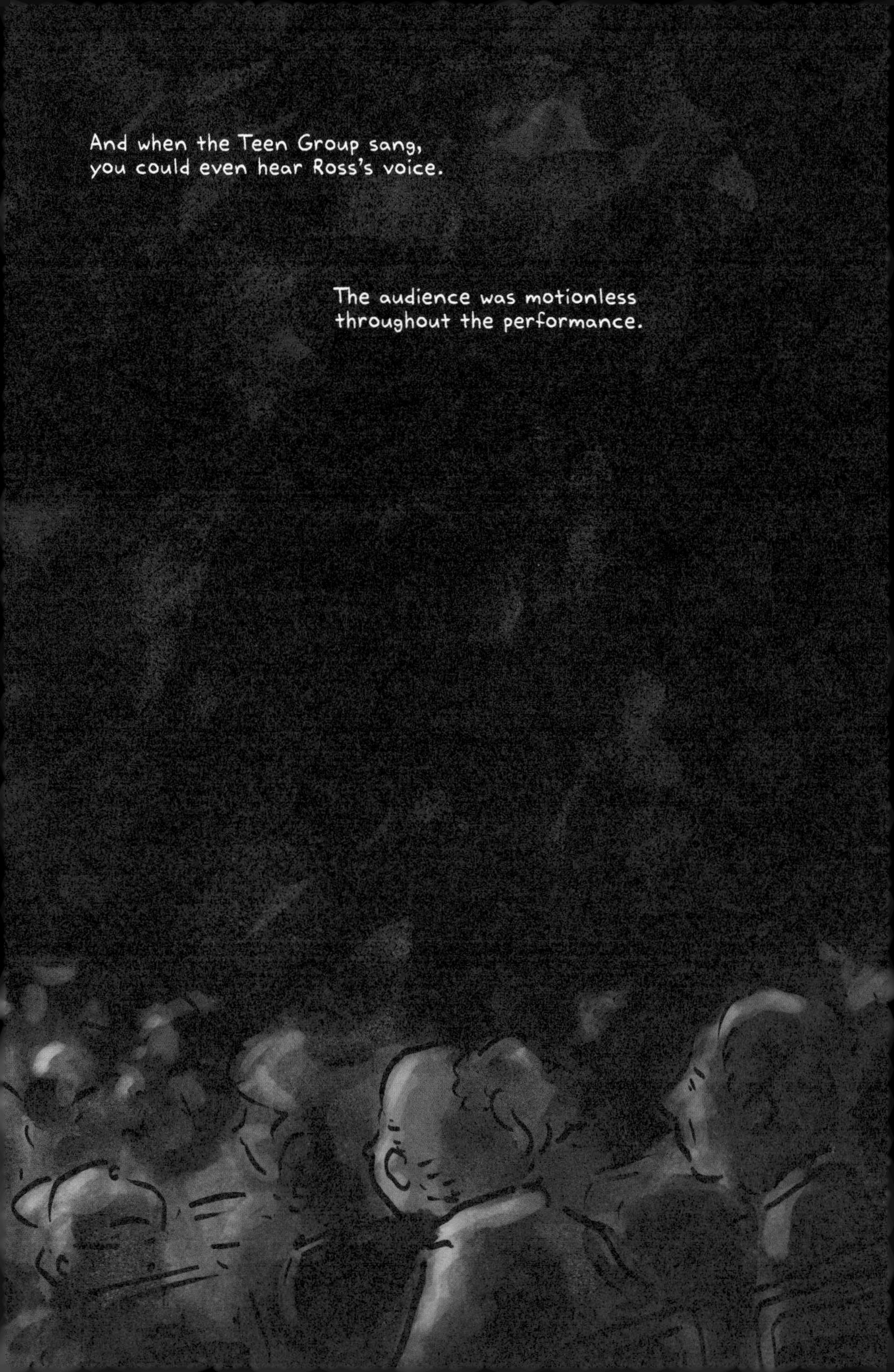
And when the Teen Group sang, you could even hear Ross's voice.
The audience was motionless throughout the performance.

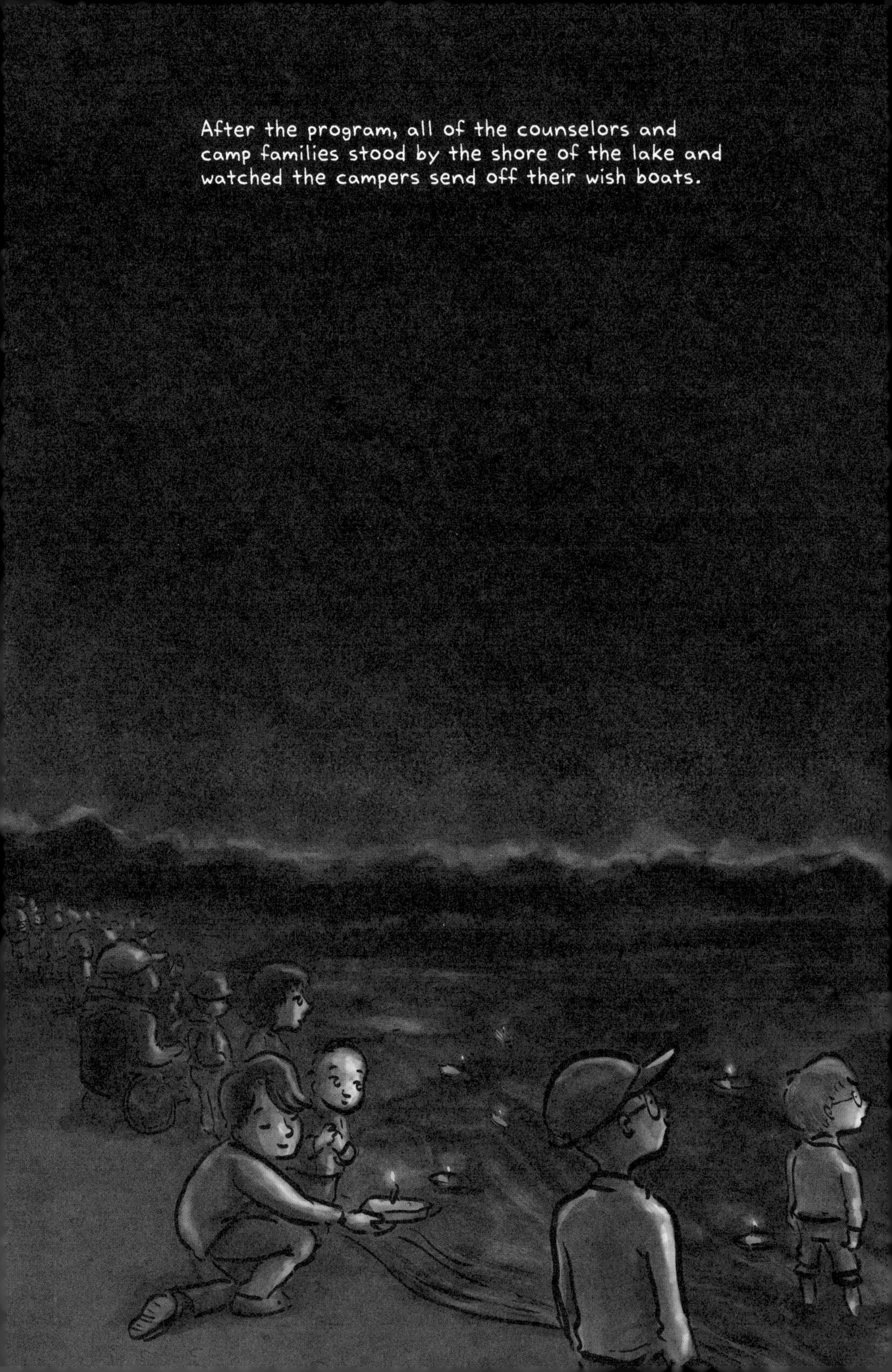
After the program, all of the counselors and camp families stood by the shore of the lake and watched the campers send off their wish boats.

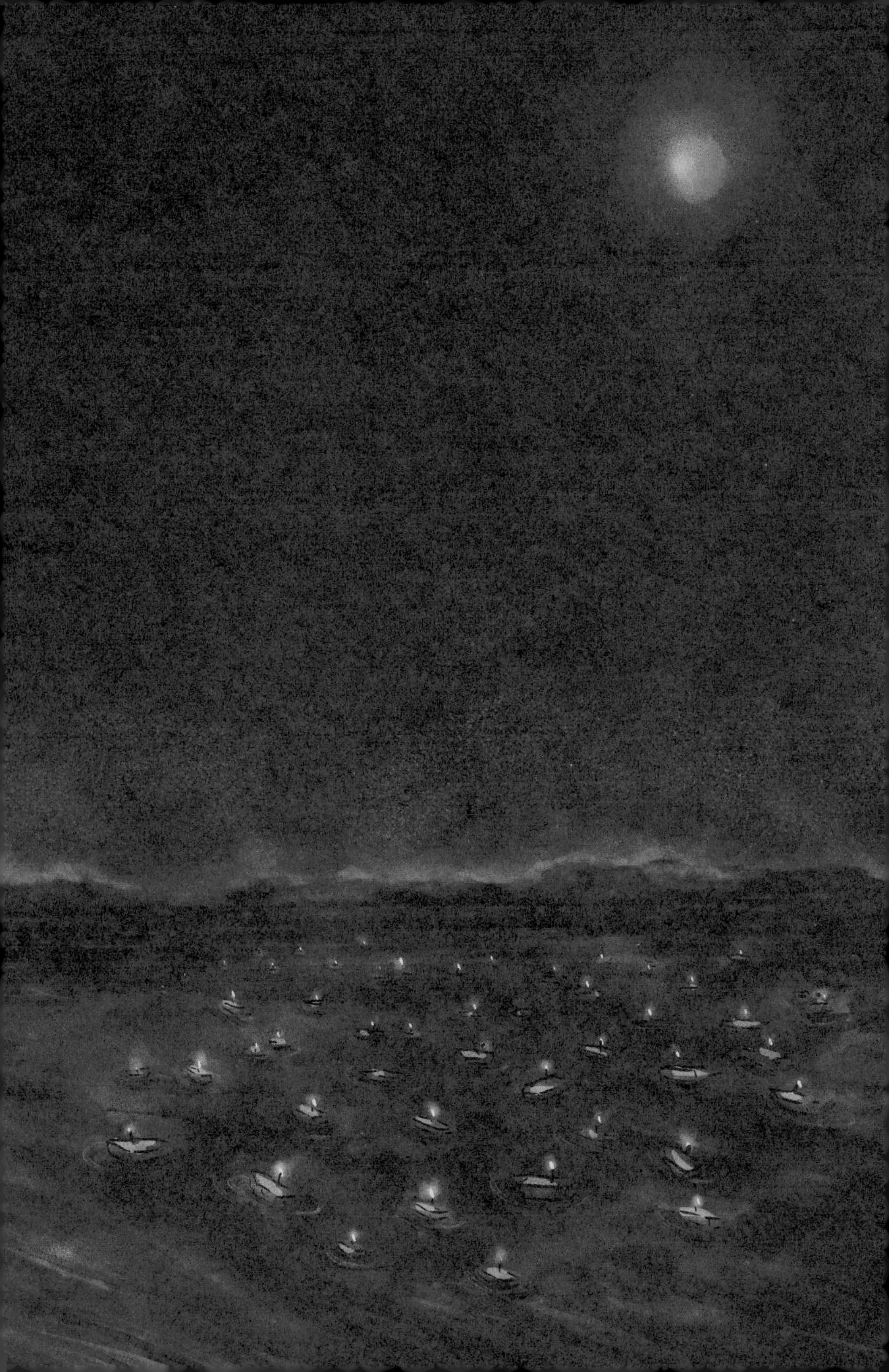

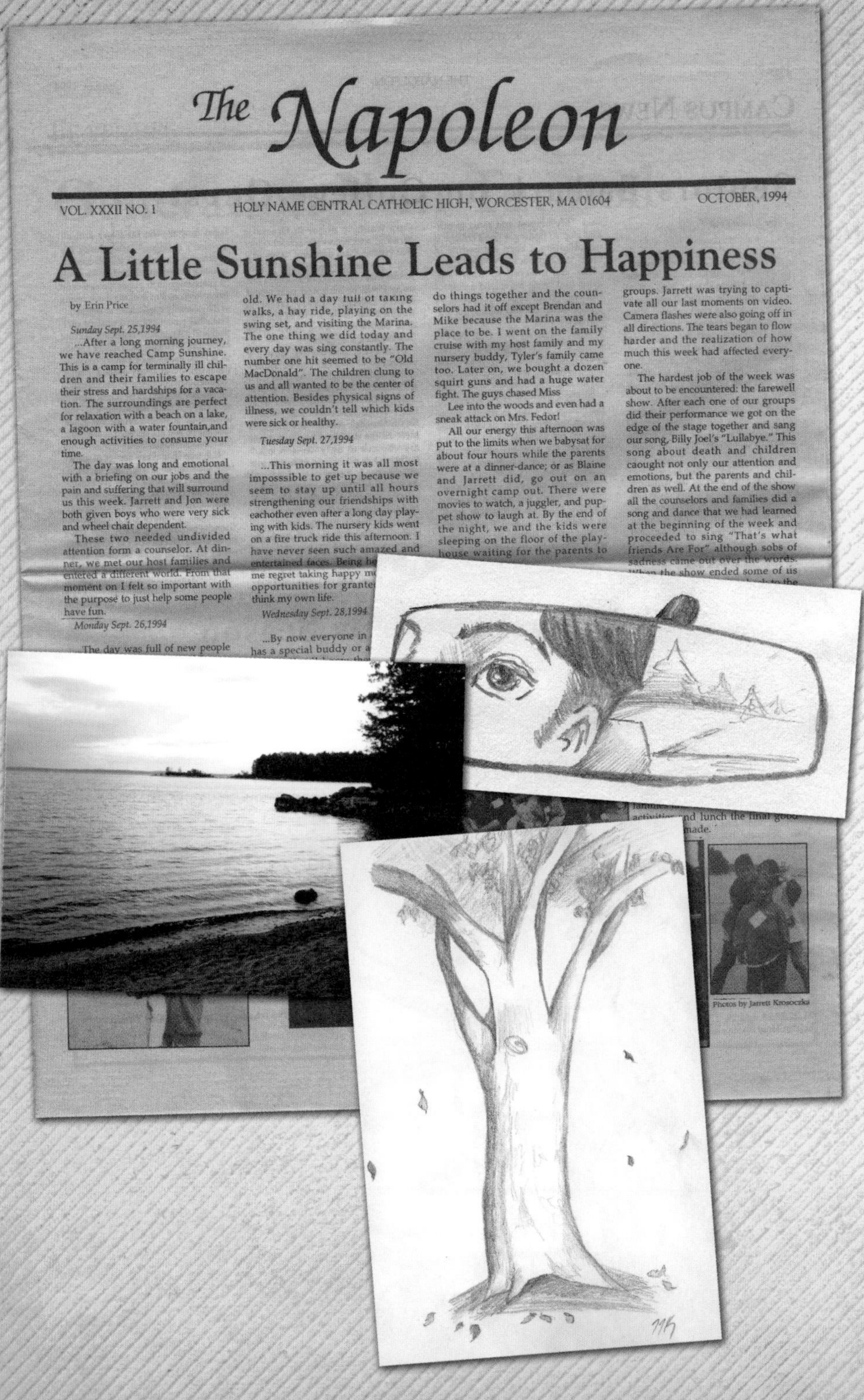

The Napoleon

VOL. XXXII NO. 1 HOLY NAME CENTRAL CATHOLIC HIGH, WORCESTER, MA 01604 OCTOBER, 1994

A Little Sunshine Leads to Happiness

by Erin Price

Sunday Sept. 25,1994

...After a long morning journey, we have reached Camp Sunshine. This is a camp for terminally ill children and their families to escape their stress and hardships for a vacation. The surroundings are perfect for relaxation with a beach on a lake, a lagoon with a water fountain,and enough activities to consume your time.

The day was long and emotional with a briefing on our jobs and the pain and suffering that will surround us this week. Jarrett and Jon were both given boys who were very sick and wheel chair dependent.

These two needed undivided attention form a counselor. At dinner, we met our host families and entered a different world. From that moment on I felt so important with the purpose to just help some people have fun.

Monday Sept. 26,1994

...The day was full of new people

old. We had a day full of taking walks, a hay ride, playing on the swing set, and visiting the Marina. The one thing we did today and every day was sing constantly. The number one hit seemed to be "Old MacDonald". The children clung to us and all wanted to be the center of attention. Besides physical signs of illness, we couldn't tell which kids were sick or healthy.

Tuesday Sept. 27,1994

...This morning it was all most impossssible to get up because we seem to stay up until all hours strengthening our friendships with eachother even after a long day playing with kids. The nursery kids went on a fire truck ride this afternoon. I have never seen such amazed and entertained faces. Being he

me regret taking happy m

opportunities for grante

think my own life.

Wednesday Sept. 28,1994

...By now everyone in

has a special buddy or a

do things together and the counselors had it off except Brendan and Mike because the Marina was the place to be. I went on the family cruise with my host family and my nursery buddy, Tyler's family came too. Later on, we bought a dozen squirt guns and had a huge water fight. The guys chased Miss

Lee into the woods and even had a sneak attack on Mrs. Fedor!

All our energy this afternoon was put to the limits when we babysat for about four hours while the parents were at a dinner-dance; or as Blaine and Jarrett did, go out on an overnight camp out. There were movies to watch, a juggler, and puppet show to laugh at. By the end of the night, we and the kids were sleeping on the floor of the playhouse waiting for the parents to

groups. Jarrett was trying to captivate all our last moments on video. Camera flashes were also going off in all directions. The tears began to flow harder and the realization of how much this week had affected everyone.

The hardest job of the week was about to be encountered: the farewell show. After each one of our groups did their performance we got on the edge of the stage together and sang our song, Billy Joel's "Lullabye." This song about death and children caought not only our attention and emotions, but the parents and children as well. At the end of the show all the counselors and families did a song and dance that we had learned at the beginning of the week and proceeded to sing "That's what friends Are For" although sobs of sadness came out over the words. When the show ended some of us

activities and lunch the final good

made.

Photos by Jarrett Krosoczka

CHAPTER 7
THE LONG
ROAD HOME

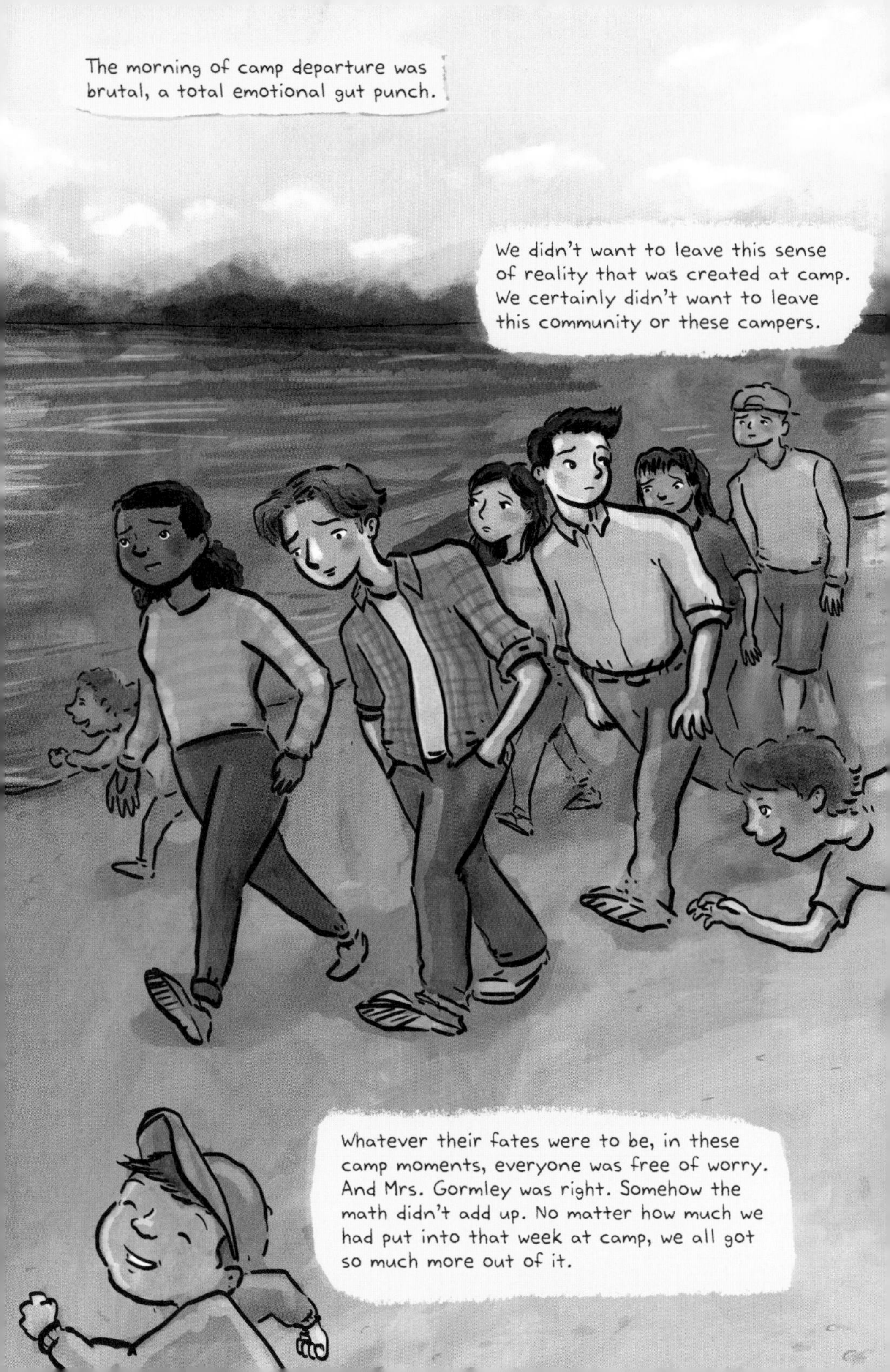
The morning of camp departure was brutal, a total emotional gut punch.
We didn't want to leave this sense of reality that was created at camp. We certainly didn't want to leave this community or these campers.
Whatever their fates were to be, in these camp moments, everyone was free of worry. And Mrs. Gormley was right. Somehow the math didn't add up. No matter how much we had put into that week at camp, we all got so much more out of it.

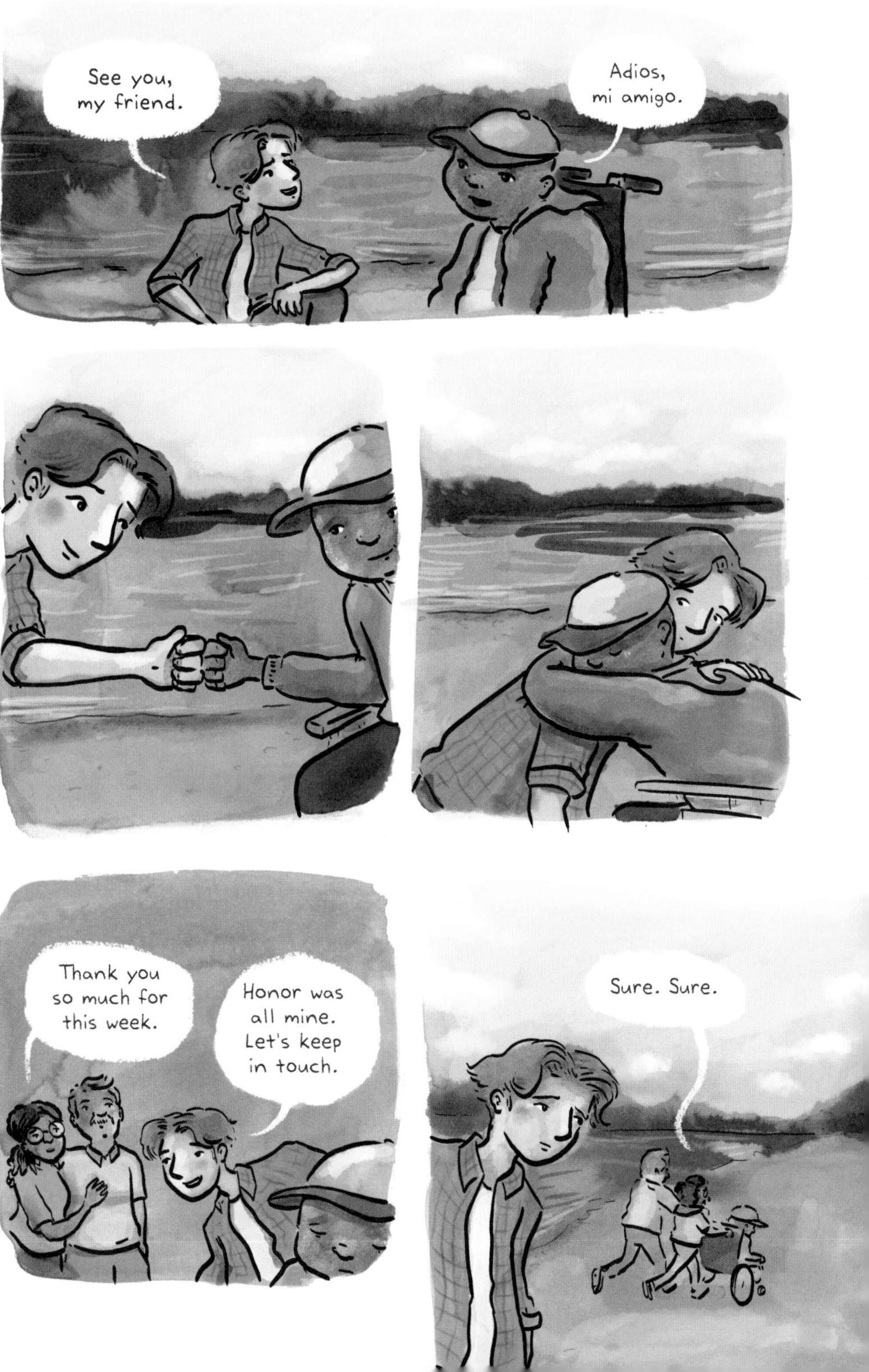
See you, my friend.
Adios, mi amigo.
Thank you so much for this week.
Honor was all mine. Let's keep in touch.
Sure. Sure.

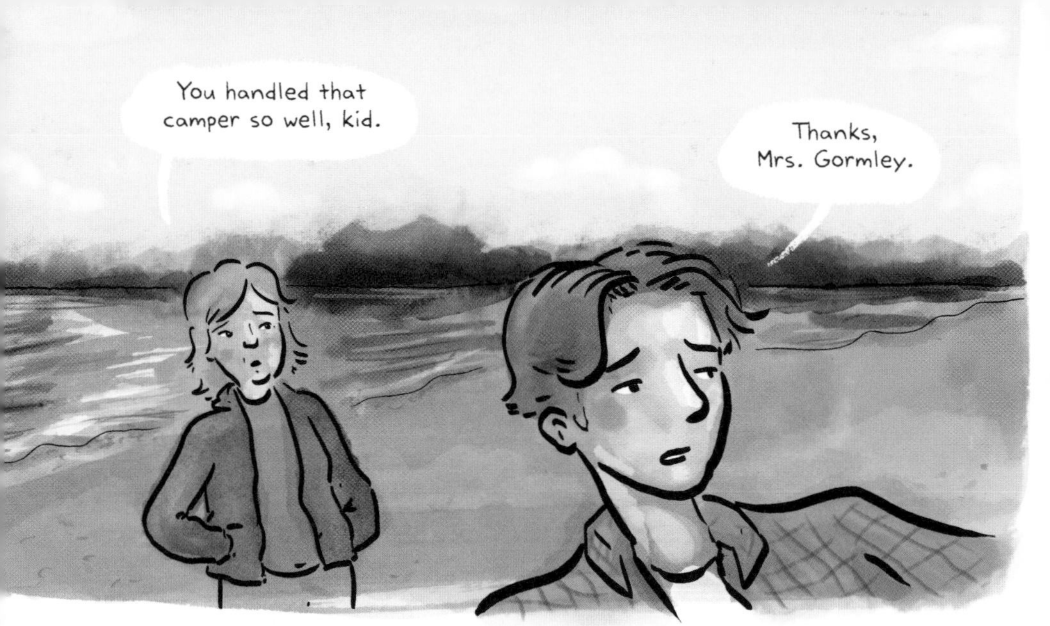
You handled that camper so well, kid.
Thanks, Mrs. Gormley.

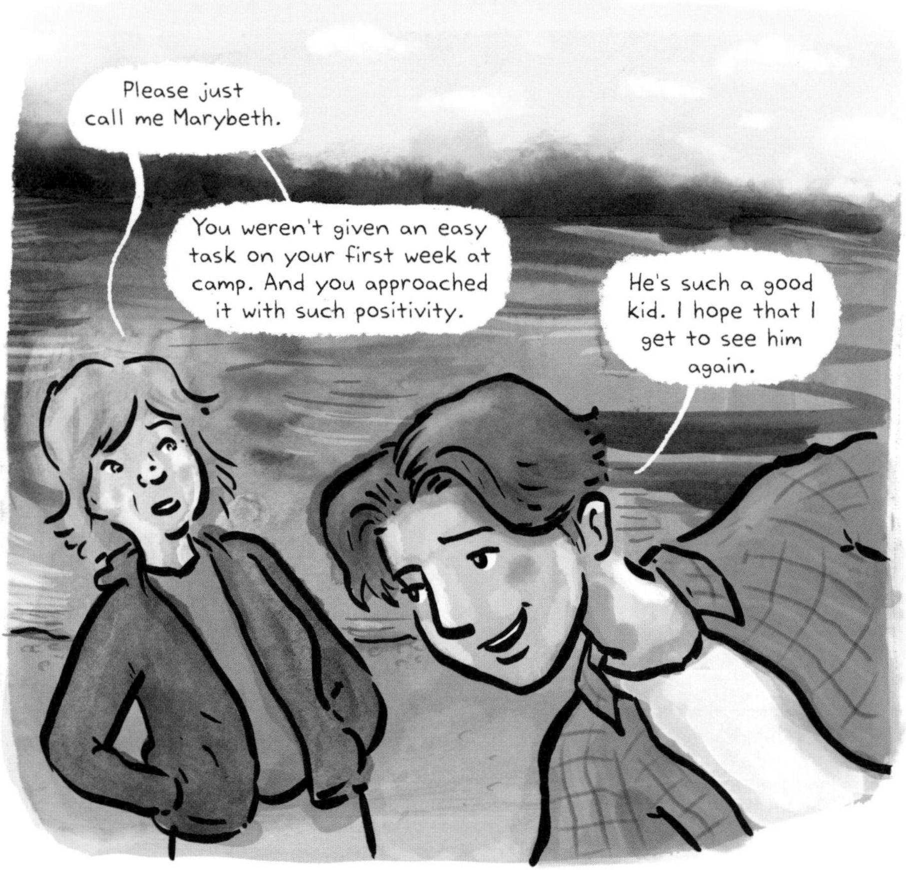
Please just call me Marybeth.
You weren't given an easy task on your first week at camp. And you approached it with such positivity.
He's such a good kid. I hope that I get to see him again.

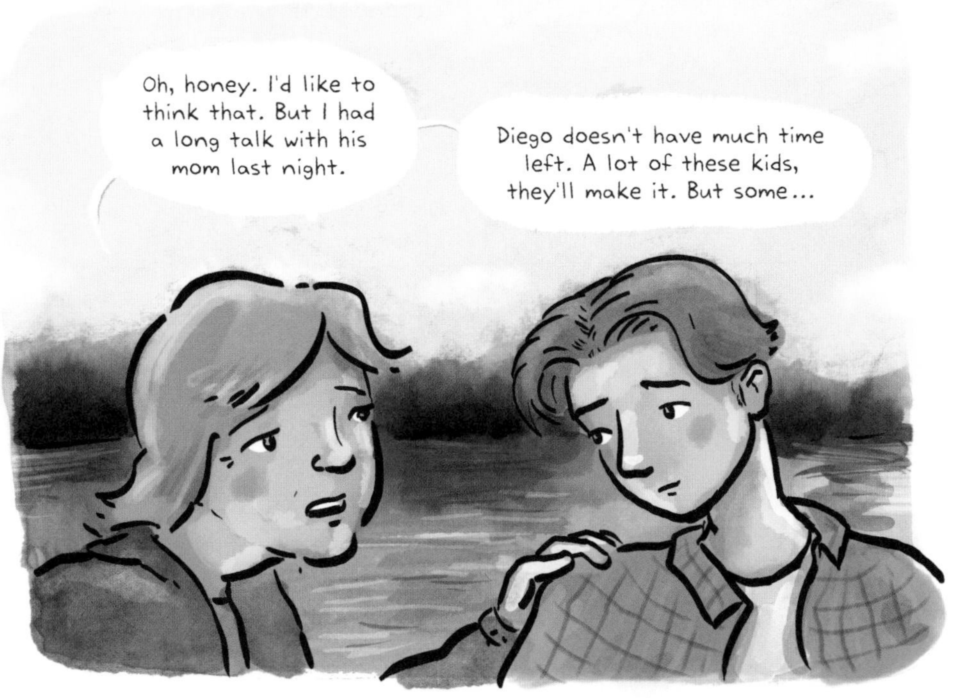
Oh, honey. I'd like to think that. But I had a long talk with his mom last night.
Diego doesn't have much time left. A lot of these kids, they'll make it. But some...

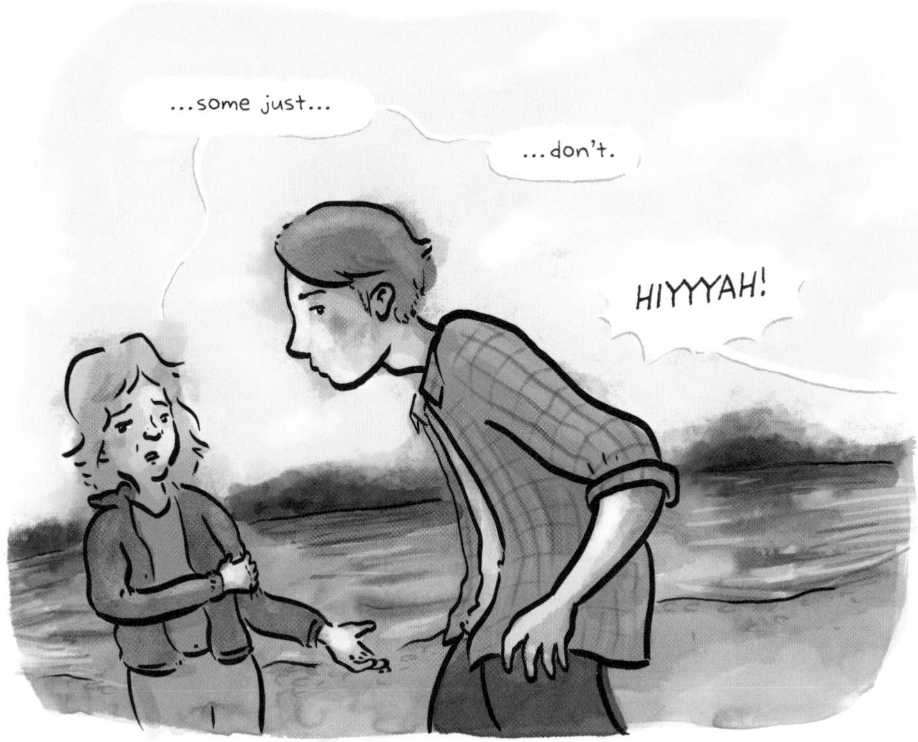
...some just...
...don't.
HIYYYAH!

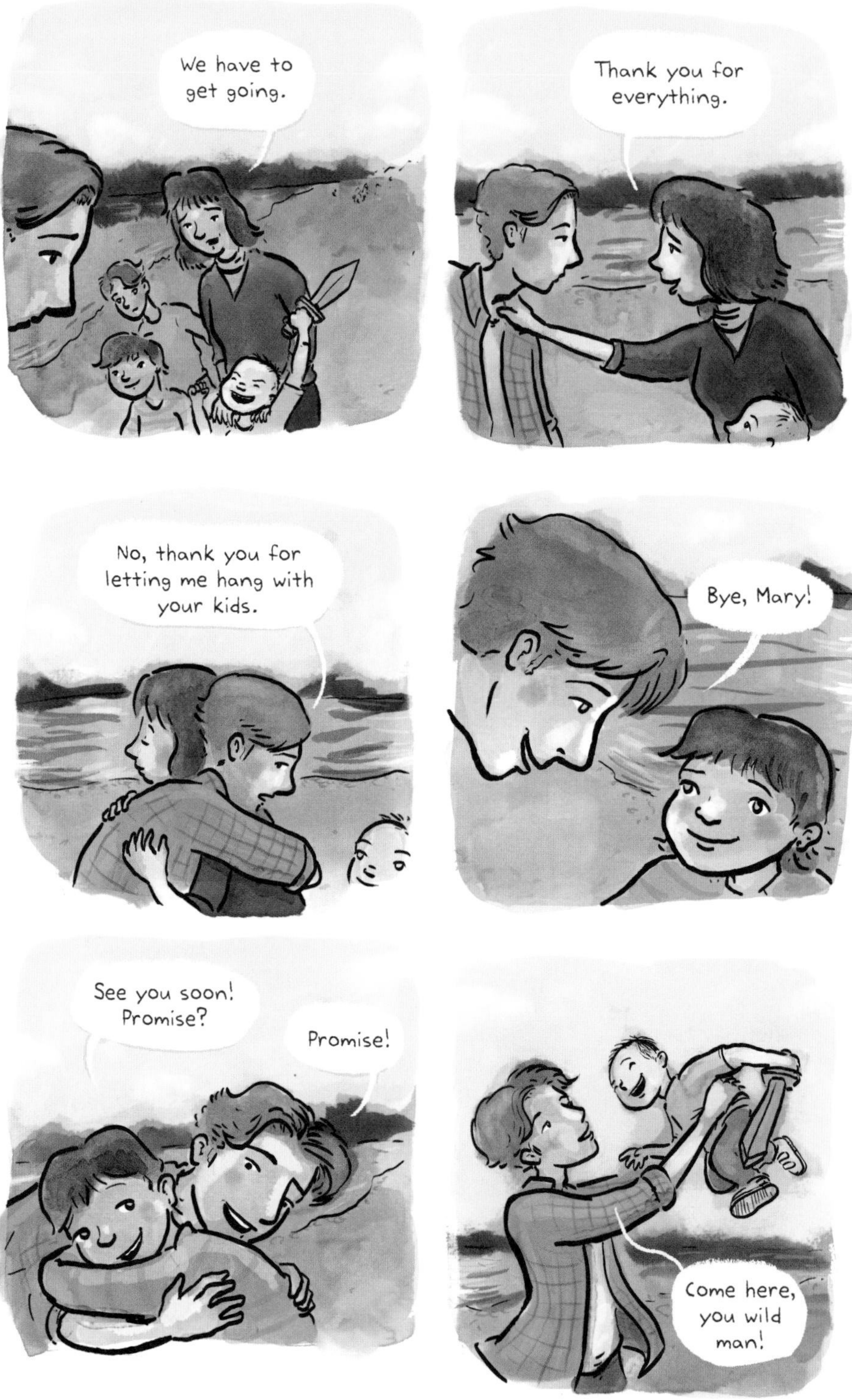

We have to get going.
Thank you for everything.
No, thank you for letting me hang with your kids.
Bye, Mary!
See you soon! Promise?
Promise!
Come here, you wild man!

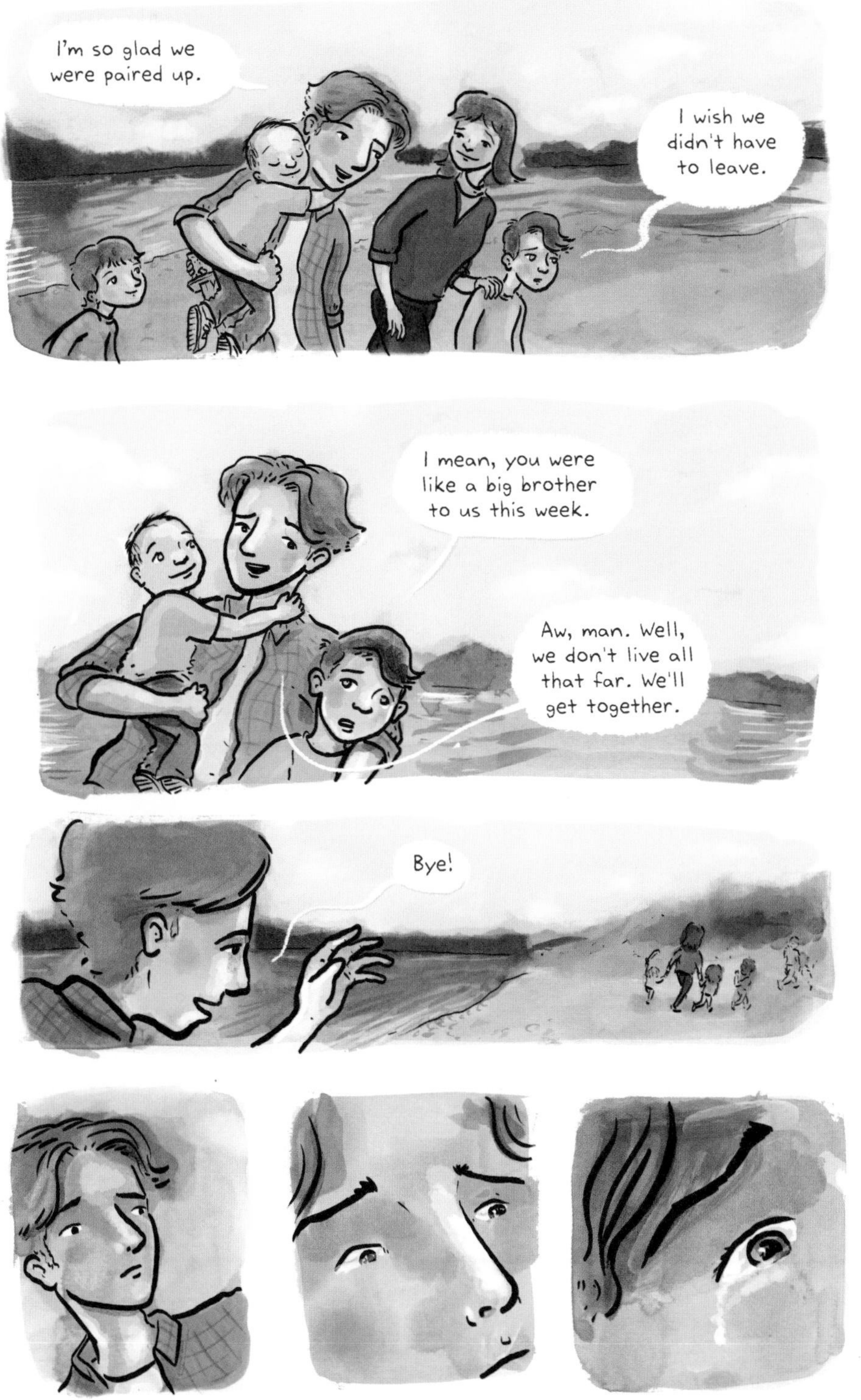
I'm so glad we were paired up.
I wish we didn't have to leave.
I mean, you were like a big brother to us this week.
Aw, man. Well, we don't live all that far. We'll get together.
Bye!

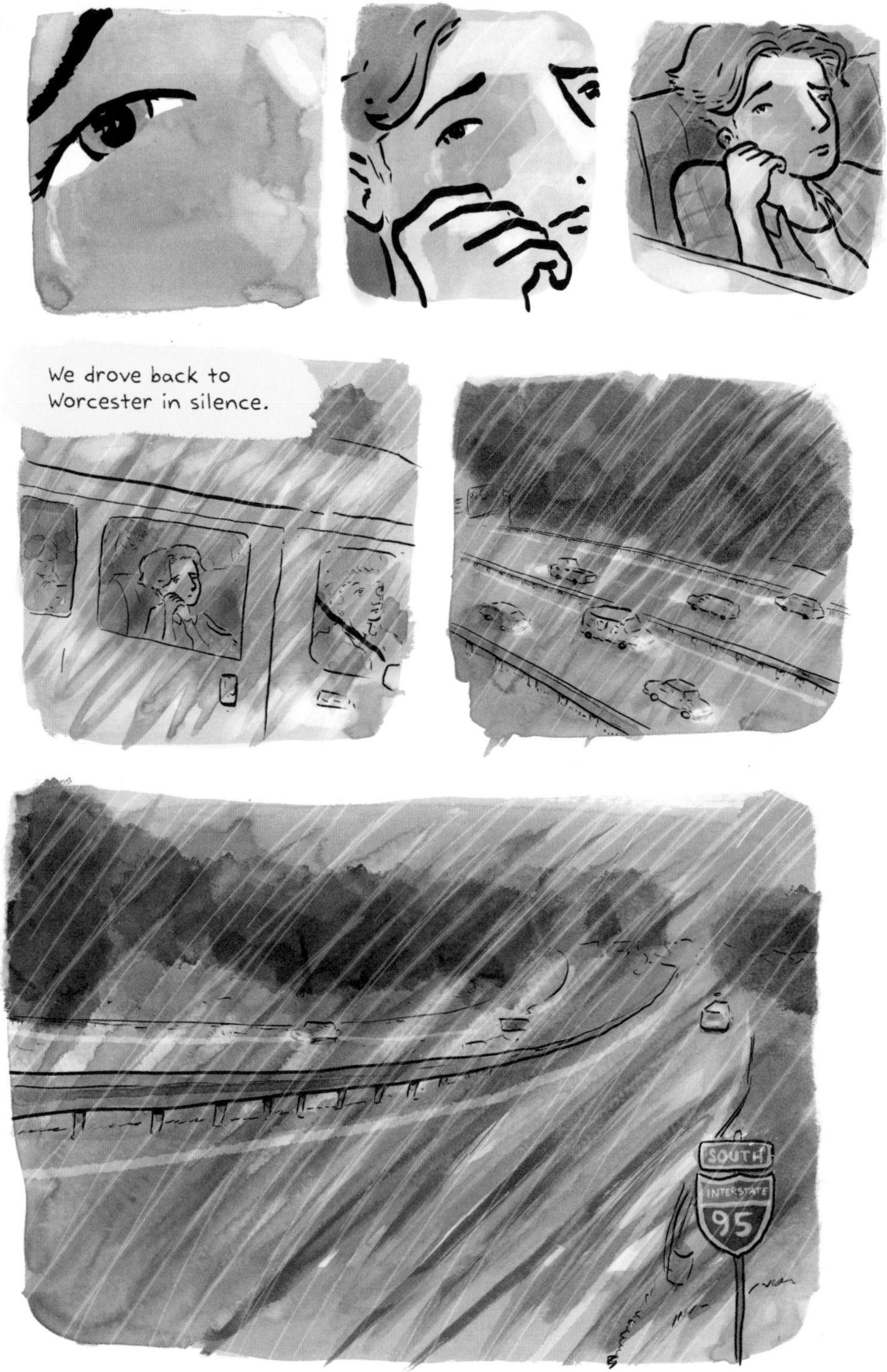
We drove back to Worcester in silence.
SOUTH
INTERSTATE
95

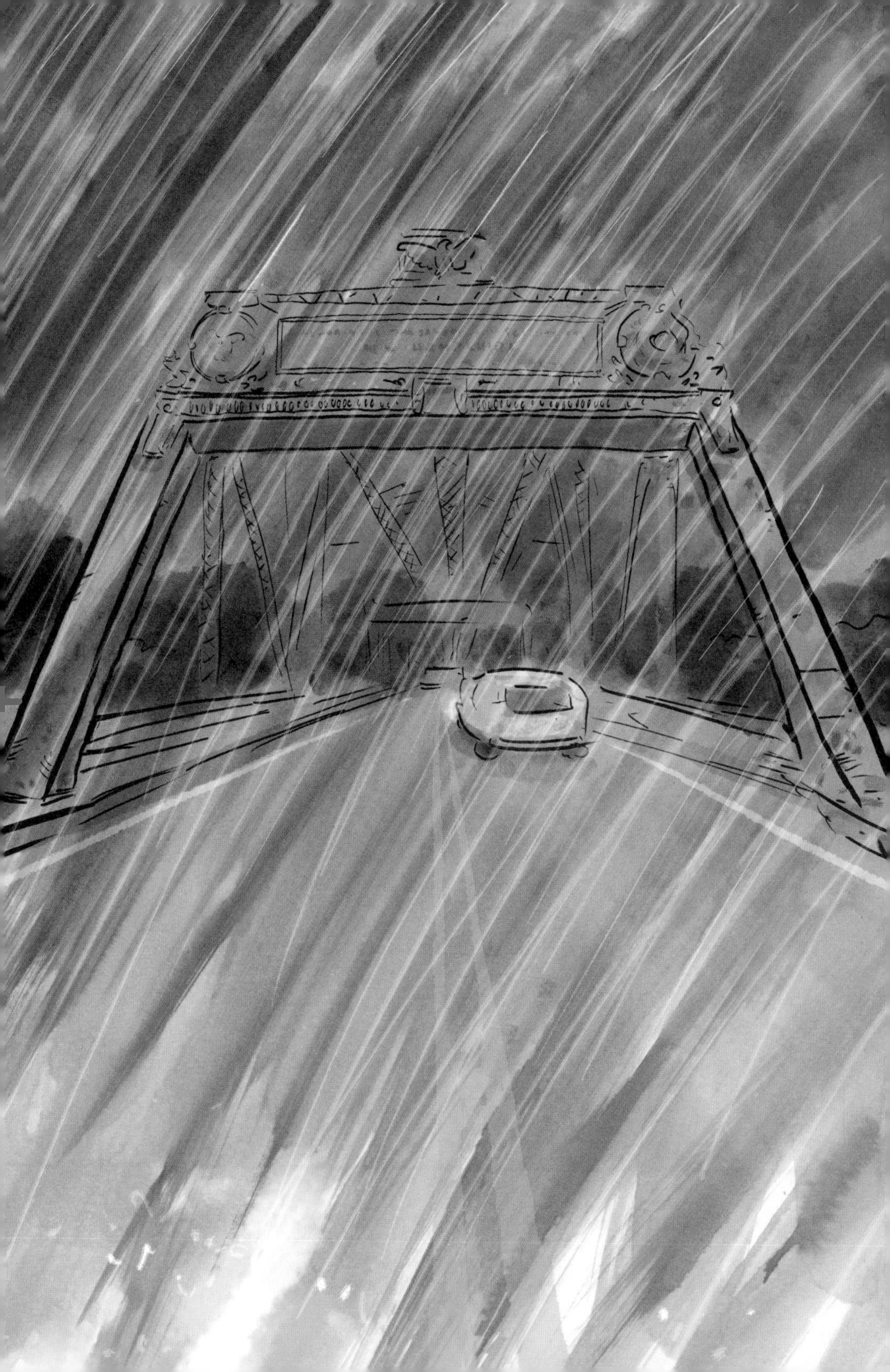

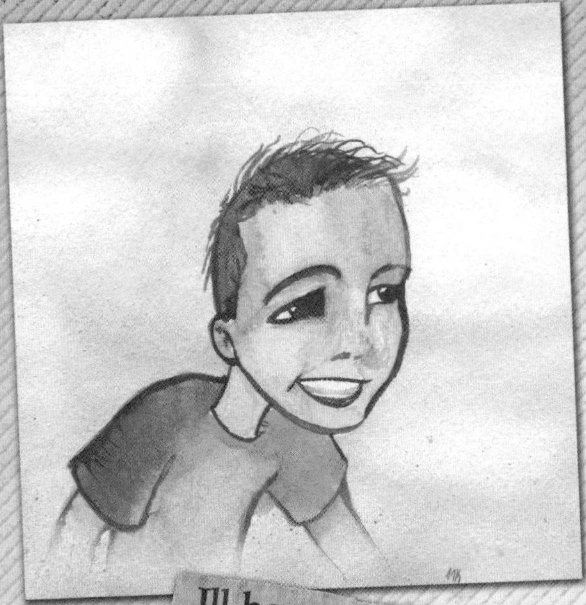

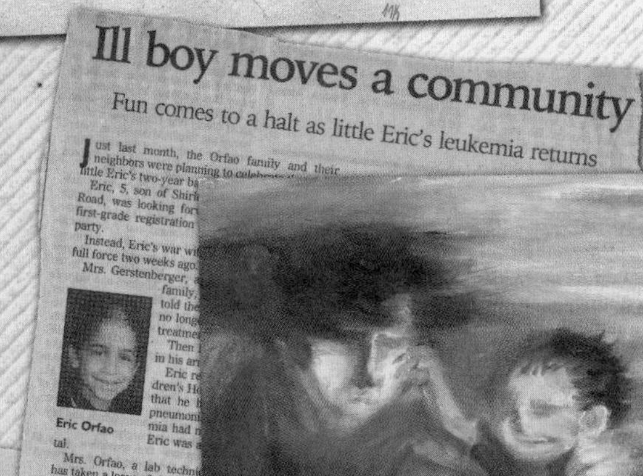

Ill boy moves a community

Fun comes to a halt as little Eric's leukemia returns

Just last month, the Orfao family and their
neighbors were planning to celebrate
little Eric's two-year ba
Eric, 5, son of Shirl
Road, was looking for
first-grade registration
party.
Instead, Eric's war wi
full force two weeks ago.
Mrs. Gerstenberger, a
family,
told the
no long
treatme
Then
in his ar
Eric re
dren's Ho
that he
pneumoni
mia had
Eric was a
tal.

Eric Orfao

Mrs. Orfao, a lab techni
has taken a leave of absence t
with Eric.
Neighbors have joined to
Orfao family with medical
expenses.
Mrs. Gerstenberger said a
dinner, co-sponsored by the C
and the community, is being pla
the elementary school. Time a
been decided.

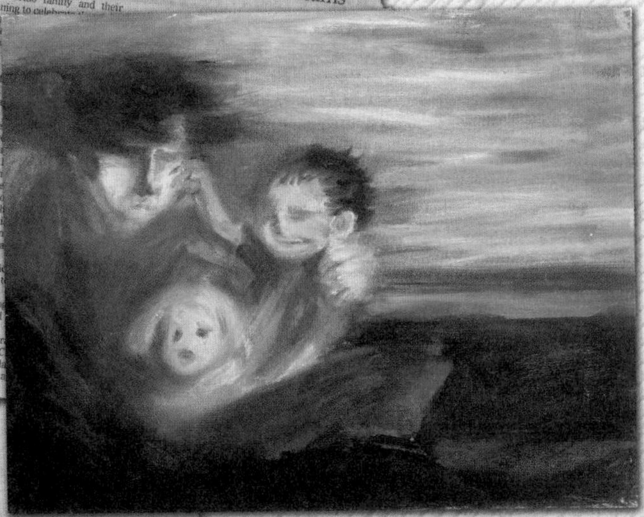

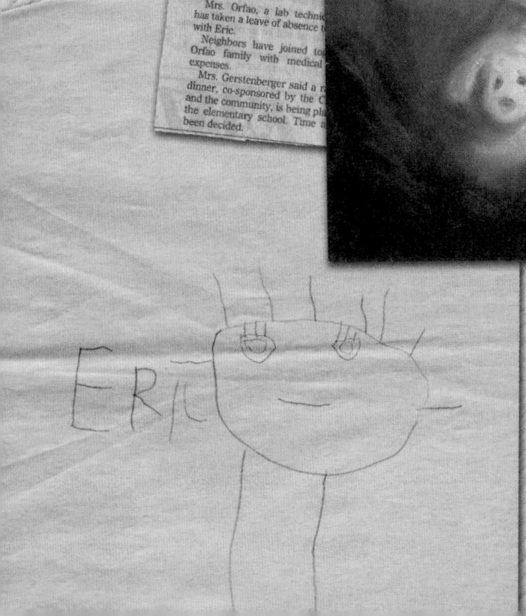
ERIC

CHAPTER 8
GOOD NIGHT
MY ANGEL

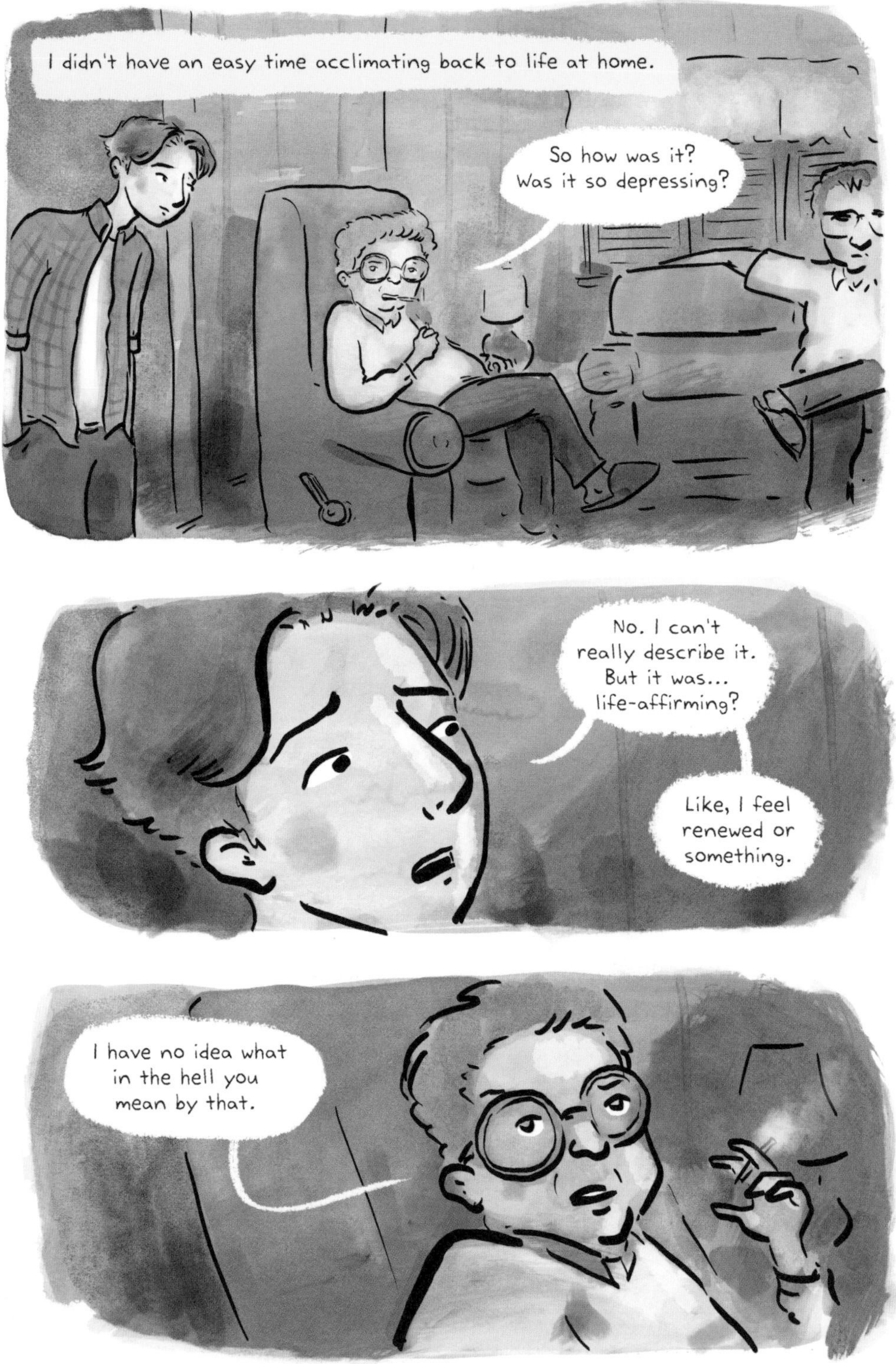
I didn't have an easy time acclimating back to life at home.
So how was it? Was it so depressing?
No. I can't really describe it. But it was... life-affirming?
Like, I feel renewed or something.
I have no idea what in the hell you mean by that.

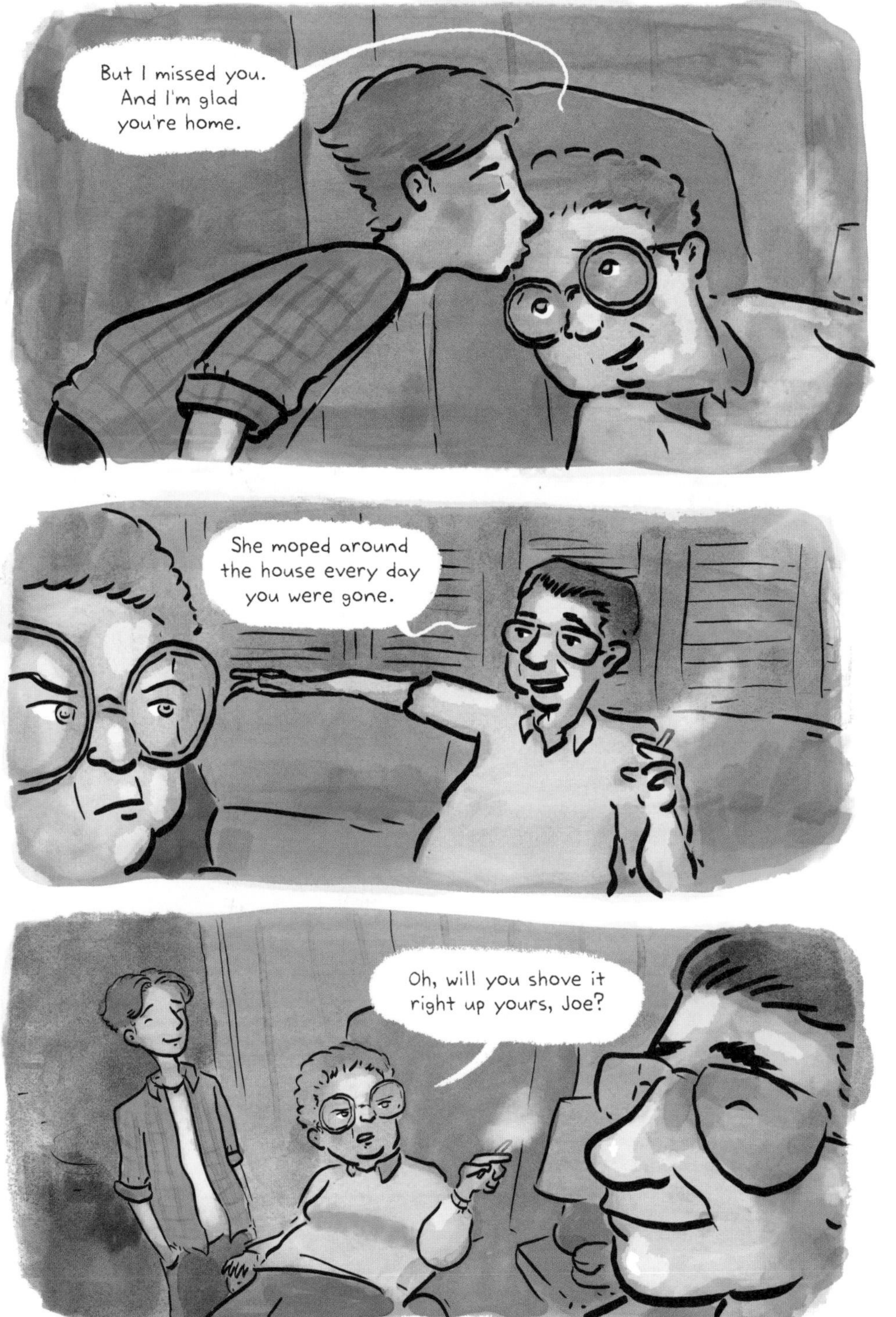
But I missed you. And I'm glad you're home.
She moped around the house every day you were gone.
Oh, will you shove it right up yours, Joe?

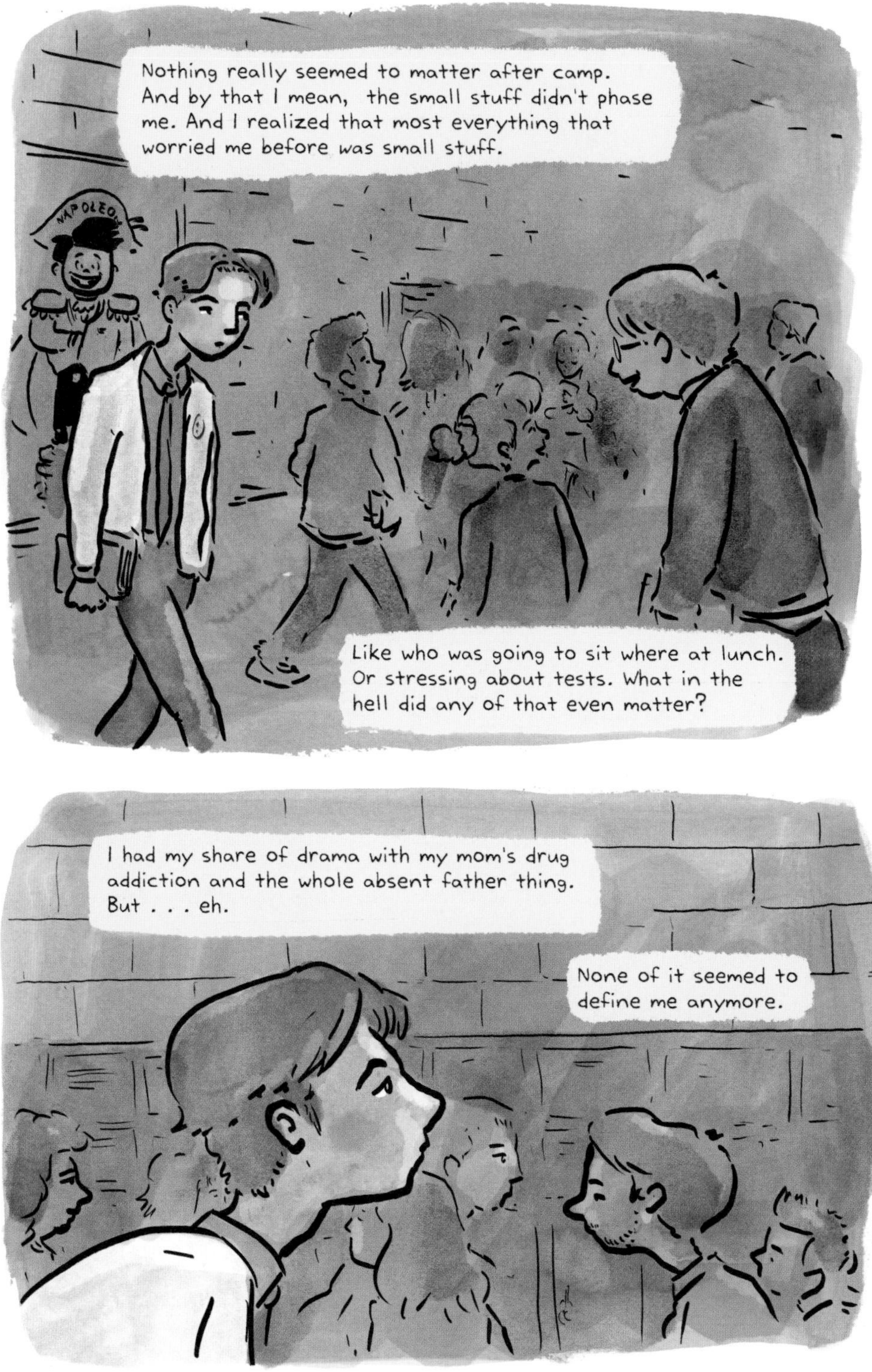

Nothing really seemed to matter after camp. And by that I mean, the small stuff didn't phase me. And I realized that most everything that worried me before was small stuff.
NAPOLEON
Like who was going to sit where at lunch. Or stressing about tests. What in the hell did any of that even matter?
I had my share of drama with my mom's drug addiction and the whole absent father thing. But . . . eh.
None of it seemed to define me anymore.

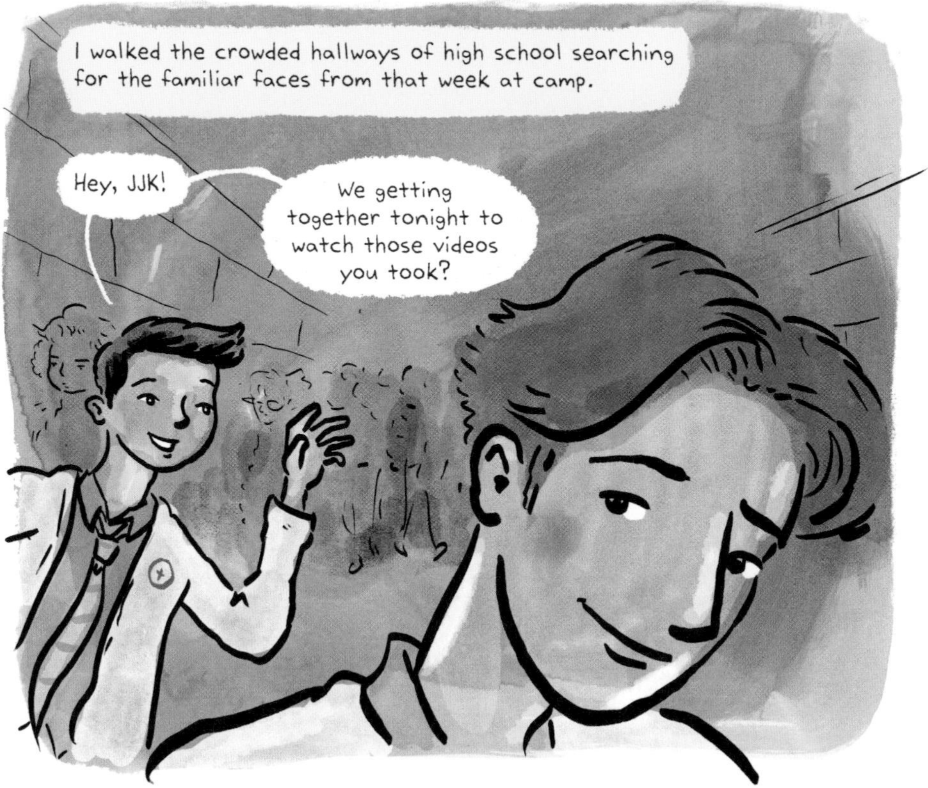
I walked the crowded hallways of high school searching for the familiar faces from that week at camp.
Hey, JJK!
We getting together tonight to watch those videos you took?

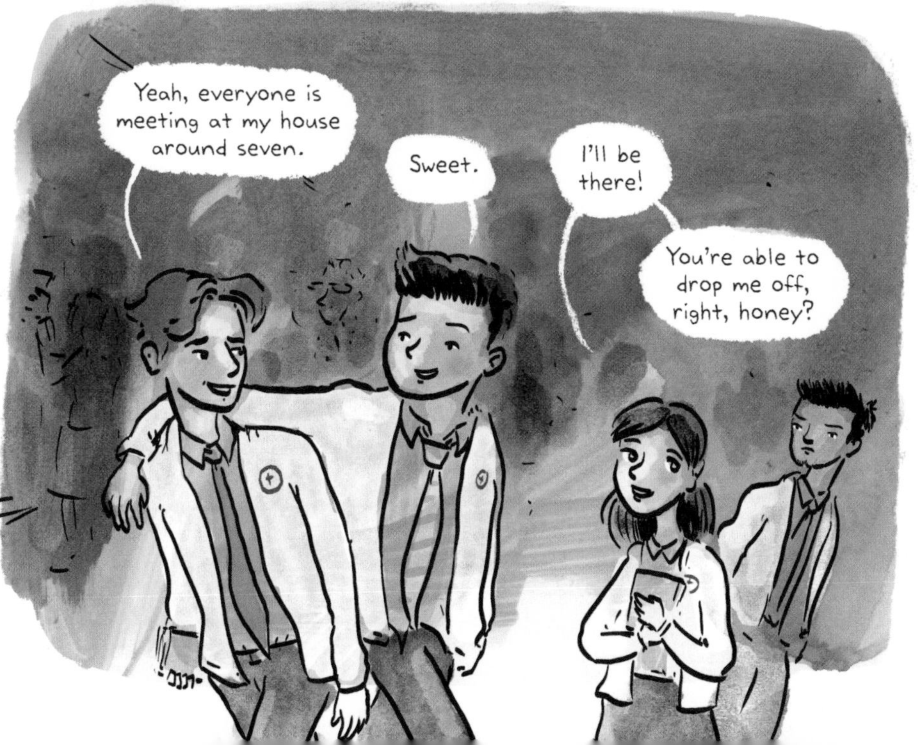
Yeah, everyone is meeting at my house around seven.
Sweet.
I'll be there!
You're able to drop me off, right, honey?

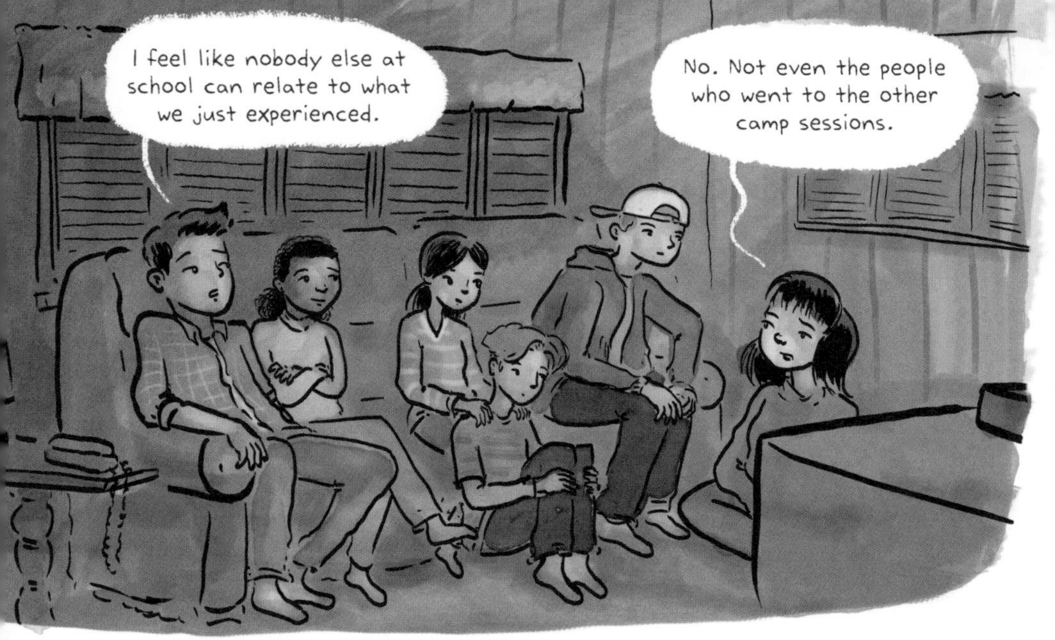
I feel like nobody else at school can relate to what we just experienced.
No. Not even the people who went to the other camp sessions.

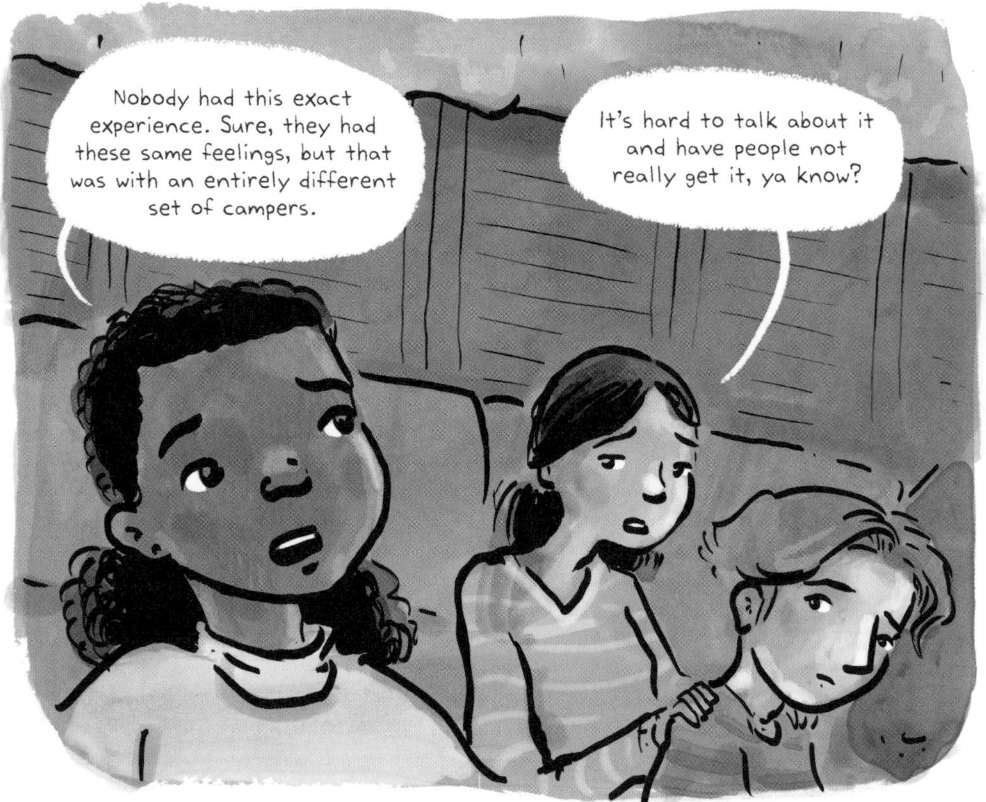
Nobody had this exact experience. Sure, they had these same feelings, but that was with an entirely different set of campers.
It's hard to talk about it and have people not really get it, ya know?

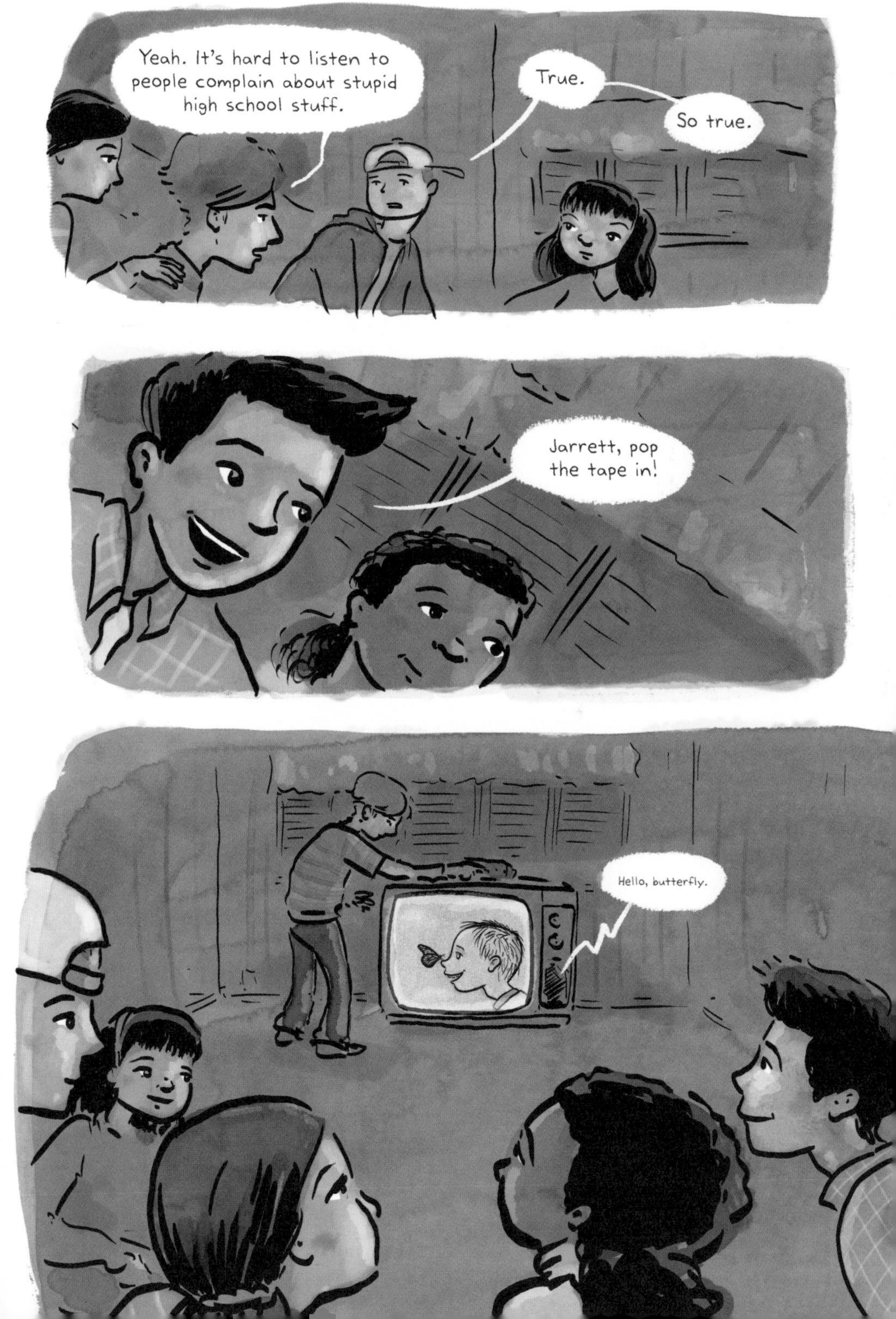
Yeah. It's hard to listen to people complain about stupid high school stuff.
True.
So true.
Jarrett, pop the tape in!
Hello, butterfly.

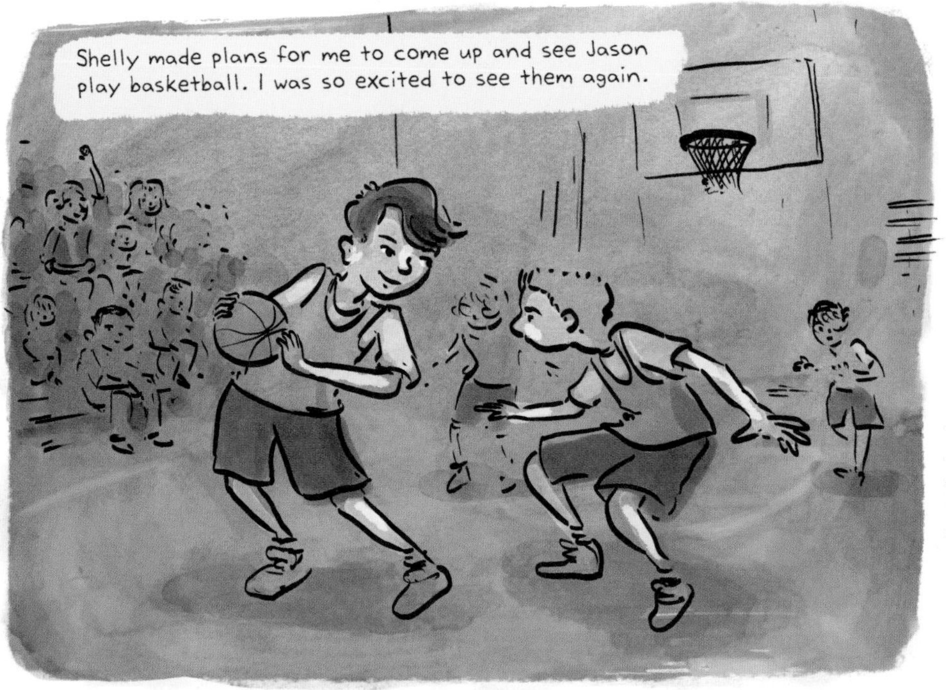
Shelly made plans for me to come up and see Jason play basketball. I was so excited to see them again.

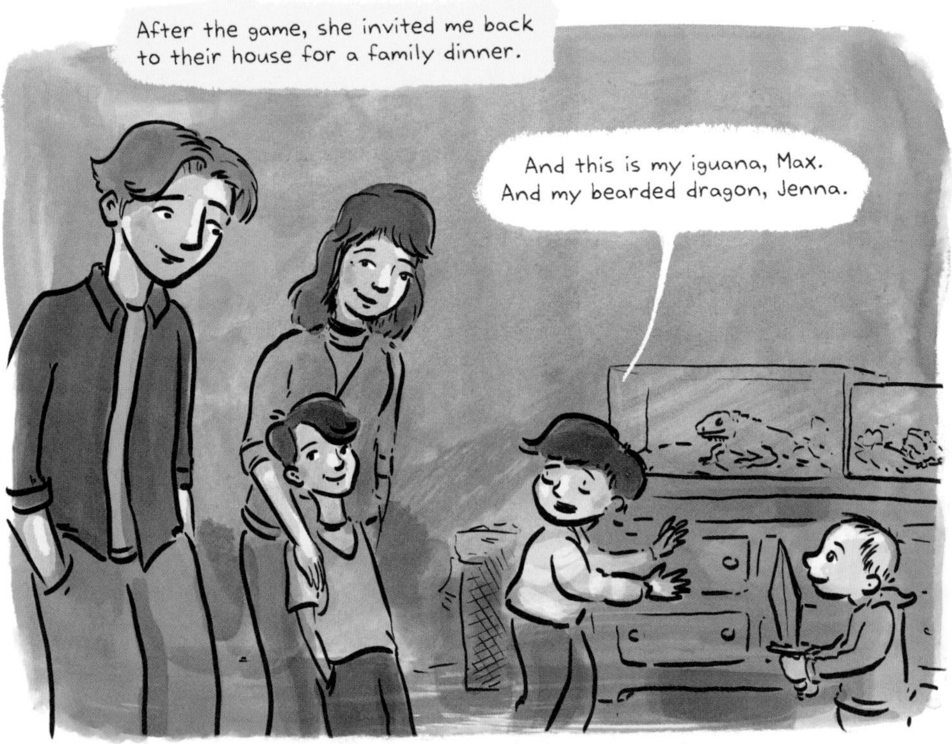
After the game, she invited me back to their house for a family dinner.
And this is my iguana, Max. And my bearded dragon, Jenna.

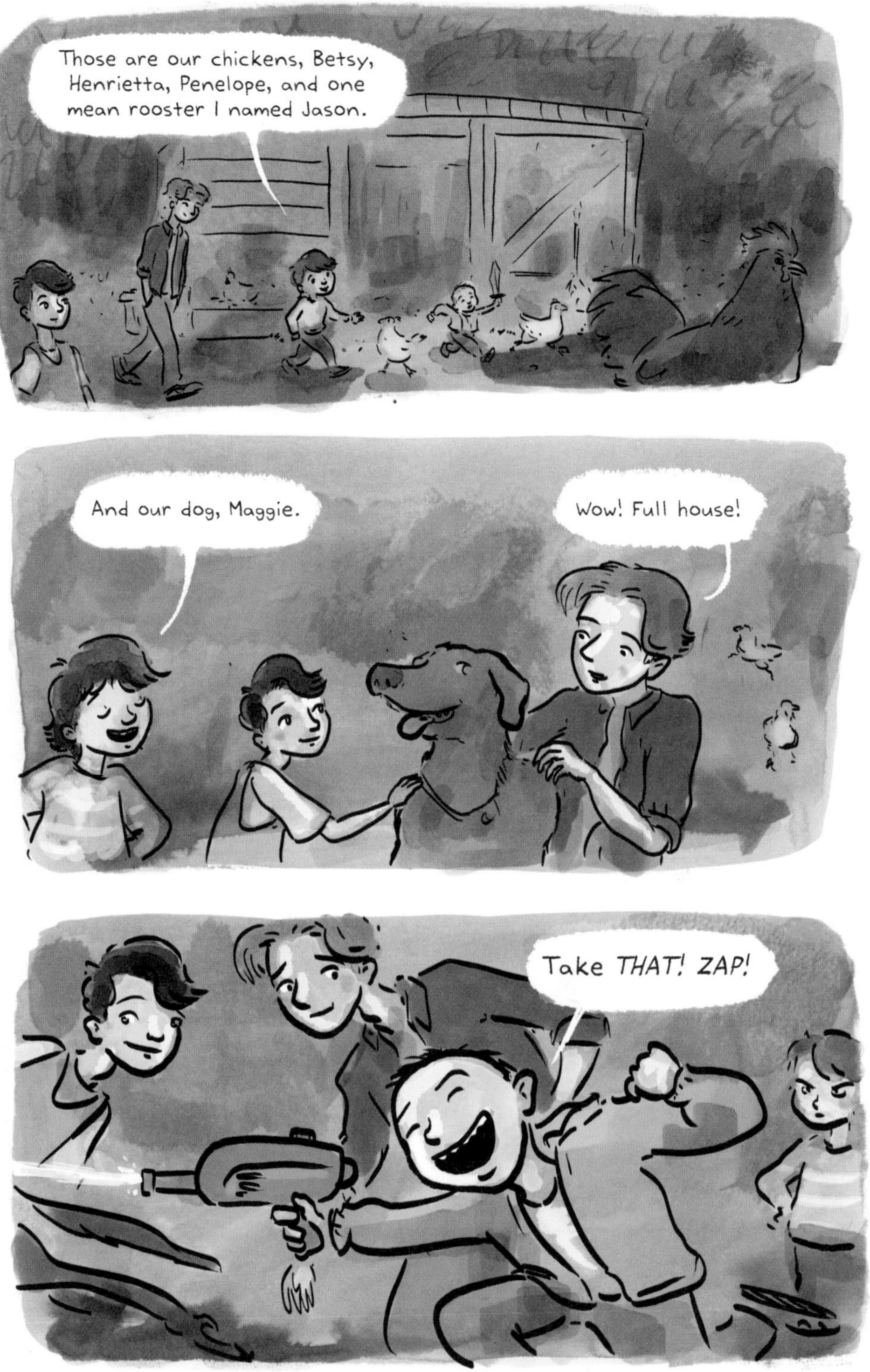
Those are our chickens, Betsy, Henrietta, Penelope, and one mean rooster I named Jason.
And our dog, Maggie.
Wow! Full house!
Take *THAT! ZAP!*

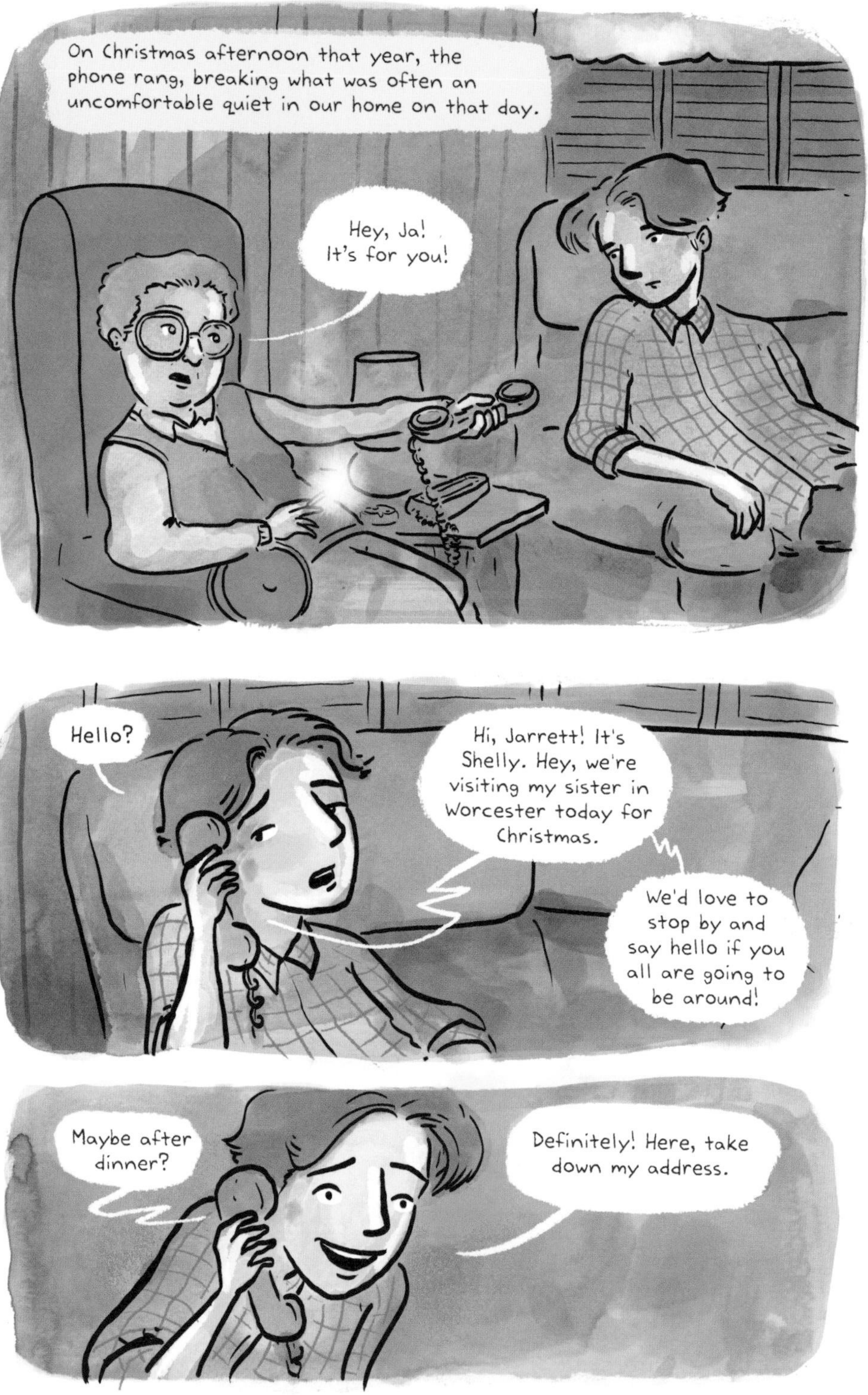
On Christmas afternoon that year, the phone rang, breaking what was often an uncomfortable quiet in our home on that day.
Hey, Ja! It's for you!
Hello?
Hi, Jarrett! It's Shelly. Hey, we're visiting my sister in Worcester today for Christmas.
We'd love to stop by and say hello if you all are going to be around!
Maybe after dinner?
Definitely! Here, take down my address.

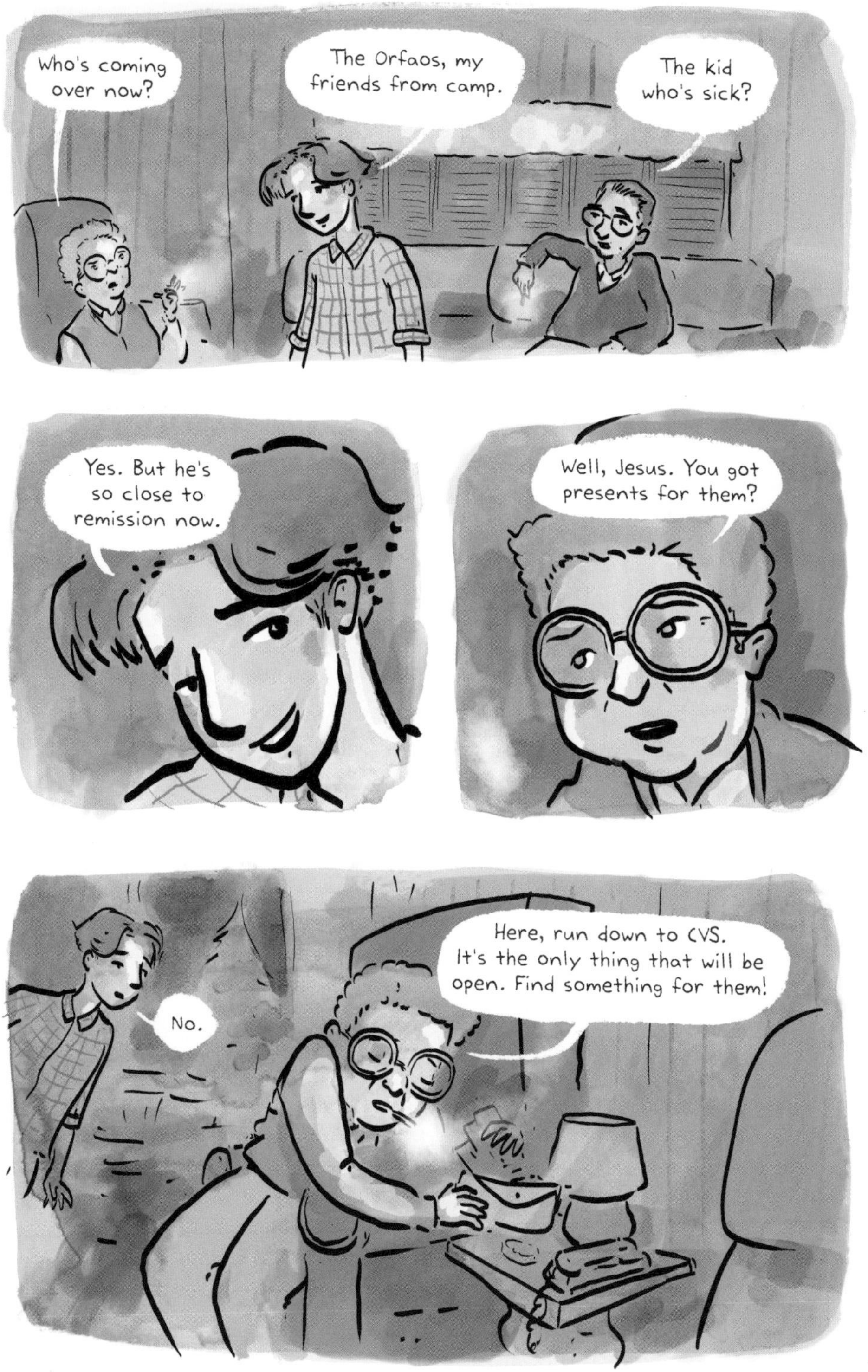
Who's coming over now?
The Orfaos, my friends from camp.
The kid who's sick?
Yes. But he's so close to remission now.
Well, Jesus. You got presents for them?
No.
Here, run down to CVS. It's the only thing that will be open. Find something for them!

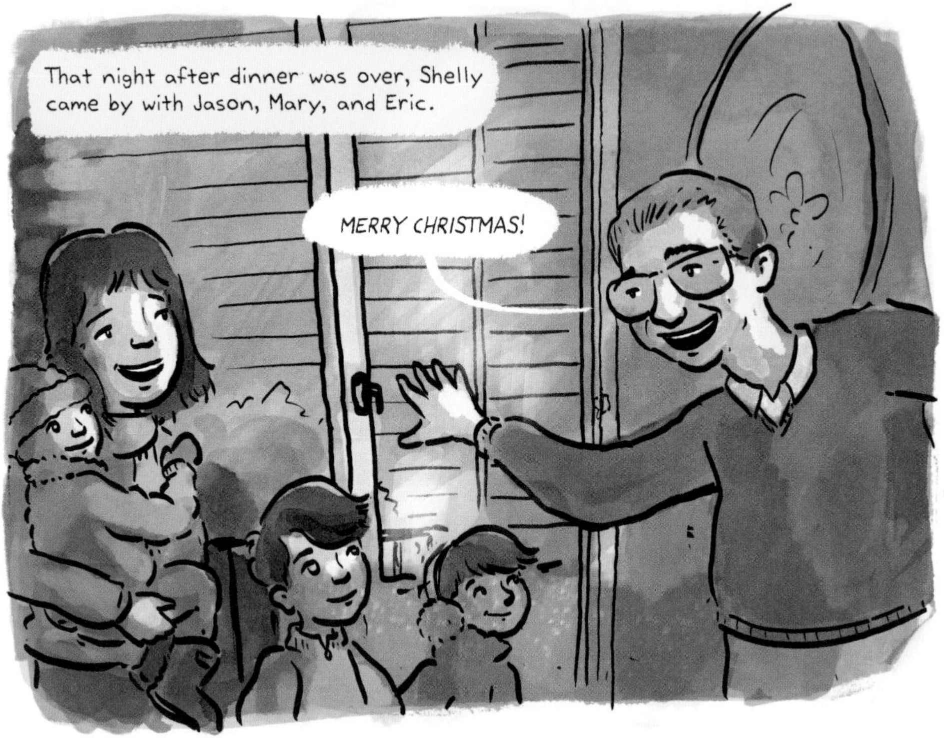
That night after dinner was over, Shelly came by with Jason, Mary, and Eric.
MERRY CHRISTMAS!

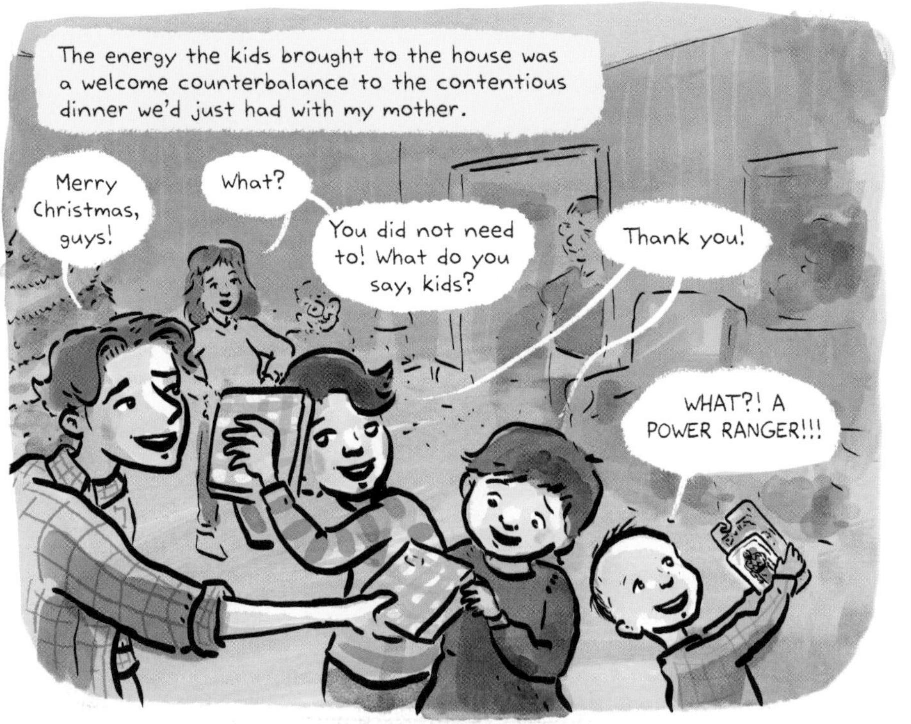
The energy the kids brought to the house was a welcome counterbalance to the contentious dinner we'd just had with my mother.
Merry Christmas, guys!
What?
You did not need to! What do you say, kids?
Thank you!
WHAT?! A POWER RANGER!!!

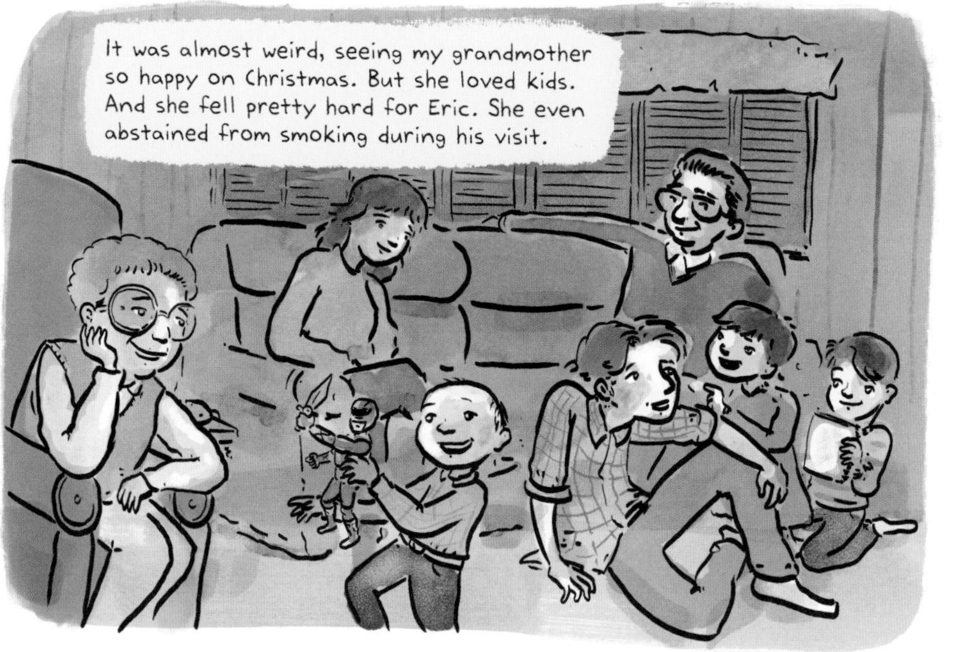
It was almost weird, seeing my grandmother so happy on Christmas. But she loved kids. And she fell pretty hard for Eric. She even abstained from smoking during his visit.

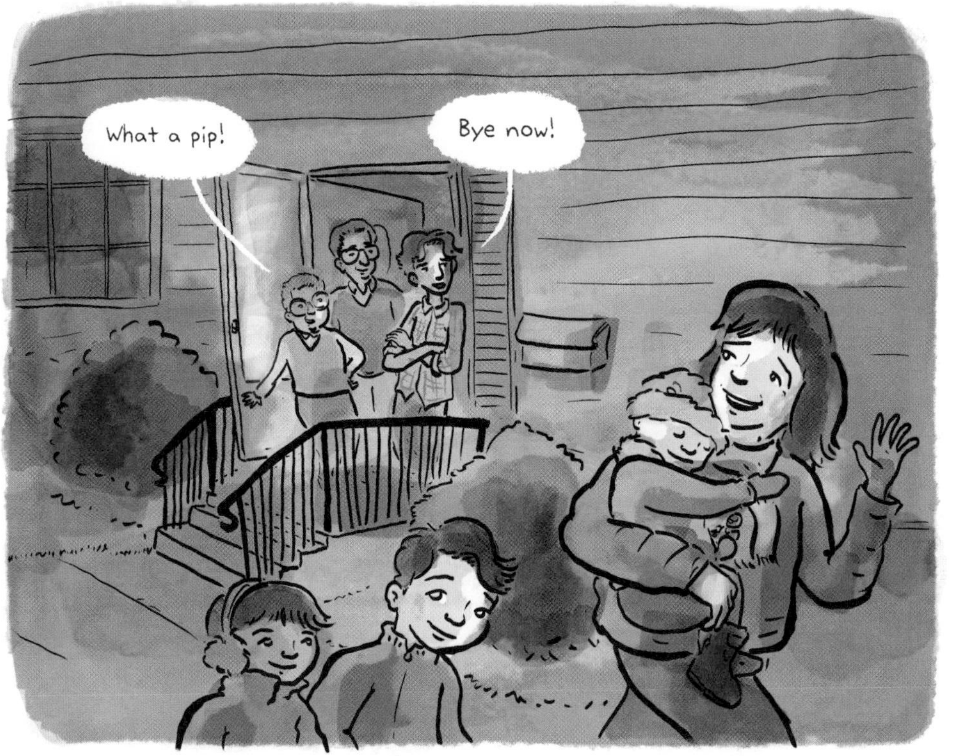
What a pip!
Bye now!

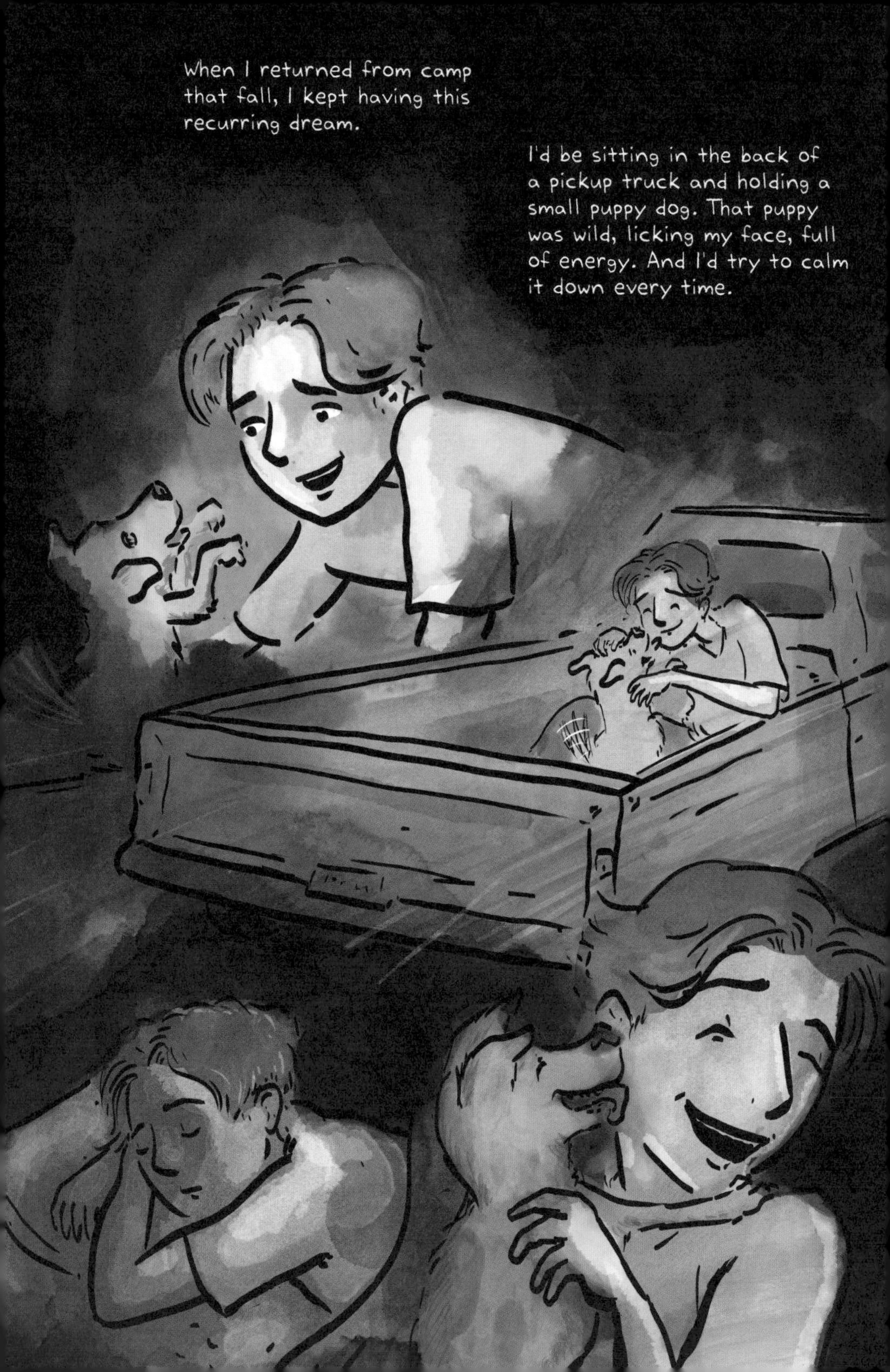
When I returned from camp that fall, I kept having this recurring dream.
I'd be sitting in the back of a pickup truck and holding a small puppy dog. That puppy was wild, licking my face, full of energy. And I'd try to calm it down every time.

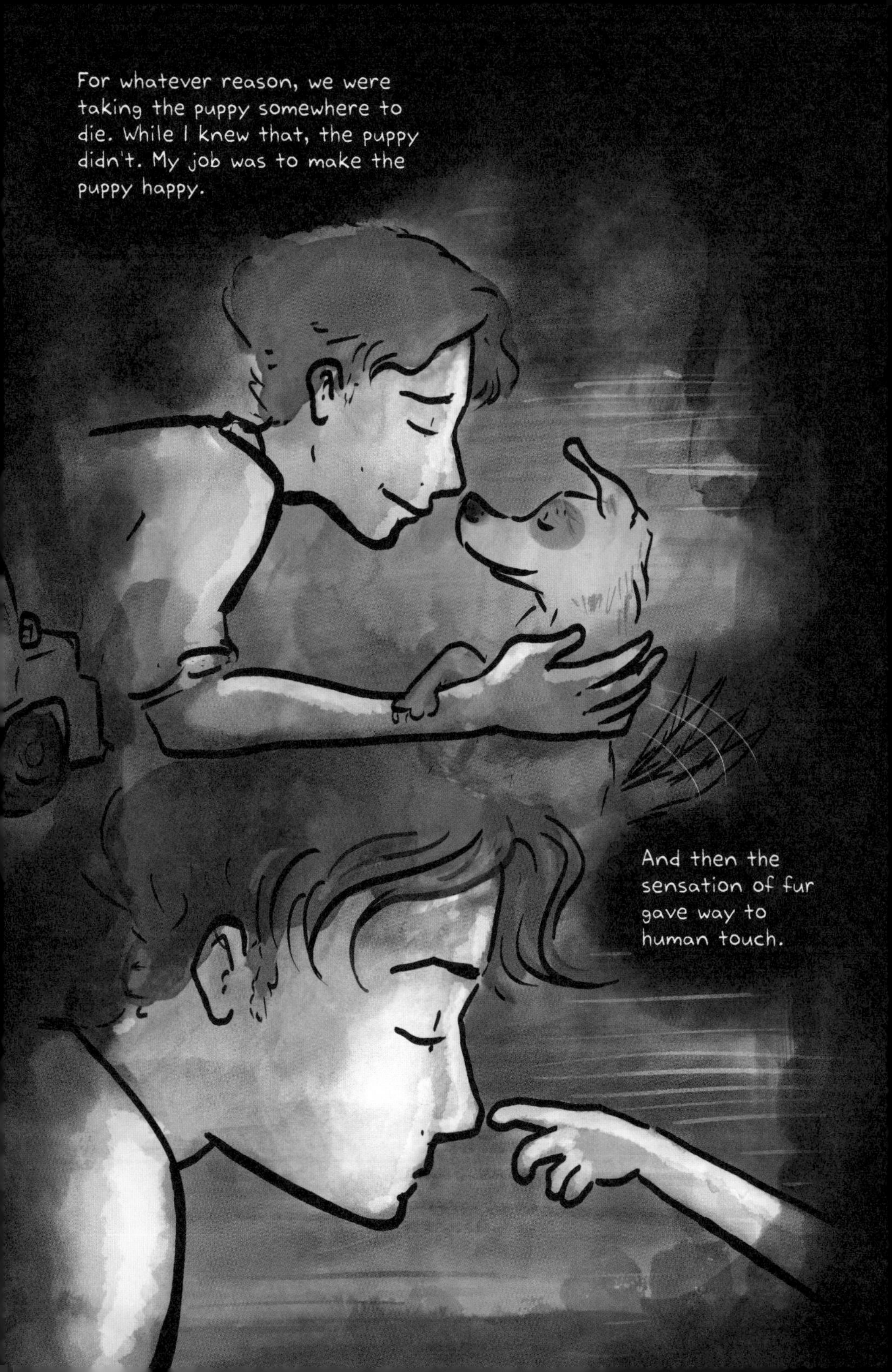
For whatever reason, we were taking the puppy somewhere to die. While I knew that, the puppy didn't. My job was to make the puppy happy.
And then the sensation of fur gave way to human touch.

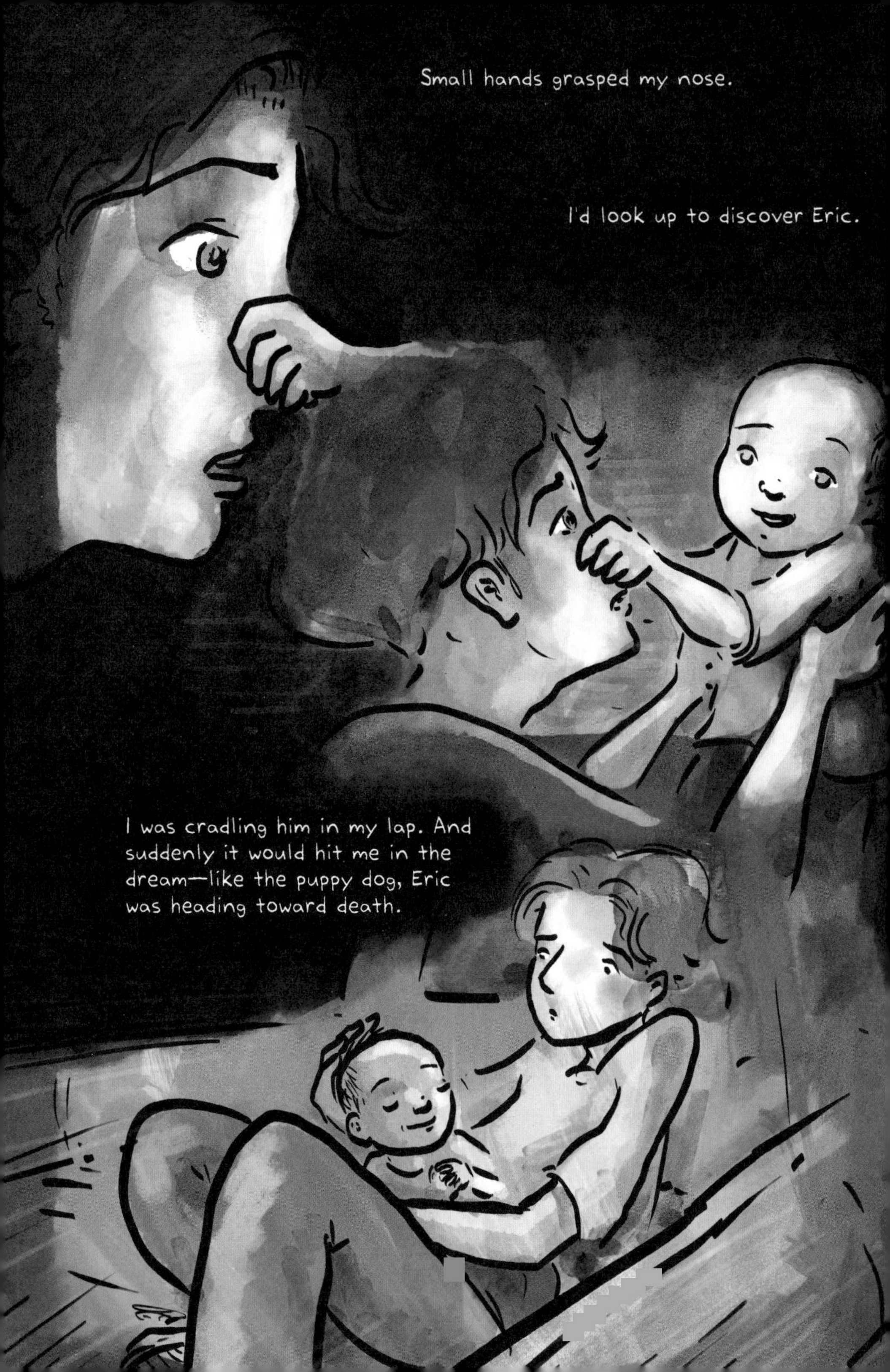
Small hands grasped my nose.
I'd look up to discover Eric.
I was cradling him in my lap. And suddenly it would hit me in the dream—like the puppy dog, Eric was heading toward death.

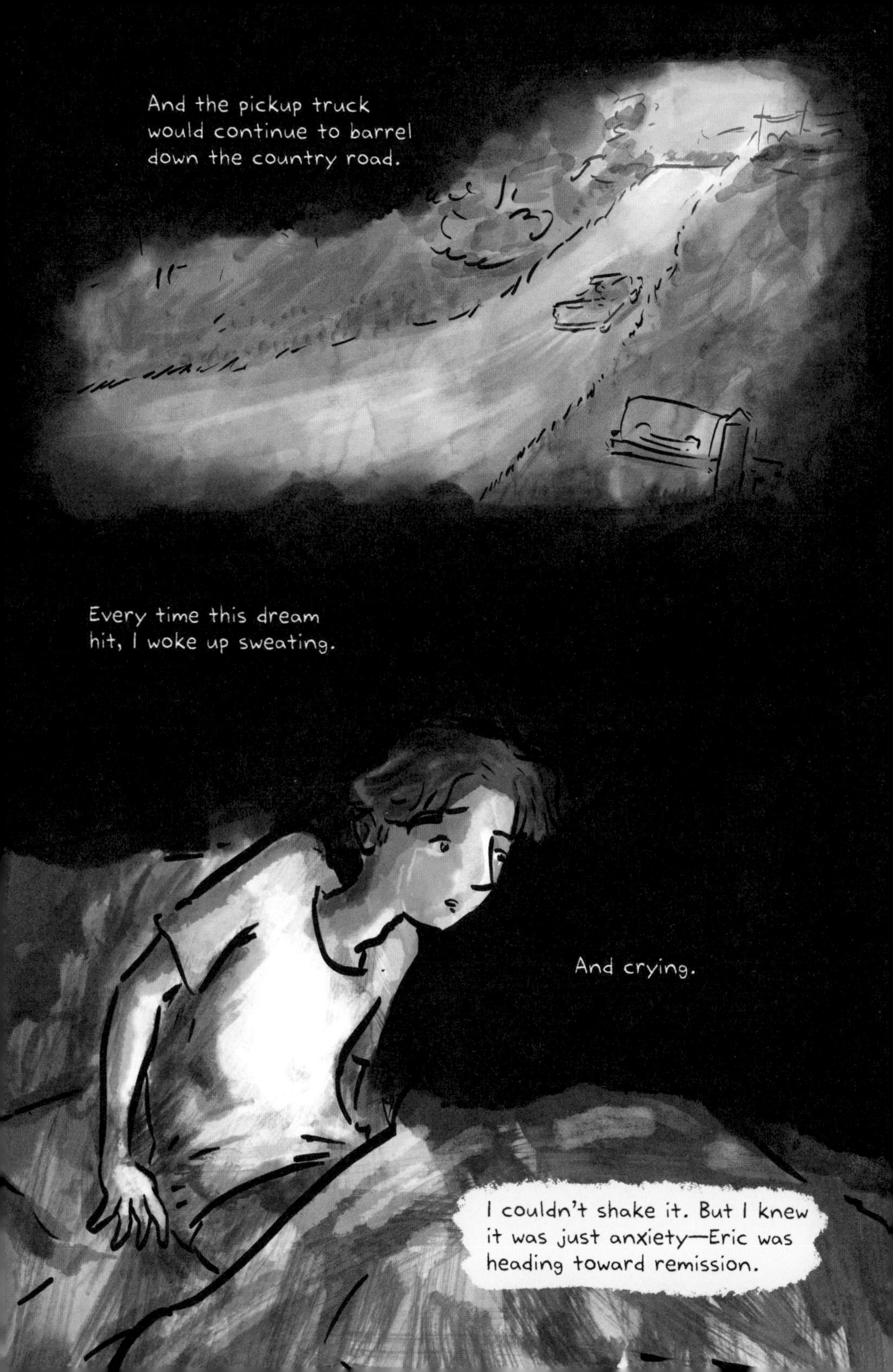
And the pickup truck would continue to barrel down the country road.
Every time this dream hit, I woke up sweating.
And crying.
I couldn't shake it. But I knew it was just anxiety—Eric was heading toward remission.

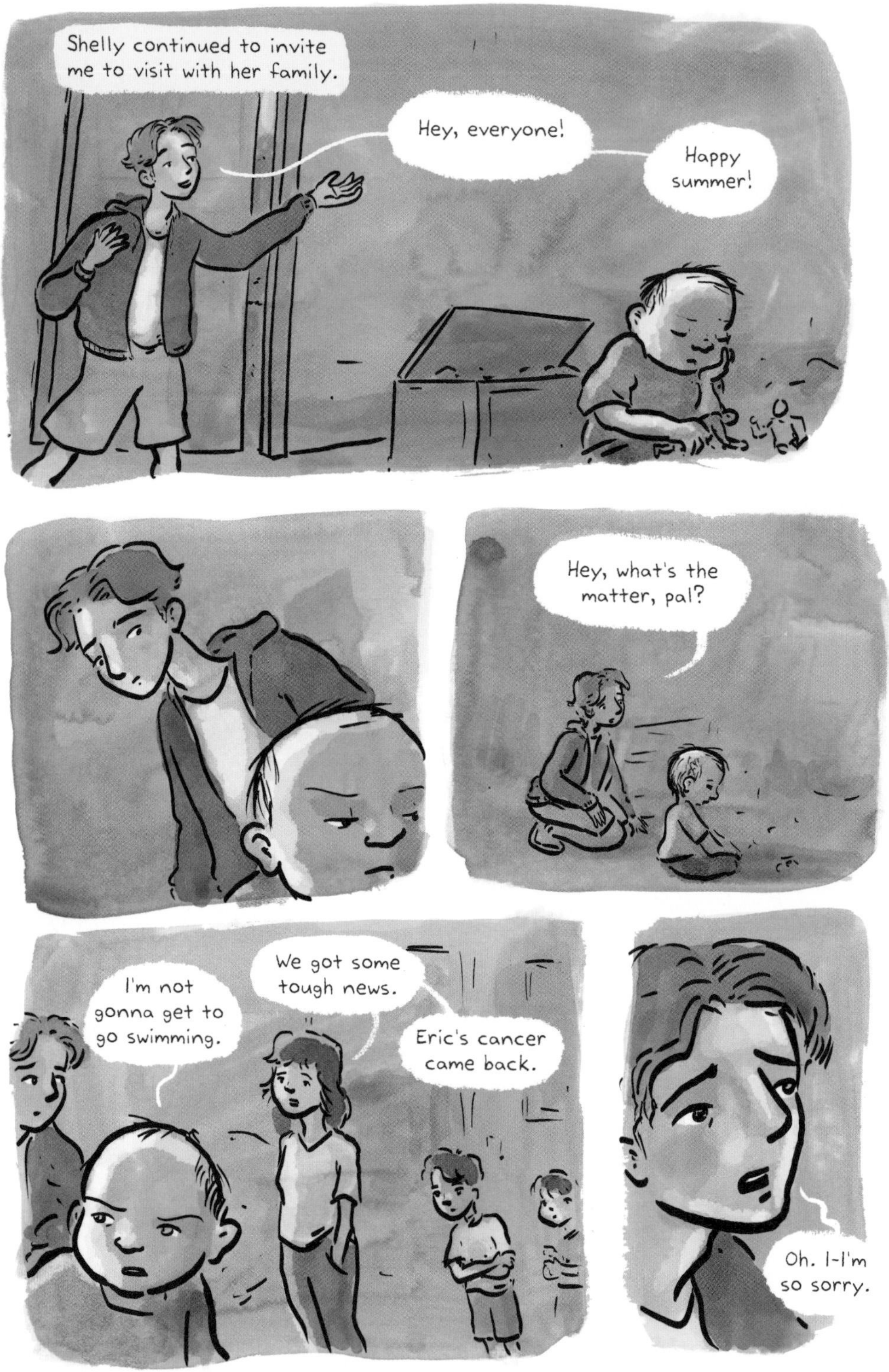
Shelly continued to invite me to visit with her family.
Hey, everyone!
Happy summer!
Hey, what's the matter, pal?
I'm not gonna get to go swimming.
We got some tough news.
Eric's cancer came back.
Oh. I-I'm so sorry.

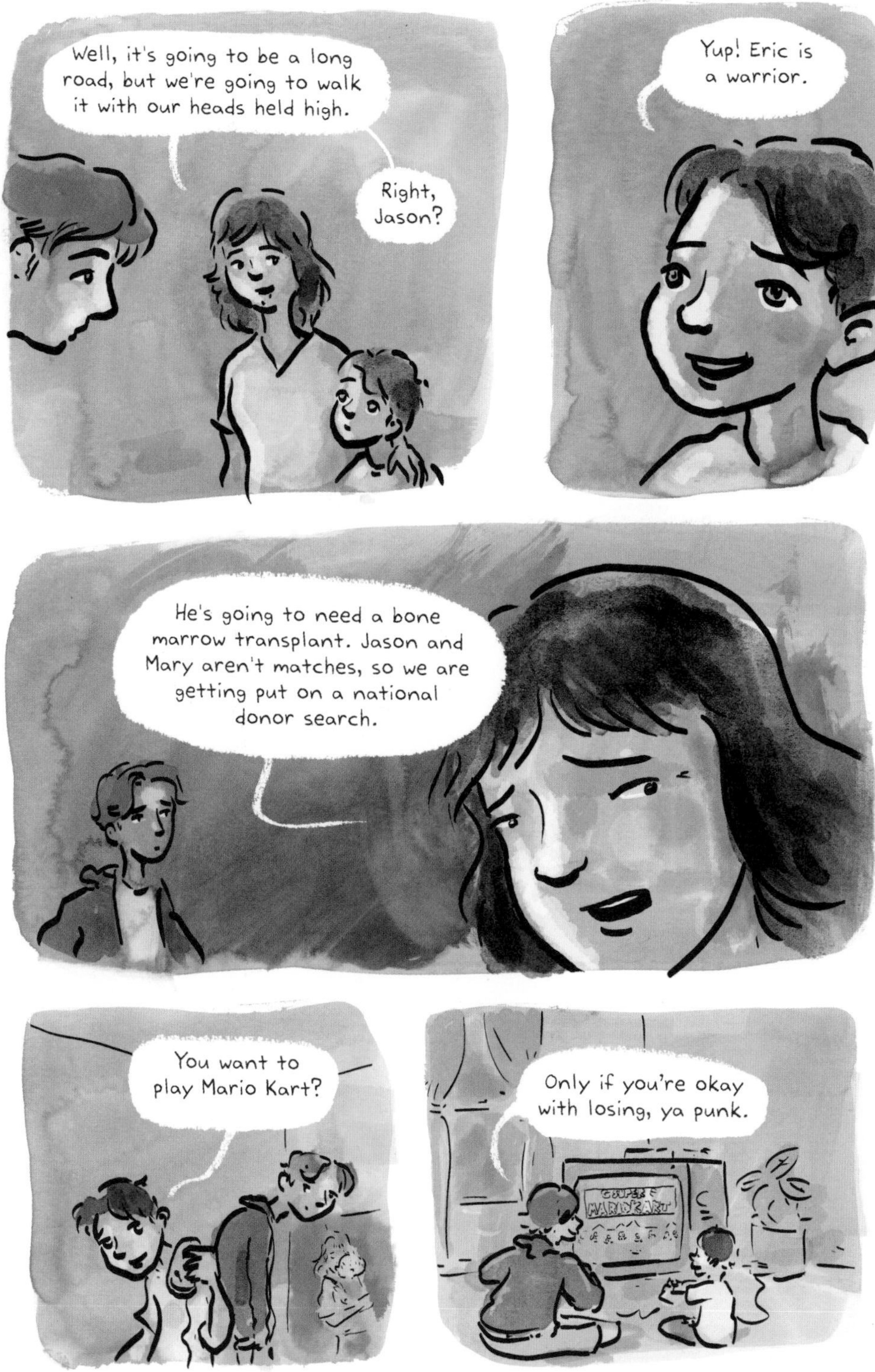
Well, it's going to be a long road, but we're going to walk it with our heads held high.
Right, Jason?
Yup! Eric is a warrior.
He's going to need a bone marrow transplant. Jason and Mary aren't matches, so we are getting put on a national donor search.
You want to play Mario Kart?
Only if you're okay with losing, ya punk.

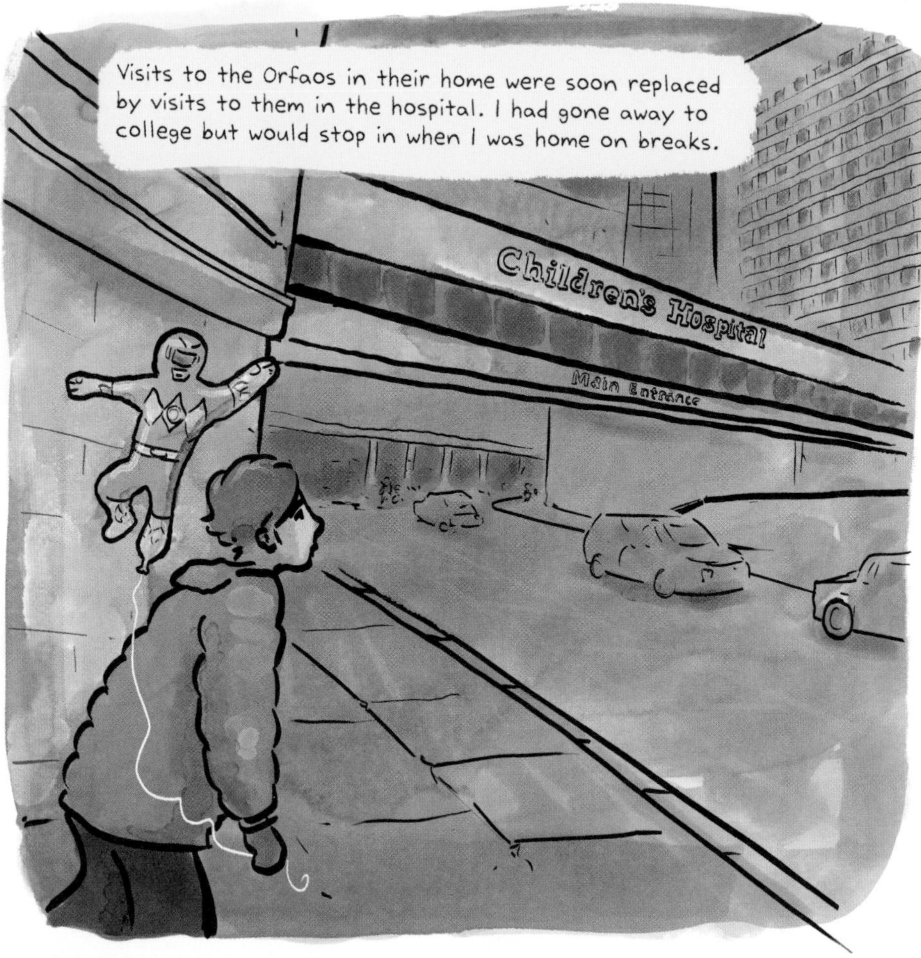
Visits to the Orfaos in their home were soon replaced by visits to them in the hospital. I had gone away to college but would stop in when I was home on breaks.
Children's Hospital
Main Entrance

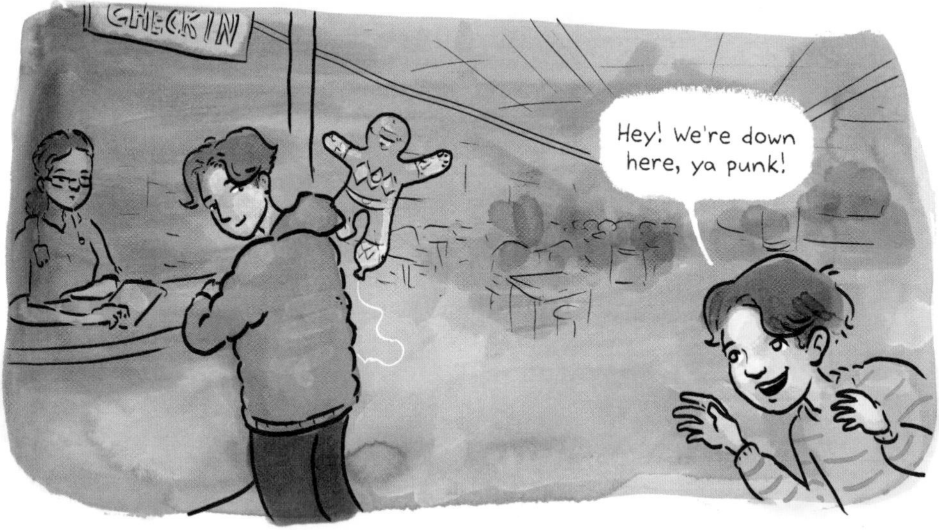
CHECKIN
Hey! We're down here, ya punk!

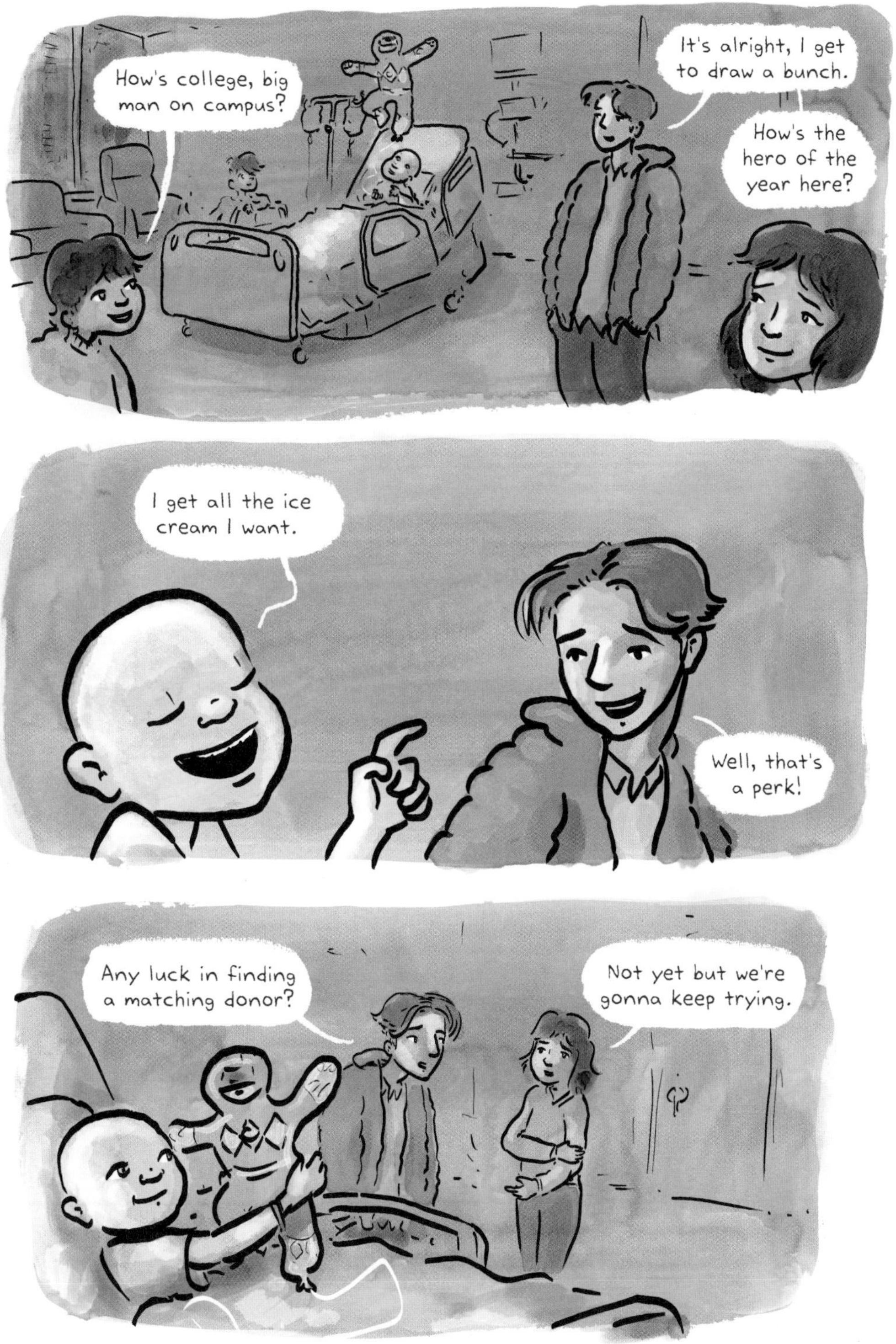
How's college, big man on campus?
It's alright, I get to draw a bunch.
How's the hero of the year here?
I get all the ice cream I want.
Well, that's a perk!
Any luck in finding a matching donor?
Not yet but we're gonna keep trying.

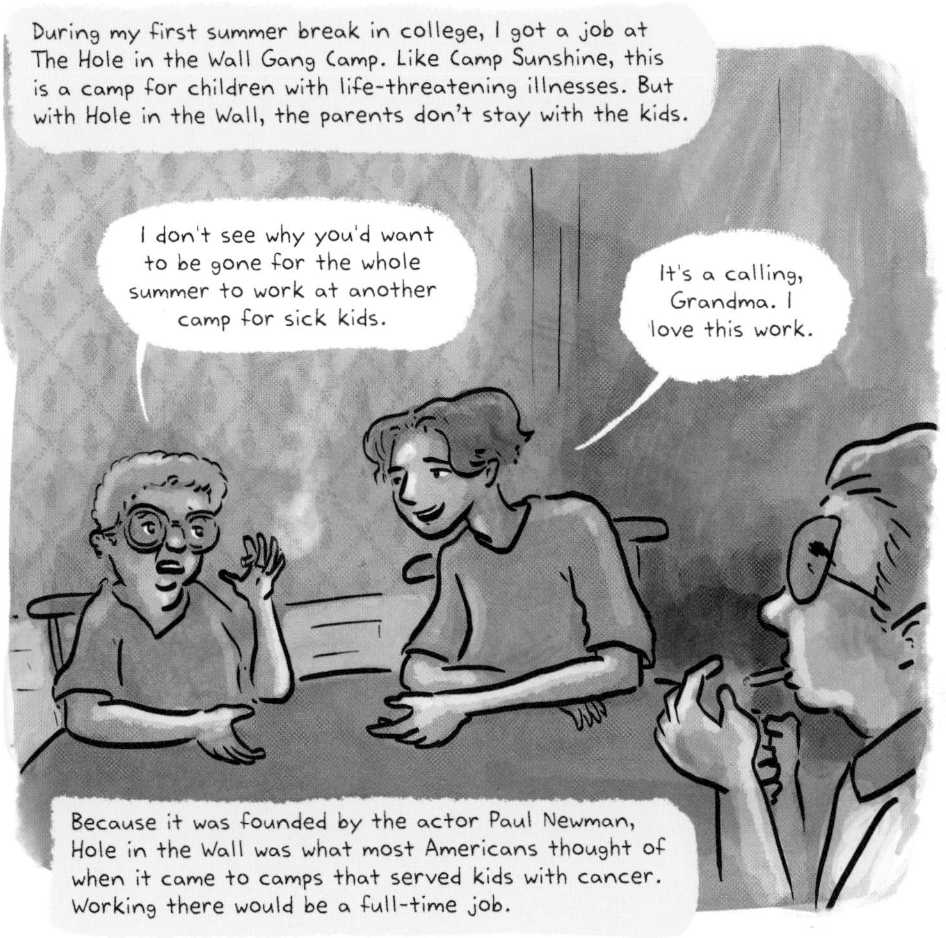
During my first summer break in college, I got a job at The Hole in the Wall Gang Camp. Like Camp Sunshine, this is a camp for children with life-threatening illnesses. But with Hole in the Wall, the parents don't stay with the kids.
I don't see why you'd want to be gone for the whole summer to work at another camp for sick kids.
It's a calling, Grandma. I love this work.
Because it was founded by the actor Paul Newman, Hole in the Wall was what most Americans thought of when it came to camps that served kids with cancer. Working there would be a full-time job.

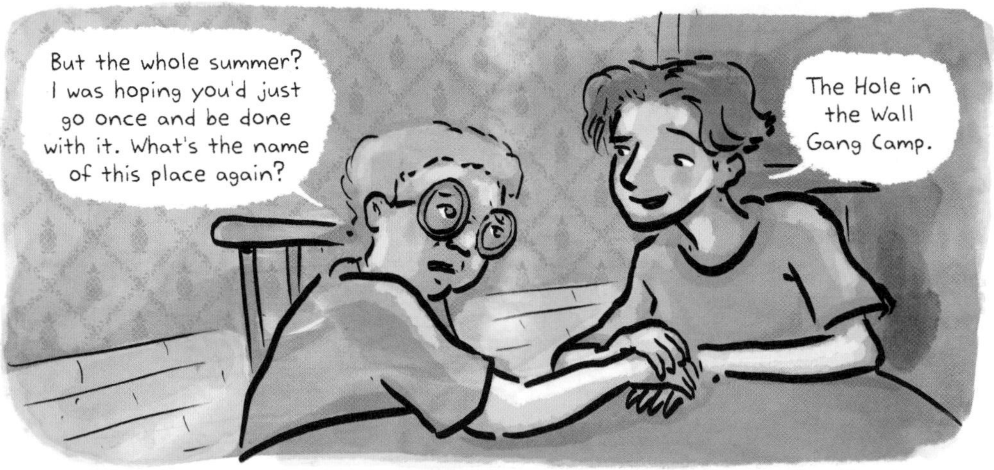
But the whole summer? I was hoping you'd just go once and be done with it. What's the name of this place again?
The Hole in the Wall Gang Camp.

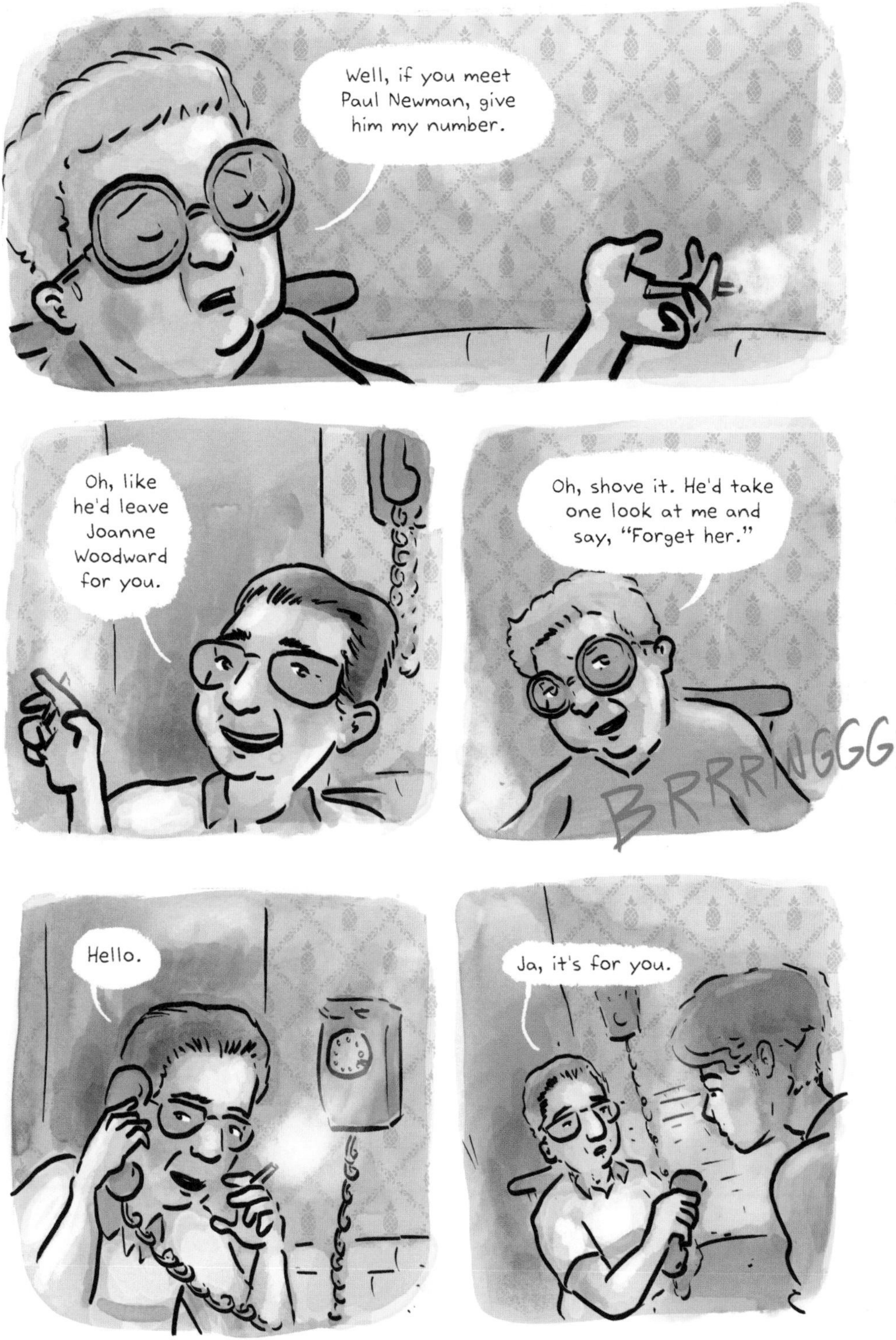
Well, if you meet Paul Newman, give him my number.
Oh, like he'd leave Joanne Woodward for you.
Oh, shove it. He'd take one look at me and say, "Forget her."
BRRRINGGG
Hello.
Ja, it's for you.

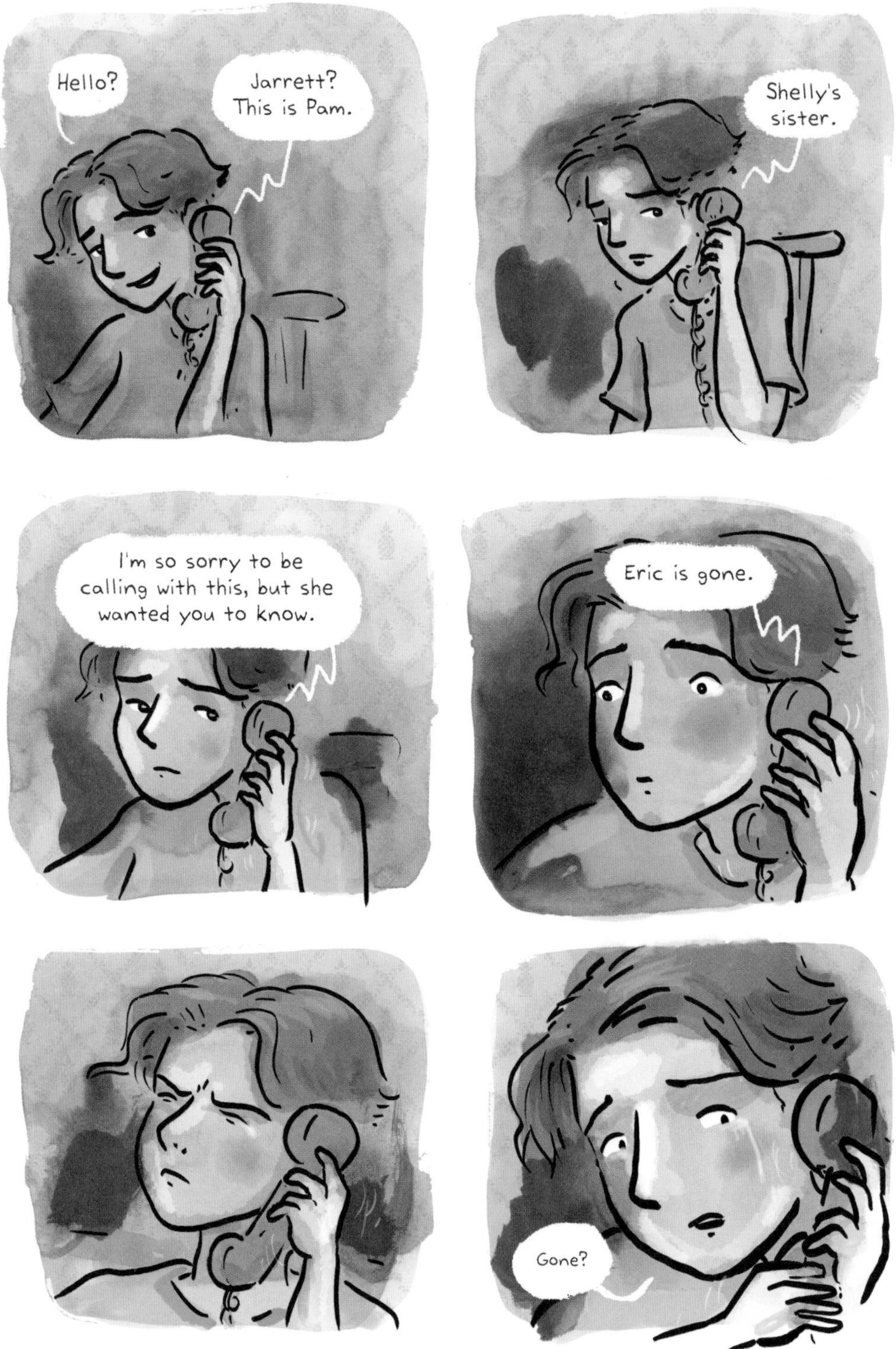
Hello?
Jarrett? This is Pam.
Shelly's sister.
I'm so sorry to be calling with this, but she wanted you to know.
Eric is gone.
Gone?

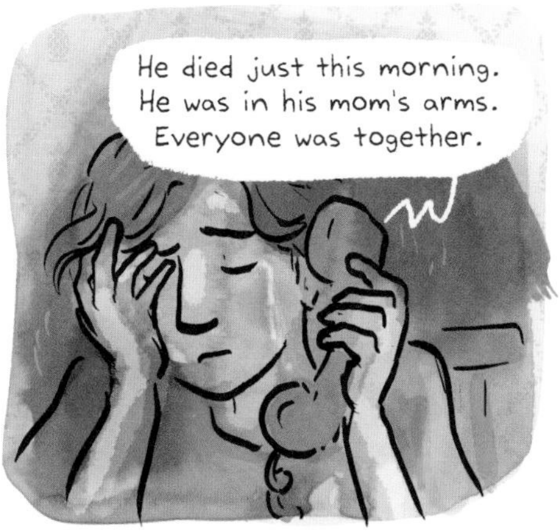
He died just this morning.
He was in his mom's arms.
Everyone was together.

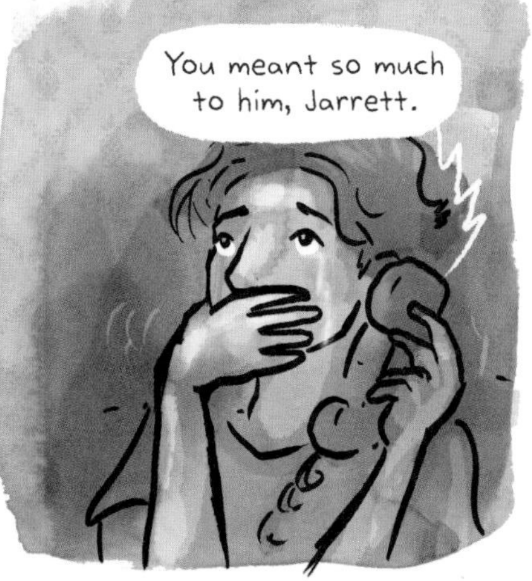
You meant so much to him, Jarrett.

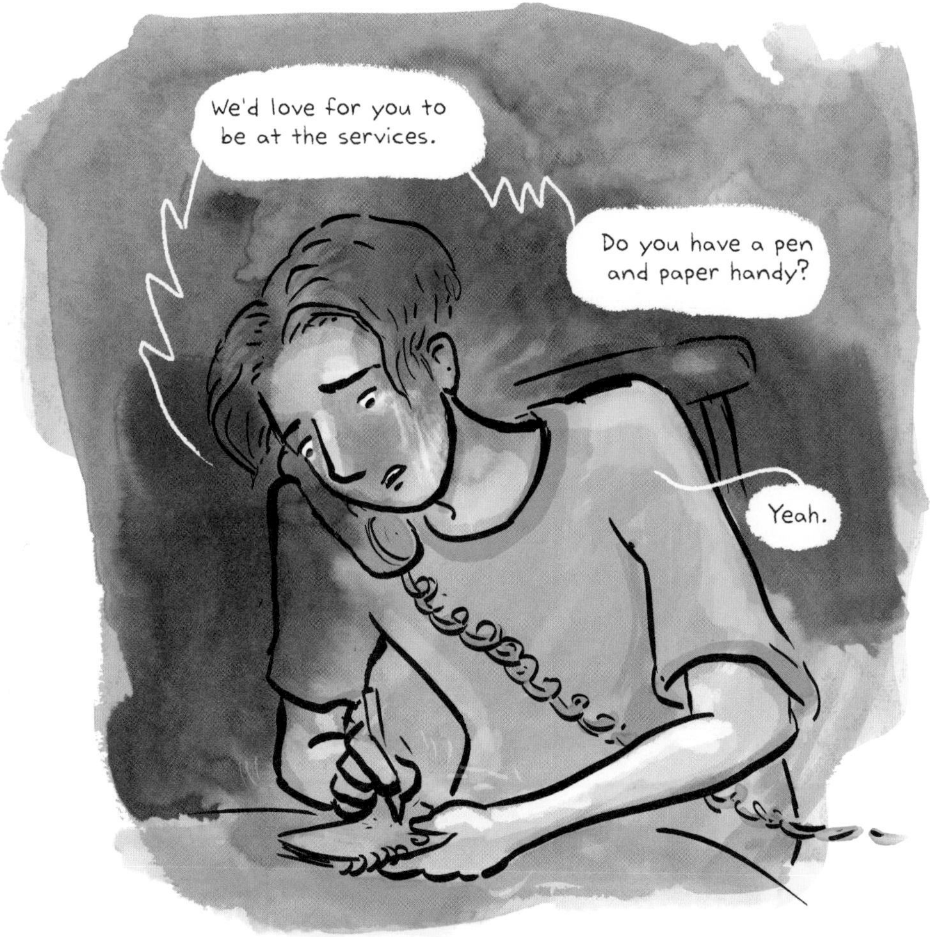
We'd love for you to be at the services.
Do you have a pen and paper handy?
Yeah.

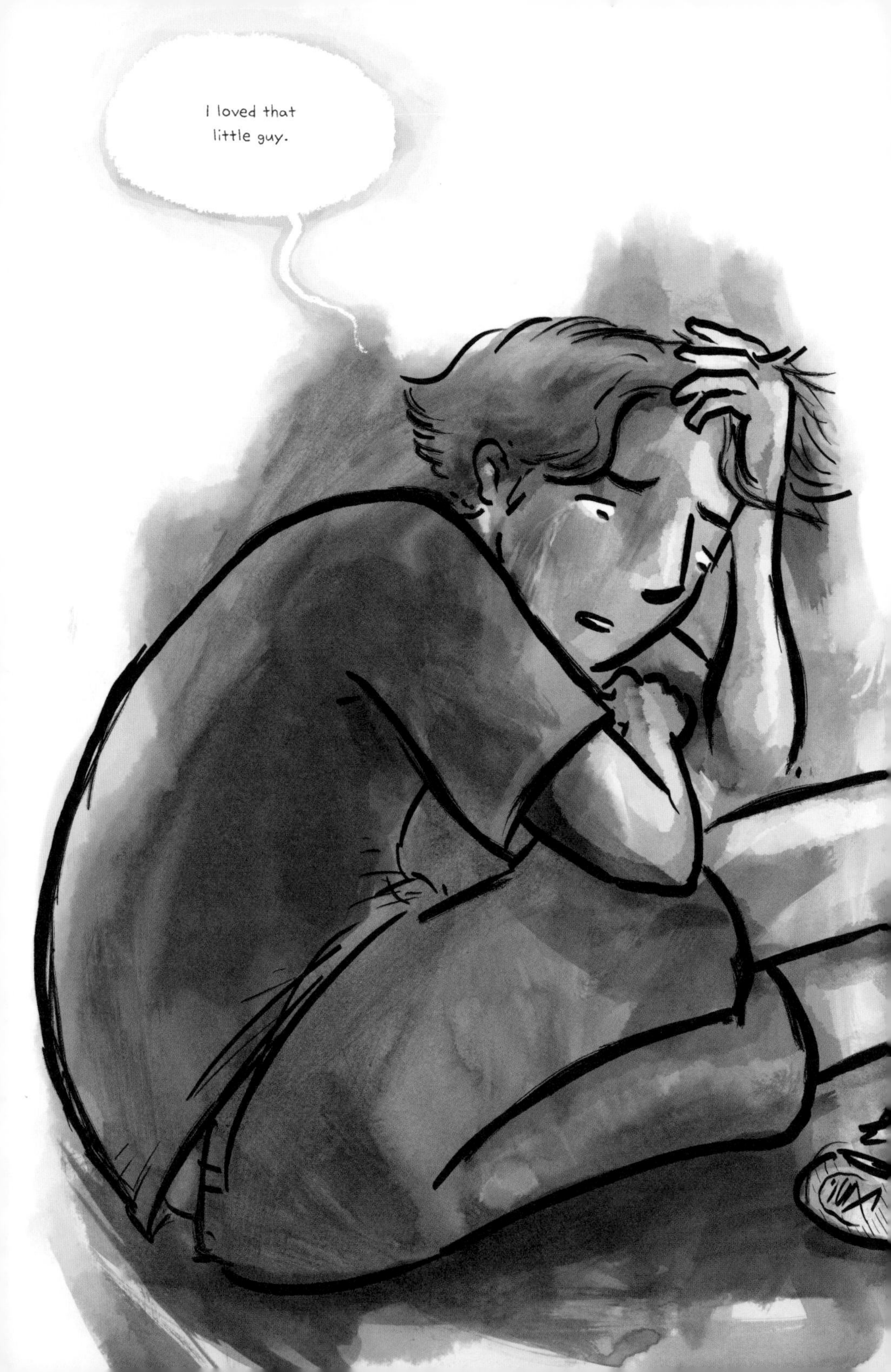
I loved that little guy.

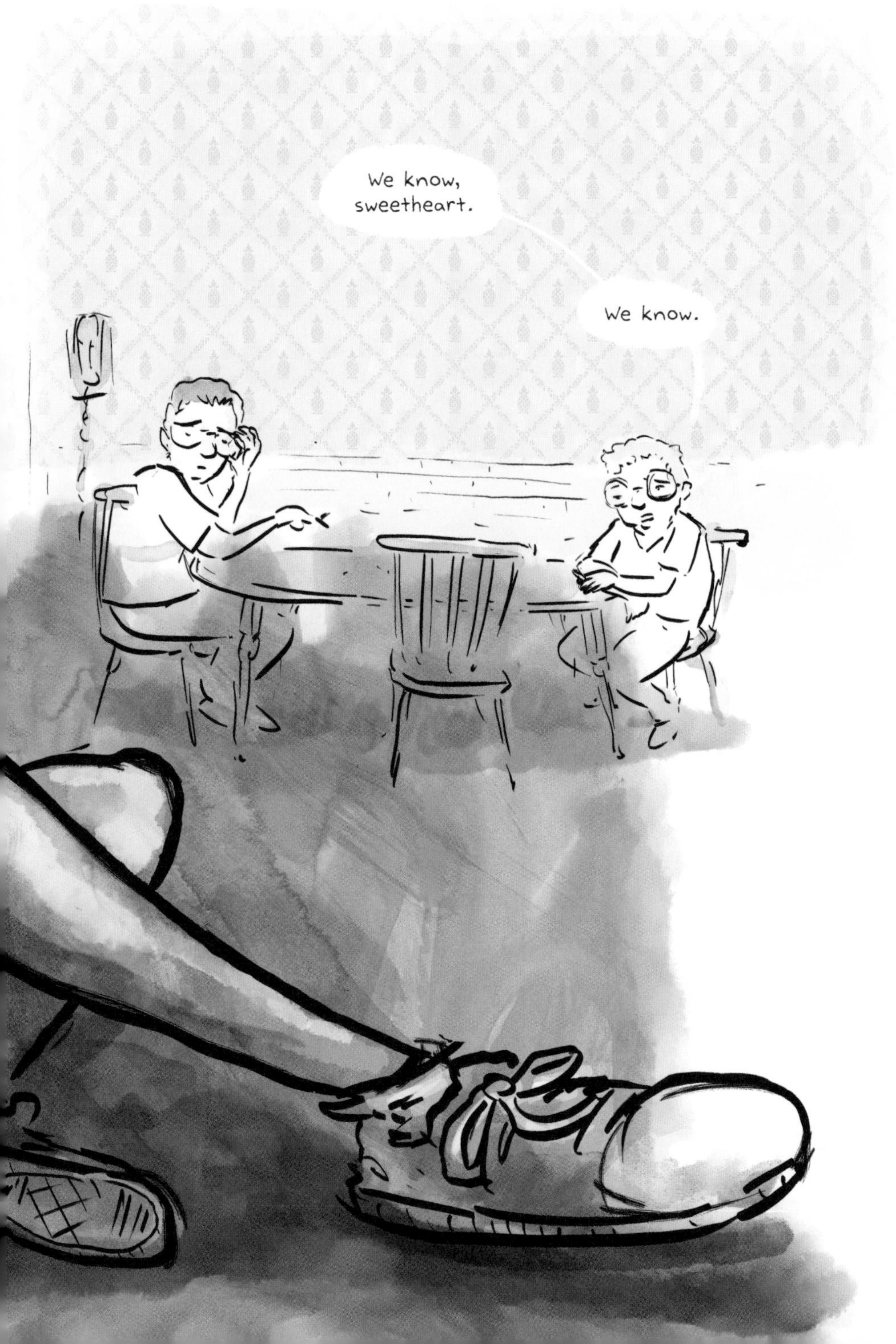
We know, sweetheart.
We know.

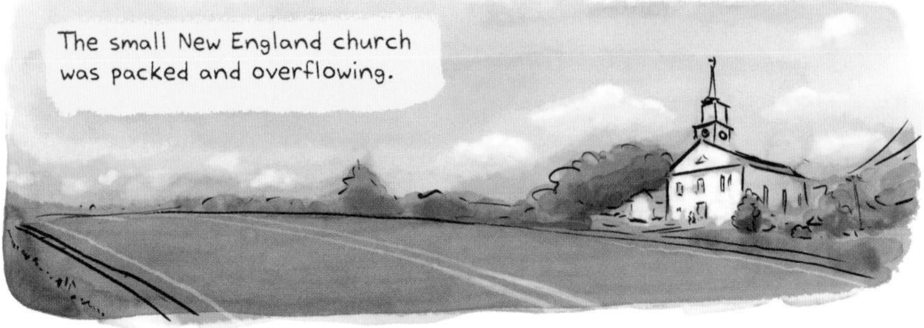
The small New England church
was packed and overflowing.

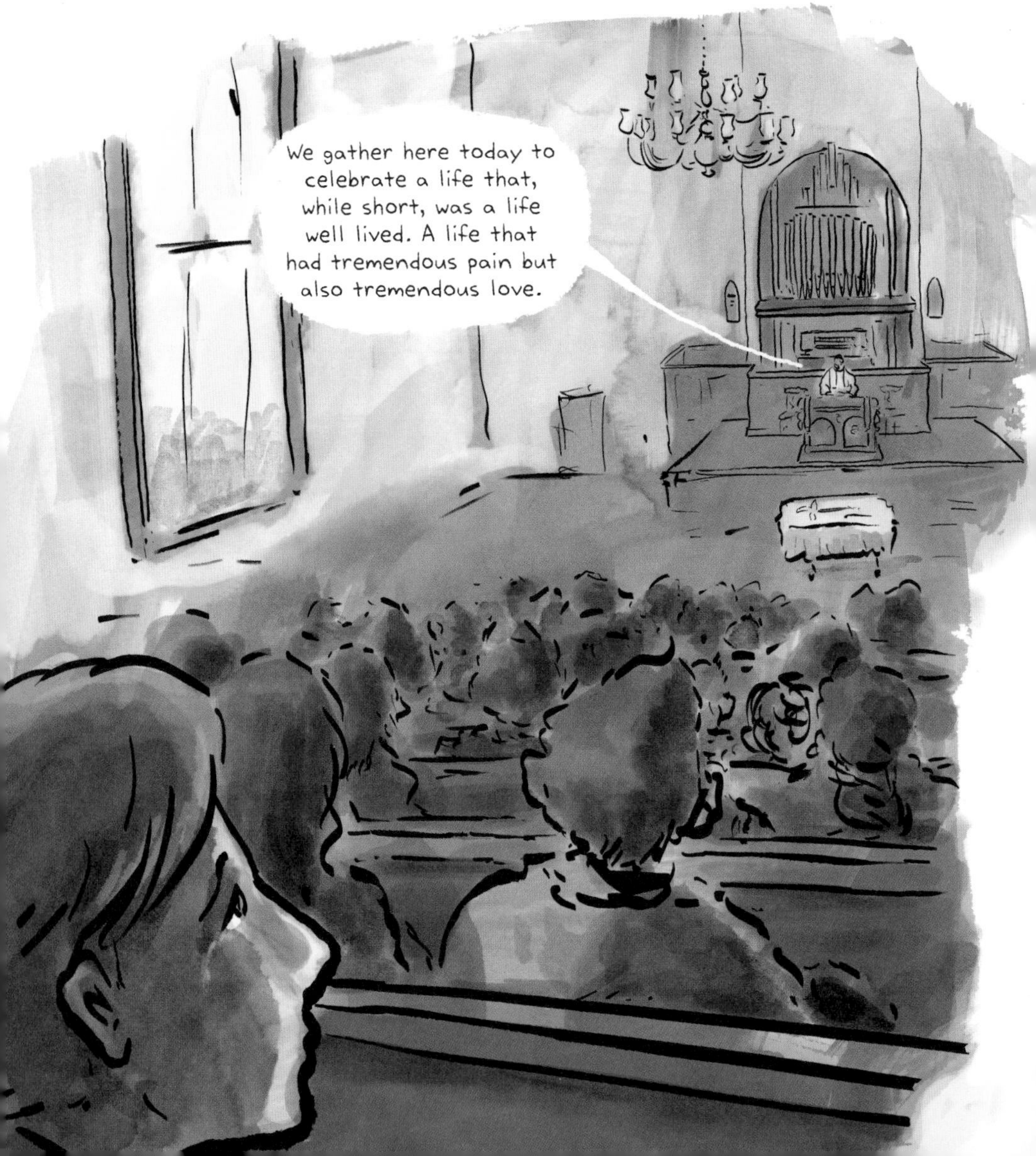
We gather here today to celebrate a life that, while short, was a life well lived. A life that had tremendous pain but also tremendous love.

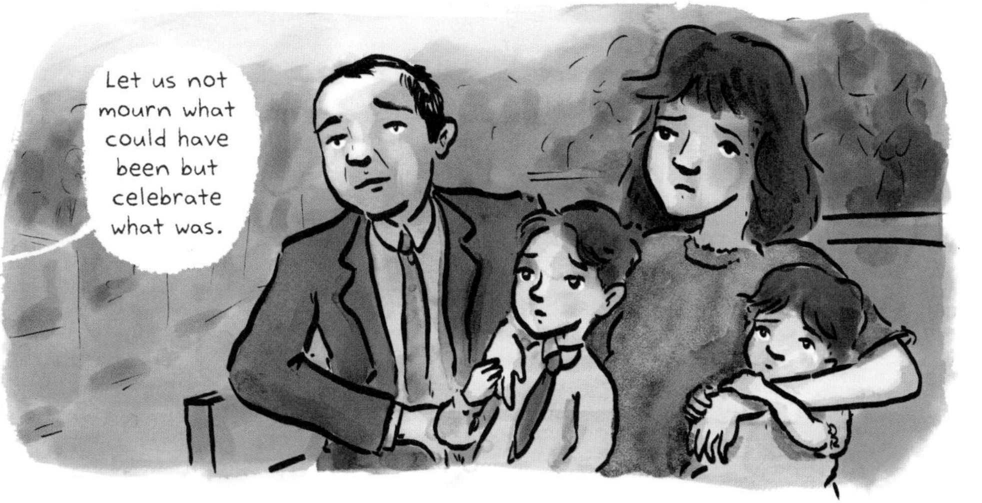
Let us not mourn what could have been but celebrate what was.

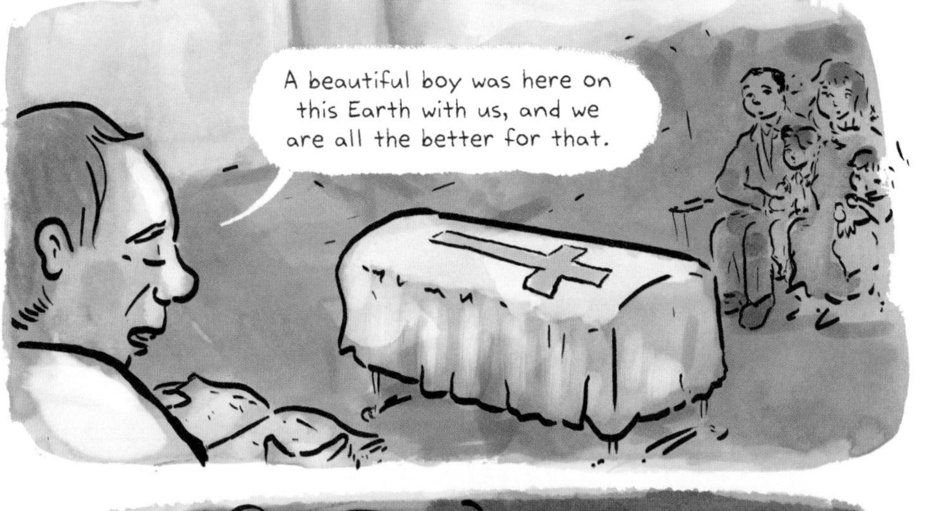
A beautiful boy was here on this Earth with us, and we are all the better for that.

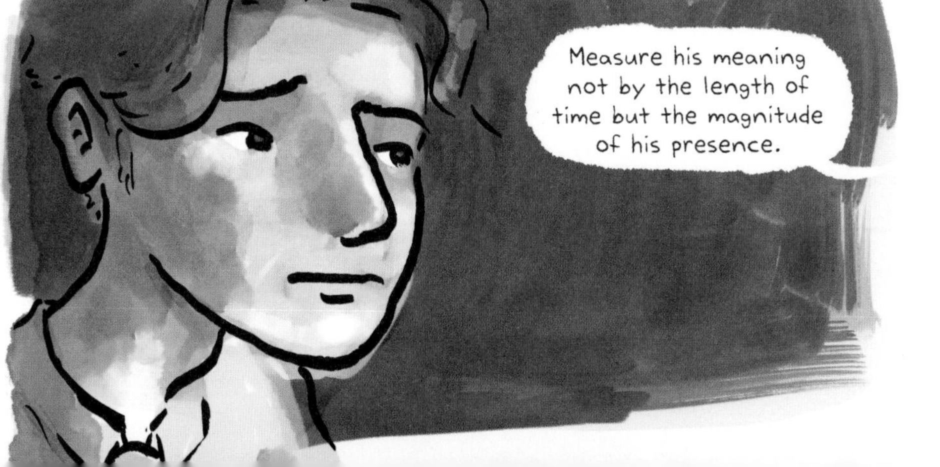
Measure his meaning not by the length of time but the magnitude of his presence.

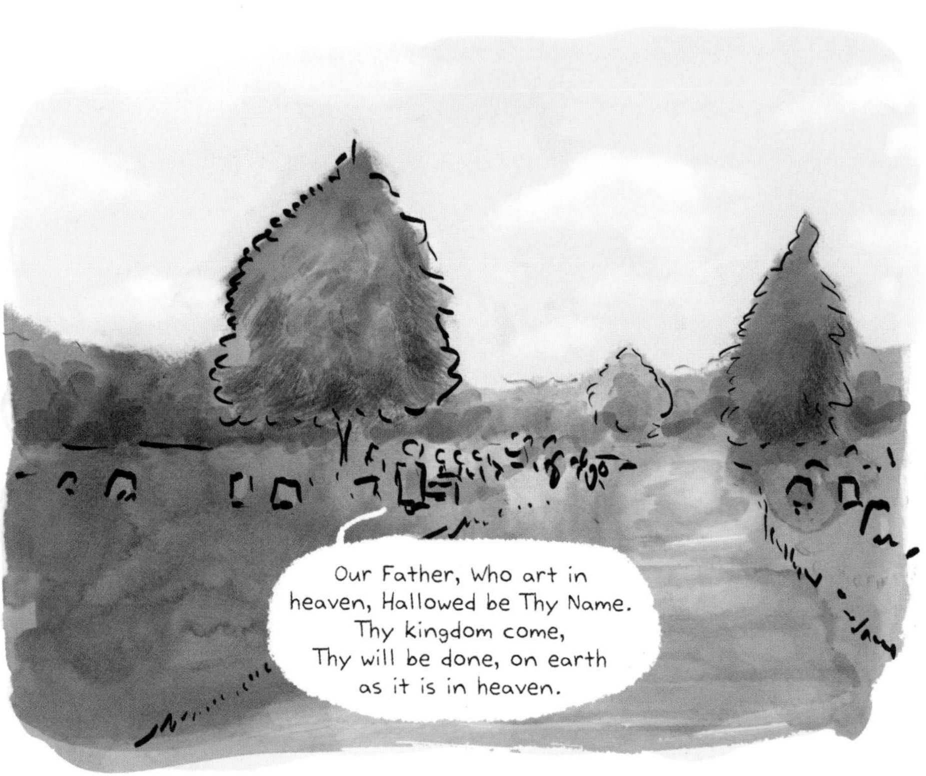
Our Father, Who art in heaven, Hallowed be Thy Name. Thy kingdom come, Thy will be done, on earth as it is in heaven.

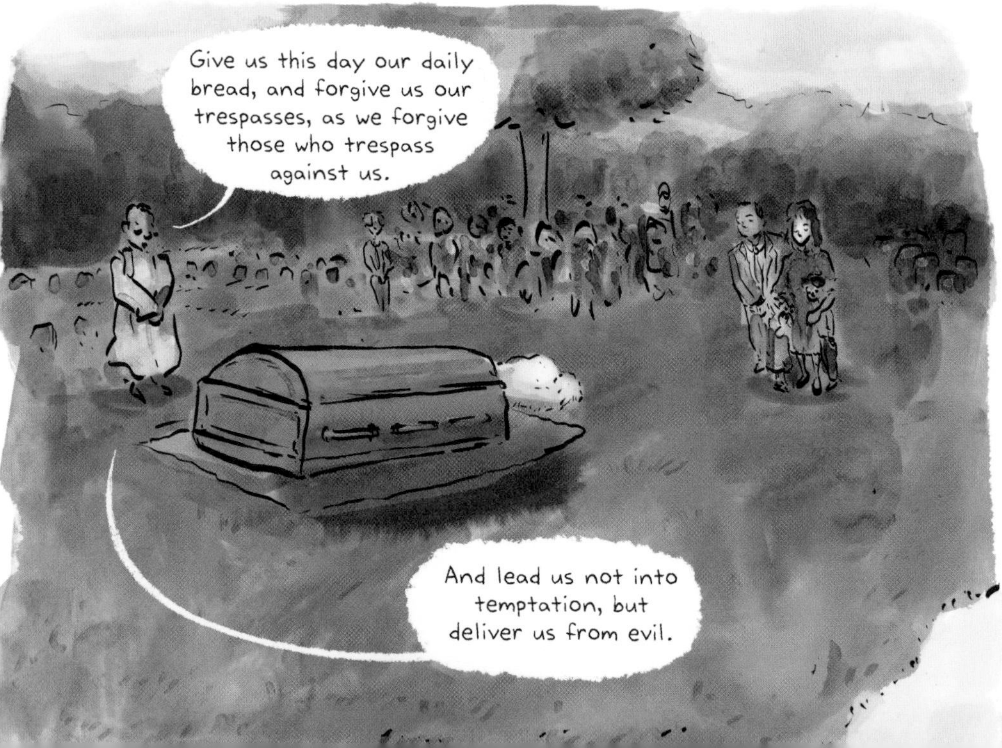
Give us this day our daily bread, and forgive us our trespasses, as we forgive those who trespass against us.
And lead us not into temptation, but deliver us from evil.

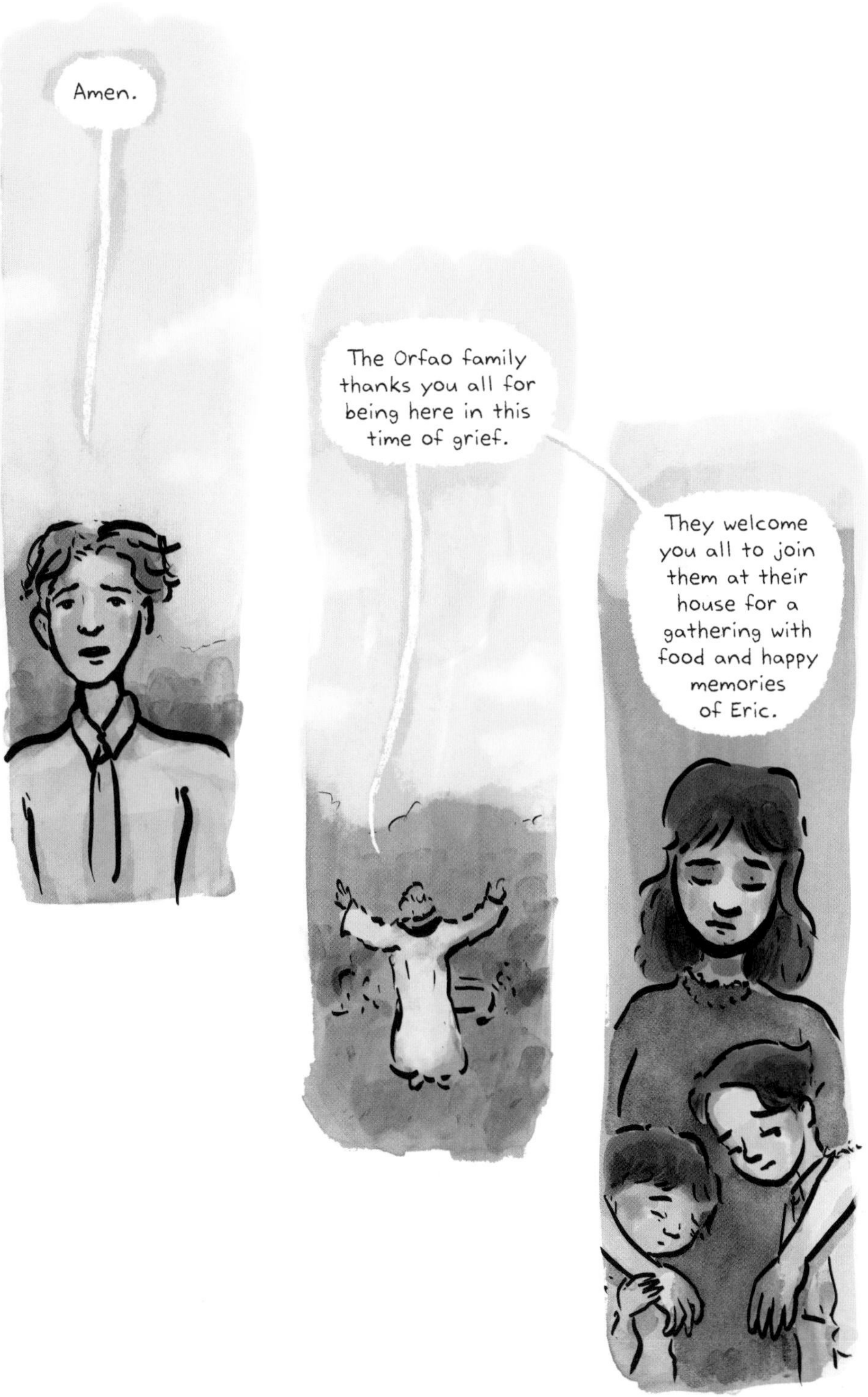
Amen.
The Orfao family thanks you all for being here in this time of grief.
They welcome you all to join them at their house for a gathering with food and happy memories of Eric.

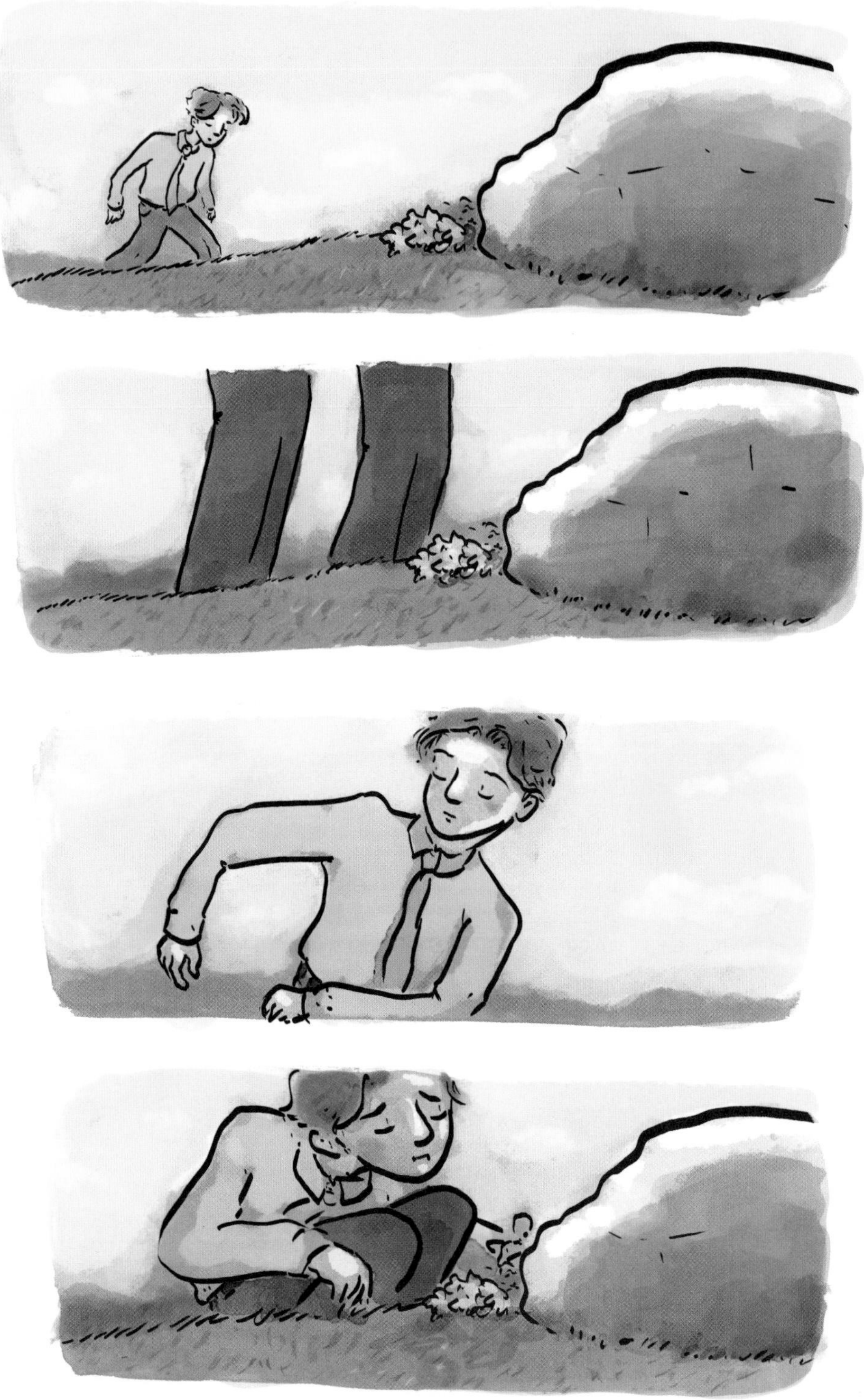

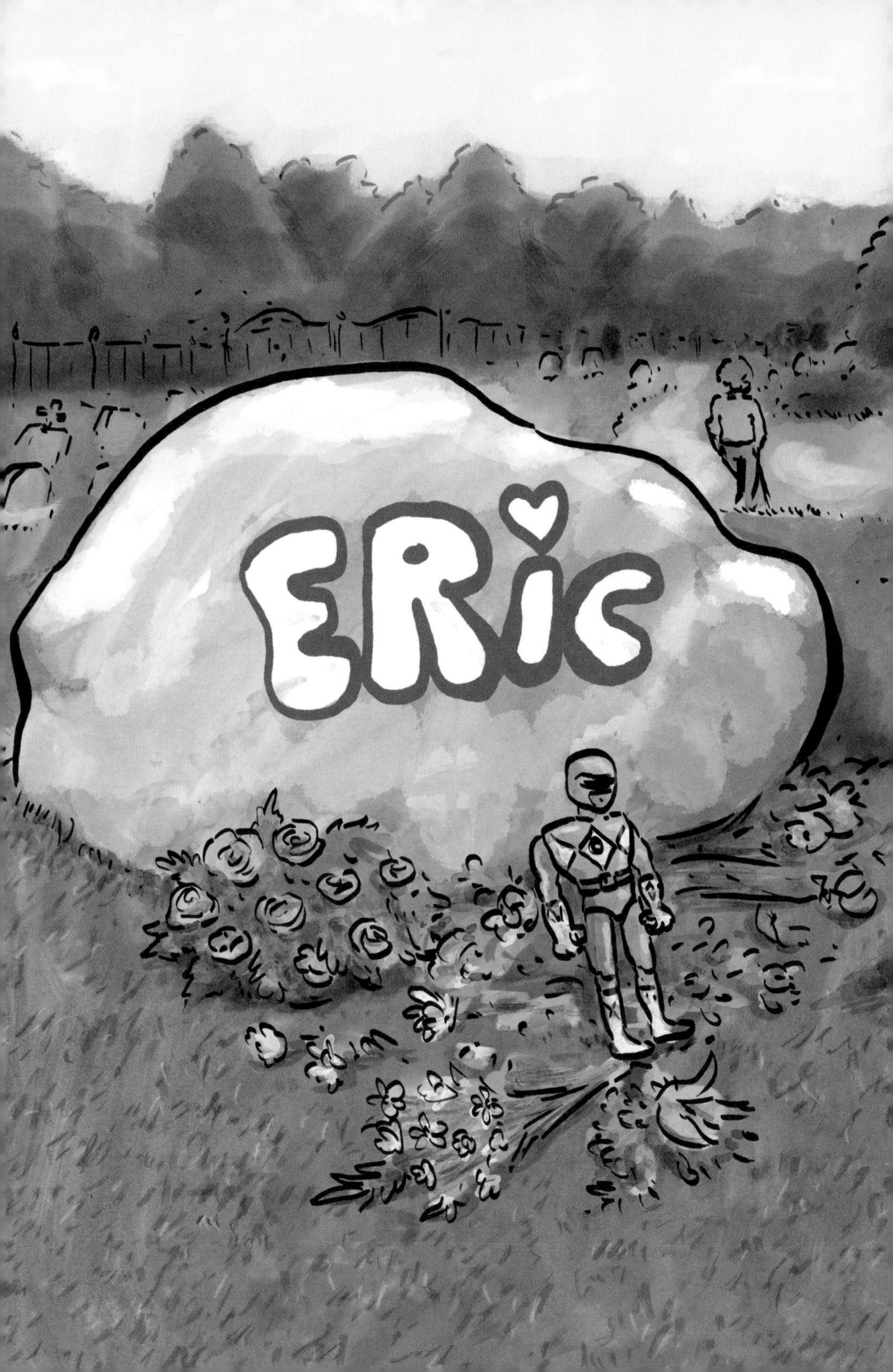
ERic

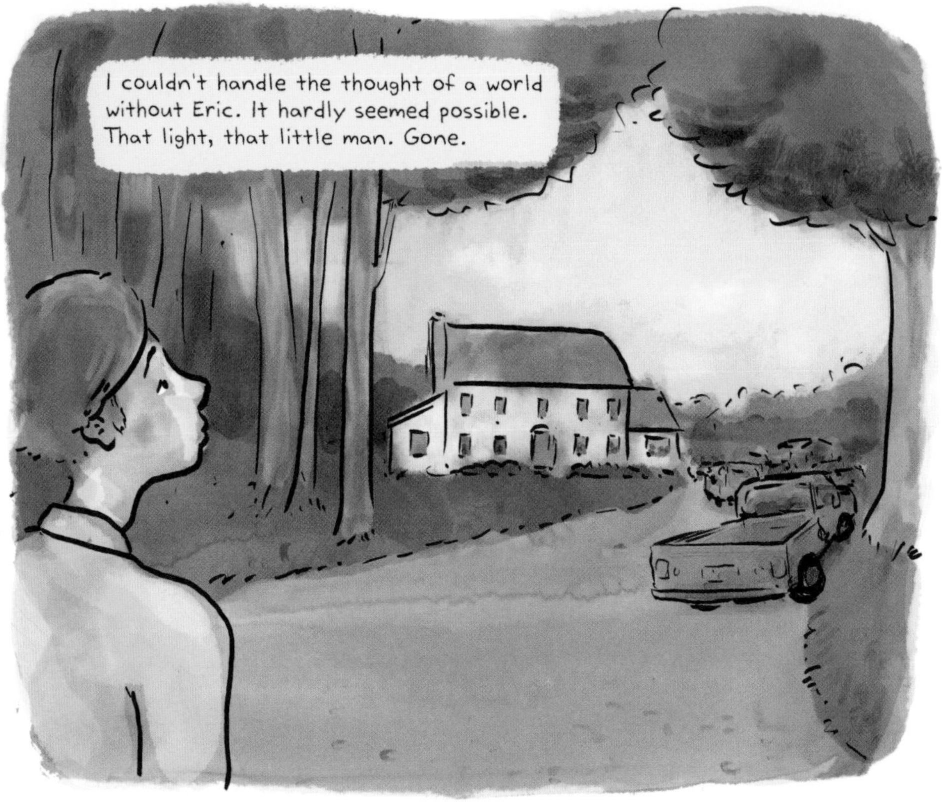
I couldn't handle the thought of a world without Eric. It hardly seemed possible. That light, that little man. Gone.

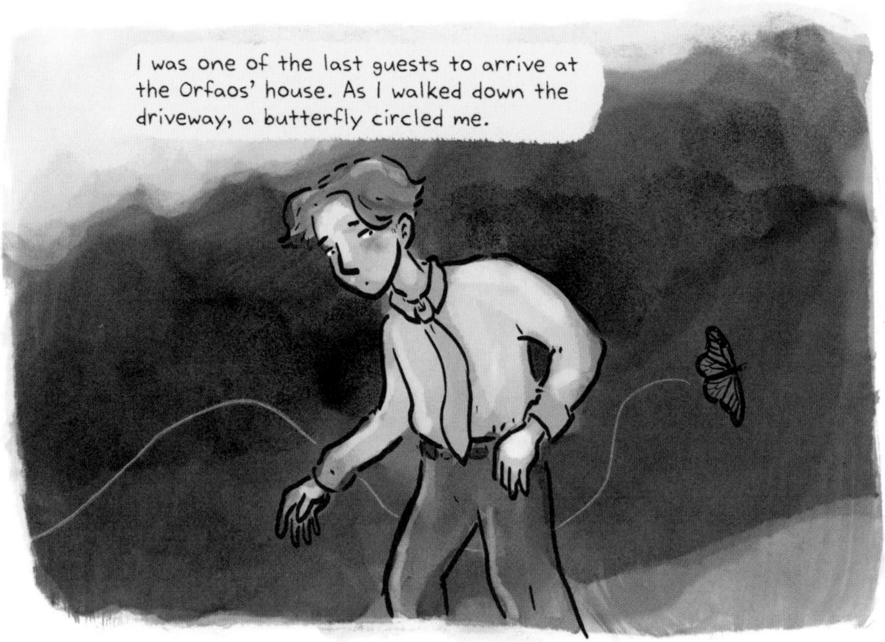
I was one of the last guests to arrive at the Orfaos' house. As I walked down the driveway, a butterfly circled me.

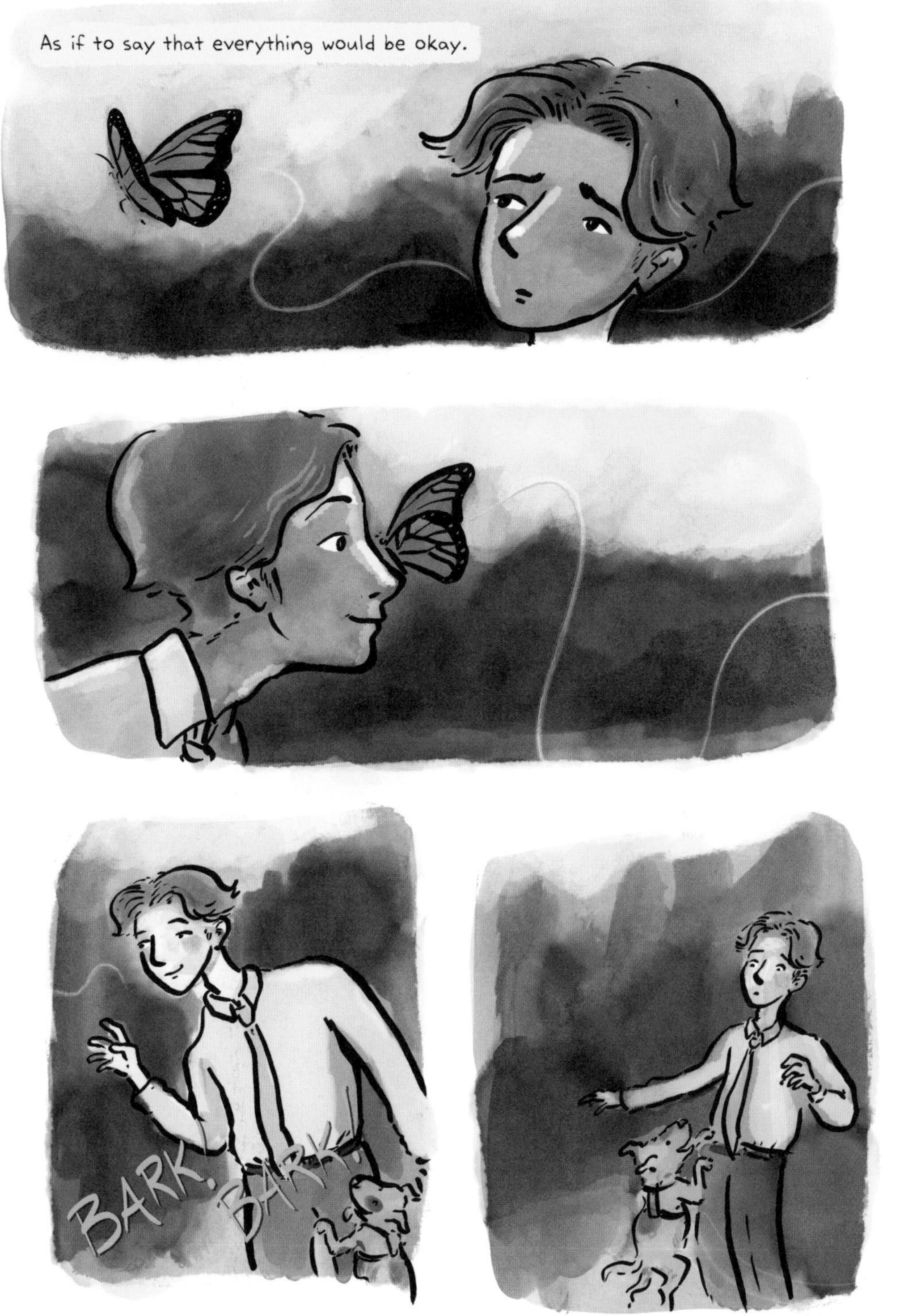
As if to say that everything would be okay.
BARK. BARK.

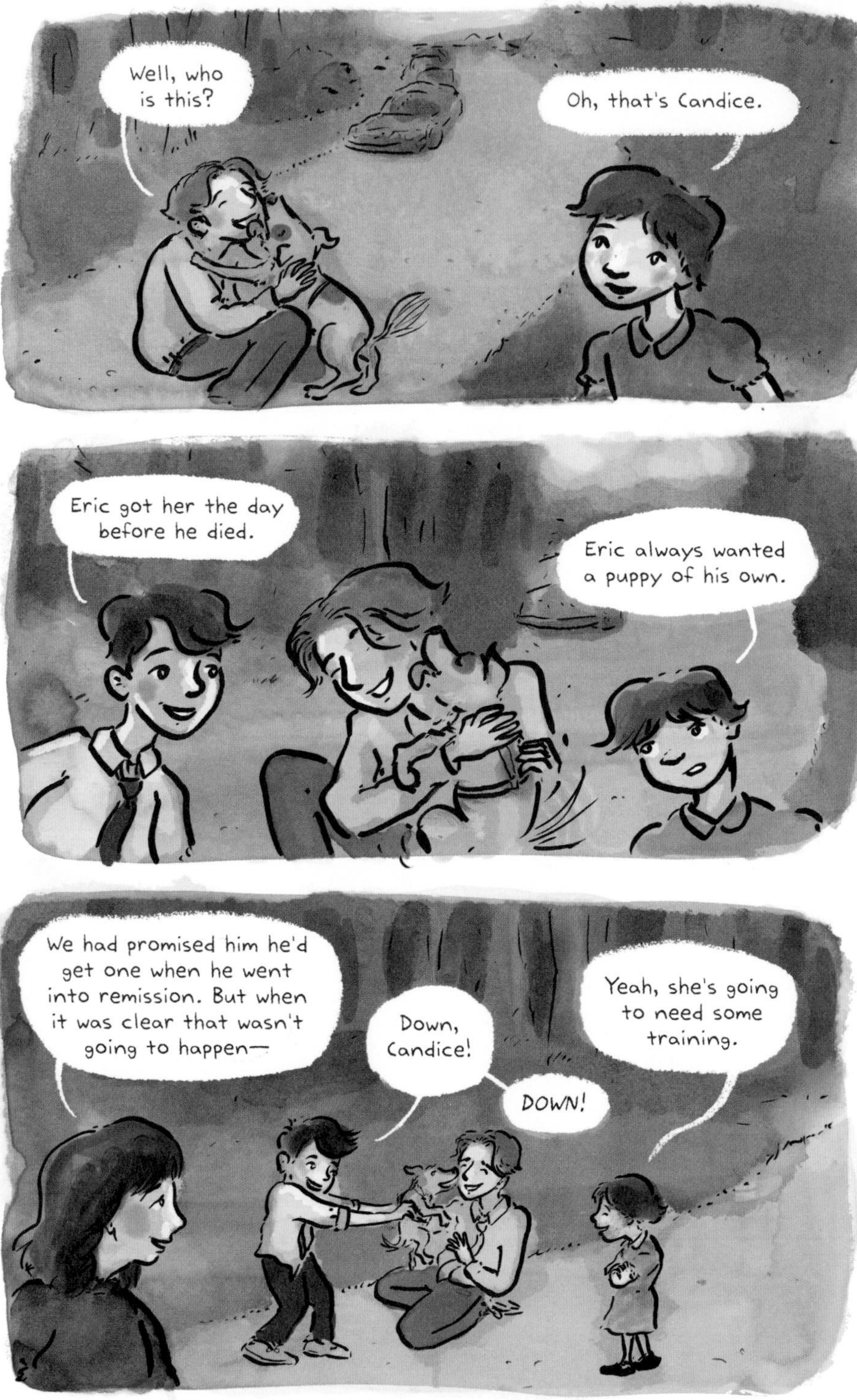
Well, who is this?
Oh, that's Candice.
Eric got her the day before he died.
Eric always wanted a puppy of his own.
We had promised him he'd get one when he went into remission. But when it was clear that wasn't going to happen—
Down, Candice!
DOWN!
Yeah, she's going to need some training.

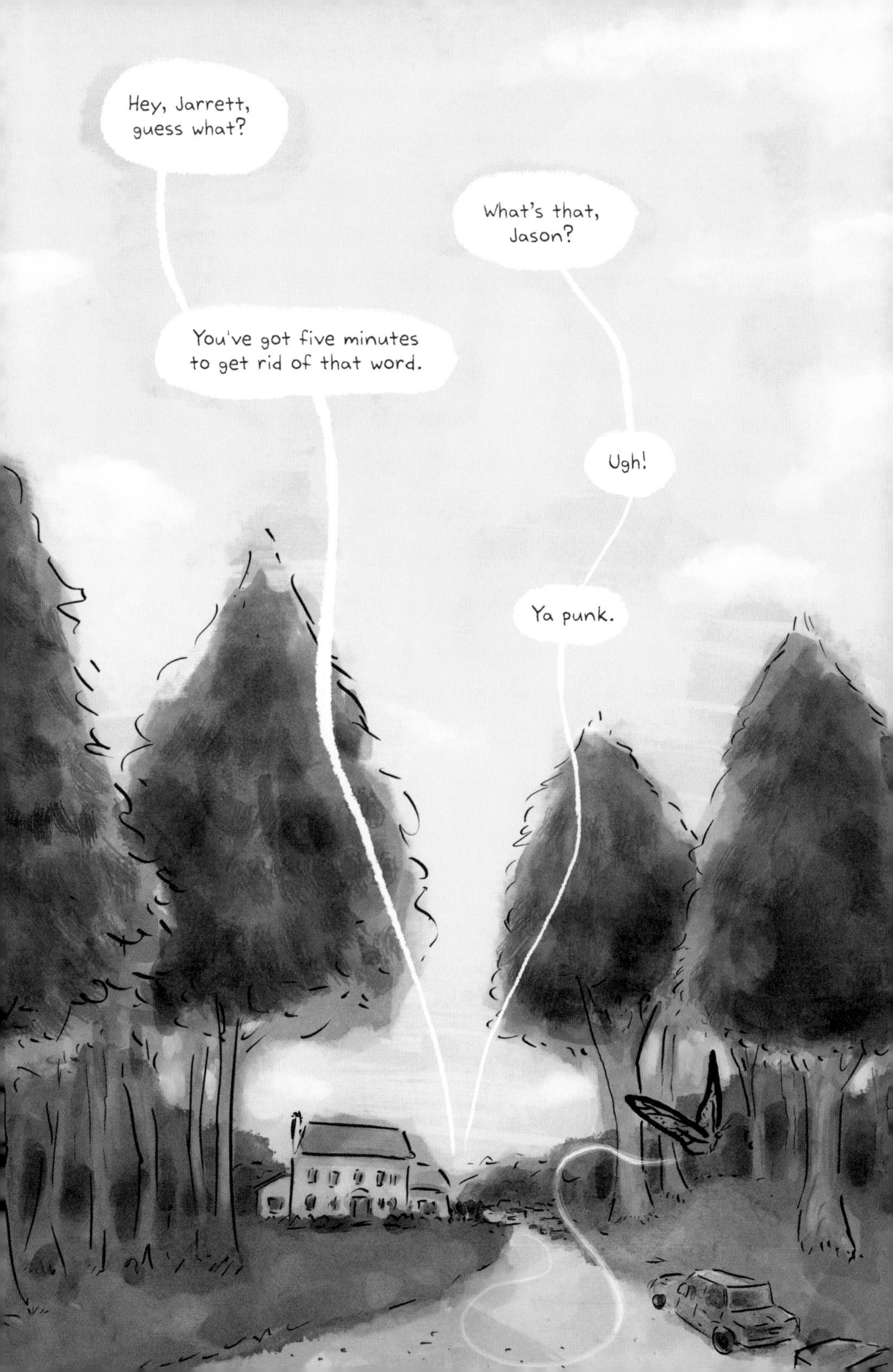
Hey, Jarrett, guess what?
You've got five minutes to get rid of that word.
What's that, Jason?
Ugh!
Ya punk.

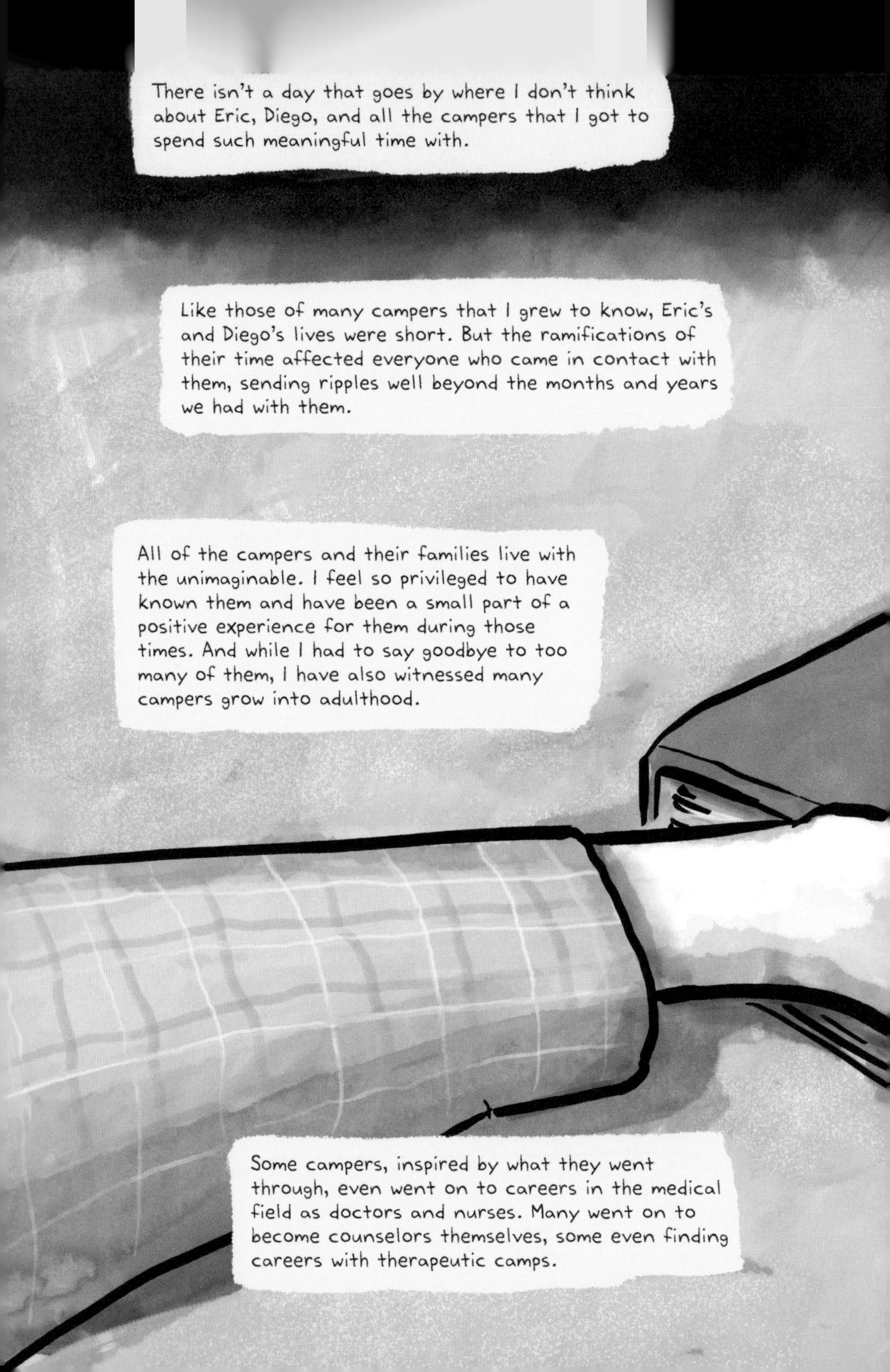
There isn't a day that goes by where I don't think about Eric, Diego, and all the campers that I got to spend such meaningful time with.
Like those of many campers that I grew to know, Eric's and Diego's lives were short. But the ramifications of their time affected everyone who came in contact with them, sending ripples well beyond the months and years we had with them.
All of the campers and their families live with the unimaginable. I feel so privileged to have known them and have been a small part of a positive experience for them during those times. And while I had to say goodbye to too many of them, I have also witnessed many campers grow into adulthood.
Some campers, inspired by what they went through, even went on to careers in the medical field as doctors and nurses. Many went on to become counselors themselves, some even finding careers with therapeutic camps.

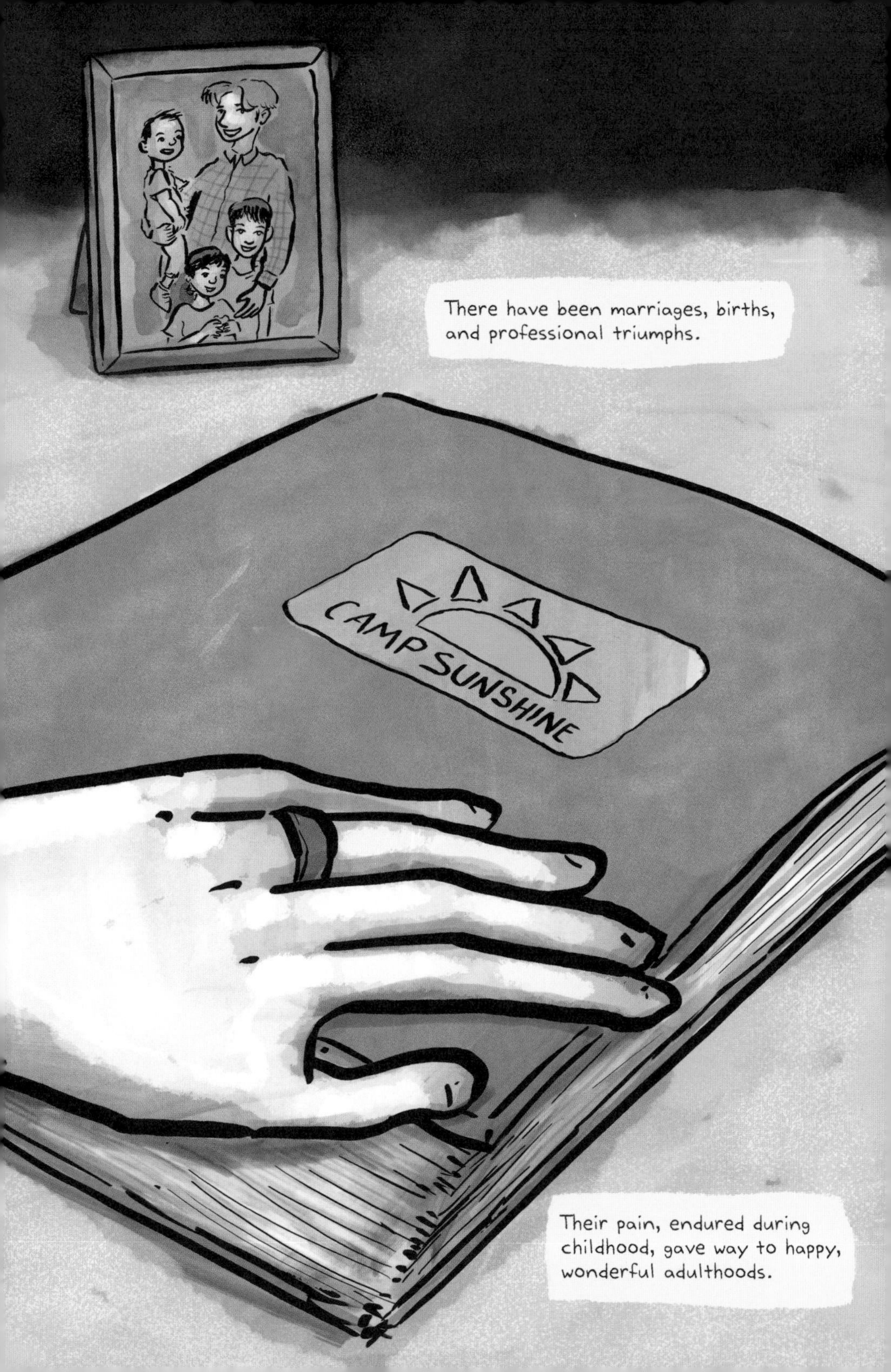

There have been marriages, births, and professional triumphs.
CAMP SUNSHINE
Their pain, endured during childhood, gave way to happy, wonderful adulthoods.

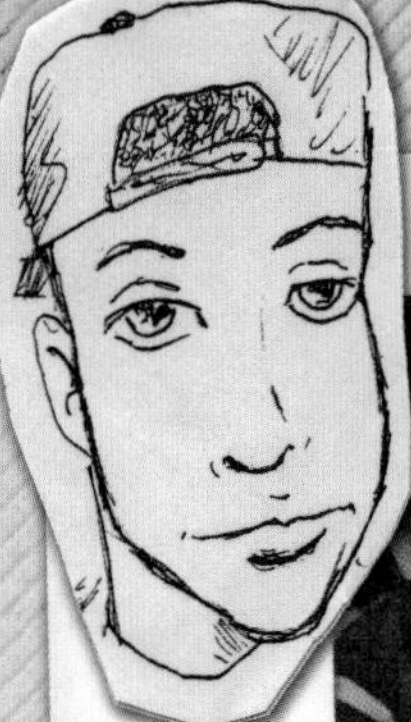
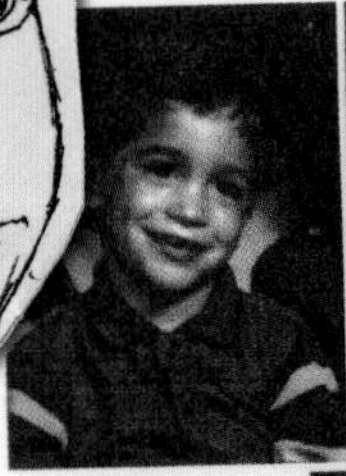
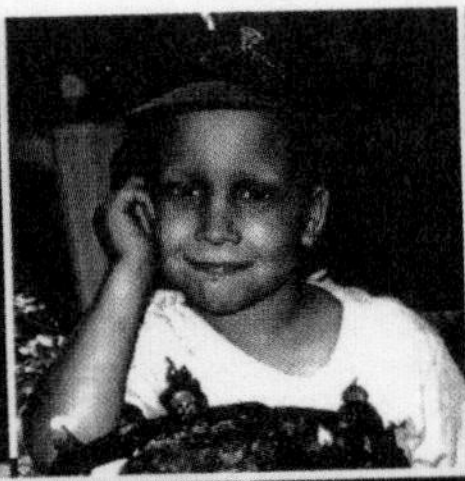
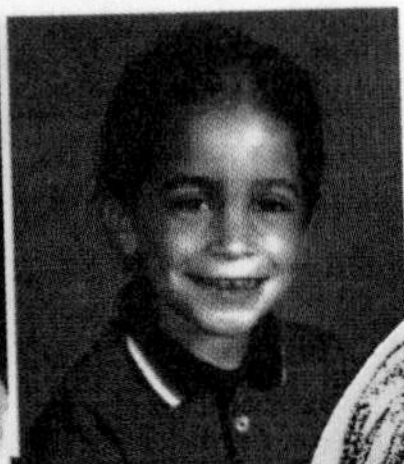
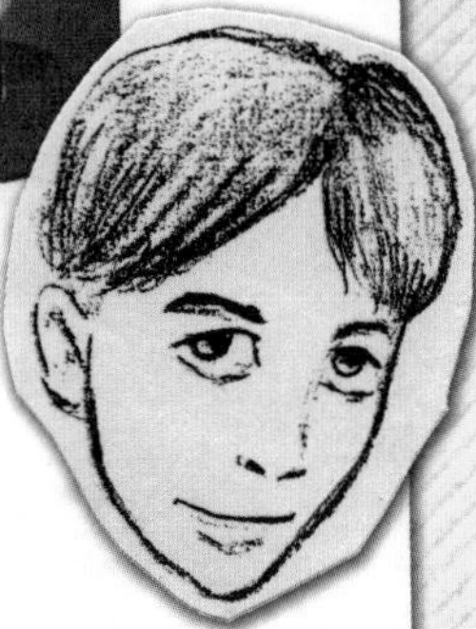
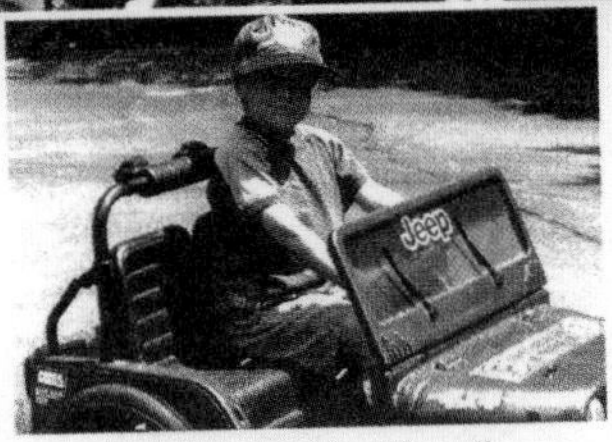
Jeep

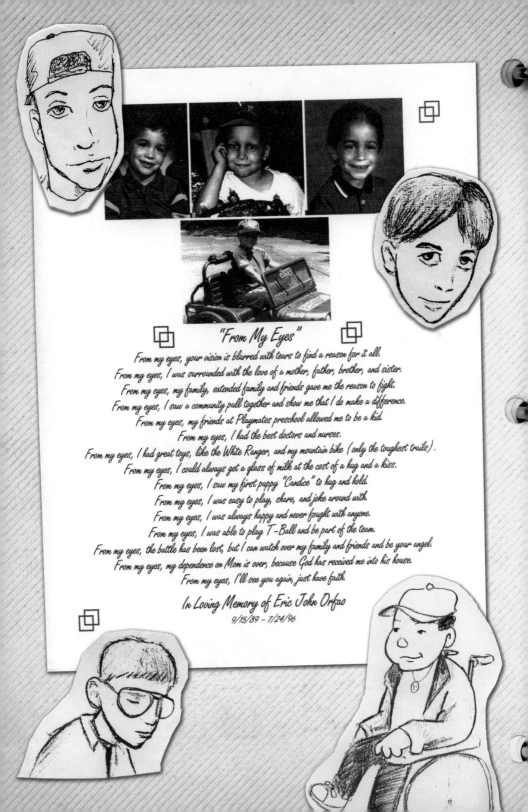

"From My Eyes"

From my eyes, your vision is blurred with tears to find a reason for it all.
From my eyes, I was surrounded with the love of a mother, father, brother, and sister.
From my eyes, my family, extended family and friends gave me the reason to fight.
From my eyes, I saw a community pull together and show me that I do make a difference.
From my eyes, my friends at Playmates preschool allowed me to be a kid.
From my eyes, I had the best doctors and nurses.
From my eyes, I had great toys, like the White Ranger, and my mountain bike (only the toughest trails).
From my eyes, I could always get a glass of milk at the cost of a hug and a kiss.
From my eyes, I saw my first puppy "Candice" to hug and hold.
From my eyes, I was easy to play, share, and joke around with.
From my eyes, I was always happy and never fought with anyone.
From my eyes, I was able to play T-Ball and be part of the team.
From my eyes, the battle has been lost, but I can watch over my family and friends and be your angel.
From my eyes, my dependence on Mom is over, because God has received me into his house.
From my eyes, I'll see you again, just have faith.

In Loving Memory of Eric John Orfao

9/15/89 - 7/24/96

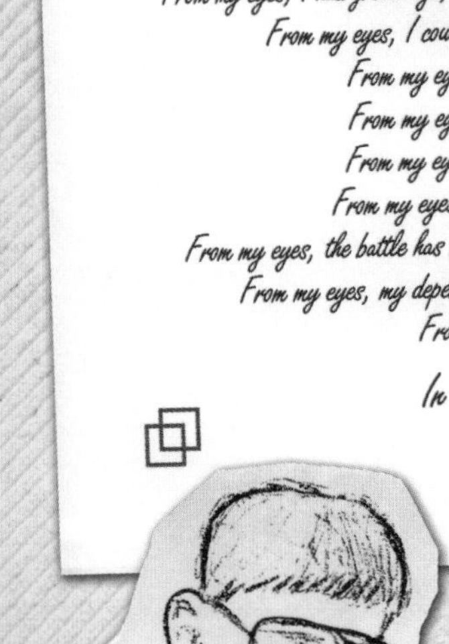
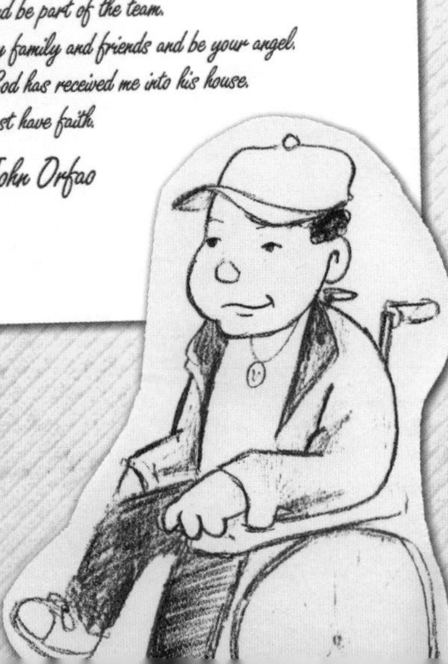

Jarrett

whaz ↑? thakes for the phatos
I finley got done bilding
my computer!!!! we hant
develaped are phatos yet.
but wen I do I'll send
some to you. how's bland
I'm haveing a grate sumor!
I just saw hunch bake of
notre Dame! It was cool.
onces I get my e-mall address
I will give it to you.

well thats all
I can think of so
write bake soon Derek

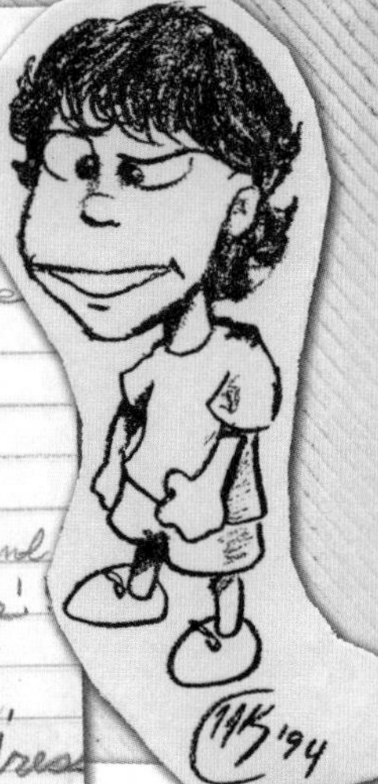

ably have a
s very nice.
fficult
pt the
om camp

ait a
ried. I think
the

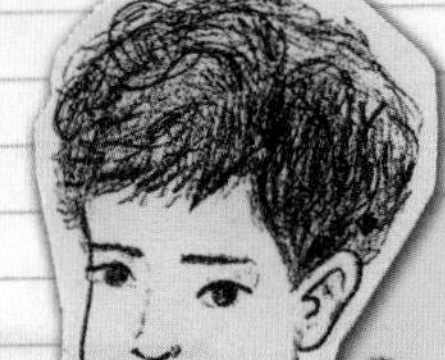

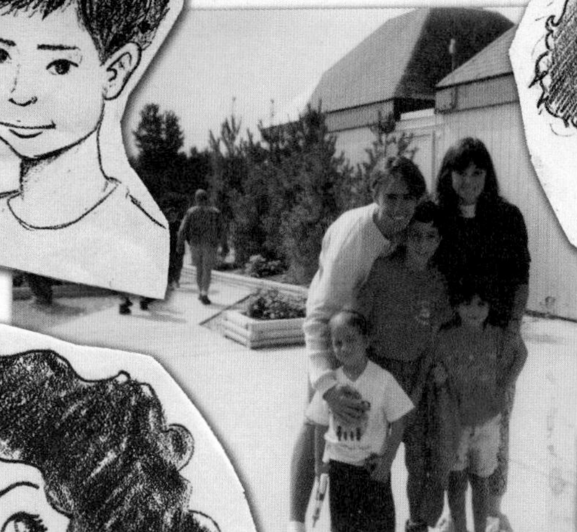

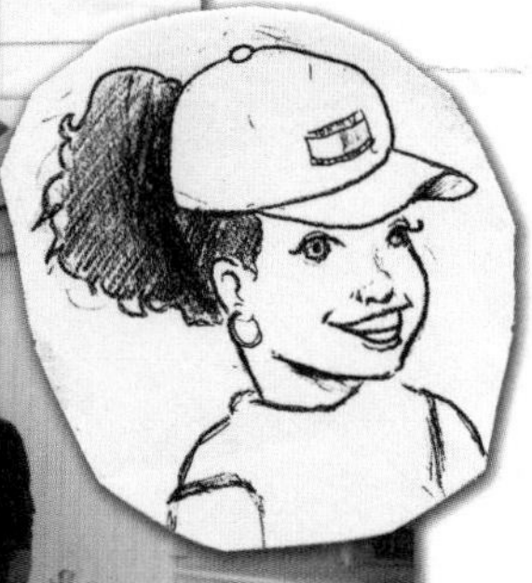

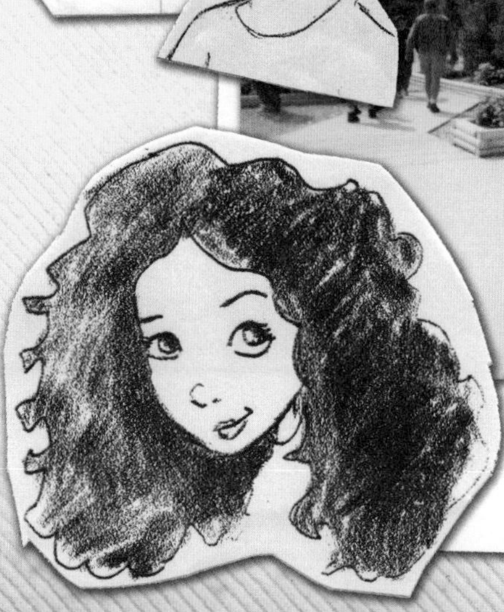

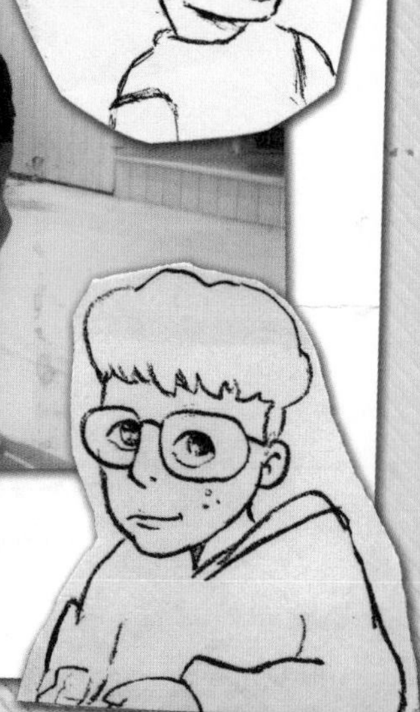

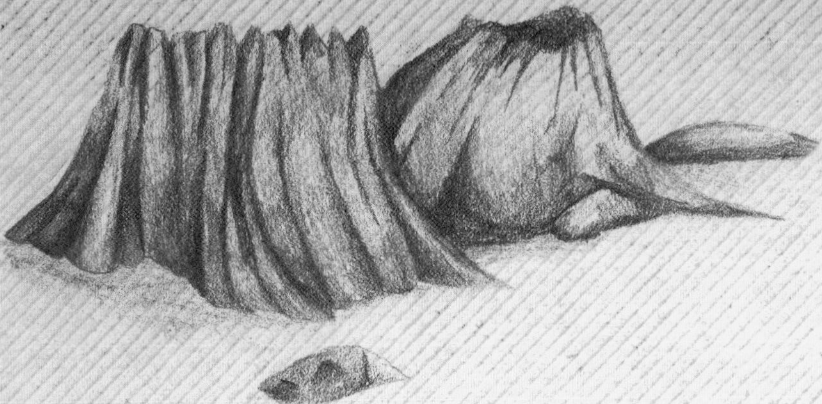

EPILOGUE

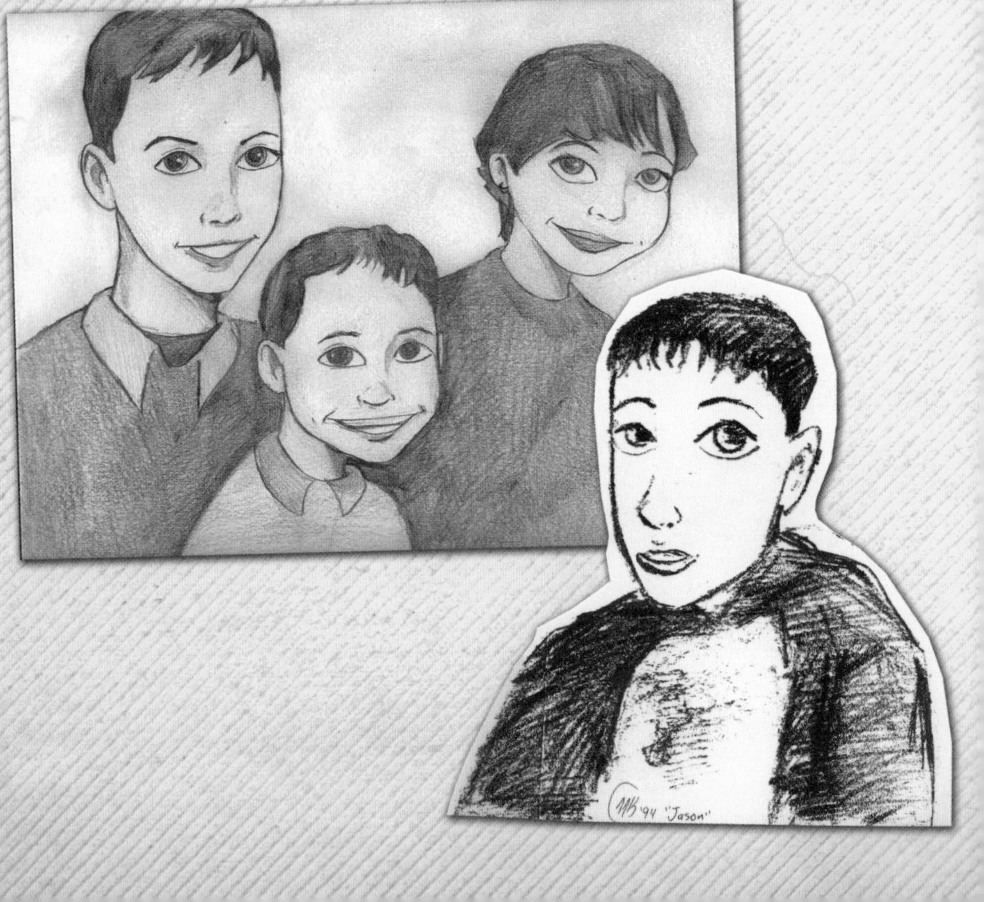
MB '94 "Jason"

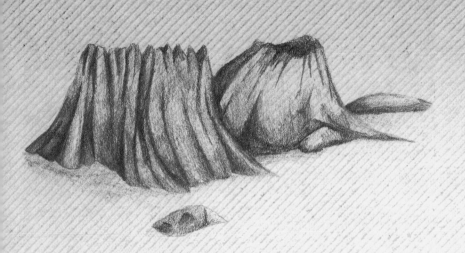

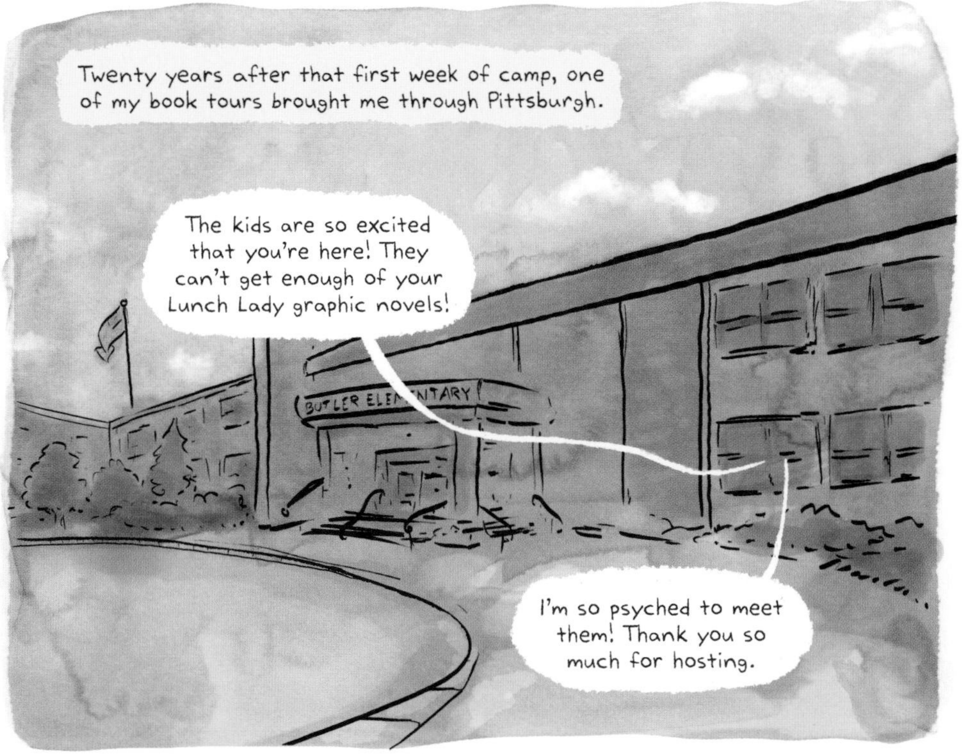
Twenty years after that first week of camp, one of my book tours brought me through Pittsburgh.
The kids are so excited that you're here! They can't get enough of your Lunch Lady graphic novels!
BUTLER ELEMENTARY
I'm so psyched to meet them! Thank you so much for hosting.

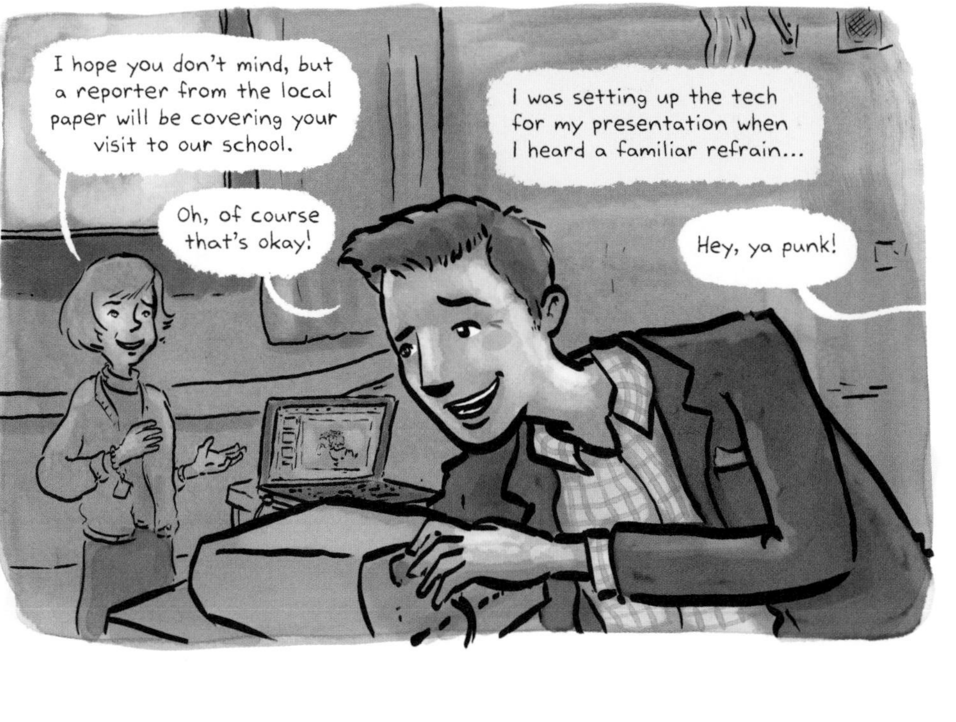
I hope you don't mind, but a reporter from the local paper will be covering your visit to our school.
Oh, of course that's okay!
I was setting up the tech for my presentation when I heard a familiar refrain...
Hey, ya punk!

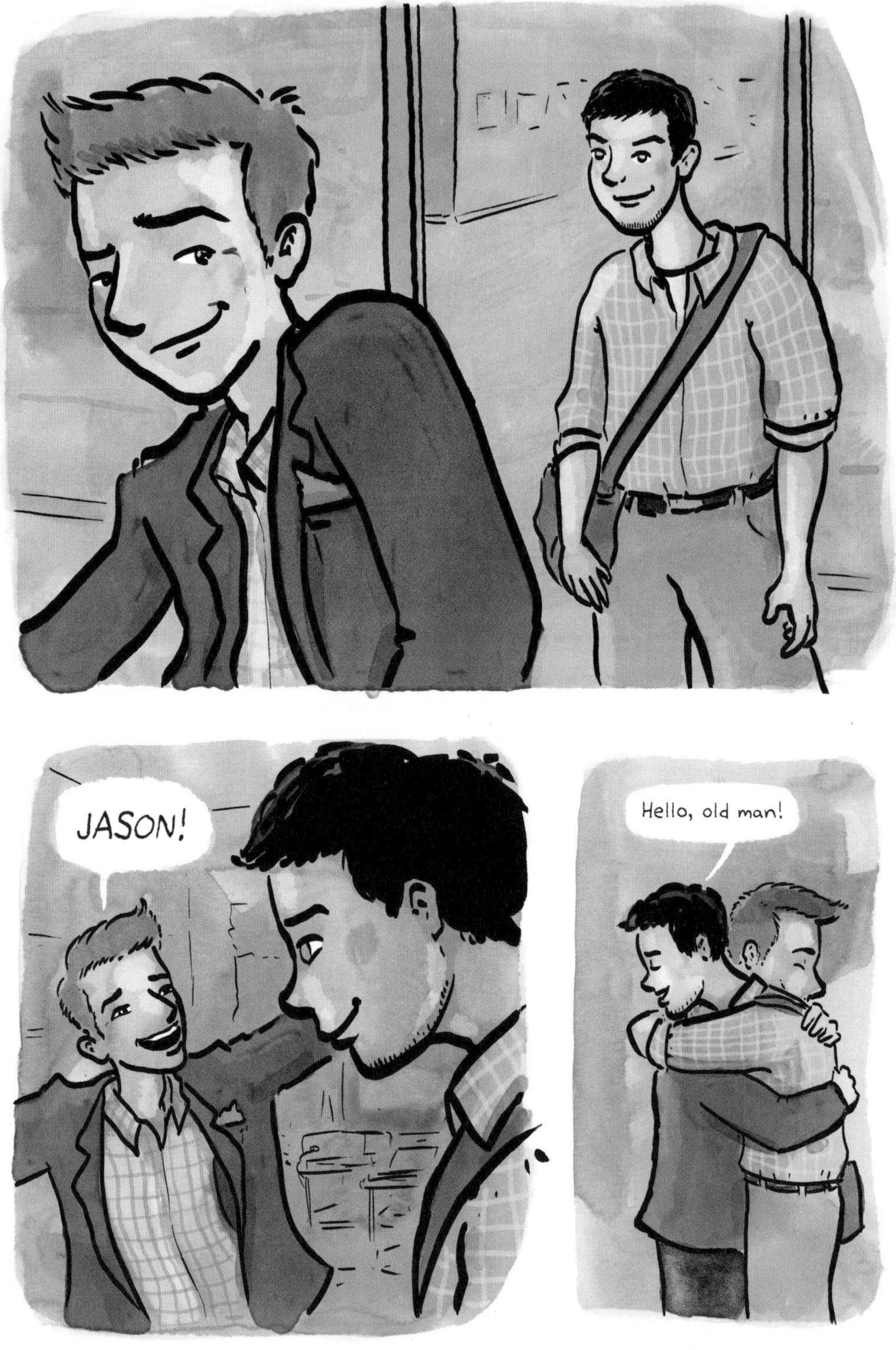
JASON!
Hello, old man!

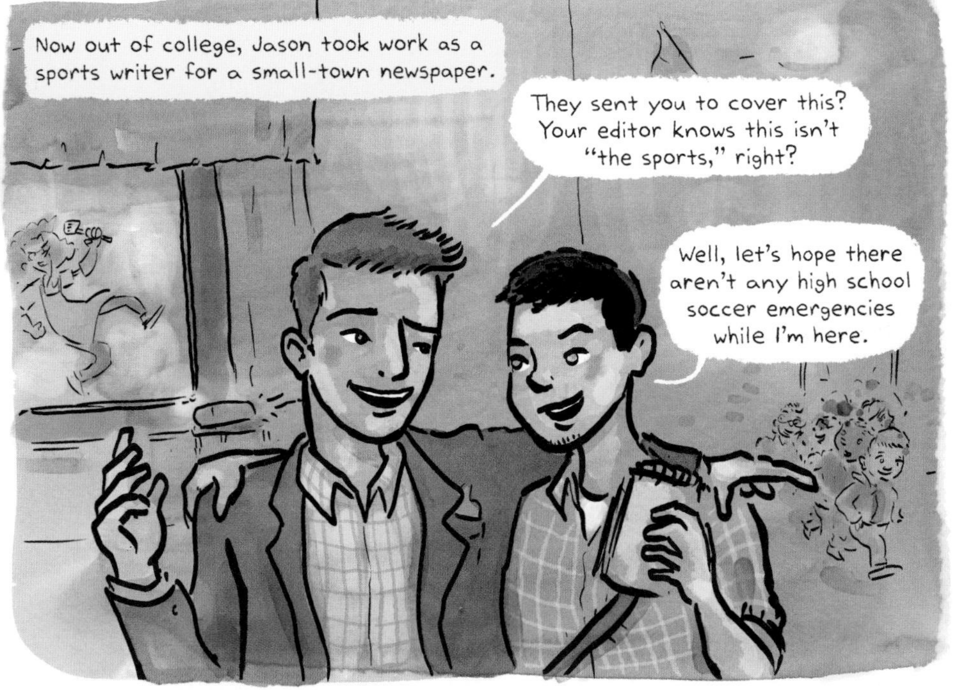
Now out of college, Jason took work as a sports writer for a small-town newspaper.
They sent you to cover this? Your editor knows this isn't "the sports," right?
Well, let's hope there aren't any high school soccer emergencies while I'm here.

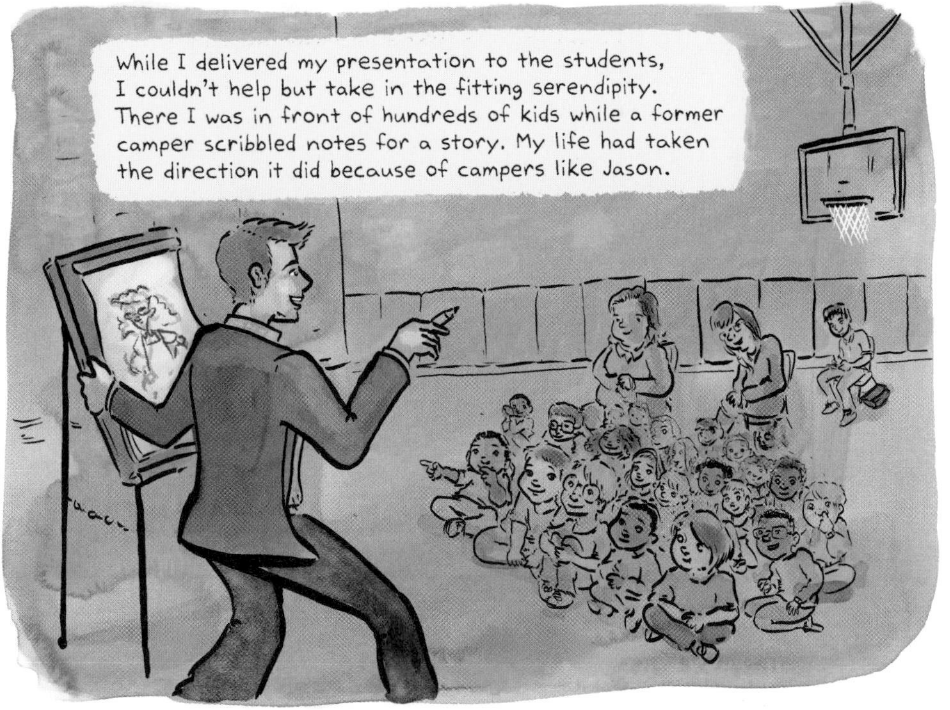
While I delivered my presentation to the students, I couldn't help but take in the fitting serendipity. There I was in front of hundreds of kids while a former camper scribbled notes for a story. My life had taken the direction it did because of campers like Jason.

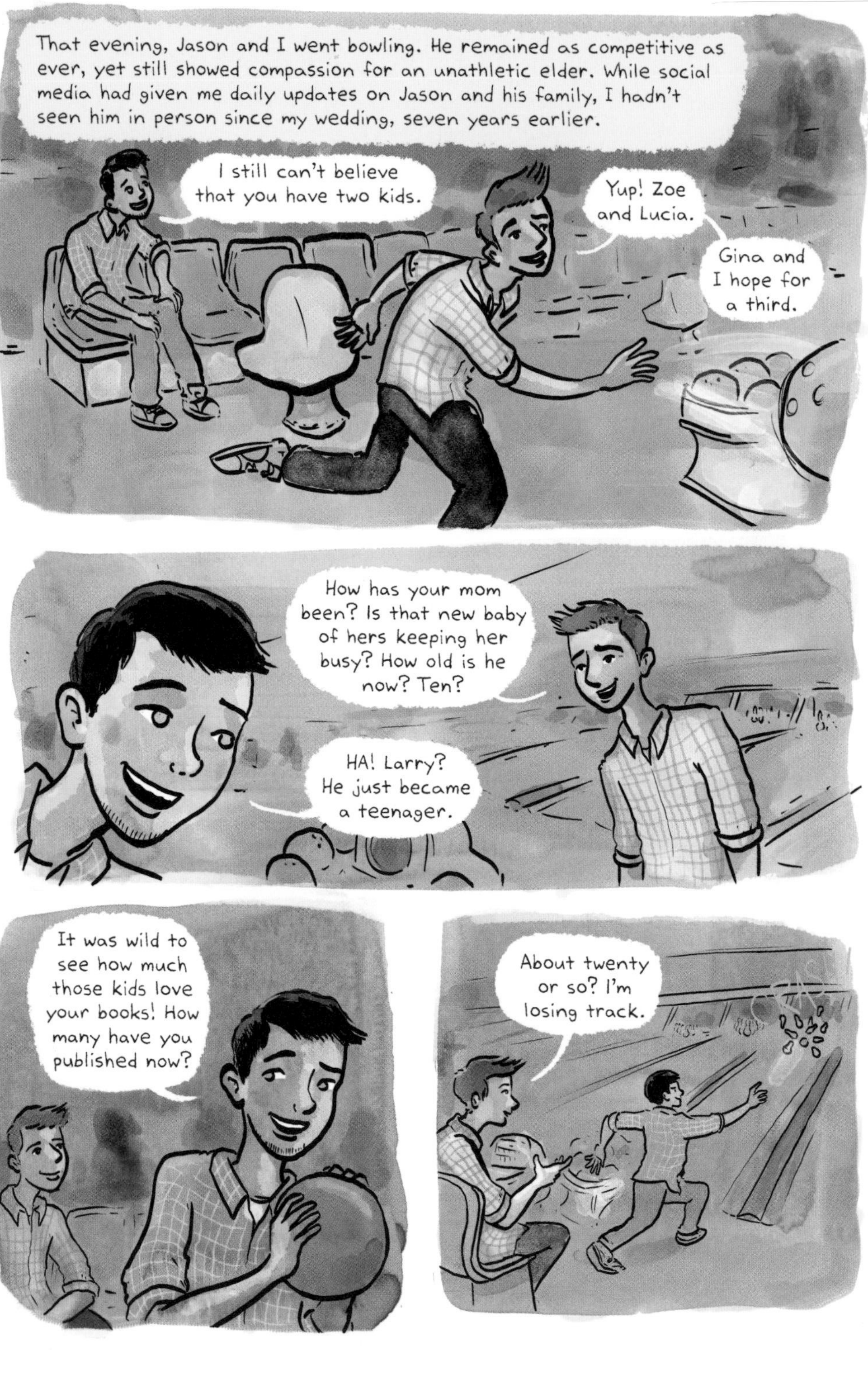
That evening, Jason and I went bowling. He remained as competitive as ever, yet still showed compassion for an unathletic elder. While social media had given me daily updates on Jason and his family, I hadn't seen him in person since my wedding, seven years earlier.
I still can't believe that you have two kids.
Yup! Zoe and Lucia.
Gina and I hope for a third.
How has your mom been? Is that new baby of hers keeping her busy? How old is he now? Ten?
HA! Larry? He just became a teenager.
It was wild to see how much those kids love your books! How many have you published now?
About twenty or so? I'm losing track.

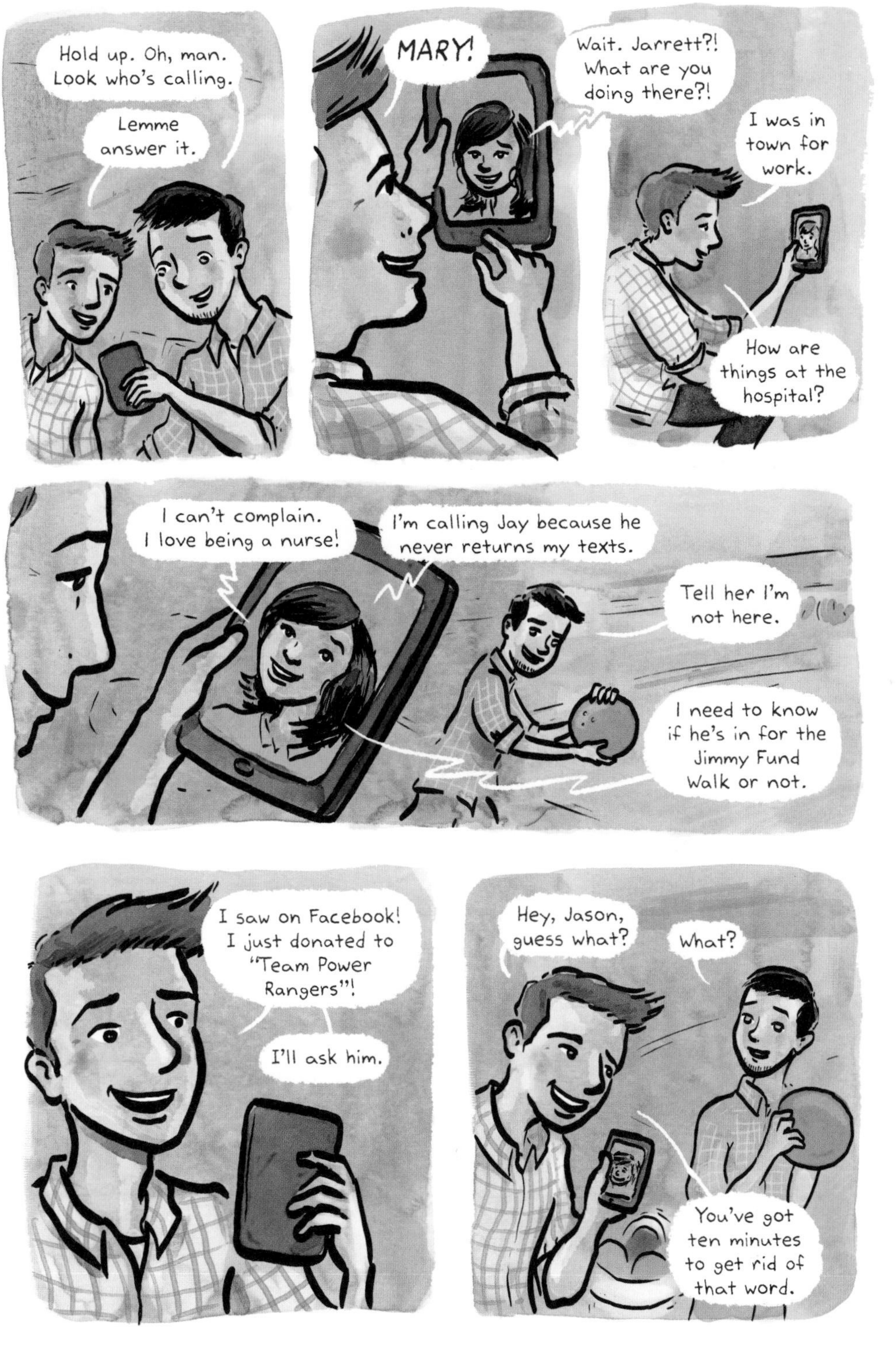
Hold up. Oh, man. Look who's calling.
Lemme answer it.
MARY!
Wait. Jarrett?! What are you doing there?!
I was in town for work.
How are things at the hospital?
I can't complain. I love being a nurse!
I'm calling Jay because he never returns my texts.
Tell her I'm not here.
I need to know if he's in for the Jimmy Fund Walk or not.
I saw on Facebook! I just donated to "Team Power Rangers"!
I'll ask him.
Hey, Jason, guess what?
What?
You've got ten minutes to get rid of that word.

AUTHOR'S NOTE & ACKNOWLEDGMENTS

It is wild to stop and think about how the short and finite time I spent at camp had such an everlasting and powerful effect on my life. I cannot fathom the direction life would have taken me had it not been for my time with those courageous campers.

Camp came to me at a period in my life when my personal problems seemed insurmountable. I often point to the saving power of art and what creating did for me as I grew up, but volunteerism proved to be an equally decisive force. Volunteerism taught me that while my difficulties were real and should be acknowledged, I was far from alone in walking a challenging path.

I began my journey at Camp Sunshine when I was sixteen and volunteered for a handful of sessions over the next few years. After finishing my first year of college, I worked as a full-summer counselor at The Hole in the Wall Gang Camp. While similar in mission to Camp Sunshine, Hole in the Wall's summer season is a sleepaway program. Like Camp Sunshine, there are programs that serve the entire family—a dedicated session for siblings and weekend retreats for parents.

I am lucky enough to still be in touch with several of the families that I worked with over the years. Perhaps I connected so quickly with them because I understood what it was like to yearn for childhood during childhood. Trauma has a way of forcing you to grow up while you are still in a small body.

While the story in this book centers on that first week that I entered into this important work, some of the incidents and stories that I included are taken from subsequent years of working at Camp Sunshine and The Hole in the Wall Gang Camp. Some of the names and likenesses in this book are true to the actual people and used with permission. Others have been changed or combined with multiple campers and moments to protect the privacy of those I couldn't gain contact with to seek consent. While I am unable to share their real names with you, those real names are held very dear to my heart.

A few thank-yous to the families that I was able to connect with while making this book:

Thank you, Susan, for allowing me to use Derek's name and likeness. It is remarkable that the one day we were able to meet up again last summer happened to be Derek's birthday. If Big D was still here, there is no doubt he would be autographing copies of this book in every bookshop that he came across.

Thank you to Matt and Josh, whose brotherly love is featured in this book. It has been a privilege and a joy to watch you grow into the husbands and fathers you both are.

And to Shirley ("Shelley"), Jason, and Mary—I am so very thankful that the stars aligned and placed us together during that fateful first week at camp. There isn't a day when Eric does not pop up in my thoughts. I am in awe of how you persevered then and weathered that storm. Jason, I have seen you grow into the man you always wanted to be with a beautiful bride and a beautiful baby. To this day, I only know that there are important local sporting events because of your social media posts. Mary, it is no surprise to me that you grew up to be a nurse. How lucky your patients are to have such a loving and caring person tending to them. It is also no surprise that you seem to have welcomed a new dog into your family every few months. And Shirley, you opened your home to me in the years after camp, and I was always so taken by how you parented your kids. They were always loved, and your house was always wild as you allowed the kids to be kids. I have taken that with me into my own adulthood and my life as a parent. And of course, thank you to all three of you for going down memory lane with me as I shared early drafts of this book.

Some other thanks:

I have three wonderful, bright, and beautiful children of my own. Parenthood has most certainly shifted my perspective on my work at camp. When each of my kids reached the age when Eric left this Earth, I would hold them just a bit closer. I am so very fortunate to be raising these three alongside an incredible co-parent—my wife, Gina.

An enormous thank-you to Gina, Zoe, Lucia, and Xavier for their patience as I finished this book. Creating a graphic memoir can be a very fraught and challenging emotional journey, and *Sunshine* certainly was all these things. I would also like to thank David, Phil, and everyone at Scholastic as well as my agent, Rebecca, for the compassion they showed me when I needed extra time to finish *Sunshine*.

Revisiting the experiences found in this book reiterated an epiphany that working at camp gave me: Time here with one another is a gift that should be acknowledged and appreciated. As I age and each new birthday rolls around, I think how fortunate I am to be here, with my collective experience of everything I've seen, felt, and shared thus far.

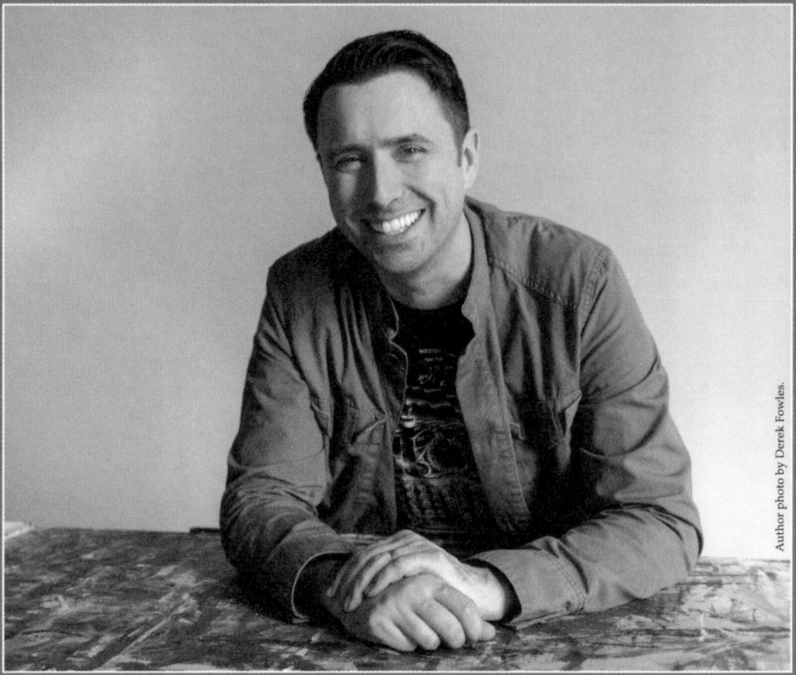
Author photo by Derek Fowles.

Jarrett J. Krosoczka is a *New York Times* bestselling author and illustrator of many books and series for children. His first graphic memoir, *Hey, Kiddo,* was a winner of the Harvey Award and the Odyssey Award and was a finalist for the National Book Award and the YALSA Nonfiction Award. His memoir was also chosen as a best book of the year by *TIME*, NPR, the *Washington Post,* and the *Boston Globe,* as well as being a TODAY Show pick. Jarrett lives with his family in western Massachusetts.